The Evolutionary Argument against Naturalism

Bloomsbury Studies in Philosophy of Religion

Series Editor: Stewart Goetz

Editorial Board: Thomas Flint, Robert Koons, Alexander Pruss, Charles Taliaferro, Roger Trigg, David Widerker, Mark Wynn

Titles in the Series

Freedom, Teleology, and Evil, by Stewart Goetz
The Image in Mind: Theism, Naturalism, and the Imagination, by Charles Taliaferro and Jil Evans
Actuality, Possibility, and Worlds, by Alexander Robert Pruss
The Rainbow of Experiences, Critical Trust, and God, by Kai-man Kwan
Philosophy and the Christian Worldview: Analysis, Assessment and Development, edited by David Werther and Mark D. Linville
Goodness, God and Evil, by David E. Alexander
Well-Being and Theism: Linking Ethics to God, by William A. Lauinger
Thinking Through Feeling: God, Emotion and Passibility, by Anastasia Philippa Scrutton
God's Final Victory: A Comparative Philosophical Case for Universalism, by John Kronen and Eric Reitan
Free Will in Philosophical Theology, by Kevin Timpe
Beyond the Control of God? edited by Paul M. Gould
The Mechanics of Divine Foreknowledge and Providence, edited by T. Ryan Byerly
The Kalām Cosmological Argument: Philosophical Arguments for the Finitude of the Past, edited by Paul Copan with William Lane Craig
The Kalām Cosmological Argument: Scientific Evidence for the Beginning of the Universe, edited by Paul Copan with William Lane Craig
Free Will and God's Universal Causality, by W. Matthews Grant
Sacred Music, Religious Desire and Knowledge of God, by Julian Perlmutter

The Evolutionary Argument against Naturalism

Context, Exposition, and Repercussions

Jim Slagle

BLOOMSBURY ACADEMIC
LONDON • NEW YORK • OXFORD • NEW DELHI • SYDNEY

BLOOMSBURY ACADEMIC
Bloomsbury Publishing Plc
50 Bedford Square, London, WC1B 3DP, UK
1385 Broadway, New York, NY 10018, USA
29 Earlsfort Terrace, Dublin 2, Ireland

BLOOMSBURY, BLOOMSBURY ACADEMIC and the Diana logo are trademarks of
Bloomsbury Publishing Plc

First published in Great Britain 2021
This paperback edition published 2023

Copyright © Jim Slagle, 2021

That Hideous Strength by CS Lewis © copyright CS Lewis Pte Ltd 1945.
Used with permission.
The Virtues by Peter Geach © copyright Cambridge University Press, 1977.
Reproduced with permission of The Licensor through PLSclear.
"Spit Out The Bone," written by James Hetfield and Lars Ulrich © copyright 2016.
Reproduced with permission of publishing Creeping Death Music (GMR).

Jim Slagle has asserted his right under the Copyright, Designs and Patents Act, 1988,
to be identified as Author of this work.

For legal purposes the Acknowledgments on p. xvi constitute an extension
of this copyright page.

Series Design by Louise Dugdale
Cover Image: Aurora Borealis in Scottish Glen © Steven Robinson Pictures/Getty Images

All rights reserved. No part of this publication may be reproduced or transmitted in
any form or by any means, electronic or mechanical, including photocopying, recording,
or any information storage or retrieval system, without prior permission in writing
from the publishers.

Bloomsbury Publishing Plc does not have any control over, or responsibility for, any
third-party websites referred to or in this book. All internet addresses given in this book
were correct at the time of going to press. The author and publisher regret any
inconvenience caused if addresses have changed or sites have ceased to exist, but can
accept no responsibility for any such changes.

A catalogue record for this book is available from the British Library.

Library of Congress Cataloging-in-Publication Data
Names: Slagle, Jim, author.
Title: The evolutionary argument against naturalism : context, exposition, and repercussions
/ Jim Slagle.
Description: London ; New York : Bloomsbury Academic, 2021. | Series: Bloomsbury
studies in philosophy of religion | Includes bibliographical references and index. |
Identifiers: LCCN 2021000343 (print) | LCCN 2021000344 (ebook) |
ISBN 9781350173118 (hardback) | ISBN 9781350173125 (ebook) |
ISBN 9781350173132 (epub)
Subjects: LCSH: Plantinga, Alvin. | Naturalism. | Evolution (Biology) | Naturalism—Religious
aspects—Christianity. | Evolution (Biology)—Religious aspects—Christianity.
Classification: LCC B945.P554 S53 2021 (print) | LCC B945.P554 (ebook) |
DDC 146—dc23
LC record available at https://lccn.loc.gov/2021000343
LC ebook record available at https://lccn.loc.gov/2021000344

ISBN:	HB:	978-1-3501-7311-8
	PB:	978-1-3502-4623-2
	ePDF:	978-1-3501-7312-5
	eBook:	978-1-3501-7313-2

Series: Bloomsbury Studies in Philosophy of Religion

Typeset by RefineCatch Limited, Bungay, Suffolk

To find out more about our authors and books visit www.bloomsbury.com
and sign up for our newsletters.

For Krista

Contents

Preface		viii
Acknowledgments		xvi

Part 1 Context

1	The Cartesian Dream	3
2	Quinean Tonic	17
3	Naturalized Epistemology Reformed	29

Part 2 Preliminaries

4	Terms of Engagement	47
5	The Evolution of the Evolutionary Argument	61
6	Elimination Game	75

Part 3 Argument

7	The Probability Thesis	91
8	The Defeater Thesis	111
9	The End of the Argument	129

Part 4 Objections

10	Analogies, Coherence, and Evolution	143
11	Expanding the Target	159
12	Loose Ends	179

Conclusions	197
Notes	207
Bibliography of the EAAN	235
Index	247

Preface

In 1939, A.E. Taylor published "Freedom and Personality" in *Philosophy*, following it up three years later in the same journal with "Freedom and Personality Again."[1] The point of both articles was to argue that determinism is self-defeating: if determinism were true, Taylor argued, then the determinist's beliefs would be entirely produced by events which preceded their reasoning about determinism, their own existence, and even the existence of the human race. So, determinism takes away anyone's justification for believing in determinism in the first place. "The guiding thought underlying the reasoning of my essay was one which I first learned long ago from F.H. Bradley, viz. that before I assert a proposition as true, I ought to be satisfied that the truth of the proposition is compatible with my knowledge that it is true."[2]

Naturally, Taylor is not the first person to make this kind of argument. It has a distinguished but disconnected history, going back at least as far as Epicurus's statement, "The man who says that all things come to pass by necessity cannot criticize one who denies that all things come to pass by necessity: for he admits that this too happens of necessity."[3] I say its history is disconnected because those who have addressed it do not seem to be aware of the others who have done so before them. And while Taylor and Epicurus focus on determinism, just as often such arguments target naturalism since it engenders some of the same problems. In *The Epistemological Skyhook: Determinism, Naturalism, and Self-Defeat*,[4] I go over many of these arguments and analyze them before concluding with my own version. "Epistemological Skyhook" is my name (after a term by Daniel Dennett) for arguments directed toward positions which posit closed systems, but which can only be defended or believed from standpoints that transcend their systems. In addition to Epicurus and Taylor, I examine Skyhooks by Kant, Kurt Gödel, William Hasker, C.S. Lewis, Arthur Lovejoy, J.R. Lucas, Norman Malcolm, Thomas Nagel, Alvin Plantinga, Karl Popper, and others. Many of the chapters could be made into independent research projects towards one particular version of the argument.

The present work is an attempt to do so by presenting an extended analysis of Plantinga's Skyhook, generally called "The Evolutionary Argument against Naturalism" or EAAN. Since his argument was initially presented in the context of his naturalized epistemology, I will first situate Plantinga's theory of knowledge by comparing it to Descartes's and Quine's in part 1. In part 2, I will go over a few preliminary issues before analyzing the argument and addressing the objections that have been raised against it in parts 3 and 4. To familiarize the reader with the broader issues, though, in the remainder of this preface I will go over what the alleged problem with naturalism is.

Religious and metaphysical beliefs

Our cognitive faculties are diverse, and some subdivisions of them are doubtless more reliable than others. We tend to think that beliefs with objects that are directly accessible or seem to be—like memory or perceptual beliefs—are more trustworthy than beliefs with objects that are more abstract or conceptual—like religious or metaphysical beliefs. The thinking is that having incorrect beliefs in the first category can have a more immediate and disastrous effect on an organism's ability to survive than incorrect beliefs in the second category. If a hominid incorrectly believed that an approaching grizzly bear was a nice, warm cinnamon roll, this would presumably impact its ability to survive more than believing, say, living creatures have vital spirits.

Nevertheless, it *could* be the case that more abstract beliefs would have some kind of survival value. Take religious beliefs: the evolutionary psychology of religion seeks to discover whether there are evolutionary benefits to religious beliefs.[5] For example, they may provide comfort resulting in better health and thus survival; or they may have played a role in social cohesion, allowing early human beings to congregate together into larger groups willing to defend each other. Naturally, some disagree: religious beliefs may be associated with other properties that allow organisms to survive. The religious beliefs are merely a side-effect or spandrel. It may even be the case that religious beliefs are *harmful*, but their harm is offset by the other property they are associated with.

Regardless, some (perhaps most) scholars of the field understand that giving an evolutionary explanation of religion effectively severs religious beliefs from their supposed objects. So, people do not believe in God because they have encountered him or because he set up our cognitive faculties to naturally produce beliefs in and about himself. Rather, they believe in God because such a belief was beneficial to the survival and procreation of our evolutionary forebears or was attached in some way to other traits which were. In these latter scenarios the purported explanation of religious beliefs effectively explains them away. People do not believe in God because God actually exists, they believe in God for some other reason, and as long as that other reason is operative, then the existence or nonexistence of God is irrelevant to their believing he does.

This type of argument is known as a debunking argument, something that has become very popular within the philosophical literature of late, where someone has beliefs but their correspondence to their objects is inexplicable by standard explanations. In these cases, we should either accept a nonstandard explanation or acknowledge that the (alleged) correspondence between the person's beliefs and reality is a coincidence.[6] With the latter option, beliefs would not amount to knowledge because their truth is accidental to them; since the person's formation and sustaining of the beliefs would be divorced from the reality they purportedly reflect, they would not be justified and may even be irrational. So, either we embrace the irrationality—which would not be a rational move itself—or we start shopping around for a nonstandard explanation. A common subcategory is *evolutionary* debunking arguments, where an evolutionary account of why people form the beliefs they do seems to dissociate the beliefs' contents with their purported objects.[7] In the present case, if religious beliefs are entirely produced by evolutionary forces (understood naturalistically) then there is a disconnect between God and belief in God, so religious beliefs would be debunked.

Plantinga, however, argues that belief in God can be innocent until proven guilty ("properly basic") since God could have set up our cognitive faculties, perhaps via evolution, so that we immediately form beliefs about him under certain circumstances. This would allow belief in God to be rational and to potentially qualify as knowledge. Plantinga spends some time discussing evolutionary psychology of religion, arguing that some forms of it (not all) are incompatible with traditional Christian belief,[8] although others have countered that Plantinga's own religious epistemology relieves the alleged incompatibilities.[9]

Regardless, there are plenty who think the evolutionary explanation *does* debunk or defeat religious beliefs. There is a big problem with this though: arguing against a position by appealing to its origin is the genetic fallacy. We cannot argue that a claim is false because people believe it for the wrong reasons. But here it gets more interesting: the origin of a belief is not relevant to that belief's *truth value*, but it is very relevant to that belief's *rationality and justification*. If a belief's truth is irrelevant to why someone believes it to be true, then they do not rationally believe it and it certainly would not be justified, even if it were true. So, if religious beliefs are in place solely due to naturalistic evolutionary forces, then their alleged truth is irrelevant to why people believe them— in which case, belief in God would be irrational whether God exists or not. Of course, if religious beliefs are formed by experiencing God or because God has arranged our cognitive faculties to innately produce theistic beliefs, then all bets are off.

It is vital here to note that evolution is not the problem: *naturalism* is the problem, in its denial of any element to reality that transcends nature. Human beings could have evolved in precisely the way that contemporary evolutionary theory argues without any issues arising about the veridicality of religious beliefs, since God could have set up the laws of nature so that, when they produce intelligent creatures, those creatures will naturally believe in God. It is only when we combine evolution with naturalism that we create a dichotomy between the existence of God and why people believe in God. This is difficult for some to accept because they think the biological theory of evolution is equivalent to (or at least strongly implies) a naturalistic interpretation thereof.

OK, well maybe religious beliefs are a gimme. It seems obvious that the denial of the supernatural would be inconsistent with belief in the supernatural. Broader metaphysics is more difficult. Despite occasional claims to the contrary, we all have numerous metaphysical beliefs that simply cannot be removed from our noetic systems. Science itself depends upon metaphysics and cannot function without it.

However, when people think of metaphysics they're usually thinking of extended discussions about whether abstract objects exist, whether human beings have souls, or detailed analyses about love or death or being which have little to no direct connection to the physical world. These subjects and systems do not have much of an empirical anchor, and this leads to rampant speculations that cannot be tested. It is not as if such speculations have *no* control, but they do not have as strong a control as speculations that are subject to empirical testing. This even leads some to deny metaphysics entirely.[10]

The problem is that metaphysical musings would have little effect, if any, on whether a creature is more adapted to its environment, so metaphysical beliefs would not go through the evolutionary grinder in order to weed out false beliefs or systems. And even if they did—even if certain metaphysical beliefs about the nature of universals, e.g., had some evolutionary benefit—they would not be selected for their truth but for the benefit they give regarding survival and procreation. As with religious beliefs, people would not believe them because they were true but because they were useful to our evolutionary forebears in some way. Again, the difficulty is not evolution but naturalism: by giving an explanation for why we hold certain metaphysical beliefs that does not take their truth value into account, we create a barrier between its truth and why people believe it is true—assuming their truth would have any effect on an organism's survival in the first place, which is highly doubtful.

Ethics and normativity

What about ethical beliefs? Here, some of those who accept that an evolutionary account of religious beliefs obviates their rationality are unwilling to say the same of ethical beliefs. Instead, they accept moral realism, the view that our moral beliefs tend to be veridical. The reason why we intuit that murder is morally wrong, for example, is because murder actually *is* wrong, and we plainly see this truth.[11] Unfortunately, the same objection applies: naturalism gives us a different explanation for why we believe moral truths. They are in place because it was useful for the survival and procreation of our evolutionary forebears to make certain judgments or classes of judgment about behavior. Incest was not evolutionarily useful and so became a moral taboo, but *ex hypothesi* there is nothing objectively immoral about it or anything else.

It's possible that there is some objective realm of moral truths, but this is insufficient. If the claims of an objective moral realm did not coincide with the moral impulses which evolution has imposed on us, we would follow the impulses. Even if they *did* coincide, the truth of the moral belief would be irrelevant to why we believe it. We would not believe love is better than hate because love actually *is* better than hate, but because it fostered the survival of our evolutionary progenitors and ended up coded into our genes. Once again, the evolutionary explanation of ethical beliefs seems to explain them away.

One issue here is that moral beliefs are prescriptive and normative. They say there are things we should and should not do, there are norms we are obligated to meet. But we cannot discover prescriptions or norms by examining the world. Such examinations could only provide us with descriptive facts (what *is* the case) not prescriptive facts (what *should be* the case). As Hume wrote, we cannot move from an "is" to an "ought" because the latter is a different kind of relation than the former.[12] So prescriptive, normative beliefs cannot be accounted for by scientific examination. That is not a problem per se: if someone thinks moral truths are real and that we can immediately intuit them, or come to know them some other way, then everything is copacetic. But it is a problem for the naturalist or anyone who thinks that science is the only source of information.

This has been excellently argued by Sharon Street,[13] who suggests it is very unlikely that ethical beliefs formed due to evolutionary pressures would somehow coincide with objective moral truths—truths which would have played no role in how our species came to have these beliefs in the first place. Maintaining moral realism in the face of this is to assert a coincidence that is literally incredible. There is no naturalistic pathway where normativity can enter the mix. "From a Darwinian perspective, the hypothesis of value realism is superfluous—a wheel that spins without being attached to anything."[14]

Value, however, cannot be confined within ethics. Street applies her arguments to all types of value and normativity. If we think we should or should not do something, we are positing a norm, and normativity's tendrils extend far beyond the obvious shouldness of ethics. Notably, it has traditionally played a significant role in epistemology.

All other beliefs?

Street specifically applies her antirealist arguments to epistemic normativity.[15] Her antirealism here is not on the same level as her antirealism about ethics though; with ethics, she is antirealist about both our reasoning about ethical claims and their alleged truth. When she looks at epistemology more broadly, she is not antirealist about the truth value of *all* claims to knowledge: notably, perceptual beliefs are exempt, they are not explained away in the same way that religious and ethical beliefs may be. But Street is still antirealist about epistemic *reasons*, since these are strongly normative in nature.[16] If epistemic reasons are ruled out of court, that prevents any belief from being rational or justified, since knowledge is "irreducibly normative."[17] Rationality and knowledge involve epistemic value, and if we reject *all* value realism, rationality and knowledge go with it. This is one of the motivations behind the development of naturalized epistemology: the elimination of normativity from epistemology.

We've seen that some think the naturalistic explanation of religious belief debunks or defeats them. The same goes for naturalistic accounts of metaphysical and ethical beliefs. These are all examples of *local* skepticism, skepticism about a particular domain of knowledge. But when the subject is expanded to knowledge in general a bigger problem arises. If all rationality or knowledge is defeated by providing a naturalistic explanation, that defeater would call virtually all beliefs into question—including beliefs about evolution, science, rationality, ourselves, etc. This is *global* skepticism rather than mere local skepticism. Moreover, if giving a naturalistic explanation of knowledge gives us a defeater for our own rationality (which is eminently debatable), it also gives us a defeater for the rational analyses that lead us to accept naturalism in the first place; it takes away any reason we had for the skepticism. So, this form of global skepticism is *self-defeating*.

Of course, we could simply deny that having a naturalistic account of knowledge gives us a defeater, but then that would apply to naturalistic accounts of religious, metaphysical, and ethical beliefs as well. Many may be perfectly willing to accept this, but we can give some strong reasons for thinking that explaining beliefs or categories of belief naturalistically does effectively defeat those beliefs. By explaining why we believe something in a way that divorces the belief from its object, we render the belief irrational because the belief's truth has no bearing on whether we believe it—believe it to be true, that is. And if *all* our beliefs are explained this way then all our beliefs are irrational. The EAAN addresses this point, and this book is an extended analysis of it.

Yet is it really plausible that we can call *everything* we believe into question like this? What about our memory beliefs about what happened five minutes ago? Or our logical and mathematical beliefs? Is it possible to have a defeater for the belief that 2 + 3 = 5? How about that the external world really exists, or that there are other minds besides one's own? Even if challenging these beliefs is theoretically possible, we cannot take these challenges seriously. Of course, the EAAN is not suggesting we *should* take them seriously; it is arguing that we should reject whatever leads to such unacceptable scenarios. But since it is such an extreme claim to suggest that everything we believe is defeated, Plantinga makes a concession: we can take his argument as just calling *metaphysical* beliefs into question, the second case we went over. And naturalism itself is a metaphysical position: it says what does and does not, can and cannot exist. These are blatantly metaphysical claims.

Scientific, logical, and mathematical beliefs

Ignoring Plantinga's concession, one pathway may still be open to the naturalist. Remember, while Street applies her conclusions to epistemic reasoning, she does not always apply them to the truth of beliefs. This is appropriate: simply forming a belief does not obviously involve normativity,[18] and normativity is her target. This seems to open the door to many theories of knowledge, such as reliabilism. If the process that produces the belief is reliable, usually producing true beliefs, then the belief is probably true, and it is appropriate—rational—to believe it. Street excludes perceptual beliefs from her antirealism because they are not produced by a reasoning process but by sensory faculties. And if perceptual beliefs are trustworthy this opens the door to scientific investigation and thus scientific knowledge, which is precisely the aspect of knowledge on which naturalism predicates itself. So perhaps we can be skeptical of knowledge in general, but we have a reason to withhold that skepticism when it comes to scientific knowledge, and that, allegedly, is the only kind of knowledge naturalism affirms.

But, again, naturalism is not merely a restatement of scientific facts, it is a metaphysical claim about what can and cannot exist. If the response is that naturalism merely accepts claims that have scientific evidence in their support and claims that are not subject to scientific investigation are excluded, the counter-response is that, in this case, one must either assume that science is comprehensive in determining what exists (otherwise we could not exclude extra-scientific claims) or at least that science is the only pathway to knowledge. The former is a metaphysical claim, and so everything already said applies to it. The latter is an epistemological claim, but it makes the metaphysical assumption that, if metaphysical realities exist, they cannot be encountered by us as emphatically as the physical world is.[19] Either way one is making a metaphysical claim. Thus, even if we are working with Plantinga's concession to only apply the EAAN to metaphysical beliefs, naturalism is still in its scope.

Another problem comes from William Talbott, one of Plantinga's critics. He argues that evolutionary forces only select for local conditions, not global conditions. This is uncontroversial: whatever issues make an organism more or less capable of survival and procreation will be those the organism and its ancestors actually encounter, unless something steps in and modifies it artificially. This will be just as true for reasoning: our ability to infer to the best explanation will develop according to the local environments in which our evolutionary progenitors evolved. This is another motivation behind naturalized epistemology: our brains evolved to address local concerns, not global concerns, and this allows the naturalized epistemologist to avoid the skepticisms that plague other theories of knowledge.

The difficulty Talbott raises is that scientific knowledge requires us to generalize from the local to the global, and as such, we need a reason to think local concerns reflect global concerns to allow us to generalize from the former to the latter. But any such reason could not be a local issue itself. Insofar as naturalistic evolution can only provide us with brains shaped by local issues, there is no naturalistic pathway for our brains to reflect global issues, and so scientific knowledge, which depends on the generalization from the local to the global, becomes impossible. Without such generalizations we would be unable to affirm evolution or any other scientific claim, and thus we could not use science as a justification for naturalism.[20]

If we grant that naturalism calls religious, metaphysical, ethical, and scientific beliefs into question, can we at least stand secure in basic logical and mathematical beliefs? Is it really possible to suggest that 2 + 3 may not equal 5? Well, first, Plantinga's argument is not calling these beliefs into question, it is arguing that *naturalism* calls these beliefs into question. The issue then becomes whether it is even possible to suggest errors on this level. If it is not, then naturalism could not lead to them. For now, we can point out that Descartes's evil demon thought experiment presents a scenario that seems to make it possible: an evil demon could have the power to make mathematical falsehoods seem as obviously true as basic mathematical truths do. This opens the door to a similar conclusion with Plantinga's argument, thus demonstrating that it functions as a form of skepticism.

Perceptual beliefs

All this just means that we cannot move from local conditions to global conditions (even when the global conditions are elementary laws of logic and mathematics), from global conditions to science, and then from science to naturalism. But are the locally based perceptual beliefs under the same cloud of suspicion as everything else? After all, it is argued, evolution would tend to select true beliefs since they will tend to produce survival-enhancing behavior. If you form the belief that grizzly bears are cinnamon rolls you probably won't survive your first encounter with a grizzly bear. Even if you don't like cinnamon rolls.[21]

There are problems with this, though. Naturalism does not allow for beliefs to influence our actions by virtue of the beliefs' contents. Most naturalistic philosophers of mind accept that the only forces available to cause action are the neural, physical processes of the brain, not the specific contents of the beliefs that are associated with them. This creates a dichotomy between the beliefs and the actions produced, and this dichotomy is not trivial. Moreover, even if evolution were able to select beliefs (or, more properly, belief-producing attributes), it would select them according to their usefulness in an organism's survival, not their truth value. While we can argue that true beliefs would promote survival more than false ones, this is not as obvious as it first appears. At the very least, in this scenario we would not ultimately believe our beliefs because they are true but because they were useful to our evolutionary ancestors. (Once again, I must point out that none of this challenges evolution. All it challenges is naturalism.)

And this is where it gets especially interesting, at least for me and anyone who happens to share my particular psychoses. The EAAN is an unusual form of skepticism that applies across the board to any theory of knowledge, including naturalized epistemology. This is radical because naturalized epistemology was formed in large part to sidestep the issue of skepticism. It merely studies the process of how sensory experiences produce beliefs and ultimately scientific theories. But if the truth of perceptual beliefs is not a given under naturalism, then the naturalized epistemologist cannot form beliefs or theories about their formation, since those beliefs are called into question along with everything else. In fact, my working title for this tome was *Naturalized Skepticism*.

Now of course our beliefs do in fact line up with our actions and we can follow the process of sensory experiences producing beliefs. *But not if naturalism is true.* Any belief the naturalized epistemologist forms while observing the relation between sensory experiences and belief production is just as suspect as everything else. If we try to hold the line at elementary logical and mathematical beliefs being reliable, then we run up against Descartes's evil demon scenario which can be modified to fit the EAAN. Therefore, the EAAN is a form of skepticism that applies to naturalized epistemology as well as every other theory of knowledge one proposes. This is why the present work begins by analyzing the epistemologies of Descartes, Quine, and Plantinga, and their responses to skepticism.

Obviously, all the above is eminently contestable. This has just been a short summary of some of the issues behind (and within, and in front of) the EAAN to prime the reader. A few chapters of this book have parallel chapters in *The Epistemological Skyhook*, and several essays I've written are used in part in the present work as well. These include "Self-Refutation and Self-Defeat," *Logique et Analyse* 56/222 (2013): 157–64; "Plantinga's Skepticism," *Philosophia* 43/4 (2015): 1133–45; "Indicators and Depictors," *The Philosophical Forum* 48/1 (2017): 91–107; and "Yes, Eliminative Materialism Is Self-Defeating," *Philosophical Investigations* 43/3 (2020): 199–213.

Acknowledgments

Among those who helped me in writing this book, most notable is Paul Herrick who has encouraged me greatly in my writing and proofread several chapters. Occasionally, I receive a package in the mail of books that Paul thought I should read. Everyone needs a Paul. Obviously, I also thank Alvin Plantinga for developing this argument, which has influenced my thinking in many subfields of philosophy: not just epistemology, but philosophy of mind, action theory, philosophy of religion, philosophy of science, and broader metaphysics. Additionally, I thank those who have commented on Plantinga's argument, positively or negatively, or come up with their own variations on it. In particular, several conversations with William Talbott were very influential, forcing me to spend more time wrestling with his objections. Even so, I fear my responses to him are insufficient.

I also want to thank all those who provided me with the context, the life, that allowed me to write this tome: first, God, for everything he has done for me, which includes (but is not exhausted by) putting me in contact with everyone *else* I'm thanking. Second, I thank my wife and dedicatee Krista for saving my life. So, if you were wondering who to blame for that, there you go. Finally, I thank my two wonderful kids, Joah the Great and Kira the Glorious, for reminding me daily that there are things more important than writing philosophy. Literally. Every day they tell me to put down the stupid computer and come play with them.

Part One

Context

1

The Cartesian Dream

And when they saw him, they worshiped him; but some doubted.

Matthew 28:17

Alfred North Whitehead famously wrote that "The safest general characterization of the European philosophical tradition is that it consists of a series of footnotes to Plato."[1] This is obviously an exaggeration, but in the same exaggerated sense, one could say Modern epistemology is a series of footnotes to Descartes. It is his development of the concept of knowledge that virtually all Modern epistemology is responding to on some level, whether positively or negatively.

Relearning the world

Descartes recognized that our systems of beliefs and reasoning are a hodgepodge of valid and invalid processes, true and false beliefs, built up from our daily experiences. He wanted to demolish our epistemic edifice and rebuild it more systematically so that the system was trustworthy and reliable as a whole. To this end he employed his Cartesian doubt as a scalpel, cutting away everything he could, regardless of how implausible it was to do so, in order to see if there was some belief he literally could not doubt.

Descartes's *Meditations on First Philosophy* is interesting, not least because of its structure: it is arranged as a series of six daily readings, in the manner of religious meditations of the day.[2] It is neither the first nor only time he drew the conclusions therein but it is his most extensive treatment of some of them.

I doubt therefore I am

He begins by reflecting on his present circumstances: sitting in front of a fire. Can he doubt this? Certainly: our senses deceive us all the time. There are visual illusions, aural illusions, etc. Yet this is too simple. An illusion does not usually involve all our senses at once. What Descartes is asking is whether it is possible to doubt that he is sitting by the fire, looking at a piece of paper in his hands. Can he doubt *all* of this? Can he look at the fire and doubt there is a fire? Can he doubt that these are his hands?

Cartesian doubt is hypothetical. He is not asking whether it is *reasonable* to doubt these things, but whether it is *possible*. There may be people who actually doubt these things, but if so, they are not merely irrational but insane. They would be on the same level as people who believe "that they are pumpkins, or made of glass."[3] So it is not a question of whether we can doubt the deliverances of our senses on a *practical* level, but whether we can doubt them on a *theoretical* level—whether we can, in Husserl's terms, bracket them and put them to the side. Descartes says yes. After all, we dream most nights, and in those dreams someone may very well find themselves sitting by a fire looking at a piece of paper. Yet in the dream, the fire is not really there, the paper is not really there. How do we know we are not dreaming right now? There seems to be no way to prove it: any alleged proof would be part of the dream, and we can very easily imagine a dream with apparent "evidences" of being awake.

Again, the issue is not that simple. Our waking world includes the dreaming world; that is, we are cognizant of our dreams as such while awake (by remembering them), as well as our waking lives. But our dreaming world generally does not include our waking world in a similar sense: we are not usually aware of the fact that we are dreaming, while remembering our waking lives all the while—and on the rare occasions when we are, we consider the dreaming world to be unreal: when dreamers say to themselves "this is a dream" they mean "this is not really happening." Thus, the dreaming and waking worlds do not seem to be parallel in significant senses, and this makes it difficult to suggest that our waking lives are just dreams.

Nevertheless, dreams often come with background information that one just "knows" and even false memories of events that do not form a part of the dream, much less of waking life. At any rate, the fact that we are not usually aware that we are dreaming shows that we mistake it as the waking world while we are experiencing it (or *would* so mistake it if the thought occurred to us). This is all that is necessary to allow Descartes's dream argument to go forward. So it seems I can doubt the deliverances of all my senses. This means that I can doubt that the physical world that they relay to me exists—it is possible to doubt the existence of the entire world.

So, what is this world that I am (theoretically) doubting? Well, obviously it would include the physical elements that comprise it. But that would include the physical elements that comprise one's own body. Again, I could be dreaming that I am sitting in front of a fire, looking at a piece of paper, but since it is a dream, the fire and paper do not exist. But what about my hands that are holding the paper? If I am dreaming, my hands are at my side in my bed, not in front of my face holding something. So, *pace* G.E. Moore, I can doubt that this hand I am holding up is my hand.[4] I can doubt this for my entire body. The dream argument that allows me to doubt the existence of the physical world also allows me to doubt the existence of my own body.

What about other people? Well, they are in an even worse state. We can, of course, doubt their physical bodies exist just as much as our own. But we can do more: we can doubt *they* exist, that their *minds* exist. We can doubt that they are sparks of self-consciousness. Certainly, when we interact with others we cannot help but believe that they are loci of first-person experiences, but it is possible, theoretically, that everyone I will ever encounter are complex automata with no minds, no self-awareness, no "there"

there. Assuming, that is, that one encounters other people via their physical bodies at all, which, staying true to Descartes's skepticism, one will not.

Descartes then moves from empirical truths to conceptual truths. Can we doubt the basic elements of logic and mathematics? Can we doubt that $2 + 3 = 5$? This is difficult, since we plainly see the truth of such claims. What would have to be the case for this to be false? Here, Descartes suggests the evil demon (*mauvais genie*), a sort of substitute God who uses all his powers to deceive us—or at least to deceive the person speculating at the moment, since this person has no assurance that anyone else exists. So, whenever someone tries to add two numbers together ($2 + 3$, say) the evil demon makes an incorrect answer seem self-evident to them, so that they "plainly see" that it is "true," but *ex hypothesi*, it is false.

Again, no one is suggesting that we take such a view seriously, least of all Descartes. It is a completely contrived claim, asserted solely in order to see whether it is possible to doubt self-evident conceptual truths. Descartes's answer, again, is yes. But note one caveat here: the evil demon is being posited to suggest that virtually all our beliefs are false. But to doubt all our beliefs, we have to accept at least one: the evil demon hypothesis itself. So, Descartes has not provided the possibility of doubting all our beliefs, because we must exclude the evil demon hypothesis from its own scope in order to make it work. Otherwise, it would give us a reason to doubt itself, and so would be self-defeating. This is a problem for most skeptical theories: for the skepticism to get any purchase, we must exclude the skeptical theory from its own application. But to exclude it will almost always be ad hoc, and thus will not be justifiable.

So, Descartes has found himself without a world, without other minds, without a body, without basic conceptual truths. Is there anything left (besides the evil demon)? Well, there is one thing: *himself*. Descartes argues that while he can doubt all these other things, he cannot doubt that he is doubting, and doubting requires a subject, an agent who is doing the doubting. If he is doubting all these things, he must exist. Since doubting is a form of thinking, this leads to the famous phrase, "cogito ergo sum": "I think therefore I am." One cannot doubt their own existence.

One immediate problem is that the evil demon hypothesis is posited in order to suggest that every conclusion, even the most self-evident, could be false. Yet Descartes is arguing "cogito *ergo* sum." How can this particular *ergo* be justified when all the others aren't? If the evil demon explains away all therefores, then it would explain away this therefore too. Moreover, if the evil demon explains away self-evident principles, it explains away the law of noncontradiction. But the claim here seems to be that Descartes cannot doubt he exists without simultaneously not doubting he exists. This, however, is just an apparent contradiction, and the evil demon hypothesis makes apparent contradictions just that: apparent.

There is some strength to this objection. It seems to be an error to make one's own existence the conclusion of an argument or to appeal to a contradiction to establish it, since the evil demon hypothesis would apply to these as well. In response, Descartes argues that his point is to illustrate, by way of argument, the immediate intuition of one's own existence, and the impossibility of doubting it. Admittedly, "cogito ergo sum" becomes misleading in this case, since it clearly has the form of an argument. Nevertheless, Descartes claims he merely intends it to be illuminative. "When someone says 'I am thinking, therefore I am, or I exist', he is not inferring existence from thought by means of a syllogism; rather, a simple intuition of his mind shows it to him as self-evident."[5]

What Descartes is claiming is that every single act of thought, including doubting, presupposes the existence of the subject doing the thinking. If I were to say, "I doubt that I exist," Descartes would ask, "Who is it that you think may not exist?" My answer would have to be: "Me. *I* am the one whose existence *I* doubt." In order to doubt I exist, I must presuppose I exist. In order to assert (or just suggest) that I do not exist, I must assert that I do. So, it is impossible, literally, to doubt that one exists, since any attempt will presuppose one's existence.

This is Descartes's Archimedean point from which he will build a lever to move the world.[6] From this foundation, he will rebuild the edifice of knowledge on much surer ground.

From oneself to one God

At this point, Descartes is left with a world containing just himself and the evil demon. No physical universe, no other people, not even his own body (because of the dream argument). This last instance shows there is conceptual space between oneself and one's body, since I can doubt my body exists but not that *I* exist. So "I" am not my body. What exactly am I then? Since the cogito asserts two things (that one thinks and exists), Descartes concludes that he is a thinking thing, "A thing that doubts, understands, affirms, denies, wants, refuses, and also imagines and senses,"[7] although he is not yet arguing that the latter are veridical. In other words, he is a *mind*.[8] And unlike the relationship between oneself and one's body, there is no conceptual space between oneself and one's mind. As the cogito shows, it is impossible to doubt the existence of one's own mind, since any attempt to do so must begin by affirming the existence of one's mind. Moreover, by referring to the mind with the terms he does—simple terms whose meanings are self-evident and do not need to be defined by reference to other terms—he avoids (supposedly) the trials and tribulations of having the evil demon hypothesis apply to them. These ideas are as self-evident as one's own existence. "[I] know plainly that I can perceive my own mind more easily and clearly than I can anything else."[9]

Since he is certain (that is, cannot doubt) that he exists, Descartes casts around for something to ground this item of knowledge. He concludes that it is because he clearly and distinctly perceives it. Therefore, any other concept he clearly and distinctly perceives is grounded in the same manner and should be accepted. "So I now seem to be able to lay it down as a general rule that *whatever I perceive very vividly and clearly is true*."[10] This, however, is a questionable move. The reason one's own existence is certain is because it is literally indubitable. It does not follow from this that dubitable beliefs that are perceived as clearly and distinctly as one's own existence are similarly certain or even true. Descartes seems to be inferring that because one member of a class has a trait, all the other class members must have it as well, even if the others do not share the element (indubitability) that establishes that that one class member has the trait in the first place. However, this, again, puts it in terms of argumentation. Descartes's whole point is that these things are directly and immediately—that is, clearly and distinctly—perceived. They are immediately present to the mind. Whether this is enough to salvage

Descartes's project is another question. If the evil demon can obviate the most elementary logical and mathematical beliefs such as that 2 + 3 = 5, which are as clear and distinct as anything, then it seems it could obviate other clear and distinct concepts as well. This subject will come back again in Descartes's epistemology.

So, one's own existence is clear and distinct. More specifically, the self, the ego, the "I," is a mental substance which has the property of thought—in fact, "The *cogito* shows that Descartes definitely believes that each person is a different individual mental substance."[11] He also looks at the concept of causality and concludes that "it is obvious by the natural light that the total cause of something must contain at least as much reality as does the effect."[12] If an effect had more reality than its cause, then that more reality would essentially be uncaused. If a cause had three aspects (C_1, C_2, and C_3), then its effect would have products of those aspects (E_1, E_2, and E_3). If we posit that the effect has *additional* aspects (say, E_4), then this additional aspect just pops into existence without a cause, since we are positing that all the effects of the cause's aspects are exhausted by E_1, E_2, and E_3.

Now Descartes observes that he has the idea of an infinite and unlimited substance which he calls "God." "By the word 'God' I understand a substance that is infinite, eternal, unchangeable, independent, supremely intelligent, supremely powerful, which created myself and anything else that may exist."[13] But if a cause must have more reality than its effect, Descartes's idea of God (the effect) must be caused by something with more reality. Descartes cannot be the cause since the effect is belief in an infinite substance, and he is a *finite* substance. Well, how can the cause have more reality than this? The only thing with more reality than *belief* in an infinite substance would be an *actually existing* infinite substance. This infinite substance caused Descartes (or, more properly, oneself) to exist and have the idea of an infinite substance. Descartes did not cause himself to exist, since then he would have made himself perfect. Even if he had always existed, and so did not need a temporal cause, he is still a finite substance, and so is contingent and dependent on something else for his continued existence. Nor could it have been his parents or some other finite cause because a) this leads to an infinite regress, since we must ask what caused these finite causes, and b) a finite cause could not have caused *everything* about himself, since one aspect of himself is his clear and distinct concept of an infinite substance, which could not be brought about by a finite substance. Nor could it be numerous causes that are not united in a single being, since "God's simplicity—that is, the unity or inseparability of all his attributes—is one of the most important of the perfections that I understand him to have."[14] Moreover, God is an infinitely perfect being, and perfection includes existence. If God did not exist, we could not have the concept of an infinitely perfect being: our concept would be of an infinitely perfect being that is not perfect (since it lacks existence), which is a contradiction.

From God to world

My goal here is not to defend these arguments but rather to point to Descartes's purpose in presenting them. Descartes argues that he could not be sure the physical world exists, nor even whether basic logical and mathematical claims were true. His skeptical exercises made these claims dubitable. But then he argues that there must be a God who is omnipotent and omnibenevolent, and infinitely and perfectly good (goodness being a perfection which any infinitely perfect being worth his salt must have). But the existence of such a God is incompatible with the existence of the evil demon. Two omnipotent beings would limit each other, and thus prevent each other from being omnipotent—unless they always agreed. And it is fair to say that a perfectly good omnipotent being and a deceptive omnipotent being would have some differences of opinion.

What if we posit that the evil demon is not omnipotent, just very, very powerful? Well, then the omnipotent being—that perfectly good God just mentioned—would not have created him. An omnibenevolent creator would not create an extremely powerful deceiver and let him ride roughshod over our cognitive faculties. Therefore, the evil demon hypothesis is refuted and can no longer be used to doubt our beliefs.

An all-powerful, all-loving God would not be a deceiver. He would create our minds so that they are, by and large, reliable. At the very least, he would ensure that our clear and distinct ideas are trustworthy. So, the existence of God not only refutes the evil demon hypothesis and any motive to think our clear and distinct ideas are not trustworthy, it gives us a reason to think they *are* trustworthy.

We are still stuck with the fact that our senses often deceive us. When one dips a stick in water, the stick appears bent. Descartes spends some time showing how it is possible for an infinite and perfect God to create finite and imperfect beings which sometimes make errors. Regardless, the fact that God created us and is perfectly good means that our senses are *generally* reliable, although not *perfectly* so. God did not create us to be infinite; we are finite, contingent beings, and this entails that we lack the perfections of God. Therefore, the God hypothesis allows Descartes to trust his senses again, and to derive a much more trustworthy system of beliefs than he had before this exercise.

Once again, this seems insufficient. From the mere premise that an infinitely good God exists it does not follow that this God will create a universe, or life, or rational beings. Just because a cause, C, *could* produce an effect, E, there is no reason to suppose that it did. For that matter, this God may have mysterious reasons for allowing our cognitive faculties to be unreliable, it may even have reasons for creating a very powerful deceiver like the evil demon, reasons that omniscience can understand but finite intellects cannot. Indeed, doesn't Descartes's Christianity posit something very much like this? The most powerful being God created turned against him and is now "the god of this age [who] has blinded the eyes" of many (2 Cor. 4:4) and deceives the whole world (Rev. 12:9). There is a logical gap between positing the existence of God and positing that our minds reliably produce true beliefs.

The Cartesian Circle

Another objection is called the Cartesian Circle. Descartes uses the fact that his clear and distinct ideas are trustworthy to show that his clear and distinct idea of God is trustworthy. But then he uses the existence of a perfectly good God to ensure that he has been created so that his clear and distinct ideas are trustworthy. It seems we need God to validate our clear and distinct ideas, but we need our clear and distinct ideas to validate our beliefs in God.

This objection was raised immediately by Antoine Arnauld, one of the scholars to whom Descartes sent the *Meditations* for review.[15] Descartes responds that this is a misunderstanding. The evil demon does not render our clear and distinct ideas suspect *when we are clearly and distinctly perceiving them*. When we attend to these ideas, we cannot help but assent to them. But when we recall them to mind—not by attending to them directly but by remembering them—then the evil demon can get to work. So, our clear and distinct idea of God guarantees his existence when we directly perceive it, and then God's existence guarantees that our clear and distinct ideas are veridical when we are not attending to them directly but just recalling them. In this way, Descartes hopes to avoid the circularity.

This raises many further questions. For example, the fact that we cannot help but believe our clear and distinct ideas when we are perceiving them is irrelevant to Cartesian doubt. I may not be able to doubt my clear and distinct ideas when I am perceiving them, but neither can I doubt the existence of the physical world when I am perceiving it. Certainly, the former are in a more stringent category than the latter, but the whole point of Descartes's project is not to find things one can doubt on a practical level but things one can doubt on a theoretical level.

While Descartes did not apply the evil demon hypothesis to clear and distinct ideas when being perceived, there is nothing to stop us from doing so. There is no reason to think a sufficiently powerful demon could not artificially produce the phenomena associated with the immediate perception of clear and distinct ideas for ideas that are false or even insane. Descartes objects that we cannot doubt such things in this moment, and if we literally cannot doubt them then to build a system upon the assumption that they are false is folly. There is some truth here, but I don't think Descartes has the epistemic right to appeal to it. Descartes has gone all the way down to the bedrock level of beliefs that we cannot doubt, but we can always ask the further question of whether those beliefs are *true*. Yes, we cannot help but think they are true, and yes, building a system on the assumption that certain beliefs that we cannot doubt are false is not going to be a system we can rationally accept. Nevertheless, the question can be asked. We cannot simply equate indubitability with truth. And Descartes, of all people, should know this, since his epistemological project is based on hyperbolic doubt that we cannot take seriously.

Cartesian epistemology

Descartes's theory of knowledge established the program for Modern epistemology, often just called Cartesian epistemology. This program involves several important elements. In the remainder of this chapter, I will examine six of them. I am not trying to be exhaustive, I am only looking at those elements most germane to the present study.

Foundationalism

The first element is *foundationalism*. This is the view that certain beliefs are the ground level and can qualify as knowledge. Nonfoundational beliefs are then derived (or at least derivable) from the foundational ones via assured pathways of inference. As

Descartes found an indubitable foundation in the cogito and built up from it, so we should look for similar indubitable beliefs and reason to further conclusions. Various contenders have been suggested for the foundations, such as observation reports and sense data statements. To say these beliefs are the foundation does not mean they are ungrounded—Descartes grounded his belief in his own existence in the fact that it was a clear and distinct idea—it just means the foundational belief is a starting point. We do not *derive* these beliefs from their grounds, their grounds are what make them true, not how we come to believe they are true.

A few issues immediately present themselves: first, the narrower the field of foundational beliefs, the more liberal the inferential rules must be by which we derive other beliefs (to allow for many objects of knowledge). Conversely, if we make the rules stricter, we must widen the category of foundational beliefs. Neither is a particularly hopeful picture, since they leave too much leeway for error to creep in. What we want is a small number of foundational beliefs and strict inferential rules linking them to other beliefs. But this does not allow for the diversity of knowledge we think we have. Second, to be "based" on foundational beliefs is a metaphor; we have to unpack it to see what it actually means. Logical deduction seems too restrictive; we should also include induction and abduction (inference to the best explanation), but these are prone to error. Hume demonstrated that with induction we can never be sure we are inferring from a skewed sample; moving from particular propositions to general ones can easily lead to erroneous conclusions since general propositions claim more than particular propositions.[16] Similarly, abduction can lead to false conclusions since in inferring to the best explanation we may not have the correct explanation in our pool of possibilities. This is Bas van Fraassen's problem of the bad lot.[17]

Is foundationalism the only option? One interesting analysis comes from Agrippa's trilemma, or the Münchhausen trilemma, which asks how any belief is justified. Ultimately, there are only three (or four, as we will see) answers we can give. First, we could say the belief is justified by another belief which is justified by another belief, etc., until one arrives at a belief that is self-justifying, requiring no independent justification. This is the aforementioned foundationalism, since it refers to a belief that functions as a foundation for the others.[18] Second, we could say the belief is justified by another belief, which is justified by another belief, etc., and we eventually circle back to the *first* belief. This is coherentism, involving circular reference, where what justifies the belief is the overall coherence of the system of beliefs being proposed. Third, we could say that it is justified by another belief, which is justified by another belief, etc., and this chain goes on to infinity without ever repeating. This is infinitism, which appeals to an infinite regress which is unending and never repeats—if it ended, that end would function as a foundation and so be foundationalism, and if it repeated, it would be circling back on itself and so be coherentism.

So, we have three possibilities: foundationalism, coherentism, and infinitism. We have given some problems with foundationalism already. One problem that Agrippa's trilemma brings out is that it is dogmatic. The foundational belief is just accepted, or just should be accepted; it is self-justified. When asked why we should believe the foundational belief, the answer is that we just should and stop asking inconvenient questions. This is not an acceptable answer. To say that some beliefs are the ground level, that some beliefs do not need to be justified by something else, is to say that we do not need to question or verify them. But virtually every class of beliefs that has been proposed for this position has been challenged precisely because it can be. We need to have a *reason* for a belief and to continue believing in the absence of a reason is dogmatic.

However, the other options fare no better. The problem with coherentism, roughly, is that each step in the chain only has *derivative* justification, derived from the step before it. But since each belief is justified by virtue of its connection to another belief, then if we are positing a closed circle, no belief in the system is justified. Circling back to a step already referred to in the process does not somehow bring the needed justification into the picture.

If we had a sequence of mirrors reflecting a beam of light on each other in turn, and they were arranged in a circle so that the beam was traveling around them, where did the beam of light come from? Mirrors *reflect* light, they do not *produce* it. Each mirror "borrows" the light from the previous mirror, but if there is no ultimate source of light, they would have nothing to reflect. Similarly, each belief in a coherentist system borrows its justification from the other beliefs in the system. But what is the source of their justification? A circle of mirrors could be in the dark; a coherent system of beliefs could be unjustified. We see here that "Circularity is the epistemic equivalent of counterfeiting,"[19] since it gives the illusion of providing a source of justification without actually doing so. The system of beliefs, even if they are coherent with each other, does not provide any justification if each belief within the system only has derived justification.

The problem with infinitism is similar. Generally, philosophers point to infinite regresses as refutations of positions. The problem with it here is that each step in the chain only has derivative justification. But without some source outside the system to input justification into it, no step will have any. If we ask where a beam of light is coming from and are pointed to a mirror, which is reflecting off another mirror, etc. on to infinity, we still have not answered the question. Just as a circular sequence of mirrors could be in the dark, so could an infinite sequence of mirrors. We ask, "Where is the light coming from?" and are being told, "There is an infinite number of mirrors." OK. So what? *Where is the light coming from?* Similarly, we can ask, "Why is this belief justified?" and the infinitist responds, "Because there is an infinite chain of beliefs. But such a chain could be unjustified, so simply saying there are an infinite number of them does not explain how any of them are justified.

If foundationalism, coherentism, and infinitism do not work, then it seems we are left with no knowledge, no justified true belief. This is the fourth option: skepticism. Unfortunately, as we will see, many forms of skepticism end up being self-defeating. If we should be skeptical of all hypotheses, we should be skeptical of the skeptical hypothesis itself. Skepticism is utterly dependent, even parasitical, on the veridicality of reason, since it *argues* that knowledge or rationality are illusory. By arguing, the skeptic is appealing to reason. Without this dependence, we would have no motive to accept the skeptical claim being made. But of course, the *point* of the skepticism is to call reason into question. So, conceding to skepticism does not seem to be a viable option either.

We are left, then, with four exhaustive possibilities regarding knowledge, one of which is just the rejection of the other three, and none of them are acceptable. Historically, foundationalism has been the near-universal position, and still is the majority view. But the last century has seen many coherentists make convincing cases,[20] and infinitism, while much rarer, has its defenders too.[21] And of course, there have always been skeptics.

Other elements of Cartesian epistemology

A second element of epistemology derived from Descartes is *internalism*. This is a complex position, but it involves the claim that knowledge is dependent on what is internally available to the cognizer. This does not mean internal *states*, per se; "the 'internal' of internalism refers to what is internal to the person's first-person cognitive perspective in the sense of being *accessible* from that perspective, not necessarily to what is internal in the sense of being metaphysically a state or feature of that person."[22] So some states that are "internal"—like physiological states—are not internal in the right sense. Conversely, *a priori* truths, which are not relevant to an individual's internal states, are still internally accessible, and so are allowed in internalist epistemologies. Exactly how accessible something must be is a matter of dispute: should we be consciously aware of the grounds for a belief, or is it enough to be able to recall them upon reflection? What if we remember that we once were consciously aware of the grounds for a belief but do not remember precisely what those grounds are now? Questions like these show that the internalist-externalist debate is not binary but involves a spectrum of possibilities.[23]

The requirement of internal accessibility usually implies that beliefs can only be justified by reference to other beliefs (or other relevantly internal conditions). In other words, knowledge is recursive: we must know the reasons for a belief for it to qualify as knowledge. In fact, a rough distinction epistemologists sometimes make is that internalism requires the cognizer to know that they know something, while externalism has no such requirement.

A third element is *infallibility*. Descartes sought to find something he could not doubt, something that was literally indubitable and thus infallible. Supposedly, if we accept that knowledge is fallible, then a belief could be completely justified or warranted, so much so that it should qualify as knowledge, and yet be false.[24] But knowledge must be true by definition. Unfortunately, we are radically fallible and, as such, infallibility is simply off the table. We either have to redefine knowledge so that it is accessible to us or acquiesce in skepticism. But both possibilities are as problematic as infallibility itself. On the one hand, if we lower our standards to the point where we are already meeting them, we are not so much redefining knowledge as abandoning it. After all, if the new definitions end up being impractical for other reasons, we can just continue moving the goalposts indefinitely. We do not accept such moves in other areas (at least we *should* not), so why should we accept it in something as important as knowledge? On the other hand, if we accept that we cannot have knowledge, then it would mean we cannot know that we cannot have knowledge—so for all we know we might be able to have knowledge.

A fourth element is *justification*. Traditionally, this was conceived as a necessary and sufficient aspect of knowledge, in addition to belief and truth. A belief is justified if one has performed their epistemic duties and obligations in verifying its truth. It is because of this concept of epistemic duty and right that epistemology in the Cartesian tradition is often called deontological epistemology (from the Greek δέον meaning duty or obligation). Again, severe problems arise, the most notable of which is that it is possible for a justified true belief to fail to be knowledge. This is demonstrated by the various Gettier cases, where one performs their epistemic duties, comes to hold a true belief, but the belief still fails to be connected to its truth (or connected to its truth in the right way). For example, someone knows that two football teams are playing a game, turns on the television, and watches one team defeat the other. They have performed their epistemic duties in observing the game, they believe that the first team won the game, and it is true that team won the game. But unknown to them, they caught the tail end of a rebroadcast from last year, in which the same team defeated the same other team. They have a justified true belief that the first team won, but it does not qualify as knowledge because their belief is not correctly connected to the fact that the first team won.[25]

The fifth element, the *quintessence*, of Cartesian epistemology is *normativity*. This is closely related to the fourth element: fulfilling one's epistemic duty means meeting some epistemic norm. The concept of normativity is, in one sense, extremely simple: it is merely "shouldness" or "oughtness." If we *ought* to do something, or if we *should not* do something, we are employing a norm, a standard to be met. In another sense, however, normativity is a mare's nest of philosophical concepts and applications. Normativity's most visible face is ethics, but it has reverberations throughout philosophy: in logic, aesthetics, philosophy of language, and, relevant to our purposes, epistemology. An epistemic norm is a *prescription* regarding knowledge or reasoning: we should think rationally, we should not believe falsehoods, etc.

How we account for epistemic norms is a topic of debate: are they conditional or unconditional? Subjective or objective? Are they reducible to a physical substrate? How do we come to be aware of them (or *can* we)? Epistemic normativity is an indispensable aspect of deontological epistemology: without normativity, there is no deontology; without deontology, there is no knowledge. As Jaegwon Kim writes, "It probably is only a historical accident that we standardly speak of 'normative ethics' but not of 'normative epistemology'. Epistemology is a normative discipline as much as, and in the same sense as, normative ethics."[26]

The sixth element we will focus on is *evidentialism*. This is the view that for a belief to qualify as knowledge, one must have sufficient evidence for believing it. This also cuts across several of the other elements of Cartesian epistemology: since someone must not only know that they know something but must also know *how* they know it (that is, what the evidence for it is), this implies internalism. To have evidence is obviously to meet a norm—namely that one must have sufficient evidence to believe something—thus implying normativity. And requiring evidence for something to qualify as knowledge means one is justified in believing it, implying justification.

One problem with evidentialism is that it fails to accurately account for many objects of knowledge. My beliefs in the past, the existence of other minds, and the existence of the external world are not based on evidence, nor should they be. My belief that I had corn flakes for breakfast is not based on any evidence that may be proposed, I simply remember having corn flakes—and "I simply remember" is not a *reason* for why I believe it, much less is it *evidence* for it: it is just a statement of the fact that I have that memory belief. Another problem that Alvin Plantinga brings out is that evidentialism seems to be self-referentially incoherent.[27] What is the evidence for evidentialism? In the absence of evidence for it, then, according to evidentialism itself, we should not accept it.

All these elements of Cartesian epistemology are interconnected. This leads some to conclude that if it fails as a theory of knowledge, every element should be rejected. Thus, in the twentieth century, when the difficulties of Descartes's project reached the point where the entire structure seemed to collapse, naturalized epistemology came forward to fill the void. The biggest problem with Cartesian epistemology was its susceptibility to global skepticism.

Cartesian epistemology and skepticism

Skeptical claims such as Descartes's evil demon, or that one is a brain in a vat being stimulated by scientists or aliens (or alien scientists) to think one has a body and is interacting with a physical world via one's senses, are deep problems in epistemology. This is because in such scenarios, our experiences would be exactly the same as if they were veridical or veracious; as such, there is no test which could disprove them.

Several elements of Cartesian epistemology are responsible for making it susceptible to global skepticism. By requiring knowledge to be infallible, for example, there is no way to satisfy the skeptic; no knowledge claim is 100 percent certain, and as long as it is not, there is room to doubt it. The skeptic steps into this gap and claims that if it is possible for something to be false, we cannot know it. If we could know something that might be false, no matter how remote the possibility, we could have a justified *true* belief of something that is not true—this is the objection to infallibilism again. Thus, Cartesian epistemology inevitably leads to global skeptical problems, where we cannot know anything about anything. If we, however, stop asking how our objects of knowledge can be infallibly true, then global skepticism becomes much less impressive.

If we give up infallibility, then we should probably give up foundationalism as well. If our foundational beliefs, those beliefs that are simply given, are fallible, then anything built upon them is fallible. Moreover, the foundational beliefs are those that are most certain; if they are not, then anything derived from them would be even *less* certain than the foundation itself, even in the best of circumstances.

Similar issues come into play for internalism and justification. According to many internalist epistemologies, one must have a reason for a belief for it to qualify as knowledge. Here, the Gettier cases spring up, although they predate Edmund Gettier's famous paper that sparked the protracted discussion. Perhaps the simplest form is someone who looks at an analog clock and forms the belief that it is noon because both hands are pointing straight up.[28] They have certainly done their epistemic duty in divining the correct time by looking at the clock; they *believe* it is noon; and, as it happens, it *is* noon. But the clock stopped at midnight last night. They have a justified true belief that it is noon, but they do not really *know* it, since their belief is not connected to its truth in an appropriate way. The problem is not with internal factors—everything there is working as it should—but with external factors. As Plantinga puts it, "What Gettier problems show, stated crudely and without necessary qualification, is that even if everything is going as it ought to with respect to what is internal (in the internalist sense), warrant may still be absent."[29] As long as justification is conceived internalistically, then it is susceptible to global skeptical arguments; indeed, this point has been one of the primary motivations for embracing externalist and naturalized epistemologies. Thus, justification, internalism, foundationalism, and infallibilism are all vulnerable to skeptical strategies. If we reject these in favor of an externalist or naturalized epistemology, there is nothing for skepticism to get any purchase on. It would behoove us, then, to assess the plausibility of naturalized epistemology.

2

Quinean Tonic

There are some remedies worse than the disease.

Publilius Syrus

Normativity and the other issues discussed in the previous chapter play large roles in Modern epistemology. However, this theory of knowledge (really, a family of them) bit off more than it could chew, and this led to a new theory being proposed and developed in the second half of the twentieth century. According to naturalized epistemology, the question of how we *should* reason and form beliefs cannot be separated from how we *do* reason and form beliefs: the prescriptive element of norms has to be at least supplemented, if not entirely replaced, with a descriptive element. Its font is Willard Van Orman Quine.

Naturalized epistemology

Quine's essay "Epistemology Naturalized" was largely a reaction against the overreaching claims of Cartesian epistemology, but it was also motivated by ontological naturalism. While Descartes argues we must presuppose God's existence for most knowledge claims to even be possible, Quine writes, "The stimulation of his sensory receptors is all the evidence anybody has had to go on, ultimately, in arriving at his picture of the world."[1] However, naturalized epistemology represents a spectrum rather than a point, and many forms of it can acknowledge the irreducible normative aspect of knowledge, merely claiming that this aspect does not exhaust knowledge. Nor must one be a naturalist in order to be a naturalized epistemologist, as we will soon see.

The place of analyticity and the a priori in naturalism

In "Two Dogmas of Empiricism," the first dogma Quine rejects is the distinction between analytic and synthetic truths.[2] Analytic truths are true by definition, for example, "all bachelors are unmarried men." Such statements require the two sides of the equation to be synonyms: analyticity presupposes synonymy. But there are no acceptable definitions of synonymy. Quine goes over several possibilities but finds them either circular or incoherent. Without synonymy there can be no analyticity, and so no truths that are true by definition. Instead, all truths are synthetic, traceable back to sense experiences. This means that even logical and mathematical laws can potentially be overturned by observations.

Of course, this is immensely problematic. Empirical truths seem to presuppose analytic truths: observations of the world can only get off the ground if we are already assuming that the laws of logic and mathematics are in effect. Any attempt to disprove them via observation would be self-refuting and any attempt to prove them would be circular. While we may need experiences of the physical world to spark our awareness of analytic truths, our knowledge of them is not *derived* from empirical observation. "My belief that things which are equal to the same thing are equal to one another is not at all based on the fact that I have never caught them behaving otherwise. I see that it 'must' be so."[3]

In going over the definition of analyticity, Quine blurs the border between analytic and *a priori* truths.[4] *A priori* truths are those we bring to experience, that are "prior" to it, in contrast with *a posteriori* truths which are learned from experience. This does not necessarily mean that *a priori* knowledge can be had in the absence of experience (as implied by Descartes's cogito), but that it is presupposed by experiential knowledge.[5] Nor must *a priori* truths be true by definition. Kant argued that there is a class of synthetic *a priori* truths that we bring to observation rather than learn from it, yet which do not involve the synonymy of analytic truths. These are his categories of thought which function as a net we throw over our experiences of the world to understand them. As such, they are not learned from experience. The law of identity is analytic whereas the law of causality is synthetic—but we do not learn causality from observation, it is just something we start with which allows us to comprehend observation. It is thus *a priori*.

Analytic and *a priori* knowledge is very difficult to reconcile with a naturalistic view of knowledge and the world: what is the ontological status of these truths? How could our brains, constructed by evolution in order to help us survive, encounter them? Certainly, evolution may have hard-wired us so that some claims are literally inconceivable for us,[6] but that only means that it would have aided our survival to think of them this way, not that analytic truths really are necessary or their denials impossible. Their very idea seems to suggest something like a Platonic world of forms, of which the physical world is simply a shadow or reflection. This is obviously incompatible with Quine's naturalism.[7]

So, Quine argues that analytic knowledge is ultimately synthetic and *a priori* knowledge is ultimately *a posteriori*. "Quine's position might be summarized by saying that he denies that there's any *a priori* knowledge to be explained."[8] While it is immensely unlikely that observation would overturn the laws of logic or mathematics, it is a possibility. Only by acknowledging this can naturalism be retained. Indeed, Quine defines naturalism as "the recognition that it is within science itself" (the *a posteriori*), "and not in some prior philosophy" (the *a priori*), "that reality is to be identified and described."[9] Having explained away the analytic and *a priori*, Quine was in a much better position to provide a completely naturalistic epistemology. However, there was one more aspect of knowledge that stood in the way.

Naturalism and normativity

Objective norms are at least as difficult to fit into a naturalistic worldview as are analytic truths.[10] Indeed, many of the problems with explaining analytic beliefs in naturalistic terms are also problems for explaining norms. If the natural world is all that exists, how could there even *be* norms? Ignoring this, how could naturalistic evolution put us in contact with them? And even ignoring *this*, if we believe them only because they helped our evolutionary ancestors, we wouldn't believe them because they are true, divorcing their truth from our belief in them. Quine's solution, therefore, was to reject norms, and reformulate epistemology accordingly—a strategy also applicable to ethics, philosophy of language, and any other field that contains normative elements.

According to naturalism, everything is explicable by empirical science and natural processes. When applied to the mind, it means everything that appears in the mind—beliefs, thoughts, chains of reasoning—are entirely produced by the natural processes on which they supervene. One would hold the belief because of the natural conditions that produced it regardless of whether the belief was actually true; similarly, if these conditions *failed* to hold, one would not hold the belief, whether it was true or false. Given this picture, how could epistemic norms governing how we *should* reason and form beliefs play any role in how we *do*? Certainly, we may believe there are norms but, as with *a priori* knowledge, this would just be because evolution deigned to provide us with such beliefs in order to aid our progenitors' survival.

The problem of normativity will not go away. However, since it plays such a large role in Cartesian epistemology, and since Quine is abandoning Cartesian epistemology in its entirety, he tries to abandon the normativity that goes with it. Given the failure of deontology, we should stop asking how we should form beliefs, and instead ask how we do, in fact, form them. Above, I quoted Quine's statement, "The stimulation of his sensory receptors is all the evidence anybody has had to go on, ultimately, in arriving at his picture of the world." He follows this up by asking, "Why not just see how this construction really proceeds? Why not settle for psychology?"[11] Science has been extraordinarily successful in explaining our world, so we should apply it to how we form beliefs. On a fundamental level, naturalized epistemology seeks to explain knowledge and belief in *non-epistemic terms*.

Thus, Quine argues that epistemology will ultimately become just another "chapter in psychology," or even that psychology will *replace* epistemology.[12] The question of how we should arrive at our beliefs asks nothing beyond how we do arrive at them. If we answer every possible question of how we form our beliefs then there is nothing further to ask. Cartesian epistemology, with its prescriptions of how we should form beliefs, has been asking the wrong questions; and if prescriptive questions are wrong, the only alternative is descriptive questions. So, normativity is simply removed from the epistemological program.

Quine's critique

The web of belief

Let's look at the six elements we specified from Cartesian epistemology and see how Quine responds to them. Quine rejects foundationalism (the first element) as an abject failure because it is dependent on infallibilism (the third element), which is untenable. Both steps in the foundationalist picture fail. We cannot establish foundational, indubitable starting points (sensory experiences for Quine), nor can we derive other beliefs (scientific hypotheses) from them via assured pathways. There are, first, no indubitable foundations, because the physical processes which produce sensory experiences do not work that way. To think otherwise is doctrinal reduction, where our senses reveal, without error or gap, the truth about the physical world (this is the second dogma of empiricism that Quine disputes[13]). Our senses, however, are fallible indicators of the physical world. Thus, there is no firm foundation on which to build our epistemology in the Cartesian sense.

Similarly, our theories cannot be infallibly derived from our sensory experiences. To think otherwise is conceptual reduction, which reduces beliefs and theories to the phenomenal experiences they seek to explain. Our theories go beyond our sensory experiences, and by going beyond are not infallible reflections of them. Observation "underdetermines" theory. So, since the two steps involved in foundationalism—the move from the world to our sensory experiences (the foundation) and from our sensory experiences to our theories (the derived beliefs)—are fallible, foundationalism, with its doctrine of infallibility, collapses, and this goes to the heart of Cartesian epistemology.

If foundationalism is not the answer, what does Quine suggest to replace it? Which of the four possibilities revealed in Agrippa's trilemma—foundationalism, coherentism, infinitism, and skepticism—does he settle on? Actually, Quine could reject all four, since he is no longer asking the question the trilemma poses ("How do you know X is true?"). However, we can still ask how our beliefs hang together, and in this regard Quine's epistemology is a form of coherentism. He maintains that our noetic faculties form a "web of belief," and that individual beliefs cannot be separated from their place within the system.[14] This holistic framework is present through much of Quine's overall philosophy. He also argues that individual sentences have meaning only in the broader context of a theory. According to the Duhem-Quine theory, individual scientific hypotheses cannot be tested in isolation, since they will have background assumptions, and the test could be confirming or disconfirming these assumptions rather than the hypothesis (observation underdetermines theory). Quine also used his holism to account for analytic knowledge. Such beliefs (e.g., elementary logical and mathematical beliefs) are close to the center of our web of belief, so denying them would entail rejecting our entire noetic systems. As such, it is literally unimaginable. Nevertheless, it remains possible that they are incorrect.

So, Quine's epistemological holism is a form of coherentism, answering questions about the process of how sensory experiences eventually lead to scientific theories by appealing to our sensory experiences. "If we are out simply to understand the link between observation and science, we are well advised to use any available information, including that provided by the very science whose link with observation we are seeking to understand."[15] This, however, is an unusual position:

> The distinctiveness of Quine's naturalism begins to emerge if we ask what justifies this naturalistic claim: what reason do we have to believe that the methods and

techniques of science are the best way to find out about the world? Quine would insist that this claim too must be based on natural science. (If this is circular, he simply accepts the circularity.) This is the revolutionary step, naturalism self-applied. There is no *foundation* for Quine's naturalism: it is not based on anything else.[16]

Quine suggests that, while his model is circular, it is not *viciously* circular. That is, it does not presuppose *as a premise* what it seeks to prove. Rather, it employs a rule in the testing of itself. The difference is that, in premise circularity (the first case), there is no doubt that by presupposing something as a premise, you will end up concluding it. As Thomas Reid writes, "Trying to prove that our reason is not deceptive by any kind of reasoning is absurd in the same way as trying to settle whether a man is honest or not by asking him."[17] Premise-circularity, then, is unacceptable.

Not so for epistemic circularity. By employing a rule in its own testing, it remains possible that the rule will not be validated. It's being tested to see how often it works, and it may not be self-confirming. The rule "could only be true if the conclusion were true,"[18] but the use of the rule *in* a premise (rather than *as* a premise) does not guarantee the conclusion that the rule is accurate. However, epistemic circularity cannot be used to establish a position, much less to defend it against objections. We cannot use epistemic circularity to "restore lost confidence" in the trustworthiness of some source.[19] Therefore, once a belief is challenged—once one is presented with a reason to deny it—we can no longer use any kind of circularity to defend it. But if one is merely asking whether the rule is consistent, some forms of circularity are acceptable. Epistemic circularity can show that a system is internally coherent but not that it is consistent with external factors.

We have already looked at Quine's response to foundationalism, infallibilism, and normativity. With regards to internalism, since Quine maintains that one need not be aware of how a belief is derived from or grounded in another belief, if it is grounded in a belief at all, his epistemology is generally considered to be externalist,[20] although this point is contested.[21] This puts Quine in the interesting position of being an externalist coherentist—interesting because coherentism is usually associated with internalism. Regarding justification, his rejection of normativity entails that there can be no obligation, what one "should" do, in developing one's web of belief. If all epistemology does is observe how the external world impacts on our senses, and how our senses impact our belief-forming capacities, then asking whether someone is "justified" in holding a belief or set of beliefs is irrelevant. As for evidentialism, since one need not know that they know something for it to qualify as an object of knowledge, they do not need to know *how* they know it either. Quine is merely looking at how things work, how the interaction between the external physical world and the brain give rise to the web of belief they do. Any evidential relation is irrelevant to such a study.

Naturalized epistemology and skepticism

One further point is naturalized epistemology's immunity to skepticism. Descartes came up with hypothetical scenarios in which our experiences and beliefs would be the same as if they were veridical but are radically deceptive. So, if we need to know why we believe something in order for it potentially to be knowledge, these skeptical hypotheses undercut all or nearly all of our beliefs. Naturalized epistemology, however, does not so much resolve such concerns as it sidesteps them. While Quine discusses extensively how our web of belief arose and became what it is (via the natural world impinging itself on our senses), his project precludes examining this in epistemic terms. But skeptical issues are only relevant in epistemic terms: how do you know X is true? Quine's answer: we believe X, now let's see how the natural processes involved in my believing X gave rise to it. So, the skeptical questions never arise.

While Quine's claims may not convince a critic, Christopher Hookway argues that they still provide sufficient room for the naturalized epistemologist to maneuver.[22] Quine seems to deny that "understand[ing] the link between observation and science"[23] needs to be defended at all: we just have the cognitive faculties we do and so use them; their use does not require any justification. Hookway, however, suggests that questioning our procedures' validity plays no role whatsoever in our cognitive lives, which is not quite the same thing. Regardless, in either case the procedures go unchallenged and the naturalized epistemologist is not irrational in continuing to use and believe them. No evaluative concepts are necessary for knowledge, shifting the burden of proof from the naturalized epistemologist to his critic. "If Quine's practice could show that the lack of this concept did not prevent him carrying out his inquiries in an ordered and responsible way, then he may be able to ignore the objection."[24]

Our intuition, says Hookway, is passive rather than active, and it tends toward simplicity and conservativism. That is, we intuitively prefer simpler explanations, and we accommodate new information in the most conservative way. Indeed, these two qualities would probably be selected in the struggle for survival, since "simplicity allows for neurological parsimony and conservativeness for reducing cognitive labor."[25] These qualities, therefore, are just given, not something we choose, and since they are the very qualities that play a major role in scientific reasoning, the scientific picture of the world—naturalistic, materialistic—is valid. Thus, we have no reason to question these qualities or the scientific worldview unless we become suspicious of the nature of these passive traits.

Moreover, since our intuitive acceptance of simplicity and conservativeness arose via evolution, they are in place to address local issues rather than global ones. These qualities are merely those that helped our evolutionary forebears survive in a particular environment; to apply them globally is inappropriate. This is precisely what allows naturalized epistemology to avoid global skeptical claims: it is not addressing global *anything* and so is not addressing skeptical charges either. As long as the naturalized epistemologist recognizes the local relevance of our cognitive equipment, no global skeptical argument can arise: one cannot question the overall reliability of our cognitive faculties or our intuitive use of simplicity and conservativism. It is

> only if we are suspicious of "passivity" rather than welcoming of it, that there is a problem. So long as we accept the "shallowness of epistemic reflection" and insist that the only normative issues that arise are local rather than global ones, there need be no normative issues arising naturally out of our practice which a naturalized epistemologist cannot address."[26]

Critique of Quine's critique

Assessing Quine's vision

Quine's problems with Cartesian epistemology are genuine issues, and many of his points against it and in favor of naturalized epistemology have some force to them. Just as quinine can prevent one from dying of malaria, so Quine's antidote to Descartes certainly allows one to avoid many of the pitfalls of the latter. There are strong reasons for agreeing with Quine that Cartesian epistemology is no longer tenable, at least as traditionally understood. Equally, there are some strong reasons for agreeing that how we should form beliefs cannot be completely separated from how we do form them. However, just as quinine tonic can produce side-effects as bad as the disease, like blindness or deafness, so the Quinean tonic creates problems of its own that are just as problematic as what it is seeking to cure.

First, it's just false that if we answer every possible question of how we form our beliefs then there is nothing further to ask. This leaves us with no way to distinguish between good and bad belief-forming processes or between true and false, correct and incorrect, rational and insane beliefs. Insofar as some beliefs are rationally preferable to others, we must be able to make a distinction between them, and this requires the normativity Quine banished.

The reduction of prescription to description is inadequate: people often reach their beliefs in inappropriate or invalid ways. Sometimes this is nearly universal; there are numerous examples in which the brain appears to be hardwired to produce false conclusions through faulty reasoning.[27] Indeed, if Quine is right about epistemology, the greatest thinkers in history were spectacularly mistaken about the nature of knowledge itself. They did not arrive at their beliefs appropriately because their beliefs were, supposedly, wrong. Yet it's odd to claim that how people do arrive at their beliefs is how they should and anyone who arrives at a contrary belief is wrong. Since being wrong means failing to meet a norm, we are apparently being told that "you should believe there are no norms"; more blatantly, "you should believe there are no 'shoulds.'"

Epistemology evolutionized

Quine appeals to evolution to explain why the way we form beliefs coincides with how we should. Specifically, he asks why the inductions we make tend to be accurate when there are any number of inductions that would not be. Just because the Xs we have observed have property Y, how do we know *all* Xs have Y? Perhaps Xs we have not observed do not have Y; or perhaps all Xs have property Z which is like Y in some ways but not in other ways. Some inductions are clearly appropriate: since the sun has risen in the east every morning so far, we can inductively infer that it will rise in the east tomorrow morning. Others, however, are clearly inappropriate: if my children have been less than fourteen years old for as long as they have existed, I should not inductively infer that they will remain under fourteen indefinitely. Such problems of induction plague the epistemologist, but Quine argues that we are asking the wrong question. We should not ask how we *justify* the inductions we make against an infinite field of possible ways of grouping properties, but just why we make the inductions we do; and this leads directly to evolution: "An answer is offered by Darwin's theory of natural selection. Individuals whose similarity groupings conduce largely to true expectations have a good chance of finding food and avoiding predators, and so a good chance of living to reproduce their kind."[28] He also writes, "There is some encouragement in Darwin. If people's innate spacing of qualities is a gene-linked trait, then the spacing that has made for the most successful inductions will have tended to predominate through natural selection. Creatures inveterately wrong in their inductions have a pathetic but praiseworthy tendency to die before reproducing their kind."[29]

Quine's faith in the power of evolution is not unique to him. Many other philosophers have argued that evolution provides the necessary mechanism to validate our claims to knowledge within a naturalistic perspective.[30] In fact, one form of naturalized epistemology is evolutionary epistemology which arose long before Quine published "Epistemology Naturalized" in 1969. Charles Darwin, T.H. Huxley, and others applied evolution to the origin of our brains almost immediately upon the publication of *On the Origin of Species* in 1859, and similar accounts were made by thinkers such as C.S. Peirce, William James, and John Dewey. Indeed, insofar as the theory of evolution did not spring fully formed from Darwin's forehead but was formulated within a specific intellectual context and history that included prior evolutionary theories (such as Lamarckism), so too does evolutionary epistemology have pre-Darwinian roots.[31] However, it was not until the 1940s when Konrad Lorenz sought to explain *a priori* knowledge in light of evolution that evolutionary epistemology began to receive fuller treatment.[32]

We must ask whether appealing to evolution explains why our cognitive faculties are reliable in general, not just regarding induction. That is precisely what the EAAN addresses, and so our answer must wait until we explore it. For now, we can suggest that there is a gap between a belief, set of beliefs, or belief-forming capacities being *useful* (so that they would be selected by evolution) and whether they are *true* or *truth-conducive*. Lorenz's account of the *a priori*, for example, shows why we would come to hold some beliefs as rigidly as we hold *a priori* beliefs, but it does not account for how we would be correct in doing so. Evolution may explain why certain beliefs are so important to our survival that we would think they are necessarily true, that we could not imagine their being false in any possible world. But that does nothing to show that such beliefs really *are* necessarily true. It does not explain the *a priori* so much as it explains it away.

Further issues

A third problem with naturalized epistemology, mentioned above, is that it is circular. This is unsurprising as it is a form of coherentism. Quine accepts epistemic circularity, since his belief in naturalism "is not based on anything else,"[33] such as evidence, reasons, or grounds. It is simply his starting point. However, it is not clear why this is acceptable since epistemic circularity still leaves it very open for false belief-forming processes to be verified. The claim here is not merely that beliefs could *possibly* be false but that they could *very probably* be false. Quine's rejection of infallibilism means it is not necessary to know something with absolute certainty, but there is a world of difference between not knowing something with 100 percent assurance and not knowing it with 50 percent assurance. Indeed, the only thing that would prevent the rule from confirming itself is if it is self-referentially incoherent. This is far too lenient a criterion, since most false beliefs and invalid belief-forming processes are not self-referentially incoherent. It is not immediately evident, for example, that using astrology to test whether astrology is accurate would show that it is not. So, while Quine's epistemology is not viciously circular, it is still circular, and this leaves too much room for accepting invalid processes. Thus, many philosophers remain unconvinced by Quine's epistemological project.

> All of this will, of course, drive the skeptic crazy. You cannot *use* perception to justify the reliability of perception! You cannot *use* memory to justify the reliability of memory! You cannot *use* induction to justify the reliability of induction! Such attempts to respond to the skeptic's concerns involve blatant, indeed pathetic, circularity.... If a philosopher starts wondering about the reliability of astrological inference, the philosopher will not allow the astrologer to read in the stars the reliability of astrology. Even if astrological inferences happen to be reliable, the astrologer is missing the point of a *philosophical* inquiry into the justifiability of astrological inference if the inquiry is answered using the techniques of astrology.... If I really am interested in knowing whether astrological inference is legitimate, if I have the kind of philosophical curiosity that leads me to raise this question in the first place, I will not for a moment suppose that further use of astrology might help me find the answer to my question. Similarly, if as a philosopher I start wondering whether perceptual beliefs are accurate reflections of the way the world really is, I would not dream of using perception to resolve my doubt. Even if there is some sense in which the reliable process of perception might yield justified beliefs about the reliability of perception, the use of perception could never satisfy a *philosophical curiosity* about the legitimacy of perceptual beliefs. When the philosopher wants an answer to the question of whether memory gives us justified beliefs about the past, that answer cannot possibly be provided by memory.[34]

Another problem with Quine's epistemology is that it reads too much into the failings of Cartesian epistemology. Most philosophers were already aware of its problems but did not think we should abandon it entirely.

> Most of us are inclined, I think, to view the situation Quine describes with no great alarm, and I rather doubt that these conclusions of Quine's came as news to most epistemologists when "Epistemology Naturalized" was first published. We are tempted to respond: of course we can't define physical concepts in terms of sense-data; of course observation "underdetermines" theory. That is why observation is observation and not theory.[35]

Quine is presenting an all-or-nothing scenario where the Cartesian epistemological project is either completely accepted or completely rejected. He's not only thrown the baby out with the bathwater, he's burned down the house, razed the village, and nuked the entire site from orbit.[36] But why can't we recognize that the Cartesian project is in dire need of reconstruction, without abandoning every aspect of it? Indeed, some of it, at least, seems necessary. The most obvious example of this is normativity.

Normativity, again

Quine does not directly address normativity in "Epistemology Naturalized," but suggesting we should replace the old model in favor of descriptive psychology implies it. By accounting for all knowledge descriptively he is removing any prescriptive element it had previously contained, and without prescriptivity there are no norms. The problem is that description and prescription do not investigate the same relation so it is difficult to see how one could replace the other. Replacement requires some point of contact or shared commonality which both positions seek to explain. "As lately noted, normative epistemology is concerned with the evidential relation properly so-called—that is, the relation of justification—and Quine's naturalized epistemology is meant to study the causal-nomological relation. For epistemology to go out of the business of justification is for it to go out of business."[37]

Often, when a tradition emerges from a single source, it develops in all directions from that source, some being more extreme, some less. Not so here: since the publication of Quine's original paper, naturalized epistemologists have continually walked back the claims being made, to the point where much of the radicalness is left behind. It is generally accepted that Quine went too far, specifically in his rejection of normativity.[38] This even includes Quine himself. In later writings, he acquiesces that some type of normativity must be affirmed. "Insofar as theoretical epistemology gets naturalized into a chapter of theoretical science, so normative epistemology gets naturalized into a chapter of engineering: the technology of anticipating sensory stimulation."[39] Elsewhere he writes,

> Naturalization of epistemology does not jettison the normative and settle for the indiscriminate description of ongoing procedures. For me normative epistemology is a branch of engineering. It is the technology of truth-seeking, or, in a more cautious epistemological term, prediction. Like any technology, it makes free use of whatever scientific findings may suit its purpose.... There is no question here of ultimate value, as there is in morals; it is a matter of efficacy for an ulterior end, truth or prediction. The normative here, as elsewhere in engineering, becomes descriptive when the terminal parameter is expressed.[40]

Quine is describing technical norms, or hypothetical imperatives.[41] These are simply the means one should employ in the pursuit of one's goals, and they are *hypothetical* because the goal in question is conditional rather than necessary. They can be rationally rejected by one's interlocutors so that the norm or imperative would not apply to them.

> Technical normativity actually prescribes only if the one to whom a technical norm is proposed shares the goal on which its prescriptivity is conditioned and has no conflicting goal to which he gives priority. This fact limits the usefulness of

technical norms in rationally excluding one of a pair of contradictory propositions. Whenever it is rational for a particular person not to share in desiring a certain purpose, then no technical norm derived from that purpose is in force for him. Thus, he is not unreasonable if he ignores the norm and any affirmation which is conditioned by it.[42]

But this is insufficient in the present case: in order to affirm that one view—naturalized epistemology, say—is rationally superior to its alternatives, we must employ a *categorical* imperative. Otherwise, we would merely be saying that one view is rationally superior if we are pursuing rationality. If we are not, then we are free to reject that view and the goal of rationality *and remain rational in doing so*. But one cannot reject rationality while remaining rational.

Cognitive suicide

With all this, we can ask whether Quine's naturalized epistemology is compatible with affirming itself or naturalism as rationally preferable to its denial. To affirm naturalism or naturalized epistemology as rationally preferable to their denials, a technical norm won't do the trick. Quine has to employ more than a hypothetical imperative, he has to employ a categorical imperative. If his naturalism and naturalized epistemology do not allow him to employ such a norm then he cannot rationally affirm them as superior or preferable to their negations.

This is not an original point: some great philosophers, foreshadowing Lynne Rudder Baker's accusation that eliminative materialism commits cognitive suicide,[43] have said the same about naturalized epistemology, that it is, in some sense, self-referentially incoherent. Thus, Hilary Putnam writes "The elimination of the normative is attempted mental suicide."[44] Similarly, Peter Geach argues that naturalized epistemology "is as incredible as McTaggart's metaphysical commitment to a denial that there is anything more than an illusory introspective appearance of discursive thought—a belief that there are no beliefs, an inference that there are no inferences."[45] And again,

> Any large-scale extrapolation to regions of space and time far distant from us, to the microscopic and the ultra-microscopic, will involve inductions that could very well be wildly unreliable without having been detrimental to the survival of the human race. The naturalist account of why our inductive procedures should be trusted is thus quite insufficient: indeed, it commits suicide, because only if large-scale extrapolation can be trusted could there be the faintest reason for believing the story of rational creatures evolving by natural selection.[46]

As with evolution, this is precisely what Plantinga's EAAN addresses, so we will defer discussion of it to later chapters. First, though, we should take a good look at Plantinga's theory of knowledge since he claims it is a form of naturalized epistemology, albeit one with an interesting twist.

3

Naturalized Epistemology Reformed

When we hear of some new attempt to explain reasoning or language or choice naturalistically, we ought to react as if we were told someone had squared the circle or proved √2 to be rational: only the mildest curiosity is in order—how well has the fallacy been concealed?

Peter Geach

We've seen some of the motivations for moving from a Cartesian to a naturalized epistemology. Since Plantinga claims his epistemology belongs squarely in the latter camp, let's go over the problems with Cartesian epistemology again to see how Plantinga answers them.

Plantinga vs. Descartes

The first element was foundationalism where some beliefs do not have to be justified by others but are self-justifying. Cartesian (or deontological) foundationalism is the first target Plantinga attacks in developing his own epistemology,[1] but he admits his position is a form of foundationalism.[2] He maintains that some beliefs are "properly basic," they do not obtain their warrant via some other belief or set of beliefs. They are simply given, and so long as our cognitive faculties are functioning properly, they are warranted, do not require justification, and function as the foundation. The interesting point in Plantinga's epistemology is that he separates this foundationalism from the other aspects of Cartesian epistemology, allowing him to avoid the problems that come with it; it is only *Cartesian* foundationalism that fails.

One reason he adopts foundationalism is the absence of any alternative: coherentism is, according to Plantinga, simply an atypical form of foundationalism.

> The coherentist does not really tout circular (or cylindrical) reasoning. What he does instead is suggest an unusual condition for proper basicality, a new source of warrant: he holds that a belief is properly basic for me if and only if it appropriately coheres with the rest of my noetic structure.... Seen from the present perspective, therefore, the coherentist reveals her true colors as a nonstandard foundationalist with unusual views about what is properly basic.... Coherentism, therefore, is a

special case (a *very* special case) of foundationalism: the variety according to which the only source of warrant is coherence.³

One issue with foundationalism is whether the number of foundational beliefs is low or high and whether the inferential rules used to derive other beliefs from them are restrictive or permissive. On the one hand, the fewer ground-level beliefs there are, the lower the probability that any of them are false, but this would require very permissive rules of inference to derive a sufficient number of beliefs from the foundational ones, and this could potentially let false beliefs in the back door. On the other hand, more restrictive rules would require having a broader base of foundational beliefs, potentially letting false beliefs in the *front* door. Plantinga essentially embraces the latter option: the number of foundational beliefs, i.e., properly basic beliefs, is large. They are the beliefs produced by our cognitive faculties when they are functioning properly, they come with some warrant, and require no further justification. This does not mean that they are ungrounded: "a belief is properly basic only in certain conditions; these conditions are, we might say, the ground of its justification and, by extension, the ground of the belief itself. In this sense basic beliefs are not, or are not necessarily, *groundless* beliefs."⁴ The problem of potentially letting in false beliefs through the front door is addressed by Plantinga's assessment of infallibility (below).

The second element of Cartesian epistemology is internalism, that a belief's justification depends upon its relations to other beliefs rather than to the world. Plantinga's epistemology fits squarely in the externalist tradition. In fact, he argues that internalism is merely the traditional view *within Modernity*; prior to this, externalism was the standard epistemological model.

> Externalism goes a long way back, to Thomas Reid, to Thomas Aquinas—back, in fact, all the way to Aristotle. Indeed, we may venture to say that (apart, perhaps, from Augustine and some of the Skeptics of the later Platonic Academy) internalists in epistemology are *rarae aves* in Western thought prior to Descartes. It is really externalism, in one form or another, that has been the dominant tradition; internalism is a recent interloper.⁵

By embracing a position more traditional than the traditional view, Plantinga avoids the usual forms of global skepticism which only apply to internalism, as well as many Gettier cases where there is justified true belief but not knowledge. According to Plantinga, these cases infect all forms of internalism. "Gettier problems afflict internalist epistemologies, and they do so essentially. The essence of the Gettier problem is that it shows internalist theories of warrant to be wanting."⁶

However, it should be remembered that an approximate rule for separating internalism from externalism is whether one must know that they know something in order to know it. On this issue, internalists say "yes," externalists say "no," and Plantinga says "sometimes."

> ... there isn't anything at all like a simple, single answer to the question whether warrant for grounded beliefs requires that the subject know that the ground is an

indicator of the belief; sometimes this is required and sometimes it is not. And the reason is not far to seek. In some cases it is perfectly in accord with proper cognitive function to believe A on the basis of B even if you have never had any views at all as to whether B is an indicator of A; in a wide variety of other cases a properly functioning human being will believe A on the basis of B only if she has first learned that B reliably indicates A.[7]

The third element of Cartesian epistemology is infallibility. Plantinga rejects this. Properly basic beliefs are innocent until proven guilty: they automatically have warrant and do not require further justification—but they *can* be overturned by considerations that have greater warrant than the basic belief. This means a non-basic belief can have more warrant than a properly basic belief.[8] In fact he thinks many of his critics have misunderstood this, and once it is corrected their criticisms no longer hold.[9]

However, he also points out that some properly basic beliefs have so much warrant that it is unlikely they could be overturned. His example is the purloined letter: A letter is stolen from someone's office, and all the evidence points to a particular person as the culprit. This person had an enormous motive for stealing the letter and has stolen such things before. Yet this person remembers taking a solitary walk through the woods when the letter was stolen and has no memory of stealing it. Should they reject their memory and accept the evidence that points to their guilt? Bear in mind, the question is not whether *other* people should judge their guilt or innocence on their memories, but whether *this* person should. It is difficult to imagine a situation where the evidence would be so great as to overrule their own memories. Yet this is not because their memory-based beliefs are infallible but because they have so much warrant—at least more warrant than can be countered by mere evidentialist considerations.

This also shows Plantinga's response to evidentialism: if properly functioning cognitive faculties produce our beliefs, then evidence need not play a role. Indeed, much of his career can be seen as the rejection of evidentialism. We do not need evidence for properly basic beliefs. The purloined letter case shows there are cases where it is irrational, even insane, to base one's belief on the evidence or to change one's belief in the face of contrary evidence.

Warrant and justification

The nature of warrant

The fourth element of Cartesian epistemology is justification. In its stead, Plantinga substitutes warrant, and this is where he devotes the most commentary. Justification is doing one's epistemic duty: we are justified in believing something if we have been responsible in coming to believe it, by doing what was within our powers to verify it, to not accept it on the basis of our desire that it be true, etc. But this has long been recognized as insufficient. Surely it is possible for someone to be responsible in forming a true belief without that belief being knowledge. These, again, are the Gettier cases, such as the person who looks at the analog clock that stopped at midnight last night and forms the belief—which happens to be true—that it is noon. They have a justified true belief it is noon, but we do not want to say they really *know* it since "it is merely *by accident* that the justified true belief in question is true."[10] Many have argued that justification is necessary for knowledge, but not sufficient; we need to add a fourth condition (like undefeatedness),[11] maybe more.

As a naturalized epistemologist, however, Plantinga scraps the whole justification project. Since epistemologists are unified in acknowledging that mere true belief is insufficient for something to qualify as knowledge,[12] he proposes the term "warrant" to refer to whatever must be added to true belief to make knowledge. "Warranted true belief," therefore, is knowledge by definition. The difference between warrant and justification is

> most clearly expressed by pointing out that justification is a property of *persons*, whereas warrant is a property of *beliefs*. In other words, for any person S and belief b, to say that a belief is justified is really to say that "person S is justified in holding belief b." On the other hand, to say that a belief is warranted is really to say that "belief b is warranted for person S."[13]

Warrant is a matter of degree, so the issue is not whether a belief has warrant, but whether it has *enough* warrant to qualify as knowledge. Moreover, warrant is transferable: if someone tells you something and you believe them, your belief is warranted if it was warranted for them, all other things being equal. If you came to believe something in a warranted way, but no longer recall the exact process of how you came to believe it, the belief is warranted for you now if it was warranted for you originally.[14]

Much of Modern epistemology, due to Descartes's influence, tries to build up to the concept of knowledge by starting with true belief and speculating about what must be added. Plantinga reverse engineers the process. He starts from genuine items of knowledge and asks how they differ from mere true belief. So, whereas Descartes tried to go back to the beginning and work forwards to the end, Plantinga starts at the end and works back to the beginning. To accomplish this, he gives several interrelated criteria for warrant which distinguish knowledge from true belief.

Proper function and proper environment

First, a belief obtains warrant if it is the product of one's cognitive faculties when they are functioning properly; or negatively, a belief lacks warrant if it is produced by cognitive malfunction.

> I therefore suggest initially that a necessary condition of a belief's having warrant for me is that my cognitive equipment, my belief-forming and belief-maintaining apparatus or powers, be free of such malfunction. A belief has warrant for you only if your cognitive apparatus is functioning properly, working the way it ought to work, in producing and sustaining it. . . .

[T]he idea of proper function is one we all have; we all grasp it in at least a preliminary rough-and-ready way; we all constantly employ it. You go to the doctor; he tells you that your thyroid isn't functioning quite as it ought (its thyroxin output is low); he prescribes a synthetic thyroxin. If you develop cataracts, the lenses of your eyes become less transparent; they can't function properly and you can't see well. A loss in elasticity of the heart muscle can lead to left ventricular malfunction. If a bird's wing is broken, it typically won't function properly; the bird won't be able to fly until the wing is healed, and then only if it heals in such a way as not to inhibit proper function. Alcohol and drugs can interfere with the proper function of various cognitive capacities, so that you can't drive properly, can't do simple addition problems, display poor social judgment, get into a fist fight, and wind up in jail.[15]

Proper function is a scientific concept, used in biology and many other fields to explain how various organs and structures work.[16] "Biological and social scientists, furthermore—psychologists, medical researchers, neuroscientists, economists, sociologists, and many others—continually give accounts of how human beings or other organisms or their parts and organs function: how they work, what their purposes are, and how they react under various circumstances."[17] According to such eminent biologists as Ernst Mayr and George Williams, virtually every advance in physiology has come from asking what an organ or structure's function is.[18]

For proper function to confer warrant on a belief, it is only necessary for the faculties producing that specific belief to be functioning properly. So it's a particular requirement, not a general one. The presence of other beliefs that are not produced by properly functioning cognitive faculties does not detract from those that are: "the rationality of my belief that China is a large country is not compromised by the fact that I harbor irrational beliefs about my neighbor's dog."[19] Moreover, the faculties involved need not work perfectly to confer warrant. And since warrant is a matter of degree, proper function is a matter of degree as well. "If warrant and proper function are properly tied together, then we may expect that they will waver together."[20]

Proper function is a very naturalistic concept. It does not privilege the mind but simply ascribes to it the same property that is ascribed to other bodily organs, organisms, and artifacts. This allows it to play a role in naturalized epistemology, since it can account for knowledge in non-epistemic terms. Thus, by employing this concept, Plantinga is cementing his epistemology in the naturalized tradition, and granting a great deal to the naturalist.

Proper function, however, is not enough. My cognitive faculties may be functioning properly but the environment in which I find myself may be unconducive to them. If I cannot see that does not imply my eyes aren't functioning properly if I'm in a dark room. If my car won't start that does not imply it's not functioning properly if it's underwater. Thus, there must be some sort of *alignment* or *fit* between my cognitive faculties and the environment for a belief to have warrant; I must be in an appropriate *cognitive environment*. A belief is warranted if it is produced by cognitive faculties functioning properly in an appropriate cognitive environment. Many Gettier cases involve one being in a misleading cognitive environment (the clock is not functioning as it should, or a person who is usually trustworthy is lying).

The design plan

This still isn't enough though. We must make a distinction between whether something is functioning properly and *what its function is*. A cognitive faculty may be functioning properly in a proper environment but not produce true beliefs because that is not what it is supposed to do. "Different parts or aspects of our cognitive apparatus have different purposes; ... some might be such as to conduce to survival, or relief from suffering, or the possibility of loyalty, or inclination to have more children, and so on."[21] Wishful thinking, for example, can produce a level of optimism that may make one more attractive and hence successful in procreation; or it may reduce anxiety resulting in greater health. But even though the "wishful thinking" faculty is functioning properly, the beliefs it produces are not warranted. So proper function in an appropriate environment is not enough to confer warrant. We need another criterion.

What is required, Plantinga argues, is that the cognitive faculties producing a belief must be aimed at producing *true* beliefs as opposed to, say, comforting beliefs. If a faculty's function is to produce true belief, then if it is functioning properly in the appropriate environment, it will produce warranted true belief. If its function is something else, such as optimism via wishful thinking, then even if the belief formed is true and the faculty that formed it is functioning properly, it would not be warranted.

Of course, this raises questions: how do we define "proper" function? How do we define an "appropriate" cognitive environment? What does it mean to say that a cognitive faculty is "aimed" at producing true beliefs? None of these concepts are synonymous with "normal" in the statistical sense. A great athlete far surpasses the normal ability of human beings, but this does not imply they are not functioning properly. If the radiation from a nuclear holocaust rendered most surviving men impotent, then the inability to procreate would be normal; it does not follow that the minority that can still procreate is not functioning properly. We need something else that explains the difference between proper function and dysfunction, between appropriate and inappropriate cognitive environments, and how an organ or organism can be aimed at truth or anything else.

Plantinga's answer is the design plan. This does not require (not yet at least) that "design" be taken literally so that we were intentionally designed by an intelligent agent or agents. It could be taken metaphorically in which case evolution designed us and our organs for particular purposes.[22] This concept of design is just as central to biological and social sciences as is function, and biologists and philosophers of science constantly use it. Plantinga notes he is using "design" in the same sense as Daniel Dennett who writes, "In the end, we want to be able to explain the intelligence of man, or beast, in terms of his design, and this in turn in terms of the natural selection of this design."[23]

This allows us to say that organs, organisms, and artifacts have functions or purposes, both proximate and ultimate. The proximate function of the heart, for example, is to pump blood. But then we must ask *why* it pumps blood. Thus, a mediate (or less proximate) function of the heart is to provide oxygen to the various parts of the body. Again, however, we must ask why it does *this*. Eventually, we reach the ultimate function, "to contribute to the health and proper function of the entire organism (some might say instead that it is to contribute to the *survival* of the individual, or the species, or even to the perpetuation of the genetic material itself)."[24] Similarly, the purpose

> of our cognitive faculties (overall) is to supply us with reliable information: about our environment, about the past, about the thoughts and feeling of others, and so on. But not just any old way of accomplishing this purpose in the case of a specific cognitive process is in accordance with our design plan. It is for this reason that it is possible for a belief to be produced by a cognitive process or belief-producing mechanism that is *accidentally* reliable.... Although such belief-producing processes are in fact reliable, the beliefs they yield have little by way of warrant; and the reason is that these processes are pathologically out of accord with the design plan for human beings.[25]

Thus, according to our design plan, when faced with certain circumstances we will form beliefs like, "there is a tree in front of me" or "I had toast for breakfast." If a friend told me last night that they were either going to study at the library or go to a party, and another tells me today that they were not at the party (and I believe it), I will form the belief that they went to the library if my relevant cognitive faculties are functioning properly.

Of course, this does not mean these beliefs are immune from defeat. The tree in front of me may be a cardboard prop for an outdoor play; the person who told me my friend was not at the party may be mistaken or lying. Plus, I will hold some beliefs more firmly than others. If I believe my friend was at the library more firmly than I believe that a proposition and its denial cannot both be true, there is cognitive dysfunction rather than proper function. Nor does it mean the formation of true beliefs must be our cognitive faculties' *sole* function. Certainly, there are fields of study characterized by wild disagreement (Plantinga suggests philosophy and biblical studies here). Moreover, just as there are visual illusions, so there are cognitive illusions, such as the gambler's fallacy or the Monty Hall problem. "Nevertheless over a vast area of cognitive terrain we take it both that the purpose (function) of our cognitive faculties is to provide us with true or verisimilitudinous beliefs, and that, for the most part, that is just what they do."[26]

For a belief to have warrant, the parts of one's cognitive faculties that produced it must be aimed at producing true beliefs. If they were not so aimed, then even if a belief were true, it would only be *accidentally* true, and an accidentally true belief is not knowledge. As long as the specific cognitive faculties are aimed at producing true beliefs—even if these faculties are not generally aimed at producing true beliefs, but in this particular instance are—then knowledge is possible. "The cognitive design plan of human beings is subtle and complicated; a source of belief might be such that *in general* it is not aimed at the formation of true belief, but in some special cases it is."[27] If the particular belief is produced by cognitive faculties aimed at truth (and the other conditions), then the belief has warrant, even if the cognitive faculties are not aimed at truth for the most part.

Trade-offs and reliabilism

Another point is that the various aspects of our cognitive faculties (or any system or organ) may have areas where they conflict. A design plan, therefore, will involve "trade-offs and compromises," which accommodate the various constraints the design entails. A cognitive system that produced true beliefs 99.9 percent of the time, for example, may have required a brain so large that the entities with it could not survive, so evolution would not select it. Instead, it selected a brain of moderate size which reliably produces true beliefs but does not endanger the individual's life. There are further trade-offs: having a brain this size requires being born much earlier in the developmental process because of the constraints on the birthing canal. This requires a longer stage of being protected by the parents or tribe, etc.

A trade-off plays a role in proper function by making some other goal possible. In other words, it is aimed *indirectly* at producing the goal. With regards to our belief-forming processes,

> a belief has warrant for you only if the segment of the design plan governing its production is *directly* rather than indirectly aimed at the production of true beliefs.... If a given response is present only because it is a part of the best compromise and not because it directly serves the purpose of producing true beliefs, then the belief in question does not have warrant.[28]

Thus far, we have the formula that a belief is warranted if it is produced by properly functioning cognitive faculties that are directly aimed at producing true beliefs in an appropriate environment for which they are intended, where "properly," "aimed at," "appropriate," and "intended" are defined in reference to the design plan. This seems fairly complete, at least in broad strokes. Yet there is still an element missing, one that is indicated by the reliabilist intuition that warranted beliefs are beliefs formed by reliable processes. We must add that the design plan in question must be a *good* plan, that it has a high probability of producing true beliefs. If incompetent aliens constructed our cognitive faculties to produce true beliefs, but their design is flawed and our faculties are unreliable, there may still be occasions where true beliefs are produced. In this case, all the conditions listed thus far would be met, yet the beliefs formed would not have warrant. This requirement is often overlooked because "we ordinarily take it for granted that when our cognitive faculties—at any rate, those whose function it is to produce true beliefs—function properly in an appropriate environment, then for the most part the beliefs they produce are true."[29] This criterion is not contained within the notion of proper function itself, and so must be specified. Thus, we now have a more complete account of warrant:

> A belief B has warrant for S if and only if the relevant segments (the segments involved in the production of B) are functioning properly in a cognitive environment sufficiently similar to that for which S's faculties are designed; and the modules of the design plan governing the production of B are (1) aimed at truth, and (2) such that there is a high objective probability that a belief formed in

accordance with those modules (in that sort of cognitive environment) is true; and the more firmly S believes B the more warrant B has for S.[30]

The design plan vs. the max plan

What makes a plan a *design* plan is three factors, or, as Plantinga puts it, "a set of triples: circumstance, response, and purpose or function"[31] where the function regulates the response in light of the circumstance. The function of an organ, organism, or artifact determines how it will respond in certain circumstances (not *all* circumstances).

> I design a radio in such a way that it has certain fail-safe features: if there is an electrical surge of moderate voltage along the line, a circuit breaker will trip, thus forestalling damage. The design plan may say nothing, however, about how it will respond (or what will happen to it) when struck by lightning, or when it sinks to the bottom of the Mindanao Trench, or is run over by a steamroller.[32]

Similarly, the heart's design plan regulates how it will respond in certain circumstances; it will increase its rate when the organism physically exerts itself, for example. And the design plan of our cognitive faculties regulates how they will respond when presented with certain circumstances; I see a tree-shaped object ahead of me and form the belief, "There is a tree." However, the design plan does not regulate how my heart or cognitive faculties will respond if I turn into a bat or am instantaneously transported to the surface of Mercury.

Something will certainly *happen* in these circumstances, but what will happen is not circumscribed by the design plan; it is circumscribed by the *max* plan. This is essentially the design plan minus the purpose or function, which allows it to describe much more diverse pairs (or doubles) of circumstance and response than if the circumstance and response are regulated by a function. A fish swimming in the ocean and a dead fish rotting on a hillside are both responding to circumstances, and so are regulated by max plans; yet the first is further regulated by a design plan that the second lacks. The set of circumstance-response pairs, however, is not unlimited. The max plan does not describe how the dead fish will respond to circumstances if all its scales spontaneously turn into marshmallows, or the strong nuclear force suddenly stops behaving in the manner to which we are accustomed. It describes how an organ, organism, or artifact will respond to circumstances "so long as it retains its approximate present structure in circumstances involving the natural laws that do in fact obtain."[33]

Doesn't the dead fish have a design plan though? Isn't there a function according to which it decomposes and feeds other animals and plants? This question shows that something can change from one design plan to another, both of which are contained by the max plan. So, the radio I construct could stop receiving radio broadcasts; I then put it on my desk and use it as a paperweight. It has a different (and much less interesting) function now, but it still has a function, a *new* one not described by its former design plan. Or to go in the other direction, say I use a metal ingot as a paperweight. One day I carry it upstairs and discover that it increases my radio's fidelity when placed in a particular location. Now it has a new function, one more interesting and complex than its old one.

This shows that a design plan can have more than one function, there can be functional multiplicity. Moreover, part of the overall design plans for organisms and some artifacts involve aspects which do not come into play unless there is *dysfunction* on some other level. That is, there are damage control functions. Blood does not coagulate when it is flowing through our veins if it is functioning properly in accordance with its design plan. But when it ceases to flow through our veins and starts flowing out of our skin, it coagulates in order to seal up the wound.

Accidental by-products

Closely related to the design vs. max plan is the issue of accidental responses or by-products. This refers to aspects of something's response to circumstances that are not regulated by the design plan but are accidental. "Accidental" here means that the response is outside of the intent of the planner (where "planner" can be understood literally or metaphorically). So, for example,

> that thumpa-thumpa sound the heart makes is (so we think) merely accidental, a by-product of how it works when it works in such a way as to fulfill its purpose or function of pumping the blood. The sound is accidental with respect to the design plan; it is no part of the design plan that it will make that sound; the circumstance-response-purpose triples that constitute the design plan will not include pairs where the response is making that sound.[34]

So, the by-product in question is not necessarily an *accident* that occasionally happens—it may usually go with the design plan without being a part of it. The by-product is accidental in the sense of being *contingent*; it is not *essential* with regards to the design plan. It may be the case that a design plan for a particular organ, organism, or artifact will reliably or generally produce a particular by-product, but that by-product does not thereby become a part of the design plan. Thus, by-products of our cognitive faculties' design plan are not a part of the design plan, and so any beliefs that are by-products or are produced by by-products do not have warrant.

Environmental issues

A common Gettier case is of one person being presented with a great deal of evidence that another person owns a car. It turns out the second person does not own a car and is trying to deceive the first; the evidence they show is misleading. However, by happy circumstance, and unknown to either one, the second person has just won a car in a sweepstakes. Then the first person will believe that the second person owns a car; they will be justified in believing it (as they have been given a great deal of misleading evidence that they do); and it turns out to be true. Nevertheless, the first person does not really *know* that the second person owns a car.

To construct a Gettier example against Plantinga, some authors have proposed a variation on this idea, in which the second person is not merely ignorant of the fact that they have just won a new car, they are also ignorant of the fact that they otherwise do not own a car (the first person thus drops out of the equation). Peter Klein suggests the following thought experiment:

> Jones believes that she owns a well-functioning Ford. She forms this belief in perfectly normal circumstances using her cognitive equipment that is functioning just perfectly. But as sometimes normally happens (no deception here), unbeknownst to Jones, her Ford is hit and virtually demolished—let's say while it's parked outside her office. But also unbeknownst to Jones, she has just won a well-functioning Ford in the Well-Functioning Ford Lottery that her company runs once a year.[35]

The point of focus here is the cognitive environment. These critics say that the environment is that for which our cognitive faculties are designed: namely Earth and its biosphere. In this case, our cognitive faculties are functioning properly in an appropriate cognitive environment according to a design plan successfully aimed at forming true beliefs. All Plantinga's criteria are met, yet Jones does not really know she owns a well-functioning Ford.

Plantinga, however, argues that the cognitive environment in question is *not* appropriate. It is not enough to form the belief in an earth-like environment, the particular circumstances must be in accord with the formation of the belief so that they are not misleading. This fails in the above example: Jones's belief that she owns a Ford is based on the Ford she drove to work that morning still existing, not on whether she had just won a new one. Her cognitive environment is thus misleading because it involves two unlikely circumstances: her car ceasing to exist, and her winning another one in a lottery.

To clarify the differences involved, Plantinga distinguishes between the global and local cognitive environments, or *maxi-environment* and *mini-environment*. The maxi-environment

> would include such features as the presence and properties of light and air, the presence of visible objects, of other objects detectable by our kind of cognitive system, of some objects not so detectable, of the regularities of nature, the existence of other people, and so on.... Our cognitive faculties are designed to function in *this* maxi-environment, the one in which we find ourselves, or one like it. They are not designed for a maxi-environment in which, e.g., the only food available contains a substance that seriously inhibits memory, or where there is constant darkness, or where there aren't any distinguishable objects, or where there is little or no regularity, at least of a kind we can detect, or where everything is in a state of constant random flux.[36]

However, there are numerous mini-environments compatible with a maxi-environment, and not all of them will be appropriate; some will be misleading. In the Jones case there is an appropriate maxi- but inappropriate mini-environment. The mini-environment relates to the particular way one believes something. In other mini-environments—say where Jones looks out the window just in time to see her car being destroyed—the problem would not arise.

An exercise of my cognitive powers, therefore, even when those powers are functioning properly (perfectly in accord with my design plan) in the maxi-environment for which they are designed, can be counted on to produce a true belief with respect to *some* cognitive mini-environments but not with respect to others. Some mini-environments are *favorable* for a given exercise of my cognitive powers; others are *misleading*, even when my faculties are functioning properly. These mini-environments, we might say, are such that my faculties are not designed to produce a true belief in or with respect to them—even though they include the maxi-environment for which my faculties have indeed been designed (by God or evolution).[37]

This difference between cognitive maxi- and mini-environments shows how a belief can lack details. If, instead of believing she owns a well-functioning Ford Jones believes she owns the specific Ford that she drove to work that day—the one with the sticky gear shift and with a particular vehicle identification number—then the chance destruction of her car and the chance winning of the lottery would not make her belief accidentally true. All beliefs have some level of irresolution and this allows a Gettier case to slip into the cracks where the belief is not detailed (the fact that it is a problem with the *belief* being imprecise verifies Plantinga's point that Gettier cases are problems for internalist epistemologies). In this case, we can point to a more specific belief so that the mini-environment is no longer misleading with regards to it.

The A/C model

Naturally, there are many more details in Plantinga's account of warrant, and its application to various types of knowledge such as perception, *a priori* knowledge, and induction. The most relevant application is Plantinga's religious epistemology, which claims belief in God can be properly basic. Given the magnitude of the issue, Plantinga devotes an entire book, *Warranted Christian Belief*, to apply his epistemology to his own beliefs in the tenets of Christianity.

For a true belief to be an item of knowledge according to Plantinga it must a) be produced by properly functioning cognitive faculties that are b) reliably and directly c) aimed at producing true beliefs d) in an appropriate epistemic environment. To apply this to Christian belief, Plantinga proposes a model derived from the theologies of Aquinas and Calvin according to which everyone has an innate sense of, or propensity for belief in, God (of course, many Christians throughout history have claimed something similar, including the biblical authors). At any rate, the basic idea behind the Aquinas/Calvin (A/C) model is that God has provided a faculty in every human being such that we immediately form beliefs about God when faced with certain situations. We see the grandeur of a beautiful landscape and spontaneously believe that God is responsible; we perform some immoral act and spontaneously believe that God disapproves of it; etc.

While many theologians have taken these beliefs to be inferential—we infer God's existence and action from, for example, the order of nature—Plantinga argues this is not usually the case.[38] He initially compares belief in God to belief in other minds: just as certain circumstances cause one to spontaneously (non-inferentially) believe that other people are loci of first-person experiences, sparks of self-consciousness, so certain circumstances cause one to spontaneously believe in God.[39] This is an interesting comparison, not least because in neither case must one directly experience what they are forming beliefs about. I do not directly experience other people's minds, I cannot enter someone else's consciousness and experience *their* first-person perspective, I can only ever experience my own. By parity of reasoning, one need not have a religious experience and base their belief in God on it,[40] unless one defines "religious experience" broadly enough to, for example, seeing a beautiful sunset and immediately forming a belief in God. (Obviously, Plantinga does not preclude someone having direct experience of God,[41] but insofar as his religious epistemology parallels knowledge of other minds, it does not require such experience.)

Thus, the A/C model entails that God has given us the *sensus divinitatis*, a cognitive faculty which causes us to immediately form beliefs about him. "In this regard, the *sensus divinitatis* resembles perception, memory, and *a priori* belief."[42] When I see a tree I do not infer from my perceptual experience and their past reliability that there is a tree; I just immediately believe that a tree is before me.

> The same goes for memory. You ask me what I had for breakfast; I think for a moment and then remember: pancakes with blueberries. I don't argue from the fact that it *seems* to me that I remember having pancakes for breakfast to the conclusion that I did; rather, you ask me what I had for breakfast, and the answer simply comes to mind. Or consider *a priori* belief. I don't infer from other things that, for example, *modus ponens* is a valid form of argument: I just see that it is so and, in fact, *must* be so. All of these, we might say, are starting points for thought. But (on the model) the same goes for the sense of divinity. It isn't a matter of making a quick and dirty inference from the grandeur of the mountains or the beauty of the flower or the sun on the treetops to the existence of God; instead, a belief about God spontaneously arises in those circumstances, the circumstances that trigger the operation of the *sensus divinitatis*. This belief is another of those starting points for thought; it too is basic in the sense that the beliefs in question are not accepted on the evidential basis of other beliefs.[43]

Moreover, such beliefs in God would not merely be basic, they would be *properly* basic,[44] regarding both justification and warrant. One would be justified—within their epistemic rights to believe in God, not flouting their epistemic duties—just as they would be justified in their perceptual, memory, or *a priori* beliefs. Being basic beliefs, there are no epistemic duties that must be performed to accept them, so they are justified. Regarding warrant, according to Plantinga's A/C model the beliefs in God produced by the *sensus divinitatis* would meet all his conditions: they are produced by properly functioning cognitive faculties, reliably and directly aimed at producing true beliefs in an appropriate cognitive environment. Indeed, the stronger one's belief in God is, the more warrant it will have.[45] Thus, the way we *do* form beliefs about God is the way we *should*—a supernaturalistic naturalized epistemology.

Of course, the mere fact that there is such a faculty does not mean it functions inerrantly. There would be trade-offs and compromises. Perhaps a cognitive system that inerrantly formed true beliefs (about God or anything else) or did so with a much higher percentage than the systems we have, would require a brain so massive it would have hindered survival. So, the compromise is cognitive systems that generally form true beliefs but occasionally err, and generally do not endanger the life of the organism. Such a compromise would be aimed at some function other than producing true beliefs, but this would not impugn those true beliefs that *are* produced by properly functioning cognitive faculties reliably and directly aimed at producing true beliefs. It would only mean that the beliefs produced due to the compromise would not have warrant and so would not qualify as knowledge even if they turn out to be true.

Moreover, according to the Judeo-Christian tradition, human beings are fallen, and thus our *sensus divinitatis* is subject to significant malfunction. Just as perceptual or memory knowledge can be hindered by cognitive malfunction, so can the *sensus divinitatis:* it can be weaker in some people, all but non-existent in others, and even if it functions as it ought, we can train ourselves to ignore it.[46]

The point is *if* God exists, a God roughly equivalent to the Judeo-Christian concept, then it is probable that the A/C model would be approximately correct, since such a God would probably bequeath us with something like a *sensus divinitatis*. In this case, belief in God would be produced by properly functioning cognitive faculties, reliably and directly aimed at producing true beliefs about God in an appropriate cognitive environment. Belief in God would be both rational and warranted, the latter qualifying it as knowledge.

Naturally, one could ask why we are privileging the Judeo-Christian tradition: what about other religions? Could their practitioners defend them in a similar manner? This is too large a subject to treat here, but there is the beginning of an interesting literature on whether Islam, Neo-Confucianism, Mormonism, some forms of Hinduism, etc., may be able to develop their own variation of an A/C model.[47] But then, some respond, why can't we just apply this method to any ridiculous belief one has? Plantinga has called these "The Great Pumpkin Objection," and argues that they fail;[48] but again, we do not have the space to treat them here.

Normativity

I began this chapter by contrasting Cartesian epistemology with Plantinga's naturalized epistemology. Most of this chapter has been on the substitution of warrant for justification, but we have not yet dealt with the quintessence of Cartesian epistemology: normativity. Quine suggested replacing normative epistemology's prescriptions with the descriptions of science, notably descriptive psychology. Unfortunately (at least for some) many sciences, including descriptive psychology, are rife with normativity. This is because the notions of function and proper function are *inherently normative*. To say that an organism, organ, or structure has a function is just to say that there is something it is *supposed* to do, and this means that, in some sense, it *should* act in accordance with that norm.

With this, we can recall Plantinga's point that basically all the life and social sciences (but not chemistry or physics) constantly appeal to the functions that various organisms, organs, and structures have.[49] Thus these fields are normative. Plantinga argues his model is a true naturalized epistemology insofar as it only employs those norms which are already used in these sciences, just as Quine's naturalized epistemology did.[50]

We are still left with the question of whether the normativity in Plantinga's epistemology consists of hypothetical imperatives (Quine's technical norms) or categorical imperatives. Hypothetical imperatives only apply if one is pursuing a particular goal that can be rationally rejected, while categorical imperatives pursue a goal that applies unconditionally. On the one hand, Plantinga is only appealing to the normativity used in science, and presumably this would be hypothetical. On the other hand, as we have already seen, the normativity involved in knowledge and rationality must be categorical: otherwise, one could not rule out a position as rationally preferable to its denial. Since the naturalist and the naturalized epistemologist are presenting their claims—namely, naturalism and naturalized epistemology—as preferable to their denials, they are applying a norm that is categorical.

Plantinga argues that function and proper function are incompatible with naturalism.[51] This gives us the clue we need: if our cognitive faculties are functioning properly in accordance with their design plan (and the other qualifications), then we have warrant, and thus knowledge. Therefore, if the designer of our cognitive faculties met the necessary criteria, knowledge is possible. *Plantinga passes off the problem of normativity onto the designer*. If the designing process or designing agent organized our cognitive faculties so that they mostly form true beliefs, then *he* or *she* (or *they* or *it*) could have done so according to whatever normativity rationality and knowledge require. So Plantinga's epistemology does have the normativity necessary for a categorical imperative, but he smuggles it in in a very interesting way.

And could the designer be an "it"? Could we have been using "design plan" throughout our discussion metaphorically to simply refer to natural processes? This is problematic: these processes, including evolutionary processes, can only provide hypothetical imperatives which are insufficient for rationality and knowledge. Being hypothetical, one can always reject the goal and retain rationality (*ceteris paribus*). Since the goal here is rationality itself, we cannot reject that goal while retaining rationality, so the imperative or norm could not be hypothetical, it must be a *categorical* imperative.[52] Since natural processes cannot provide categorical imperatives, Plantinga's epistemology requires a *literal* designer who *intentionally* designed our cognitive faculties to produce mostly true beliefs.

Thus, to call Plantinga's epistemology "naturalized," is unusual. It meets all the definitions of a naturalized epistemology but rejects one of the primary motives for embracing it in the first place: ontological naturalism. Some argue that, merely on these grounds, Plantinga's epistemology is not a naturalized epistemology.[53] It certainly puts Plantinga in the unique position of arguing that "naturalistic epistemology flourishes best in the garden of supernaturalistic metaphysics."[54]

Recall the reason Descartes's appeal to God does not work: by working from cause to effect—from the existence of a trustworthy God to our having reliable cognitive faculties—he leaves too much of a logical gap. The cause could have any number of effects and specifying the one we want would be a case of special pleading. Plantinga, however, works from *effect* to *cause*. Since our cognitive faculties are reliable (at least sometimes), what makes this possible? And here the answer is very different. While the cause could have any number of effects, there may be only one way for the effect in question to have been caused. Naturalism, Plantinga argues, cannot account for it. Therefore, his argument that naturalism is self-defeating because it is incompatible with knowledge, including knowledge of naturalism, is not a mere addendum to his overall epistemology: it is an expression of its very essence. To this we now turn.

Part Two

Preliminaries

4

Terms of Engagement

... definitions are hazardous.

Samuel Johnson

Plantinga's "official and final version (I hope)"[1] of the EAAN is as follows:

(1) P(R/N&E) is low.
(2) Anyone who accepts (believes) N&E and sees that P(R/N&E) is low has a defeater for R.
(3) Anyone who has a defeater for R has a defeater for any other belief she thinks she has, including N&E itself.
(4) If one who accepts N&E thereby acquires a defeater for N&E, N&E is self-defeating and can't rationally be accepted.
Conclusion: N&E can't rationally be accepted.[2]

The argument hinges on the equation P(R/N&E). P means probability, R means one's cognitive faculties are reliable, N means naturalism, and E means evolution. N&E, then, refers to the conjunction of naturalism and evolution. Thus P(R/N&E) means "the probability that naturalistic evolution would produce reliable cognitive faculties." Plantinga argues the probability is low and that this produces a defeater for (a reason to withhold belief in) any belief, including belief in naturalism and evolution. Below we will define some of these terms more fully, while also spelling out some of their consequences.

P, R, and some N

P refers to objective probability not epistemic probability—although there are connections between the two so it could be reformulated in epistemic probabilistic terms.[3] Plantinga goes into detail about the nature of probability, rejecting Bayesian and Kyburgian (or statistical) accounts in favor of logical probability. To be sure, logical probability has its own problems, but he responds to some of the most potent objections.[4]

N refers to naturalism. Unfortunately, naturalism does not have a set definition in contemporary philosophy, so instead of defining it, Plantinga gives some entailments or corollaries of it. I will start with two: first, Plantinga says naturalism involves "the belief that there are not any supernatural beings—no such person as God, for example."[5] Second, he argues that "nearly all naturalists are also *materialists* with respect to human beings; they hold that human beings are material objects."[6] This second criterion allows him to take a rudimentary type of naturalism without all the bells and whistles a more rigorous account would require.[7] Note that naturalism is a universal claim: *all* objects and states are natural (or material), *no* object or states are other than natural (or immaterial). In fact, it is even more drastic: according to naturalism, *there can be no* object or state that is other than natural, where "natural" is defined in light of contemporary science.

Reliability

R means our cognitive faculties are reliable. By cognitive faculties, Plantinga means "those faculties, or powers, or processes that produce beliefs or knowledge in us,"[8] where "beliefs" refer to those mental items that have propositional content. Perhaps a cognitive scientist has a more technical definition of cognitive faculties than this; if so, they may substitute another term—"belief producing attributes" or something. Or perhaps they mean something else by belief: then they may substitute another term for the mental items which have propositional content and can be true or false.[9] But what *Plantinga* means by cognitive faculties is those faculties or properties that produce beliefs, and what *Plantinga* means by beliefs is mental items with propositional content.

So, what would it mean to say the faculties that produce beliefs in us are *reliable*? This cannot be given a precise figure, but Plantinga estimates they are reliable if they produce true beliefs between two-thirds and three-fourths of the time.[10] This is a conservative estimate because producing false beliefs one-third or one-fourth of the time would not be considered "reliable" in most appraisals. At any rate, saying our faculties are this reliable is a general statement: there are contexts where they are more reliable or less. There is also cognitive malfunction. Plus, our faculties are reliable within a certain range; outside it they are less reliable. Nevertheless, despite these qualifications, we take their reliability to be a general truth.

> We suppose, for example, that most of the deliverances of memory are at least approximately correct. True, if you ask five witnesses how the accident happened, you may get five different stories. Still, they will agree that there was indeed an *accident*, and that it was an *automobile* accident (as opposed, say, to a naval disaster or a volcanic eruption); there will usually be agreement as to the number of vehicles involved (particularly if it is a small number), as well as the rough location of the accident (Aberdeen, Scotland, as opposed to Aberdeen, South Dakota), and so on. And all this is against the background of massive and much deeper agreement: that there are automobiles; that they do not disappear when no one is looking; that if released from a helicopter they fall down rather than up, that they are driven by people who use them to go places, that they are seldom driven by three-year-olds, that their drivers have purposes, hold beliefs, and often act on those purposes and beliefs, that few of them (or their drivers) have been more than

a few miles from the surface of the earth, that the world has existed for a good long time—much longer than ten minutes, say—and a million more such Moorean truisms.[11]

Again, this is what *Plantinga* means by reliability. Others may have different definitions with different criteria. But since we are examining Plantinga's argument, to use other definitions would erect a strawman. We have to see what his argument is before we critique it, and this requires us to use his definitions. In fact, there *is* another definition of reliability I suspect Plantinga would approve of, but it is not something that relates directly to truth values. It comes into play in chapter 7.

What P(R/N&E) does not mean

Now that we have a grip on what R means, the first thing to note is that when we ask what P(R/N&E) is, we are *not* asking how probable it is that we have reliable cognitive faculties *per se*. P(R/N&E) ≠ P(R). Again, we take for granted that our cognitive faculties are generally reliable. Certainly, there are areas where they are less than stellar (philosophy perhaps), even subject to widespread error or illusion, and even under the best of circumstances they are painfully fallible. Nevertheless, we still take them to be trustworthy. This is not what is at issue and any contrary suggestion is a misunderstanding.

> We are not asking about how things *are*, but about *what things would be like if both evolution and naturalism . . . were true*. We are asking about P(R/N&E), not about P(R/the way things actually are). Like everyone else, I believe that our cognitive faculties are for the most part reliable, and that true beliefs are more likely to issue in successful action than false. But that's not the question. The question is what things would be like if N&E were true; and in this context we can't just assume, of course, that if N&E . . . were true, then things would still be the way they are. That is, we can't assume that if materialism were true, it would still be the case that true beliefs are more likely to cause successful action than false beliefs.[12]

Neither are we asking what the probability is that we have reliable cognitive faculties *given evolution*. P(R/N&E) ≠ P(R/E). This gets into more controversial territory, namely, how to define evolution. Plantinga lists five criteria: (1) "the ancient earth thesis"; (2) the progression of life "from relatively simple to relatively complex forms"; (3) "descent with modification"; (4) "the common ancestry thesis"; and (5) that "natural selection operating on random genetic mutation" is the mechanism by which descent with modification takes place.[13] For Plantinga, conditions 1 to 4 constitute evolution and adding condition 5 constitutes Darwinism. He also suggests abiogenesis as a potential sixth point but argues that it "isn't really part of the theory of evolution,"[14] presumably as it is chemistry rather than biology. But then Plantinga's first criterion, the ancient earth thesis, while perhaps being a necessary condition for evolution, should not be considered a part of evolutionary theory either.

The fifth criterion, natural selection operating on random genetic mutation, is what allegedly supports the claim that evolution, E, should be understood as naturalism-plus-evolution, N&E, and thus that P(R/N&E) *does* equal P(R/E). The randomness of mutation and the law of natural selection both imply that there are no additional forces involved in the evolution of the diversity of life. Specifically, there are no intentional agents, like God, involved; and to claim that the only forces involved in evolution are natural just is N&E.

How do randomness and natural selection imply that God is not involved? First, if God intentionally causes an event, it's not random. Second, evolution posits a law (natural selection) which determines which organisms will survive. If natural processes are doing the determining then God is not: it is fully accounted for, and to appeal to another cause is gratuitous. Traditional theism, therefore, is ostensibly incompatible with the a) production and b) ordering of the elements involved in the evolution of humanity and the rest of the living world. We can avoid all this by positing a view like naturalism in which such compatibility issues do not arise. Naturalism, in other words, should be the default position.

Naturalism and randomness

To say something occurs randomly, without a purpose or goal, means it was not directed by any agent, including God. But it is a traditional theistic principle common to Judaism, Christianity, and Islam (not to mention other theisms) that God had a hand in the creation of the various forms of life including human beings. If Darwinian evolution is random it precludes this doctrine.

In response, Plantinga argues that "randomness, as construed by contemporary biologists, doesn't have this implication."[15] According to philosopher of biology Elliot Sober, "random" mutations means there is no physical mechanism in the environment or the organism which foresees which mutations would be beneficial and then causes just those mutations to occur.[16] But this concept of randomness does not imply or even suggest the mutations were not caused by God, since God is neither physical nor a mechanism. This is not some fine point of definition: a physical mechanism could be observed in conjunction with its effects; something which is not *physical* could not be. Moreover, something which is not a *mechanism* would not produce its effect with nomological necessity and so could fail to do so. Thus, a nonphysical, nonmechanistic cause would be invisible to science. Yes, there is no physical mechanism that foresees which mutations would benefit the organism, but no theist is claiming there is. So, although some scientists think evolution means there has been no superintendence by God or anyone else in the history of terrestrial life, such a claim is actually metaphysical, not scientific.

Could we simply redefine evolution? Rather than just excluding mechanisms that foresee and cause beneficial mutations, why not exclude *anything*—mechanisms, minds, what-have-you—that foresee and cause beneficial mutations? But Sober did not come up with his definition arbitrarily. As we've seen, we cannot exclude such considerations because they are metaphysical. Science must *presuppose* metaphysics, but it cannot draw metaphysical *conclusions* and still be considered science.

Of course, there is much more that should be said here, it deserves its own extended analysis. For now, it is enough to say that the randomness of evolutionary biology does not preclude God's involvement in the evolutionary process.

Naturalism and natural selection

However, there is a longstanding response to this. Perhaps we cannot scientifically rule out such claims, but insofar as we can explain a phenomenon without appealing to God's (or anyone else's) intentions, any such appeal is ad hoc and can be ignored. Ockham's Razor teaches us not to multiply entities beyond necessity when formulating explanatory hypotheses, so if we can explain the diversity of species solely by the efficient causes involved in the evolutionary process, the Razor cuts away the extras and leaves us with the explanation that makes no appeal to a designer. Hence, in his debate with Plantinga, Dennett concedes that evolution is perfectly compatible with theism's claims that God created the various forms of life, but that it "is an entirely gratuitous fantasy."[17] This is most strongly felt in the alleged incompatibility between theism and natural selection: if natural processes are doing the ordering, appealing to God is gratuitous.

We can frame this as an antilogism of three incompatible premises: traditional theism, Darwinian evolution, and Ockham's Razor. Supposedly, we can accept any two of these premises, but not all three. If we accept evolution and Ockham's Razor, then we can no longer accept the gratuitous addition of theism and its doctrine of creation. If we accept evolution and theism, then we should reject Ockham's Razor, since by including two sufficient causes of the same event (natural selection and God) we are unnecessarily multiplying causes. If we accept theistic creation and Ockham's Razor, then the phenomena are completely explained and appealing to natural processes would be gratuitous. Whence then is evolution?

In response, we can point to Jaegwon Kim's claim (in a different context) that there are only a few possibilities regarding the relationship between two types of causes or explanations of an effect. First, they may be identical, resolving the tension by indicating that there is only one cause. Second, one may be dependent on the other in some way, such as when one explanation supervenes on another. "We do not have in cases of this kind two *independent* causal explanations of the same event. The two explanations can coexist because one of them is dependent, reductively or by supervenience, on the other."[18] Third, both may be partial causes, indispensable parts of an overarching cause—or one may be a partial explanation and the other the overarching cause. Fourth, the two causes may not be simultaneous but "different links in the same causal chain."[19] Fifth, the two causes may be sufficient and independent causes of the effect. This is causal overdetermination and it is possible—Kim's examples are a building that catches fire because of faulty wiring and a simultaneous lightning strike; or a man who is shot through the heart by two assassins at the same time. However, overdetermined events are rare and unique; in a word, they are *coincidences*, and remarkable ones at that. Thus, they cannot explain a general relationship that regularly connects two entities, states, or processes.

If God and natural processes are the two types of causes, only the fifth possibility makes one of them gratuitous. However, using this to argue God is gratuitous is a strawman argument since it is contrary to traditional theism's concept of God as the author of the "fixed laws of heaven and earth" (Jer. 33:25) who frequently uses these laws to accomplish his goals. So, it would not be a case of two complete and independent explanations competing to explain the same phenomena. This is not an ad hoc attempt to insert God into a picture from which science has banished him: this has *always* been the theist's claim. Arguing against theism by suggesting that God and natural processes are both sufficient and independent causes of the same effects won't address any form of theism that has actually been suggested.[20]

Some analogies can illustrate the issues here. Imagine a world where it rains hammers, saws, nails, and other tools and building materials. Imagine further we discover a cabin in the woods. One could argue that the obliging precipitation was bound to construct such an edifice, given enough time. Appealing to a builder who used the falling tools to build the cabin is gratuitous and violates Ockham's Razor. Or consider a player piano. Since the inner workings of the piano are responsible for the effect (the melody), why appeal to an agent? To appeal to a builder who constructed the piano—and a composer who wrote the melody—is gratuitous. If the mechanics inside the piano are responsible for the production of the melody, then (allegedly) the builder and composer are not. Or take a third analogy: we can explain how an automobile gets made without appealing to anything except the machines on the assembly line. Appealing to other causes (like those who built the machines, the company's CEO, or Henry Ford) adds more causes and Ockham's Razor cuts them away.

These cases roughly parallel the theist's who sees evolution as the method God used to create the diversity of life, so they allow the nontheist to see the issue through the theist's eyes. The natural laws, such as natural selection, parallel the unusual precipitation, the inner workings of the player piano, and the machines on the assembly line. The role of God would parallel the cabin's builders, the player piano's builders and the composer of the melody, and the builders of the assembly line machines as well as other people involved in the larger process. Plantinga argues that if someone already believes in God, if they have the concept of God in their noetic system, then it is not gratuitous. Naturally, the nontheist—along with those who deny there are builders of the cabin, player piano, and machines on the assembly line—will want to know why they should accept these entities. But the only claim at this point is that the existence of builders is not gratuitous, contrived, or ad hoc.

Obviously, there are explanations which genuinely run afoul of Ockham's Razor, but not all charges of being gratuitous are equal. Plantinga argues at length that the "deep roots of science" must presuppose something like theism to explain the physical laws and their continuance. Without this, it is inexplicable that the universe is ordered by laws, and our confidence these laws will persist is unfounded.[21] This makes appealing to God even less gratuitous than the builders in the analogies above. We only need to appeal to builders to explain the *origin* of the cabin, piano, and machines, not their continued existence. So before charging theism with positing gratuitous causes, one must explain how appealing to God is more analogous to genuine cases of gratuitousness and how it is not analogous to the analogies above.

Naturalism as the default position

Some object that the naturalist is not really positing anything beyond the evidence, they are simply taking the evidence as "complete." Nothing has to be "compatibilized" with evolution to assert naturalism so they are not asserting any metaphysical concepts transcending the scientific evidence. "Naturalism," Dennett writes, "is the *null hypothesis*" which does not assert anything, thereby placing the burden of proof on those who aver additional entities.[22]

This, however, is false. A motorcycle mechanic need not appeal to God, but this does not mean they are excluding him. There is a world of difference between a) "the art of motorcycle mechanics" and b) "the art of motorcycle mechanics and God does not exist." Obviously, b) claims more than a), so one can accept a) without accepting b). More than that, there is nothing inherent in a) that would lead one to b): if someone tried to argue that adding God to a) is gratuitous and so b) should be accepted by default, they would obviously be wrong. Saying a) does not explicitly *include* God does not suggest it *excludes* him or asserts his nonexistence. We need more evidence for this beyond the claim that God is not necessary for a).

We can ask the same question of physical laws. As Plantinga writes, the conjunction of Newton's laws with atheism claims more than Newton's laws alone claim, and one can accept Newton's laws without accepting its amalgamation with atheism.[23] We can certainly supplement the scientific theory with atheism or naturalism if we wish, but then it would obviously be the *supplement* that conflicts with theism, not the science.

For precisely the same reasons there's a difference between evolution and evolution-plus-naturalism. Evolution-plus-naturalism claims more than evolution and one can accept evolution without accepting its conjunction with naturalism. Granted, evolution-plus-naturalism is incompatible with theism. For that matter, seventeenth-century-French-shipbuilding-plus-naturalism is incompatible with theism; *anything*-plus-naturalism is incompatible with theism. And obviously what *makes* them incompatible is the "plus-naturalism" part. It is, again, adding naturalism that makes it incompatible with theism.

Naturalism, therefore, is not a null hypothesis. It is definitely a metaphysical claim, something over and above the scientific theory. Plantinga even argues that, although naturalism is not a religion,[24] it can function as an "honorary" or "quasi-religion" since it serves

> one of the main functions of a religion: it offers a master narrative, it answers deep and important human questions. Immanuel Kant identified three great human questions: Is there such a person as God? Do we human beings have significant freedom? And can we human beings expect life after death? Naturalism gives answers to these questions: there is no God, there is no immortality, and the case for genuine freedom is at best dicey. Naturalism tells us what reality is ultimately like, where we fit into the universe, how we are related to other creatures, and how it happens that we came to be. Naturalism is therefore in competition with the great theistic religions: even if it is not itself a religion, it plays one of the main roles of a religion.[25]

Naturalism is a metaphysical addition to the scientific evidence for evolution, and as with Newton's laws, if we add naturalism to evolution then it is the addition (naturalism) that conflicts with theism, not the science (evolution). The theist can affirm evolution with no concerns (at least no *philosophical* concerns) as to whether it poses a problem for their belief in God.

The target of the EAAN

Some may object that while Darwinian evolution may not be strictly *incompatible* with theism, it at least makes more sense, is more to be expected, under naturalism than theism. This is where much of the ink is spilled in this issue, and again it deserves a fuller response than I can give here. For now, I will say that Plantinga's argument repudiates this claim by arguing that N and E are incompatible with each other. If his argument is sound, then evolution, science, and rationality itself are incompatible with naturalism, so none of them are more to be expected under naturalism than theism.

The Evolutionary Argument against Naturalism is (spoiler) an argument against *naturalism*. It is not challenging evolution. It claims that if naturalism is true, then our beliefs—including beliefs in evolution, naturalism, and evolution-plus-naturalism (E, N, and N&E)—are unreliably formed. Saying belief in E is thereby unreliably formed is not the point of the argument but the point of the dagger: it prevents the naturalist from appealing to E to justify N.

Plantinga's argument presents a dilemma: we can accept either N or E but not both. Plantinga argues that we should accept the second horn and reject N. Theoretically, however, a naturalist could accept the first horn and reject E. But rejecting E would not reestablish R. Moreover, without E to buttress it, the naturalist has no motive to accept N in the first place, although perhaps they could follow Quine in starting from N without basing it on anything else.[26] But ignoring these, there is still the problem that N gives them a reason to withhold belief in any belief they have, *including N*. So they cannot just reject E and accept N in the basic way because N itself gives them a defeater for N. But if they reject N, then R is (or at least can be) reinstated.

Thus, the EAAN is not addressing the viability of E, which, after all, is established by scientific evidence not philosophical argument. Plantinga explicitly says as much:

> Of course I am *not* attacking the theory of evolution, or the claim that human beings have evolved from simian ancestors, or anything in that neighborhood; I am instead attacking the conjunction of *naturalism* with the view that human beings have evolved in that way. I see no similar problems with the conjunction of *theism* and the idea that human beings have evolved in the way contemporary evolutionary science suggests.[27]

I will not address whether Plantinga actually accepts E once it is divorced from N, mostly because I don't know. But he can at least be *taken* as accepting E and only rejecting its confluence with N.[28] Regardless, whether Plantinga does or not, *I* accept evolution, and nothing I write here should be taken as challenging it.

This has been a lengthy (but necessary) excursus defining E and N and asking whether P(R/N&E) is equivalent to P(R/E). It is not. And the reason it is not is because E, by itself, is neutral regarding whether God (or anyone else) had a hand in our creation, while N&E is not neutral since N entails God's nonexistence and inaction. In fact, we could supplement E with a different metaphysical theory such as theism (T). Depending on our concept of God, P(R/T&E) would be very different from P(R/N&E), and not in the naturalist's favor.[29] Yet the scientific claims and evidences would be identical in both T&E and N&E. In other words, E covers both N&E and T&E (and numerous-other-claims&E) all of which are empirically equivalent, so we cannot simply equate N&E with E. Obviously other considerations (such as explanatory power, ad hocness, etc.) come into play in determining which option is superior, but even so, having one option be superior in one case does not mean that it is superior overall.

At any rate, we have seen that N is a metaphysical addition one can append to E. So just as the naturalist asks the theist if T is compatible with E, so Plantinga's argument asks the naturalist if N is compatible with E. The EAAN answers this in the negative. In this case, N cannot be a successful hypothesis to explain evolution, science, or any kind of knowledge.

Defeat

A defeater is a reason to not believe something. If someone has a belief and is presented with a defeater for it, they have a reason to relinquish their belief. A defeater can be another belief, an experience, or some other kind of mental state, providing it constitutes a reason to refrain from believing something. Of course, there are more details to flesh out: what if someone does not *accept* the defeater? What if they accept it but do not recognize that it defeats the belief? Can a defeater be defeated itself? To answer these questions, we must make several distinctions.

1. A defeater that gives one a reason to *disbelieve* a belief, to believe the belief is false, is a rebutting defeater. A defeater that takes away one's reason or justification or ground for believing a belief, and thus to *withhold belief* in it without necessarily disbelieving it, is an undercutting defeater.

To take the standard illustration, say someone is in a warehouse and sees red widgets emerging from a machine on a conveyer belt.[30] They will naturally form the belief that the widgets are red. But then someone else tells them that the widgets are irradiated with a red light when they emerge from the machine to reveal hairline cracks. This new information is an *undercutting defeater* for their belief that the widgets are red.[31] They have not been given a reason to think they are *not* red—they may be. But their reason for believing they are red (their appearance) is taken away so they cannot rationally believe they are red. They have a reason to withhold belief that they are red, to be agnostic about it, but not to disbelieve it.

Now say they take a widget outside and look at it in the sunlight. The widget appears white. This gives them a *rebutting defeater* for their belief that the widgets are red. They have a reason to believe that the widgets are not red. Now they have a reason to disbelieve they are red, not just to withhold belief in it.

2. A defeater that makes someone believe something less firmly is a partial defeater. If they would still put the belief's probability above .5, the defeater is only partial. If they would put it at .5 or lower, it is a total defeater, since at that point it is no longer rational to continue holding the belief.[32] Note that "total" is not referring to the probability, that it is 0. It means it is lowered to the point of withholding the belief, i.e., .5 (an undercutting defeater) or to the point of disbelieving it, < .5 (a rebutting defeater).

What if someone finds the probability inscrutable or informulable (this played an important part in Plantinga's early versions of the argument)? In this case, they have no idea what the probability is or should be, and so should suspend judgment, neither believing nor disbelieving it. But suspending judgment "is a species of not believing."[33] If someone thinks the probability of a belief's truth is inscrutable, if they have no idea how probable it is, they have a total, undercutting defeater for that belief. It is not as if they disbelieve it—it is not a rebutting defeater—they are merely agnostic about it. But being agnostic about something qualifies as not believing it. Therefore, judging a belief's probability as inscrutable is a total defeater of that belief, all other things being equal (which they never are). I will make some qualifications of this later, however, since I think, as it stands, it is too strict a criterion.

3. Another distinction is the difference between rationality and warrant defeaters.[34] A rationality defeater makes it irrational to continue believing what it defeats. Rationality, however, is a difficult concept to nail down. Plantinga variously describes it as "elusive," "multifarious," "baffling," "pluriform," "many things to many people," "multiply ambiguous," "protean," "many-sided," "polyphonous," "legion," and "one of the slipperiest terms in the philosophical lexicon."[35] Fortunately (for us at least) we can narrow it down since we are looking at the EAAN, and Plantinga conceives of rationality in terms of proper function: to be rational is for one's cognitive faculties to function properly and to be irrational is for them to malfunction or function improperly. If a person's cognitive faculties are functioning properly, then a proper function rationality defeater will require them to withhold belief in (or believe less firmly) whatever the defeater is defeating.

This does not mean proper function defeaters are the *only* kind of rationality defeaters. Hume argued that he had no reason to think his cognitive faculties were truth-directed and this gave him a defeater for R. In his philosophical reflections in his study this could hit pretty hard. But then he would shake his head and go out to play backgammon with his friends. While out living his life he could not take the skepticism seriously anymore. He had no problem thinking *other* people would have a defeater for R if their cognitive faculties weren't truth-directed, but he could not apply it to himself. So, a *Humean* rationality defeater makes it irrational to believe something because the forces behind it are not truth-directed. We *would* think it does so for someone else, but we cannot seriously relinquish the belief in our own cases.—except, perhaps, in the quiet of our studies.

Warrant defeaters, on the other hand, are associated with *warrant*, and thus address knowledge rather than rationality. They point to what the function of something *is* rather than whether it is functioning properly—specifically whether the function is to form true beliefs. If it is not, then the belief is not warranted, and it has a defeater. For example, if someone is diagnosed with a usually fatal disease, an "optimistic overrider" may kick in and they may form the belief that they will be one of the lucky few that survive.[36] The optimism function (or wishful thinking function if we are in a more cynical mood) will be functioning properly, but since the purpose is not to produce true beliefs, their belief that they will survive will not have warrant.

So, whereas a proper function defeater addresses whether someone's cognitive faculties are functioning properly, a warrant defeater addresses *what that function is*. Will the continued belief in the face of a defeater be produced by properly functioning cognitive faculties aimed at producing true beliefs? A proper function defeater would say no because the cognitive faculties will not be functioning properly, whereas a warrant defeater would say no because, even if the cognitive faculties are functioning properly, the function in question is not to produce true beliefs, and so the belief could not qualify as knowledge (warranted true belief).

Rationality and warrant defeaters are closely intertwined. If one has a rationality defeater, then one automatically has a warrant defeater, since warrant would be absent if one's cognitive faculties were functioning improperly. In other words, rationality defeaters are also warrant defeaters. The converse does not hold though: having a warrant defeater does not necessarily entail having a rationality defeater. However, if one is *aware* of a warrant defeater, in most circumstances they would also have a rationality defeater.[37] If someone realizes their belief was produced by processes which do not have the function of producing true beliefs—either they have a different function or no function at all—then generally, their cognitive faculties would not be functioning properly if they continued to believe it. They would know they do not believe the belief because it is true but for some other reason. To continue believing it—to continue thinking it is true when they know its truth is irrelevant to why they believe it—would be irrational.

4. A believed defeater is a mental state that is *taken to be* a defeater, leaving aside the question of whether it actually is. It is believed in the same sense that an alleged crime is alleged: whether it is an *actual* defeater is another question.[38] This means (according to Plantinga) that an irrational defeater can defeat a rational belief. Plantinga mentions Descartes's madman who thinks his head is made of glass, and so wears a football helmet to protect it.[39] Wearing the helmet is rational in a sense, since *given* his belief that his head is made of glass, he should do what is necessary to keep it from shattering.

This is the difference between internal and external rationality. Something is internally rational if it is rational given one's other beliefs, regardless of whether those other beliefs are true, plausible, or even sane. It is rational relative to *a given system of beliefs*.

> Internal rationality has to do with proper function, proper cognitive response downstream from experience, including doxastic experience; external rationality has to do with proper function upstream from experience.... Under this conception, a belief that is acquired and held in a way that is externally irrational can nevertheless be a defeater of a belief that is acquired and held rationally, both internally and externally. By virtue of paranoia I come to think you are out to destroy my academic reputation; this gives me a defeater for my previous belief that you are well disposed toward me, even though it is irrationally acquired.

Under this conception, defeaterhood has to do with what the design plan requires, *once you acquire a new belief*; it does not have to do with the rationality, for you, of this new belief.[40]

The EAAN operates in internal rationality. We may be dissatisfied by this: we want some beliefs to be defeated regardless of whether anyone believes them; we want them to operate in external rationality, not just conditioned on a given system of beliefs.[41] But being conditional like this does not mean it is different for each person. Conditional probability doesn't work that way. This is precisely why Plantinga rejects Bayesian probabilistic accounts: they relativize probability to the person. "Conditional probability," however, "is *not* thus relative to persons."[42] Moreover, the system of beliefs the probability assessments are conditioned on in the EAAN is simply R, N, and E. The argument claims that N defeats R, E, and N itself. These are the only elements we need consider. And if someone gives up belief in N, they no longer have a defeater for their belief in R and E.

5. A defeater can be defeated itself, and this second order defeater can be defeated, and this pattern continues indefinitely. So, I believe the widgets are red based on their appearance, but then someone tells me they are irradiated with a red light and this defeats the belief that they are red. Then someone else tells me that the person who told me they are irradiated with a red light is a compulsive liar. Now I have a defeater-defeater: ignoring any other considerations, if my cognitive processes are aimed at truth and functioning properly, I will believe the widgets are red again. Then *that* defeater gets defeated, and the pattern keeps going. Note that even though the defeaters are going on to infinity, all that is happening is that the original belief is wavering back and forth between being defeated and not defeated.

6. It is possible for a belief (or other mental state) to defeat itself; there are self-defeating beliefs. This may seem odd[43] but it is easy to generate examples. If someone argues that arguments are all invalid, then that argument itself would be invalid as well. If someone believes that there are no beliefs, then that belief would constitute a counterexample to itself. We can distinguish three different concepts of self-referential beliefs here.[44]

First, a belief may not be true in any possible world. This amounts to a logical contradiction; such a belief is self-*refuting*. So, for example, the belief that there is a set of sets that do not belong to themselves is a self-refuting belief, since if there were such a set, it would belong to itself if it did not, and it would not belong to itself if it did. A self-refuting belief, therefore, is a belief that is incompatible with itself. It functions as a rebutting defeater of itself; it gives one a reason for rejecting itself.

Second, there may be possible worlds where the belief is true (and therefore it is not a logical contradiction), but there are no possible worlds where the belief is true and rationally believed. Such a belief is self-*defeating*. For example, there are possible worlds where the statement "There are no beliefs" is true—namely, worlds with no conscious agents to have any beliefs—but there is no possible world in which that statement is true, and someone *believes* it, since such a belief would constitute a counterexample to itself. As such, the problem here is not that the belief is incompatible with its own *content*, strictly speaking, as is the case with self-refutation. Rather a self-defeating belief is incompatible with the nature of *belief* itself (or knowledge, assertion, argumentation, etc., depending on how the issue is framed).

Self-defeat falls into two categories: inherent and accidental. An accidental self-defeating claim or belief can be rephrased to avoid the problem. So, if I scream at the top of my lungs, "I ALWAYS SPEAK SOFTLY!!!" it is accidentally self-defeating since my presentation of the claim is a counterexample to itself. There is no possible world where I *shout* it and it is true—but of course, I could whisper the same proposition, and then it is no longer self-defeating. There may even be possible worlds where it is true. An inherently self-defeating claim or belief, however, cannot be presented differently to avoid self-defeat. There may be possible worlds with no affirmations (e.g., worlds with no one to affirm anything) but there are no possible worlds where the affirmation "There are no affirmations" is affirmed and true.

Third, a belief may be neither self-refuting nor self-defeating. Not only are there possible worlds where it can be true, there are possible worlds where it can be true and rationally believed. But the actual world is not one of them. The technical philosophical term for such a belief is "false." For example, whispering that I always speak softly. Just ask my kids if that's true.

The EAAN does not merely argue that naturalism is false, but neither does it argue it is self-refuting. It argues that naturalism is (inherently) self-defeating. This makes it an undercutting, believed, complete defeater,[45] and can be taken as either a rationality defeater or a warrant defeater.

7. Bringing together defeater-defeaters and self-defeat leads to the possibility of an ultimately unresolved defeater. In this case, once the belief is made rational again, it automatically produces a next-level defeater. The next-level defeater then defeats the belief, but in doing so also defeats itself, thus rendering the original belief rational again, but also rendering the defeater effective again, and on the cycle goes. This type of chronic defeat is associated with Hume's skepticism and is sometimes called a Humean loop. As he argues, we go back and forth between two poles. First, we accept reason, see the valid reasoning behind the skeptical argument, and reject reason. Second, having rejected reason, we realize we no longer have a motive to accept the reasoning in support of the skeptical argument, and so the motive for rejecting reason is taken away, and we accept reason again. But as soon as we do so, we see the valid reasoning behind the skeptical argument again, and so on, "till at last they both vanish away into nothing."[46] The rational response when we see a Humean loop approaching is to avoid it by rejecting whatever leads to it.

It is also possible to have an ultimately *undefeated* defeater. Here, when the defeater is defeated, it is somehow still capable of defeating the original belief.[47] In this case, it functions like a Humean loop, with the caveat that reason remains defeated throughout the process. We will see how this is cashed out in chapter 9 when we contrast Plantinga's diachronic loop with his synchronic regress.

5

The Evolution of the Evolutionary Argument

The man who represents all thought as an accident of environment is simply smashing and discrediting all his own thoughts—including that one.

G.K. Chesterton

Background of the argument

Plantinga first presented the EAAN in print in a 1991 essay, "An Evolutionary Argument against Naturalism," which was reproduced with some changes as chapter 12 ("Is Naturalism Irrational?") of *Warrant and Proper Function*.[1] Objections were made immediately in the philosophical literature, and Plantinga responded in kind, as well as online with his essay "Naturalism Defeated." He refined the argument in 2000 in *Warranted Christian Belief*, and in 2002 James Beilby edited the volume *Naturalism Defeated?* with numerous essays by (mostly) critics and a lengthy response by Plantinga.[2] The debate continued for the next decade, literally in some cases, with Plantinga publishing debates with Paul Draper, Michael Tooley, and Daniel Dennett.[3] Finally, in 2011, Plantinga published *Where the Conflict Really Lies* which presents "the official and final version" of his argument.[4]

Before going over this final version, we need to look at the first two stages of the argument, not least because many objections are responding to an earlier form rather than the current form.

The first argument

Having defined the constants (P, R, N, and E)[5] in the previous chapter, we can see how to form a rough argument. (1) If, "Among the crucially important facts, with respect to the question of the reliability of a group of cognitive faculties, are facts about their origin";[6] and (2) if it is improbable that naturalism should provide us with reliable cognitive faculties—if $P(R/N\&E)$ is low—then (3) N may defeat R. But why think this? To reiterate, this does *not* mean it is improbable that we have reliable cognitive faculties or that it is improbable for evolution to have produced them. It is only when we add naturalism to the mix that the probability becomes low, less than or equal to .5. Not impossible, just improbable.[7]

But again, why think it's improbable? Specifically, why does *Plantinga* think it's improbable? He is certainly not alone in this. He points to several high-profile nontheistic philosophers who have alluded to the apparent absurdity in affirming we have reliable cognitive faculties given naturalism, such as Friedrich Nietzsche, Stephen Stich, Barry Stroud, Thomas Nagel, and Patricia Churchland.[8] Churchland argues that naturalistic evolution would only select for *behavior* not belief contents, behavior being what makes an organism more fit in an evolutionary sense. "Boiled down to essentials, a nervous system enables the organism to succeed in the four F's: feeding, fleeing, fighting and reproducing. The principal chore of nervous systems is to get the body parts where they should be in order that the organism may survive. . . . Truth, whatever that is, definitely takes the hindmost."[9]

Churchland's quote has become famous, perhaps because of Plantinga's use of it. But since Plantinga clearly enjoys turning the tables on people, he uses the naturalists' chief weapon against them with a more poignant example: Charles Darwin.

Darwin's Doubt

In 1881, Darwin wrote a letter to William Graham to praise the latter's *Creed of Science*.[10] Darwin writes, "with me the horrid doubt always arises whether the convictions of man's mind, which has been developed from the mind of the lower animals, are of any value or at all trustworthy. Would any one trust in the convictions of a monkey's mind, if there are any convictions in such a mind?"[11] So Darwin himself seemed to recognize a disconnect between our brains being the product of naturalistic evolution and our beliefs ("convictions") being mostly true—that is, that P(R/N&E) is low. Plantinga proceeds to call this concern "Darwin's Doubt."[12]

Note, however, that Darwin only articulated this concern in a specific area. In the sentence preceding the quote above, he writes, "you have expressed my inward conviction, though far more vividly and clearly than I could have done *that the Universe is not the result of chance*."[13] So his concern was not whether he trusted his mind regarding evolution or science but only regarding his "inward conviction" that something intentionally made the universe. It is unclear why Darwin applied this argument to the one but not the other—indeed, perhaps he did. Or perhaps he thought his conviction in a cosmic Orderer was an intuition rather than a reasoned conclusion, and naturalistic evolution only calls the former into question; it only touches our immediate beliefs or impressions before we turn a critical eye on them.[14] In fact, this seems likely: in a footnote to the letter, Francis Darwin (Charles's son) writes,

> The Duke of Argyll ("Good Words," Ap. 1885, p. 244) has recorded a few words on this subject, spoken by my father in the last year of his life. '. . . in the course of that conversation I said to Mr. Darwin, with reference to some of his own remarkable works on the "Fertilisation of Orchids," and upon "The Earthworms," and various other observations he made of the wonderful contrivances for certain purposes in nature—I said it was impossible to look at these without seeing that they were the effect and the expression of mind. I shall never forget Mr. Darwin's answer. He looked at me very hard and said, "Well, that often comes over me with overwhelming

force; but at other times," and he shook his head vaguely, adding, "it seems to go away."¹⁵

So, Darwin may have just been questioning the validity of intuitions that sprang into his mind unbidden when he observed the universe and perceived it is the result of intelligence, not blind chance. Nevertheless, there is no reason to limit its application this way: *we* can certainly apply it beyond this sphere, and Plantinga, in fact, does.[16]

Following Stephen Stich, Plantinga writes that thinking N&E would produce reliable cognitive faculties breaks down into two assumptions: (1) N&E "produces organisms with good approximations to optimally well-designed characteristics or systems," and (2) "an optimally well-designed cognitive system is a rational cognitive system."[17] Neither of these is very plausible. There is no reason to think that natural selection would even have the *opportunity* to select a preferable characteristic, there are simply too many variables. The products of evolution do not have to be optimal or anything approaching it, they just have to stave off death long enough to reproduce, and this can be accomplished with organisms and systems that fall far short of optimality.[18]

Ignoring this, there is the further assumption that an optimal cognitive system would be a rational one, that is, a *reliable* system in Plantinga's sense, one that produces mostly true beliefs. But reliability could cost too much in terms of energy expenditure or memory storage, while a less reliable system could cost less and offset its production of false beliefs. Plus, evolution often bets on overgeneralizations. Suppose there is an animal species that often falls prey to a predator. The predator has evolved to closely resemble several other animals that are harmless to the species; it is not until the predator is close that it becomes distinguishable from these other animals. One member of this species instinctively flees upon seeing any of these similar animals while another flees only once the animal is close enough to be recognized as the predator. The instincts of the former species member would be less accurate since it treats the various animals as if they were all predators when only one is. The instincts of the latter species member would be more accurate, but it also decreases its chances of survival since it would not flee from the predator until it is close enough to make escape less probable. If the two species members had beliefs which corresponded to these instincts, it would be the latter's that would be reliable and the former's that would be unreliable. Yet evolution would choose the former since it increases the organism's chances of survival.[19]

Five possibilities

From here, Plantinga goes over five possible relations between mind and body that "are mutually exclusive and jointly exhaustive,"[20] and asks whether they would likely lead to a propensity for forming true beliefs (that is, R). However, just as Darwin asked this about monkeys first rather than ourselves, so Plantinga asks this about "a hypothetical population of creatures a lot like ourselves on a planet similar to Earth"[21]—"like ourselves" in that they arose via evolutionary processes and have beliefs—and then posit that naturalism holds for them. Ultimately the point will be to apply this to ourselves since what would be true of them would be true of us, but that is a later step.

This move to a hypothetical population is important and wards off several objections to the EAAN.

First, beliefs could be free floating, neither causing nor being caused by behavior. In this case, the probability that most of the beliefs formed (that is, two-thirds to three-fourths of them) would be true would be low. There would be no control, no connection between the beliefs and the circumstances of the organism's body and environment. Without such a control, any given belief would be a coin toss: either it or its negation is true. So, under this scenario, it is very improbable that their belief-forming capacities would reliably produce true beliefs.

Second, beliefs could be caused by behavior, or caused by whatever also causes behavior. Here there would be a one-way connection between body and mind. The body produces the beliefs, but the beliefs are not causes themselves, they are dead end streets. This may seem better since there is at least *some* connection between behavior and beliefs, but since the direction only goes in one direction, from behavior to beliefs, there is no reason to think that the beliefs are true. The organism's environment impresses itself on the body, the body responds with behavior, and, *ex hypothesi*, beliefs are produced. But these beliefs would be mere epiphenomena: why think they correspond with the organism's actual situation? Whatever control we want to posit would have no influence on the beliefs' contents. Without such a control, the probability of any belief being true would still be .5, and the probability of most beliefs being true would be low.

Third, beliefs could be caused by and cause behavior. The connection is a two-way street. Beliefs respond to circumstances and behavior, but then beliefs can themselves cause behavior. This definitely seems better, but there is an added wrinkle: beliefs' *contents* do not cause behavior, it is the neurological processes they embody that do so. It is analogous to an opera singer breaking a glass with her voice. What breaks the glass is her voice's resonance frequency, but the propositional content—the words she is singing—is irrelevant.[22] Similarly, while the brain's neurological processes cause survival-enhancing behavior, the propositional content those processes embody is irrelevant. In philosophical parlance, a belief's semantics does not cause behavior, its syntax does. As Dennett puts it, "It is true that every belief state is what it is, and locally causes whatever it causes, independently of whether it is true or false. As I have said, our brains are *syntactic engines*, not *semantic engines*, which, like perpetual motion machines, are impossible."[23] This is significant as this position corresponds to the computational theory (or theories) of mind, a very popular view in philosophy of mind today.

Unfortunately, under this scenario there would still be no control on what beliefs' contents would be. The syntax of beliefs could bring about the appropriate behavior that allows the hypothetical population to survive, thrive, and evolve, but the semantics of beliefs could be just about anything. Therefore, as above, the probability of any belief being true would be .5 and the probability of most of our beliefs being true would be low.

The fourth possibility is that beliefs cause behavior and do so by virtue of their propositional content (they are genuine semantic engines), but are, nevertheless, maladaptive. Perhaps beliefs are a genetic side-effect, the genes that code for them also coding for survival-enhancing behavior. If the benefits of the coded behavior outweigh the disadvantages wreaked by beliefs, then a propensity to form beliefs could survive despite being harmful. There still would not be a control over belief contents in this scenario, since beliefs could be false, both individually and *en masse*, but the beneficial behavior the genes code for offsets the harmful behavior the false beliefs bring about. The situation here is no better than before: any particular belief would only have a .5 probability of being true, since there is nothing exerting control over beliefs' contents to make false beliefs less common and true beliefs more common.

Fifth and finally, beliefs could be causally efficacious—semantic engines—as before, but their effects are beneficial, not maladaptive. This is what most people believe (excluding philosophers of mind) because we intuitively tend to think false beliefs would cause harmful behavior and true beliefs would cause beneficial behavior. So, there *would* be a control over beliefs' contents. What is the probability that most beliefs formed by members of the hypothetical population are true?

"Not as high as you might think."[24] Behavior, after all, is not *merely* produced by beliefs but by many other factors. If these other factors combine with beliefs to produce survival-enhancing behavior, the beliefs need not be true. For example, say a member of the hypothetical population encounters their planet's version of an angry grizzly bear during their morning constitutional. We would normally assume they believe they are in danger of being killed and so undertake whatever maneuvers are necessary to avoid the bear; not only because that is the commonsense view but because if they did not, they would not have survived to pass on their genes to future generations. But remember Churchland's point: evolution would *only* select for behavior, not for the beliefs that lead to it. Plantinga demonstrates this by positing parallel circumstances where the hypothetical population member engages in identical behavior but for different reasons. Perhaps they want to be eaten by the bear but think the best way to accomplish this is to hide from it. Perhaps they think the bear is a big slab of bacon but want to avoid temptation and so every time they see tasty foods they turn around and run away. The point is straightforward: the number of false beliefs that produce adaptive behavior is greater than the number of true beliefs that produce that same adaptive behavior.[25] This "belief-cum-desire"[26] scenario still leaves too much room for beliefs to be false while producing beneficial behavior, and since evolution only selects for behavior, the survival of the fittest is no guarantee that, of any particular belief we choose, it is probably correct.

At this point, however, Plantinga is unwilling to say the probability of any belief is only .5, and the probability of most beliefs being true is low. Perhaps we just cannot formulate a probability here, it is *inscrutable*. So for this fifth possibility, the probability that the hypothetical population has reliable cognitive faculties is either low or inscrutable.

So, we have five exhaustive possibilities: "exhaustive" since—given Plantinga's definitions of "belief," "cognitive faculties," and "reliability"—any scenario we can imagine will fall into one of these categories. Sometimes Plantinga reformulates them, collapsing the first two into epiphenomenalism, a position he says is "widely popular among those enthusiastic about the 'scientific' study of human beings."[27] The third can stand as-is and represents the most common view among philosophers of mind. And the last two can also be collapsed into "the commonsense (folk psychological) view as to the causal relation between behavior and belief."[28] Elsewhere, he telescopes them further, according to whether beliefs cause behavior by virtue of their contents or not. In this case, the first three possibilities—which are much more plausible under naturalism, something most naturalistic philosophers accept—say no and the latter two say yes.

When we look at all five (or three, or two) possibilities taken together, then, we can say that the probability that the hypothetical population has reliable cognitive faculties is either low or inscrutable, and the likelihood of it being inscrutable as opposed to low depends upon how likely we think that fifth scenario would be *given naturalism* as opposed to the other four possibilities. To use our constants, $P/R(N\&E) \leq .5$. If you knew someone who chose their positions on various issues by flipping a coin, they would have a .5 chance of being correct on any given belief. Would you trust their conclusions? To ask this question is to answer it: if the mechanism by which they arrive at their beliefs has only a .5 chance of being true, it is not a reliable one.[29]

The EAAN version 0

Before presenting his first argument that naturalism is self-defeating, Plantinga uses Darwin's Doubt to present a Bayesian argument that naturalism is *false*.[30]

$$P(N\&E/R) = \frac{P(N\&E) \times P(R/N\&E)}{P(R)}$$

If we grant R (which should not be too controversial), we should assess P(R) at 1. Darwin's Doubt argues that we should assess P(R/N&E) as .5 or lower. If we set that at the highest possibility, the second half of the equation would be

$$\frac{P(N\&E) \times .5}{1}$$

With this, no matter what probability we assign to N&E, even 1 (absolute certainty), the total number in the numerator will not be greater than .5, and so the total number of the equation will not be greater than .5. So, at best, P(N&E/R) is .5 and almost certainly lower. In order to raise P(R/N&E) higher than .5, we would have to make P(R) lower than P(N&E). But since P(N&E) is *dependent* on P(R) (that is, our rational assessment of N&E can only *be* rational if R holds for us), this is not a genuine alternative.

"A very pretty little argument," writes Plantinga, "too bad it contains a serious flaw."[31] This was brought to his attention by Branden Fitelson and Elliot Sober.[32] Plantinga's error was to exclude a necessary factor, namely the background information (B) on which we conditionalize our probabilities. Otherwise, we would be making an absolute probability assessment, conditionalized only on necessary truths. But then P(R) is not 1 since it is not necessary (there are logically possible worlds where R does not hold). Adding B to the equation gives us

$$P(N\&E/R\&B) = \frac{P(N\&E/B) \times P(R/N\&E\&B)}{P(R\&B)}$$

which does not make the case.

Conditionalization plays a role in Plantinga's main argument.[33] For the present case he suggests a quick fix: instead of determining the absolute probability of R on N&E, we should instead compare naturalism with theism (T), or

$$P(N/R) = \frac{P(N) \times P(R/N)}{P(R)}$$

and

$$P(T/R) = \frac{P(T) \times P(R/T)}{P(R)}$$

This does not strike me as a quick fix so much as a completely different argument. Regardless, it allows Plantinga to effectively ignore P(R), since it will be the same in both equations, thus leaving the two numerators. The first terms in both are difficult to assess (the probabilities of naturalism and theism on our total evidence), so Plantinga ignores it as well, leaving us with P(R/N) and P(R/T). On N we have a reason—namely, Darwin's Doubt—to assess the probability of R as low. But we do not have a comparable reason to assess the probability of R as low on T. Indeed, we have some reason, Plantinga argues, for assessing it as relatively high.[34] Thus P(R/T) > P(R/N). "So we have a reason to prefer T to N. Not perhaps a very *strong* reason … but a reason nonetheless. (It's the same sort of reason the atheologian has for preferring atheism to theism, given that he thinks it unlikely that a world created by God would display all the evil the world does, in fact, display.)"[35]

In the rest of this work we will focus on the argument that naturalism is self-defeating rather than false since I think the former is preferable. In this I am joined by Plantinga's critics who have focused almost exclusively on the self-defeat version. Plantinga, it would seem, agrees, since he spends less than a page arguing that naturalism is false, and only two pages reframing it in response to the paltry few objections made to it,[36] while spilling considerably more ink arguing and defending the argument that naturalism is self-defeating. In fact, at this point I'm starting to fear my word count on the initial argument is higher than his.

The EAAN version 1.0

We are still looking at the hypothetical population who have beliefs and evolved by naturalistic processes. When considering the five possible ways that action and belief content can be connected (or disconnected) under N, we would assess P(R) as low or inscrutable. What we have here is a case where the only source of information is shown to be unreliable.

The hypothetical population is one analogy, but Plantinga uses others, such as the red widgets. Someone sees widgets on a conveyer belt but told they only look red because they are irradiated in a red light. Rationally, they could assess the probability they are red as low or inscrutable. They could *not* rationally conclude it is still probable they are red, since their only source of information is not reliable. Another analogy is a theist who, "perhaps through an injudicious reading of Freud,"[37] comes to believe (1) belief in God is produced by wish-fulfillment and (2) wish-fulfillment does not reliably produce true beliefs. They could draw similar conclusions as the widgeteer, that the probability their theistic beliefs are true is improbable or inscrutable. In either case, the rational response is to refrain from believing theism. "That is not to say, of course, that she would in fact be *able* to do so; but it remains the rational course."[38]

Plantinga argues that in cases where a belief is solely produced by unreliable sources, the low probability translates into a defeater. The Freudian theist believes that wishful thinking does not reliably produce true beliefs (beliefs so produced are true .5 or less of the time), so if they think their belief in God is solely produced by wishful thinking, their belief in God is defeated. The widget observer thinks the probability that a widget is red is .5 or less, their belief the widget is red is defeated. The hypothetical population realizes that P(R/N&E) is low or inscrutable, and so acquire a defeater for any belief they think is exclusively produced by R. But of course, that would be all their beliefs. Obviously, there are multiple sources of information, but in order to become beliefs (mental items that have propositional content) any information gleaned must go through the cognitive faculties (the faculties, powers, or processes that produce beliefs).[39] And if they have a defeater for the proposition that their cognitive faculties are reliable (R), they have a defeater for all their beliefs, since all of them must go through that gatekeeper.

The kicker, is that what is true of the hypothetical population is also true of us, if we assume that we are also produced by naturalistic evolution. Insofar as we are in the same situation as them, we have a defeater for the belief that our cognitive faculties are reliable. Plantinga concludes that belief in naturalism and evolution (N&E) would be among the defeated beliefs, therefore naturalism is self-defeating. And just as the Freudian theist would not be able to simply give up their belief in God, so too the naturalist may not be able to give up their belief in naturalism. Nevertheless, "it remains the rational course."[40]

Any belief vs. all beliefs

Much of the criticism directed toward Plantinga's first argument that naturalism is self-defeating is that his analyses of the commonsense options (where beliefs cause actions by virtue of their contents) are not sufficiently defended. His scheme of combining absurd beliefs with absurd desires or other factors would only allow a member of the hypothetical population to survive a very particular set of circumstances. Perhaps believing falsely that a bear is a cuddly kitten combined with a desire to avoid kittens or another belief that you pet kittens by running from them would produce survival-enhancing behavior in very particular circumstances, but it will not allow them to survive a world with a multitude of dangers in innumerable permutations. This does not demonstrate a *general* unreliability in forming true beliefs. Certainly, there can be widespread false beliefs, but what someone believes about one thing will influence what they believe about many other things. The question is whether the hypothetical population could have *systems* of false beliefs. Plantinga has proposed an ad hoc situation, and systematizing ad hoc situations is almost a contradiction in terms.

> Suppose, for example, that to reach food you need to survive, you need to engage in some team activity with other members of your species—e.g., negotiating some tricky terrain that includes a narrow ledge and a poisonous snake. Someone has to distract the snake while someone else crawls carefully along the ledge and leaps over the snake at the exact moment it is distracted.
>
> Now try to imagine a perceptual mechanism ... that produces mostly false beliefs about your surroundings, but beliefs that, when paired with certain desires with which evolution has pre-equipped your species, will result in the required adaptive behavior from you and your team-mates.
>
> You must not believe that there is a snake and a ledge and some food and some team-mates with whom you must co-operate. And nor [sic] must your team-mates. You, and they, must have mostly false beliefs about your environment, but beliefs that, nevertheless, when paired with desires with which evolution has collectively furnished you, lead you to act in tandem with your other team members to retrieve and eat the food.[41]

Modifying the target

In response to this objection Plantinga develops the EAAN mark 2 which I will treat below, and some take this as a concession on his part.[42] However, Plantinga also provided a response in his original presentation: our cognitive faculties are very diverse, so some subdivisions of them may be more reliable than others. The EAAN applies more obviously to faculties that produce metaphysical beliefs, for example, than those that produce perceptual beliefs. So Plantinga makes a peace offer: instead of saying R is defeated, we can say instead that MR is defeated, MR being the claim that those cognitive faculties that produce metaphysical beliefs in us are reliable. The present objection to the belief-cum-desire argument would not touch this modified claim since there are plenty of systems of mostly false metaphysical beliefs already in circulation. This also has the added benefit that, once we are no longer addressing R *simpliciter*, there is no need to come up with weird scenarios like a hominid who thinks seeing a bear indicates the start of a ten-kilometer race in the opposite direction. Of course, we could easily come up with weird metaphysical beliefs, but we don't need to: we would just need to come up with eminently plausible but false metaphysical beliefs for the argument to proceed.[43]

Plantinga is not granting that the EAAN may not apply to R *simpliciter*, he is just making it more palatable. Denying R involves denying the most immediate claims to knowledge we have, such as perceptual and memory beliefs. Since we cannot make ourselves suspicious of such claims, this presents a stumbling block to accepting the argument. So Plantinga tries to remove the stumbling block while still allowing the argument to do its work. Since N is a metaphysical belief (it says what does and does not, can and cannot exist), by limiting the EAAN's applicability to that class of beliefs to which naturalism belongs, the argument still works. Anyone who cannot take the argument seriously because of its universal scope can change the target from R to MR and proceed apace.

Plantinga's second argument

Another way Plantinga responds to this objection is to reformulate the EAAN so that it does apply to systems of beliefs, specifically systems that are a) as expansive as the ones we seem to have, b) as internally coherent as the ones we seem to have, but which c) consist mostly of false beliefs. This is not an easy task. Descartes's evil demon could make us hold only false beliefs, but it is not obvious that it could make us hold coherent and expansive *systems* of false beliefs because it is not obvious there could *be* such a system. Certainly, the evil demon could make someone falsely believe that their belief system is coherent and expansive, but the question is whether an actual system like this is even possible. To muddy the waters, some add a further condition that is especially relevant to the EAAN: d) the system of beliefs must be evolutionarily adaptive, so that it connects to behavior in a way that did not impede the survival and procreation of our evolutionary forebears.

Many philosophers think the idea of a system that meets these conditions is an absurdity. Dennett lists Quine, Hilary Putnam, Sydney Shoemaker, Donald Davidson, and himself among those who find it obvious that any coherent and expansive system of beliefs must be composed of true beliefs for the most part,[44] especially if it is the product of evolution. If we take an ancient Greek whose physics and cosmology were almost entirely incorrect, we would still say that most of his beliefs involving his daily life were correct: otherwise, how could he even function? Or, to put it another way, if the Greek changed his physics and adopted a more accurate one, wouldn't most of his beliefs—"about which house he lived in, what to look for in a good pair of sandals, and so forth"[45]—remain as they were before?

Certainly, producing such a system in an ad hoc manner seems all but impossible. If we start with one of Plantinga's absurd beliefs—say that the appearance of bears indicates the start of a ten-kilometer race in the opposite direction—trying to hold that belief in numerous circumstances, and constructing other beliefs, also false, that will counteract the negative impact the first false belief would have on the organism's survivability, would be a Herculean task. It is a bit like taking medication for a health condition, but the medication has severe side-effects, so the patient must take other medications to treat the side-effects, but these new medications have severe side-effects of their own, and the situation multiplies. However, this analogy only goes so far: taking more medications may bring some degree of health to the body. With false beliefs, trying to compensate for negative consequences by constructing a system of mostly false beliefs in ad hoc fashion is clearly beyond our abilities—perhaps not impossible, but at least impossible for us.

Witches, creatures, and dimensions

Fortunately, we do not have to resort to such methods. Plantinga suggests we introduce a false belief at the essential or definitional level that touches all other beliefs. For example, the hypothetical population could falsely believe that everything is a witch. If they use definite description to invoke reference, understood in Bertrand Russell's sense,[46] and such references were expressible by singular sentences (such as "That witch-cloud is blocking out the witch-sun"), such descriptions would be false and so render all of their beliefs false. "If they ascribe the right properties to the right witches, their beliefs could be adaptive while nonetheless (assuming that in fact there aren't any witches) false."[47] By piggybacking on the system of beliefs we already have, he is thus able to construct a system of beliefs as expansive, internally coherent, and evolutionarily adaptive as ours (because the added condition could be such that it does not alter the creatures' behavior) but contains mostly false beliefs. We can even do this without using bizarre examples. Plantinga points to a real-world example that is particularly apropos: theists believe that everything other than God is literally a creature—that is, created by God. Nontheists deny this. So, we can substitute "creature" for "witch" in the above formulation to get "That cloud-creature is blocking out the sun-creature." Whichever side is correct, it follows that just about everything the other side believes is false.

> There are plenty of other ways in which systems of mainly false beliefs can be adaptive.... Michael Rea argues that naturalism implies an ontology of gunk, an ontology according to which there really aren't any *objects* (although there is a sort of continuous gunk or goo which may, as they say, be 'propertied' differently in different places). Suppose Rea is right: then since most of our beliefs imply that there are objects, most of our beliefs will be false. Still our natural way of cutting the world up into objects could be adaptive; if so, most of our beliefs would be false but adaptive.[48]

Despite this, many philosophers would still maintain the hypothetical population's beliefs about witch-clouds and sun-creatures would be fundamentally correct.[49] Here, I think Plantinga's penchant for fanciful examples has come back to haunt him: by choosing something most people cannot take seriously, he renders his argument less plausible, at least on a rhetorical level. While believing everything is a witch would render the hypothetical population's beliefs incorrect, they still have a belief about the physical world that tracks a true belief; ascribing "witch-ness" to everything may be technically incorrect, but a critic may argue that, in some sense, their beliefs are still roughly correct. The differences between clouds, witch-clouds, and cloud-creatures does not seem like enough of a difference to call beliefs about such objects incorrect.

Rea's claim that dividing the universe into discrete objects would be false given naturalism appears more dramatic, since we share the definitional belief that there are discrete objects. Claiming there are not does seem more significant an error than thinking everything is a witch and would render most of our beliefs false. Nevertheless, in this example, the universe is the way we perceive it to be, it is just a way of conceiving it that is incorrect. The objects we perceive exist but not *qua* objects. So, once again, beliefs would be approximately correct in this scenario. They may be incorrect in a *technical* sense, "But we do not, and ought not, think of this as a *pernicious* skeptical scenario akin to deception by an evil demon or ensconcement of one's brain in a vat. It's incumbent on the defender of the EAAN to show that, given naturalism, cognitive disaster is likely."[50] For example, Jerry Fodor argues that his ability to brush his teeth is "prompted and guided by a host of true beliefs," at least some of which are so basic that denying them would constitute a cognitive disaster: "true beliefs about the spatiotemporal location of my toothbrush, true beliefs about the spatiotemporal location of my teeth, true beliefs about the spatiotemporal location of my limbs with respect to my toothbrush and my teeth, and so on."[51] Believing my toothbrush is a witch-toothbrush does not generate a catastrophe radical enough for Plantinga's argument to go forward (supposedly).

However, we can construct examples that would constitute cognitive disasters. As a starting point, take the following passage from *The Orange Catholic Bible*: "Think you of the fact that a deaf person cannot hear. Then, what deafness may we not all possess? What senses do we lack that we cannot see and cannot hear another world all around us?"[52] This sentiment finds more prosaic expression in the writings of Konrad Lorenz who argues "we must assume that reality also has many other aspects which are not vital for us ... to know, and for which we have no 'organ', because we have not been compelled in the course of our evolution to develop means of adapting to them."[53]

> ... many realities which appear completely comprehensible to us humans, are insurmountably transcendent for more simply constructed organisms. Deeply convinced of the organic nature of my own cognitive apparatus, it therefore seemed to me a wanton arrogance to see the boundaries of our human cognitive capabilities as absolute, and to want to pronounce a final "to this point and no farther." Slipper animalcule live in a world of only one dimension, belly-haired infusoria live in a world with two, and all spatially-oriented living creatures obviously live in the same three-dimensional space as we ourselves; who would dare to assert that this must be the last possible orientation in space?[54]

Lorenz's creatures are not literally one- or two-dimensional but let's make his example stricter by proposing another hypothetical population of creatures that are actually two-dimensional,[55] yet which live in a three-dimensional universe. If they had beliefs about the world would they be mostly true? Perhaps their beliefs should be qualified as the world *they experience*, and so only apply to the two dimensions they perceive. Yet they would leave so much out, we would want to say that their beliefs are *not* correct, not even approximately correct. Here the difficulty is almost the opposite of Plantinga's witches: the two-dimensional creatures' beliefs may be technically correct, since they are only about the aspects of the world they experience, but in another sense, we want to say that their beliefs are false since they leave out so much. Indeed, some theories of knowledge rely on just such a criterion, that "One knows P if and only if one has accurate enough beliefs about P and also comprehensive enough beliefs about P."[56] Obviously, two-dimensional creatures in a three-dimensional world would not have "comprehensive enough beliefs" about nearly anything to qualify as knowledge. Just as Plantinga's hypothetical population attach "witch-ness" to every belief, so these attach "two-dimensional" to every belief; and since they live in a three-dimensional world, that qualification would render most of their beliefs radically incomplete. Once again, the reason for the difference is that Plantinga's hypothetical population added something we believe to be false to our conception of the world (witches), while Lorenz's two-dimensional creatures removed something that we believe to be true (a third spatial dimension).

To get the worst of all possible worlds, we would have to add something false which, by doing so, arrives at our conception of the world. So, let's propose two-dimensional beings who live and move and have their being in a two-dimensional universe with no third spatial dimension. However, evolution has deigned to provide them with the illusion that they are three-dimensional beings in a three-dimensional world. For whatever reason, it was helpful (or at least not harmful) for their evolutionary ancestors to add an illusory spatial dimension to their perception and conception of the world on top of the two that they actually experience. This third dimension need not be what an actual third dimension would be if it existed, it can be erroneous, although it would seem perfectly real to them. Having such a belief does not affect their ability to survive and propagate in their two dimensions since they respond appositely to them. Those elements they perceive as involving another spatial dimension either do not exist or form a part of their two-dimensional world, and they misperceive them as operating in a third dimension.

This belief attaches to virtually everything they believe in the Russellian manner Plantinga describes. Are their beliefs mostly true? They see a two-dimensional counterpart to a cloud and form the belief, "That three-dimensional cloud is blocking out the three-dimensional sun." Of course, they do not realize they are adding such an element to their beliefs: they think they are merely forming the belief, "That cloud is blocking out the sun," but their conceptions of clouds and suns and everything else are inherently (or essentially or definitionally) three-dimensional—remembering that *ex hypothesi* there *is* no third dimension. Therefore, their beliefs would almost always be false, and not in the seemingly innocuous way that beliefs in witch-clouds would be. This would constitute a cognitive disaster.

And here's the kicker: as with Plantinga's hypothetical population, what is true of them is true of us, since *we* believe that we exist and move in three spatial dimensions. How do we know our experiences of three dimensions are not illusory and we actually only exist in two? Just as the two-dimensional creatures misperceive two-dimensional objects as existing and operating in three spatial dimensions, so might we.

Someone might find it odd that we were all discombobulated about the implausibility of a population of hominids believing everything is a witch and our search for a closer analogy has led us to two-dimensional beings in a two-dimensional universe. But this misfires in two ways. First, as we've seen, the witches analogy adds something false to our conception of the world, while the two-dimensional analogy removes something true from our conception. Second, the analogy does not have to be *metaphysically* similar to us but *epistemologically* similar. On that point, the two-dimensional analogy is closer since the two-dimensional beings share our conception of the world while the witches analogy has a significant element in their conception that we lack. To bring these two points together, the witches analogy adds something false to our system of beliefs while leaving the world identical, whereas the two-dimensional analogy removes something true from the world while leaving our system of beliefs identical.

Remember Dennett's Greek? We asked: if he abandoned his false physical and cosmological theories in favor of true ones, wouldn't most of his beliefs about his daily life remain unchanged? We can now ask the same thing of our two-dimensional beings. If one of them corrected their false three-dimensional space and accepted a true two-dimensional space, would most of their beliefs be significantly altered? Obviously they would. Some beliefs may remain untouched, but most of their three-dimensional beliefs would be radically incongruent with the actual two-dimensional world in which they live. Their system of beliefs would be, by and large, unreliably produced, and the majority of their beliefs false—and again, we can qualify this as merely referring to their metaphysical beliefs. Since what is true of them is true of us, it seems perfectly possible for most of our beliefs to be false.

Representations and regresses

I have not gone into as much detail about Plantinga's second argument as the first because many elements new to the second argument play a role in the third, and the third is what most of the remainder of this work is about. I will introduce them as they become relevant. These include the distinction between two types of mental representations, indicative and depictive, as well as the move from presenting the argument as a Humean loop to an infinite regress. First, however, we must deal with a potential escape route: the rejection of beliefs as Plantinga defines them.

6

Elimination Game

The nearest thing to a human passion which still existed in him was a sort of cold fury against all who believe in the mind. There was no tolerating such an illusion. There were not, and must not be, such things as men.

C.S. Lewis

Remove your thought, 'cause it's only for deceiving
Deceiving thoughts destroy within
Disappear like man was never here

Metallica

Eliminative materialism denies that certain self-evident properties of mind—notably beliefs and propositional content—are real or veridical. There are no beliefs and there never have been, because materialism cannot accommodate them. If belief content is abandoned, then any claims of truth value go with it.[1] Such concepts ("belief," "truth," and "concepts" itself) constitute the commonsense way of thinking about our minds. Eliminativists call it "folk psychology" and reject it as a failed theory of mind. The elements of folk psychology will be eliminated, not merely reduced, as we discover via neurological studies what is really happening in the brain when we think we're thinking.

Plantinga never applies the EAAN to eliminative materialism,[2] and for good reason: his argument deals with the truth and falsity of mental items with propositional content, i.e., beliefs.[3] The eliminativist can grant that P/R(N&E) is low because Plantinga defines R in terms of the truth value of beliefs, and he defines beliefs in terms of propositional content—and the eliminativist denies there can be such properties. Thus, eliminativism does not allow the argument to proceed because it does not grant that N&E (or R, or eliminativism for that matter) are beliefs. Moreover, the EAAN focuses on the hypothetical population who is relevantly similar to us, and Plantinga states that this would include that they have beliefs. If they didn't, a critic could argue they are not sufficiently analogous to us. The eliminativist, however, would think it is only if they lack beliefs that they become analogous.

Content and natural selection

Nevertheless, Plantinga does bring up eliminativism in the context of the argument. "Most naturalists," he writes, "accept *materialism* with respect to human beings: the claim that human beings are material objects. On this view human beings have no immaterial parts—no immaterial soul, or mind, or self, for example."[4] But propositional content is not a material property: how could material objects—like asteroids, carburetors, blocks of cheese, or neural configurations—have propositional content? This is why eliminativists deny there are beliefs. For one material object or event (or set of objects or events) to be "about" another is incoherent. Trees are not about puddles. Rocks are not about clouds. How can neural events be about anything?

Plantinga argues that ascribing propositional content to material objects is simply a category mistake and considers it an insurmountable problem for the materialist. He quotes a passage from Leibniz envisioning "a machine whose structure produced thought, feeling, and perception."[5] If we enlarged it and went inside (like a mill, Leibniz suggests) and observed all the various motions and parts, all we would observe is motions and parts—not thoughts, sensations, perceptions, or anything characteristic of mentality. In particular, we would not find *beliefs*. Observing all these parts, we would still ask, where is the content? How does that part moving in relation to those parts have a content? If physical objects and processes are not "about" anything, the physical objects and processes in Leibniz's thinking machine are not about anything.

Hume argues we cannot get a prescription from a description, an "ought" from an "is," since the former "expresses some new relation or affirmation."[6] Likewise, Leibniz and Plantinga argue we cannot get content from physical objects and processes, since content ("aboutness") expresses a new relation or affirmation. For Hume, if we multiply descriptions so that we have an enormously complex system that we cannot keep track of, we are no closer to a prescription (an "ought") than we were with a single description (an "is"). Similarly, we can make Leibniz's machine larger and more complicated, but this does not change anything. Having many physical connections between many physical parts may be difficult to keep track of, but a complex series of movements among complex parts has no more claim on content than a simple series of movements among simple parts. Thinking the complexity, the large number of interacting parts, may produce content is like thinking if you walk far enough, if you take enough steps, you'll eventually walk to the Moon.

As Plantinga notes, the problem is not merely that we do not see how material objects could have content; it is that we *do* see that they *could not* have content. That is why it is a category mistake to think material objects could have content.

> It's a little like trying to understand what it would be for the number seven, e.g., to weigh five pounds (or for an elephant to be a proposition). We can't see how that could happen; more exactly, we can see that it *couldn't* happen. A number just isn't the sort of thing that can have weight; there is no way in which that number or any other number could weigh anything at all. (The same goes for elephants and propositions.) Similarly, we can see, I think, that physical activity among neurons can't generate content. These neurons are clicking away, sending electrical impulses

hither and yon. But what has this to do with content? How is content or aboutness supposed to arise from this neuronal activity? How can such a thing be a belief? You might as well say that thought arises from the activity of the wind or the waves.[7]

In his debate with Plantinga, Michael Tooley responds that this is based on Plantinga's (and Leibniz's and many others') intuition that material objects don't have content. But obviously contemporary materialists, or at least materialist philosophers (or at least materialist philosophers who aren't eliminativists), do not share this intuition: "one should view the conflicting intuitions of other thoughtful philosophers as defeaters, at least if such conflicting intuitions are very common—as they are in the present case, where the intuition that things other than immaterial substances can have beliefs is very widespread indeed."[8] Appealing to this intuition to rebut materialism and naturalism, therefore, begs the question.

One would think the better part of valor would involve allowing one's opponents to define their own intuitions. Plantinga apparently disagrees: he is unwilling to grant this point to Tooley. He names some prominent materialists who argue that mind-body dualism is the "natural" position to take, and that empirical evidence indicates most people share this intuition.[9] Certainly, materialists may think the negatives of accepting the intuition that material objects cannot have content outweigh its strengths, but that does not mean they do not share the intuition. Denying the veridicality of the intuition is not the same as not having it.

So, if naturalists really are materialists about human beings, they should reject the possibility of content and beliefs. "Materialists, I say, should agree with eliminativists in thinking there aren't any beliefs."[10] So, Plantinga and eliminativists agree on what the dilemma is, they just disagree on which horn to grasp. Moreover, Plantinga's phrasing takes away an interlocutor's attempt to say the same of him: we cannot imagine, after all, how an *immaterial* thing could have content either. But here it is not a case of seeing that it could not happen, we just do not see how it would. This would not stop us from seeing *that* it does, it would just stop us from seeing *how* it does—in the same way we do not see how electrons have negative charges (by what process? Why can't protons have this property? Or elephants?) even though we see they do; we do not see how sets have members even though we see they do; we do not see how propositions have content even though we see they do; etc. Thought may be mysterious in many ways, but the reason it appears mysterious here is because we are trying to explain it in materialistic terms. "But that's not a problem for thought; it's a problem for materialism."[11]

However, there is an obvious response to this: computers are material objects operating on material principles yet their processes have content. I type "The state of Oregon is larger than the United Kingdom" on my computer and it appears on my screen. That sentence expresses a proposition, and that proposition has content. Ergo material objects can have content. In fact, this shows we don't even have to appeal to computers: *sentences* are material objects, composed of vocal sounds or physical marks on paper or computer screens, and have, as their contents, propositions. Obviously material objects can have content.

This moves too quickly, however. Sentences can be understood in terms of their material components—as marks on a page—or in terms of their content, what they *mean*.[12] Yet a sentence can only have content if it is assigned by a mind. If, on an alien planet, some extraterrestrial slug crawled in the dirt and its slime trail just happened to spell out a coherent sentence—say, "*cogito ergo sum*"—it would not have any meaning without a mind to assign meaning to it. Or take Richard Taylor's example of white rocks on a hillside that spell "The British Railways welcomes you to Wales."[13] If the rocks just fell into those positions by natural processes and were not placed there by a mind intending to communicate that proposition, we would have no reason for thinking the sentence is true. We would have no reason for thinking we *were* entering Wales, or even that such a place exists. The rocks' configuration wouldn't really have content, it would only appear so because they happened to fall into a formation we *would* ascribe content to if it *had* been arranged by an intelligent agent.

This illustrates the difference between original content and secondary or derived content.[14] A material object can have derived content because we can assign content to it—just as we can see a random configuration of objects and designate that it symbolizes something, even though, in and of themselves, the objects' configuration does not mean anything because they do not have original content. And you cannot produce original content by starting with derived content and building up, since derived content only has content by virtue of its relationship to original content. We have to start with original content in order for anything to have any content at all. We have to work top-down rather than bottom-up.[15]

However, *this* moves too quickly in the opposite direction. Certainly, we can assign meaning to some random configuration of objects, but what if the objects' configuration is not random? What if they signify something about their environment or history? A string of small rocks on a beach could indicate how far the tide came in.[16] Tracks indicate that some creature has walked past. Smoke indicates fire. These indicative representations do not require a mind to assign meaning to them, they just mean what they mean regardless of whether there are any minds around to comprehend them.[17] We can assign arbitrary meaning to random objects, but there are also objects and configurations that naturally and non-arbitrarily indicate something. So, again, material objects can indicate something about their environment and their history, what has happened to them. Our bodies are replete with structures that indicate various conditions such as temperature, blood pressure, etc. In the same way, the neurons and neurological processes in our brains can indicate something about the environment and history of the organism and its brain, and that is all that is necessary for various mental processes to take place.

Conspicuously absent from this, however, is *propositional content*. Yes, we can form a proposition around what a given structure indicates, but that does not imply the structure just has that propositional content. Thus, Plantinga makes a distinction between indicative representations which indicate something about an organism or environment and depictive representations which depict something, have propositional content, and can be true or false. I'll deal with this in more detail in the following chapter.

So, Plantinga argues, naturalists should be eliminativists because of the incongruity of material objects having propositional content. To get to the EAAN, however, he ignores this for the sake of argument and just argues that the probability that our beliefs would mostly be true on naturalism (P(R/N&E)) is low. Granting the existence of beliefs is not question-begging on his part since most materialists do not accept the extreme claims of eliminativism. In fact, we can argue that eliminativism is just as self-defeating as naturalism. The eliminativist seems to be arguing for, asserting, claiming to believe and asking *us* to believe eliminativism. Since argument, assertion, and belief are denied by the eliminativist, this renders their position self-defeating.

Two false starts[18]

Believing there are no beliefs

Two common ways of charging eliminativism with self-defeat are misleading. The first is probably the response most people have to the claim there are no beliefs: "Do they expect me to *believe* that?" To be consistent, eliminativists would have to say they are not asking us to believe eliminativism, they do not even believe it themselves, and regardless, eliminativism is not true (truth being one of the things scheduled for elimination). But then it becomes exceedingly difficult to continue paying attention to them.

There are three possible responses eliminativists could make.[19] First, they could recognize they cannot discuss this without presupposing folk psychology's validity, and so they lapse into silence. Unfortunately, this won't work, since they can hold inner dialogues with themselves, and this will lead them directly into self-defeat.[20] They could try to not think about it (although trying not to think about something is the surest way to think about it even more), but if eliminativism requires that we not think about eliminativism, we can have no motive, rational or otherwise, to accept it. Plus, what would be required is not that someone stop thinking about eliminativism but that they stop thinking about *everything*. But how exactly would the eliminativist give up thinking?

> Suicide would be too drastic. Although it would stop him deliberating, it would also stop him believing in [eliminativism]. On the other hand, nothing less than suicide would be drastic enough. Drugs or drink might induce a temporary suspension of his practical reason, but as soon as their effects wear off the inconsistency will reappear. This inconsistency therefore requires him to abandon [eliminativism].[21]

Second, the eliminativist could deny that our normal view of assertion means what we think it means. The claim here is not merely that we are mistaken about what is actually going on when we assert something (which is, after all, the eliminativist thesis), but that our *normal view* of assertion is wrong, a thesis that denies we mean what we think we mean.[22]

This denial, however, is greatly lacking in plausibility. It seems to virtually all of us that, for example, the difference between genuine assertion and playacting is that in one case, but not in the other, one intends to convey to the hearer that one is uttering sentences one believes to express truths. To deny this is to say in effect that while we do have the concept of assertion, we are completely mistaken about what the implications of the concept are. In the absence of any plausible alternative analysis it is difficult to take this seriously.[23]

The third response is that eliminativism will supply successor concepts that replace the elements of folk psychology with neurophysiological descriptions and processes—that is, they will describe what's *really* going on when we say "believe" or "belief." Call "belief" as conceived in folk psychology "belief$_{fp}$," and the eliminativist replacement as "belief$_{em}$," where the $_{fp}$ subscript refers to the concept within folk psychology and the $_{em}$ subscript refers to the whatever will eventually replace it when science has advanced sufficiently to provide us with successor concepts. The eliminativist can say, "No I do not believe$_{fp}$ there are no beliefs$_{fp}$. I *believe*$_{em}$ there are no beliefs$_{fp}$." Since they are not using the same concept or term that they are denying in their statement of eliminativism, they are not presenting a self-defeating thesis.

This move is, and should be, highly contentious. I doubt an eliminativist would grant to their opponent the use of terms that have no meaning to argue that eliminativism is false—especially if the argument's validity hinges on those terms. Nevertheless, it is sufficient to show that eliminativism is not self-defeating in the sense of believing there are no beliefs. However, I will ultimately argue that we can reframe this type of objection to demonstrate that eliminativism is genuinely self-defeating.

Eliminativism's dependence on naïve scientific realism

The second misleading way eliminativism could be charged with self-defeat is to show how it is derived from naïve scientific realism, "the view that science aspires to show us the real structure of the objective world, and our best present-day science is at least roughly successful in doing this."[24] Over and over eliminativists say they are just taking science seriously, and any criticism of them is motivated by the fear of science taking over some sacred aspect of life we do not wish to surrender. As such, they compare folk psychology to pseudosciences like astrology or alchemy and eliminativism to genuine science like astronomy or chemistry.[25]

Sometimes, eliminativists make this point by tying their views to the "conflict thesis," the claim that science and religion are at war, and science is winning.[26] Just as science has shown that the earth is not the center of the universe—just as science has shown we are tiny specks in a vast cosmos—just as science has shown we are evolved animals rather than the creation of a loving God—so science will show that our mental processes are just material processes and nothing more. We are no longer justified in having the exalted view of ourselves that religion expressed through geocentrism and creation in the light of scientific discovery.[27] And just as religion has stood in the way of these scientific discoveries, so it is at the heart of the rejection of eliminativism. So, again, eliminativists compare folk psychology to geocentrism and young-earth creationism and compare eliminativism to the scientific revolutions brought about by Copernicus and Darwin. Indeed, the very label "folk psychology" is a slur, intending to condemn by association with unscientific, commonsense beliefs.

Once more, this is highly contentious. Noting that other people have had false views of the universe does not advance one's claims in the face of contrary evidence. Moreover, the conflict thesis is almost completely rejected by historians of science; it is simply an inaccurate view of how science and religion have historically interacted.[28] Additionally, appealing to a future science that would exonerate their claims would be available to virtually any statement about anything, including those of the astrologist, alchemist, and geocentrist.

However, another objection is that eliminativism is only put forth within the framework of naïve scientific realism, but ultimately requires its rejection. This looks like another self-defeating scenario: the eliminativist presupposes naïve scientific realism, but their conclusions are incompatible with this presupposition. If this realism is unacceptable to eliminativists, whatever plausibility they had is lost. Our only motive to accept their claim is undercut since science is permeated with the elements to be eliminated, and scientific realism takes these elements at face value. Eliminativists recognize this: Patricia Churchland argues that evolution would not have produced brains that reliably pursue truth,[29] and Paul Churchland argues the ultimate goal of science should not be to discover truth and reality because this cannot be accommodated within eliminativism.[30] But then "why be materialists at all, let alone eliminativists?"[31]

There is a kernel of truth here, but we must be wary of taking it too far. The kernel is that, in point of fact, no one accepts eliminativism except as an extreme extension of naïve scientific realism. However, this does not mean that there cannot be other valid motives. It's possible once someone is led to eliminativism via scientific realism, they continue to believe it based on other grounds compatible with eliminativism.[32] Being led to a position for a reason (which may be a *bad* reason) does not mean that reason is the only one possible. Thinking otherwise commits the circumstantial ad hominem fallacy. It is necessary to distinguish between how we come to believe something and whether the object of that belief is true. I conclude that while this point remains very interesting, it does not yet amount to self-defeat, although a little fine-tuning may be able to make it so.

So, what *is* the problem?

The two false starts—or maybe near misses—point us toward what the real problem is. It is that eliminativists cannot express their claims without extensive use of the folk psychology they decry. Removing such references leads to others cropping up in their places. So, the eliminativist is forced to presuppose the validity of folk psychology in order to express their rejection of folk psychology. This really halts the discussion before the eliminativist can say anything. The eliminativist cannot even *begin* to express their position without granting a great deal to the folk psychology they reject.

Recall the three possible responses above: the eliminativist could stop talking and thinking, deny folk psychology's concept of assertion means what we think it means, or provide successor concepts. Ceasing to talk or think are problematic, as is the second alternative, and regardless, eliminativists have not embraced those options, so we are stuck with successor concepts. Thus, the eliminativist makes a distinction between beliefs$_{fp}$ and beliefs$_{em}$, rational$_{fp}$ and rational$_{em}$, argument$_{fp}$ and argument$_{em}$, etc.

Yet how are we to understand the difference between rational$_{fp}$ and rational$_{em}$? The only option for an eliminativist is to use rational$_{fp}$; that is, they must employ rational$_{fp}$ to explain rational$_{em}$, and so must *presuppose* rational$_{fp}$'s viability to reject it. If rational$_{fp}$ is invalid, then their elucidation of rational$_{em}$ via rational$_{fp}$ is similarly invalid. This means these successor concepts are empty: we literally have no idea what they might entail. And the eliminativist freely admits this: otherwise, it would be incumbent upon them to explain what they really mean. But insofar as these concepts are empty, they cannot use them to explain their theory.

> We simply *have no grasp* of these successor concepts, and cannot use them to make any assertions, no matter how they are named. Indeed, we have no assurance (as Churchland's scenario makes clear) that the roles played by the successor concepts will be even "remotely analogous" to those occupied by the concepts of our present scheme. No. The concepts involved ... the only concepts available to him, are precisely the concepts of the commonsense conception renounced by eliminativism. The charge of falsehood and contradiction remains. And if a theory which admittedly contains self-contradiction and massive falsehood is not self-refuting, what more does it take?[33]

It's not just when eliminativists try to express their position that this problem arises, it's also when they contemplate the possibility of eliminativism in their own minds. Every potential reason, argument, or motive for accepting eliminativism would only have force within folk psychology. Nor can we say that once someone accepts eliminativism and abandons folk psychology they can find some other basis for affirming eliminativism. Because of the discontinuity they place between eliminativism and the folk psychology that leads them to it, whatever position they affirm *would not be eliminativism*. Their position will inevitably be premised on the veridicality of folk psychology and so will be an implementation of it and its categories. They *cannot* abandon folk psychology, no matter what they say. We cannot shift from folk psychology to eliminativism like we move from one language to another. When we study a new language, the underlying claim that communication is possible is not being challenged. The eliminativist, however, is challenging the underlying claim. Even if we encountered extraterrestrials with an eliminativist vocabulary, they could not communicate it to us, much less convince us of it. Any attempt on our part to understand them would be, solely and exclusively, an exercise in folk psychology.

What I'm arguing here is similar to Hilary Putnam's refutation of brain-in-a-vat skepticism according to which my brain is being stimulated to think there is an external world I am not actually experiencing.[34] Putnam argues that if I am a brain in a vat, my concepts of brains and vats would be based on my specious experiences as a brain in a vat. I would not have any experience of actual brains and actual vats, just experiences of what the scientists in charge of the electrical impulses want me to experience. There would be no causal connection between my concept of a vat and an actual vat. So, when I consider whether I am a brain in a vat I would not be using the concept of actual vats—I *could* not use this concept since I cannot have it in the first place. But of course, the whole idea of the brain-in-a-vat hypothesis is that I am an actual brain in an actual vat. Therefore, Putnam concludes, the whole scenario is incoherent.

The weakness of Putnam's argument is its dependence upon semantic externalism, where a term's meaning is based on conditions external to the cognizer, specifically a causal theory of reference to establish the proper connection between external objects and the concepts of them. These are eminently defensible positions, but it leaves plenty of wiggle room for the skeptic to maneuver. But this option is not available for the eliminativist. We don't have to adopt a particular, finely-tuned metaphysical theory of meaning that might be alien to the eliminativist to argue against eliminativism: we only need folk psychology, the position eliminativists themselves use and on which they base their claims. Yes, their position is the rejection of folk psychology, but folk psychology is the foundation upon which eliminativism is built. That is why I'm charging eliminativism with self-defeat instead of mere falsity.

Objections

Begging the question

The eliminativist's primary response is that this begs the question. They compare it to a vitalist who thinks life requires vital spirits, and so argues that any contrary position is self-defeating.[35] The anti-vitalist would not be alive to deny vitalism unless they had a vital spirit, after all. This supposedly parallels the folk psychologist accusing eliminativism of self-defeat. Both the vitalist and folk psychologist criticize their opponents for failing to meet the criteria they explicitly reject. To critique them via these criteria, therefore, begs the question.

However, a similar argument could be used against any charge of self-defeat, since such a charge claims a position is incompatible with its own presuppositions, it has consequences that undermine its own presentation or acceptance. Someone could always reply that this begs the question since it applies standards (the position's presuppositions) that the position denies. If the eliminativist's counterargument were successful, it would rebut all claims of self-defeat.

For example, take a naïve Freudian who thinks psychological evidence and analysis proves that all beliefs are produced by irrational psychological processes brought about by childhood traumas and so are not rational. A critic points out that this would apply to the Freudian's belief in Freudianism too. Could the Freudian object that this begs the question? After all, the critic is claiming that Freudianism is not rational, but since the Freudian thinks their position is proven by evidence and analysis, they think it *is* rational. The critic is judging Freudianism's claim to rationality from the standpoint that it is not rational. It's not too surprising, then, that they find it self-defeating and irrational, since this was the starting position.

Such a response is obviously inadequate. The critic is not assuming that Freudianism is irrational, they are *arguing* that Freudianism is irrational. The irrationality of Freudianism is their *conclusion*, not their starting point. On the contrary, their starting point is that Freudianism is rational (this is what allows it to be comprehensible and analyzable). They then apply Freudianism's claims to itself, and find that, by its own lights, it is *not* rational. Hence, it is self-defeating. That's how we show anything is self-defeating: we take the position as true, valid, rational, or whatever, and apply its own standards of truth, validity, rationality, etc., to itself.

Of course, there are question-begging arguments, and the anti-vitalist case seems to be one. However, as Victor Reppert demonstrates, the vitalist scenario does not parallel the anti-eliminativist scenario. He gives three conditions that make the vitalist's argument question-begging:

(i) Vitalism is an explanatory theory for the purpose of explaining life.
(ii) Vital spirits are supposed to exist *solely* by virtue of the fact that they are needed to explain the existence of life.
(iii) Whether or not there is life cannot be disputed. Life is a publicly observable phenomenon, and any theory that takes life to be an illusion simply fails to save the appearances.[36]

These conditions would be accepted by both the vitalist and the anti-vitalist. Since they are uncontroversial, the vitalist begs the question by assuming the truth of vitalism in their critique of anti-vitalism. By presupposing a theory which exists solely to explain the given data (point ii) to argue against that theory's denial is question-begging.

The parallel conditions for folk psychology would be:

(iv) Folk psychology is an empirical theory, employed to explain various aspects of human behavior (such as assertion).
(v) Beliefs and desires, the posits of folk psychology, are supposed to exist *solely* in virtue of the fact that they are needed to explain these aspects of human behavior.
(vi) Whether or not there are assertions cannot be disputed. Assertion is a publicly observable phenomenon, and any theory that takes assertion to be an illusion simply fails to save the appearances.[37]

None of these, however, would be held by both sides of the debate so none of them would be uncontroversial. Folk psychologists—everyone who denies eliminativism—reject (iv) since critics of eliminativism do not believe folk psychology constitutes a theory. Theories explain data. What the eliminativist calls folk psychology is the data itself: beliefs, concepts, chains of reasoning, etc. We directly experience these things, they're simply given. Any theory, therefore, must explain *them*. Eliminativists reject (vi): their position, after all, denies there are assertions. And the larger point here is that the posits of folk psychology are necessary for intelligibility and coherence, beyond any explanatory power they have regarding human behavior. Therefore (v) would not be accepted by the folk psychologist.

Since these claims are denied by one side in the debate, neither the anti-eliminativist nor their argument begs the question. In particular, the anti-eliminativist is not presupposing a theory which exists solely to explain the given data (which is what makes the vitalist case self-defeating). As such, the eliminativist's supposed parallel case is not parallel, and the question-begging nature of the vitalist case does not transfer to the anti-eliminativist case.

Reducing the argument

William Ramsey suggests arguments that eliminativism is self-defeating are reducible to other objections, and so do not present us with an independent challenge. He modifies Lynne Rudder Baker's anti-eliminativism arguments[38] to form a *modus tollens*:

(T1) If there are no propositional attitudes, then nothing is asserted.
(T2) Eliminativism has been asserted.
(T3) Therefore, there must be propositional attitudes.
(T4) Therefore, eliminativism is false.[39]

But this just amounts to a counterexample to eliminativism, and the overabundance of counterexamples is the primary objection to eliminativism. Why, Ramsey asks, would the counterexample that an eliminativist (unintentionally) presents have more relevance than any other? What would the counterexample's *source* have to do with anything? It only takes one case to refute a position.

In response, it is more relevant because it shows that eliminativism is *necessarily falsified*.[40] Any attempted statement of it, argument, even to merely *entertain* it in one's own mind can only begin by presupposing its falsity. Positions which are not self-referentially incoherent do not suffer from this infirmity of being false by necessity. This is the difference between positions that are self-defeating and those that are false. Therefore, Ramsey's claim that charging eliminativism with self-defeat offers nothing more than a counterexample is incorrect.

He then proposes a *modus ponens*:

(R1) If there are no propositional attitudes, then no thesis is asserted.
(R2) There are no propositional attitudes (the eliminativist thesis).
(R3) Therefore, no thesis is asserted.[41]

But if no thesis is asserted, *eliminativism* has not been asserted, which leaves us with no way to interpret the eliminativist's claims. Their position undermines our interpretation of what they are saying. Yet this, Ramsey argues, is the "promissory note objection," which accuses eliminativists of pinning their case on a future science justifying their claims, leaving them without justification in the interim. We will be able to interpret their claims when we have accomplished a reasonably complete neurological science (supposedly). This is not self-defeating, because they may be right: a future science *may* accomplish what they say.

But the claim isn't that we merely *do* not have a way to interpret eliminativism, it's that we *could* not. It is impossible to move from folk psychology, with its tools of interpretation, to eliminativism, since any move would rely on the very tools of folk psychology we are being told to abandon. The eliminativist wants us to be patient but can only do so by embracing the folk psychology they profess to reject. This is self-defeating. Moreover, as noted above, virtually any position could be defended by appealing to the possible discoveries of some future science, including flat-earthism and geocentrism.

Ramsey suggests we can conclude the *modus ponens* as follows:

(R4) The claim that nothing is asserted is obviously false.
(R5) Therefore, eliminativism is false.[42]

But this is just the "reductio objection" which says eliminativism's consequences are so radical (e.g., nothing is asserted) that it would always be more plausible to reject eliminativism instead. Obviously, though, eliminativists disagree; they are perfectly comfortable with the idea that nothing is asserted.

Here Ramsey conflates two types of absurdity. The charge is not merely that eliminativism leads to a silly conclusion, it's that it leads to *self-defeat*: it's absurd in a *logical* sense, not in the mundane sense of "something I can't take seriously." It *is* a reductio—any claim that something is self-defeating is a claim that it is absurd—but it's not the same type of absurdity that Ramsey has in mind, where we are simply asked to believe some bizarre proposition.

To his credit, Ramsey recognizes this and constructs a similar argument replacing (R4) with a premise that applies eliminativism to itself.

(P1) If there are no propositional attitudes, then no thesis is asserted.
(P2) There are no propositional attitudes (the eliminativist thesis).
(P3) Therefore, no thesis is asserted.
(P4) Therefore, eliminativism (P2) isn't asserted.
(P5) Therefore, eliminativism cannot be interpreted.[43]

At this point, Ramsey concedes self-defeat is present, since if eliminativism is unassertible and uninterpretable, we can no longer use premises (P2) and (P3) in the argument, as their meaning is permanently impenetrable. Moreover, in this form, the argument is not reducible to another type of objection. However, Ramsey argues that once this argument is formulated to be genuinely self-defeating it no longer has any teeth, since the charge that no thesis is asserted would not be a failing particular to the eliminativist thesis, it would apply to *all* theses.

> If the eliminativist isn't bothered by the claim that *no* thesis is asserted (or interpreted), I see little reason why she should be bothered by the claim that her own thesis isn't asserted either. If eliminativism entails that *nothing* is asserted (or interpreted), then on this score it is no worse off than any other theory or statement—including the theories and statements of the defenders of folk psychology. If it turns out that being asserted is a virtue that *no* thesis possesses, then it is hard to see how being *un*asserted could be much of a vice. Thus, this last construal of self-refutationist objection doesn't really buy the advocates of folk psychology anything that can be used against the eliminativist.

Although it appears that eliminativism entails its own downfall, under more careful consideration it turns out that what eliminativism really entails is that such a failing *wouldn't* be a failing, since the alleged shortcoming would be shared by *all* theories.[44]

This, however, is a highly unusual claim. The charge is that if eliminativism is true, we can have no reason or motive for accepting eliminativism. Ramsey agrees, but asks, so what? The answer is to repeat the point: *we can have no reason or motive for accepting eliminativism*. Remember, this is all under the shadow of an "if" clause: *If* eliminativism is true, no thesis is asserted or interpreted, including eliminativism. But if eliminativism is *not* true, there could be theses which are assertible and interpretable. Saying that all these other theses are in the same boat forgets that this is only the case *if eliminativism is true*. Insofar as all theses being in the same boat is unacceptable—not least because it takes away any rationale or motive for believing all theses are in the same boat— eliminativism should not be accepted.[45] If eliminativism were true, we could have no motive for accepting it, nor would we be able to distinguish truth from falsity, rationality from irrationality, reason from insanity. Thus, we would have no way of knowing into which category we should put eliminativism. This makes it self-defeating.

Wittgenstein's Ladder

Another potential objection the eliminativist might make, hinted at above in the discussion of naïve scientific realism, is that once someone accepts eliminativism they can find some other basis for it other than folk psychology. This is similar to Wittgenstein's claim that "My propositions are elucidatory in this way: he who understands me finally recognizes them as senseless, when he has climbed out through them, on them, over them. (He must so to speak throw away the ladder, after he has climbed up on it.)"[46] So the eliminativist can use the steps of folk psychology to climb above them, and then kick the ladder away when they reach the top.

The problem (and this may be a problem with Wittgenstein's Ladder in general) is that the analogy does not work. Climbing a ladder to reach the top of some structure assumes the structure is built with material solid enough to hold your weight. If you step off the ladder onto a structure made of shaving cream, well, good luck. But the conditions that make the structure capable of supporting your weight must also be true of the *ladder;* otherwise, you could not climb up it. The analogy may be salvageable if the claim is merely that, once someone reaches the top, they recognize the ladder is faulty and find another, better method of reaching the top—just as one can reach a conclusion for irrational reasons, but find good rational grounds (i.e. another ladder) for continuing to affirm it. But this better method would have to have the same principles that the structure has. I don't know if this is compatible with Wittgenstein's Ladder, but it is not compatible with eliminativism. The conditions that allow the ladder and structure to exist and be connected so that you can reach one via the other are precisely the conditions the eliminativist is denying. They are climbing the ladder of folk psychology into midair and kicking it away, expecting to remain hovering in nothing. How can they expect anything but to fall?

Conclusions

The eliminativist has crawled out of Plato's cave and tried to convince us that the world of light and color, sun and sky, is a massive illusion, and the real world is the cave and its shadows. Of course, "light," "color," "sky," and the rest are all categories of the outside world, and will no longer apply once we're back, safe and sound, in the dark. If eliminativists cannot present (to others or themselves) the eliminativism thesis—and if this is by necessity since their thesis precludes the possibility of presenting anything—then eliminativism is self-defeating. Any presentation of it must covertly presuppose the veridicality of those elements of folk psychology that eliminativism is overtly rejecting.

Some eliminativists respond to this charge with sheer disbelief$_{em}$: it's *insulting* to suggest they have embraced a position that commits so blatant a fallacy as being self-referentially incoherent.[47] However, without intending to remove the charge of self-defeat, I would like to extend an olive branch (or fig leaf, as the case may be). I suspect they are looking at the first false start and think that this superficial objection has been rebutted. Or perhaps, they are taking "self-defeat" more broadly, and so are rightly rejecting the suggestion that eliminativism entails a logical contradiction. They are therefore skeptical that any similar charge is not equally superficial and false. But this skepticism is unwarranted: positions can be subtly self-defeating, and our noetic faculties are enormously complex, so it need not be an aspersion on one's intellectual integrity to be guilty of inadvertently falling into incoherence. If it happened to as great a logician as Frege, we mere mortals should be humble about our own abilities.

It's not unusual for a well-thought-out position to be self-defeating, even in an obvious sense. Verificationism, the claim that only empirically verifiable statements and logical tautologies have meaning, was a popular project for decades despite the fact that verificationism is neither empirically verifiable nor tautological. And one of most interesting fields in philosophy is nonclassical logic, which self-consciously begins by rejecting one or more of the basic laws of logic. It's not a slur against its practitioners to say that their positions are self-refuting, and obviously so: they are brilliant and their theories fascinating. They are also incoherent. Eliminativism is self-defeating, but this is no slight against its advocates.

Of course, many naturalists could happily concede this self-defeat, and argue that it merely applies to eliminativism not naturalism.[48] But Plantinga argues another premise, that if naturalism is true, eliminativism is true: those who think the human being is entirely material, "should agree with eliminativists in thinking there aren't any beliefs."[49] Eliminativists may agree with this, but non-eliminative naturalists will not. This allows them to avoid the self-defeat of eliminativism, but then they will have to face the EAAN—just as the eliminativist can avoid the EAAN, but then is faced with their own self-defeat.

Part Three

Argument

7

The Probability Thesis

It is very certain that, when it is not in our power to determine what is true, we ought to act according to what is most probable.

René Descartes

Plantinga's "official and final version"[1] of the EAAN, it will be recalled, is as follows:

(1) P(R/N&E) is low.
(2) Anyone who accepts (believes) N&E and sees that P(R/N&E) is low has a defeater for R.
(3) Anyone who has a defeater for R has a defeater for any other belief she thinks she has, including N&E itself.
(4) If one who accepts N&E thereby acquires a defeater for N&E, N&E is self-defeating and can't rationally be accepted.
Conclusion: N&E can't rationally be accepted.[2]

The first premise, sometimes called the Probability Thesis, is the premise that has received the most attention. Also recall that if challenging R is a sticking point, we can just substitute MR (that our faculties do not reliably produce true *metaphysical* beliefs). Since N is a metaphysical belief, calling MR into question will allow the argument to proceed without loss.

Indicators and depictors[3]

Plantinga uses the hypothetical population to argue that P(R/N&E) is low. Leibniz's mill analogy from chapter 6 illustrates the category error of ascribing content to physical objects and processes. Yes, a *type* of representation can be naturally associated with physical objects, but the representations would not have propositional content. So Plantinga distinguishes between indicative representations, or indicators, and depictive representations, which by analogy we can call depictors.

Depictors depict something as being a certain way and so have propositional content. If the way they depict something is correct then they are true, and if the way they depict something is incorrect, they are false. *Indicators* do not represent things "*as being* this or that"[4] because they do not have propositional content. If what they indicate about something is incorrect, they are not false, merely idiosyncratic or, in a qualified sense, inaccurate. A thermometer indicates the temperature, and we may even say that it is accurate "in a Pickwickian sense: a representation *r*, of this sort, is accurate if the state that *r* is in is the one with which *r* is correlated—in this case, the ambient temperature. Representations of this sort will therefore be *trivially* accurate."[5] But they would not be *true*. A thermometer that reads thirty degrees when it is thirty degrees is accurate; the correlation between the indication and what it indicates is normal or nonanomalous. "Of course the representation isn't *true* (or false); the mechanism is not speaking truly when it attains the state that matches the ambient temperature, and it isn't speaking falsely either."[6] As Anthony O'Hear argues,

> It is certainly true that what an animal finds salient in its present experience will be to some degree idiosyncratic, depending on just what its past experience has been. But this will simply be a matter of causation. That Munchie refuses to go into his trailer may well be due to unpleasant experiences he has had in the past. If the new trailer is perfectly safe and very different from the old one in which he was bashed about, or even if his trailer-phobia was bought [*sic*] about by bad experiences in a narrow loose-box, rather than a trailer, there is no sense that his present stroppiness is a *mistake*. It just exists, and it has the causal antecedents it does; it may be more or less idiosyncratic.[7]

The question at hand is whether material objects (like neurons or neurological arrays) can have propositional content and be true or false. The reason this is the question at hand is because that is what *beliefs* are: beliefs have propositional content and are true or false. Material objects may indicate something (smoke may indicate fire) but they do not depict something (such as the proposition "there is fire on the mountain"). To represent something depictively is to have content, and material objects do not have content—just as numbers do not weigh a certain amount and elephants are not propositions.

Certainly, we could redefine content to apply to the trivial accuracy or inaccuracy of indicators, but then we are not addressing Plantinga's argument. What he means by content is *propositional* content, and we can't get around this by redefining the terms and pretending that, since the new definition is accessible to materialism, the old definition is too, just by virtue of being called by the same word.

Reducing agents

So Plantinga says most naturalists are materialists about human beings, and they should be *eliminative* materialists because Leibniz's mill analogy shows that material objects and processes do not have (original) propositional content. Since neural structures and processes are material, they do not have propositional content and so cannot be beliefs. But eliminativism has *problems*, beyond the fact that it is mind-bogglingly counterintuitive. The next step up is reductive materialism where depictors with propositional content (i.e., beliefs) exist, but they are not anything over and above the physical neurological workings of the brain. Rather, content is, or is reducible to, neurological states. So we'll just ignore Leibniz's mill analogy and say the material components of the brain can and do have content, but having content is a kind, perhaps a special kind, of neurological property. Essentially, beliefs are complex combinations of physical processes.[8]

We are still discussing the hypothetical population who have beliefs. If they live in a reductive materialistic world, how probable is it that the preponderance of their beliefs are true? Perhaps we should first ask: how probable is it for any particular belief—say, "The state of Oregon is larger than the United Kingdom"—is true?

> That belief is a neuronal event, a congeries of neurons connected in complex ways and firing away in the fashion neurons are wont to do. This neuronal event displays a lot of NP [neurophysiological] properties. Again, we may suppose that it is adaptively useful for a creature of the kind in question to harbor neuronal structures of the sort in question in the circumstances in question. The event's having the NP properties it does have is fitness-enhancing in that by virtue of having these properties, the organism is caused to perform adaptively useful action—fleeing, for example. Since the event is a belief, some subset of these NP properties together constitute its having the content it does in fact display. That is, there will be some proposition that is the content of the belief; the belief will therefore have the property of having that proposition as its content; and that property, the property of having such and such a proposition as its content, will be a (no doubt complex) NP property of the belief.[9]

At first blush this paints a positive picture. Reductive materialism locates a belief's contents in the brain's neural properties, so it is not removed from the body's physical components that have been selected in the struggle for survival.

However, another difference between depictors and indicators is that *natural selection can "see" indicators and select them*. Our body has many indicators unrelated to cognition, where physical attributes respond to their surroundings based on what those surroundings are. "In the human body there are indicators for blood pressure, temperature, saline content, insulin level, and much else; in these cases neither the blood, nor its owner, nor anything else in the neighborhood ordinarily holds beliefs on the topic."[10] Indicators are just the kind of thing evolution *would* see, that natural selection *would* select, since it is exactly such traits that make an organism (or gene or population or whatever the agent of evolutionary success is posited to be) more capable of surviving and passing on its genetic material.

When an indicator is neural it is just as "visible" to natural selection. An animal must be able to recognize predators and avoid them. It must be able to recognize food and consume it. If it were unable to do these things evolution would not select it. We can fill in the blanks with as much detail as we want: light waves bounce off a cheetah and go through a gazelle's pupils to its lenses. The lenses reflect the light (upside-down and inverted) on the retinas, which pass the information along to the bipolar and ganglion cells, and on to the thalamus, the optic nerve, and the visual cortex. This triggers a neural structure to fire which prompts the leg muscles to move in a direction that increases the gazelle's chances of survival. This registering of where the danger lies and where it is going—or where the food is and where *it* is going if one is the predator—is obviously part of the brain. So, evolution could see these indicators and select the more accurate ones: those organisms with more accurate neural indicators would have a greater chance of survival than those with less accurate neural indicators.[11]

Again, these are indicators not depictors: they do not require beliefs since animals could (and many do) evade predators and hunt for food with just the indicators in place. Nevertheless, unlike the indicators for blood pressure, temperature, et al., neural indicators are certainly "in the neighborhood" of beliefs, since both are mental representations. It doesn't seem much of a stretch to suggest that neural structures *can* have propositional content, can depict something, and so be beliefs (ignoring Leibniz's mill analogy). In this case, natural selection could select certain neural patterns, events, and structures which serve as indicators, and these neural patterns could also serve as depictors and be beliefs. Thus, beliefs could be visible to natural selection, with survival-enhancing ones being selected over survival-inhibiting ones.

There is still a big problem, though. Under this scenario beliefs would not be selected for their depictive properties but their indicative properties. This is obvious from the fact that the depictive properties could be entirely absent, from the materialist point of view, and if the indicative properties are accurate, the organism would engage in the same fitness-enhancing behavior. Indeed, the depictive properties could be something completely different. The indicator could indicate there is a predator 200 meters to the left while the depictor depicts there is *food* 200 meters to the left; or there is a predator two meters to the *right*; or the state of Oregon is larger than the United Kingdom; or the swallows have returned to Capistrano. As long as the indicator reliably indicates the circumstances and causes the survival-enhancing behavior then it simply does not matter what the depictor is.

So, while natural selection can see and select indicators, it cannot see and select depictors. Plantinga argues this is not controversial: the view that belief contents cannot influence behavior is "widely popular among those enthusiastic about the 'scientific' study of human beings" as well as most contemporary philosophers of mind.[12] For a naturalist, even granting that depictors are materialistically reducible, the depictive properties are not those that natural selection can "observe" and select.

Indeed, the difficulty here is related to the mind-body problem. To rebut the EAAN we would have to solve the mind-body problem within a naturalistic framework. In fact, Plantinga's argument is more recalcitrant than this: even if we had a naturalistic explanation of how belief content interacts with the body, we must ask the further question whether the contents of those beliefs are true and relevant. Simply having a connection between them is not enough, they must have the *right kind* of connection. Given naturalism, the depictors would be irrelevant to the fitness of the organism because they can be completely absent or completely random—just so long as the indicators are accurate.

An analogy raised earlier was a singer who sings at just the right pitch to cause a glass to shatter. It isn't the meaning of the words they are singing that breaks the glass, it is the resonance frequency of their voice. In the same way, given naturalism, the indicative properties of a belief may be causally efficacious, but the depictive properties would not be. With the singer, the glass does not break because she sings the word "shatter." That would be magical thinking. But by the same token, under naturalism, a person does not pick up a book because they believe the proposition, "I want that book." The propositional content of the belief is as irrelevant here as the propositional content of the song is to the shattering of the glass. In either case, to think that depictive content plays a role is magical thinking.

But why couldn't evolution see the content of belief if content is one of the physical, material properties of a given neural pattern? Remember Dennett's claim: brains are syntactic engines, i.e., based entirely on indicators, yet seem to be semantic engines, i.e., based on depictors. But from a naturalistic perspective a semantic engine is as ludicrous as a perpetual motion machine.[13] As Leibniz and Plantinga argue we can just "see" that material objects and processes cannot have content, so Dennett is arguing we can just "see" that naturalism precludes content attaching to matter such that belief content causes action. So even ignoring Leibniz's mill analogy and granting that purely material (neural) processes can have propositional content, the problem just pops up again at another level.

There are two ways to look at this: for any proposition, there is one correct answer and any other is incorrect, although for most cases, close approximations would be sufficient. So, $2 + 3 = 5$ is true, $2 + 3 = 6$ is false, $2 + 3 = 7$ is false, etc. On this account the probability of a belief being true, even though it is associated with an accurate indicator, is low.[14] However, a better assessment is available: for any proposition on offer, its negation is also on offer. We can certainly propose an infinite number of false mathematical equations, but then we can just substitute "$\neq$" for "$=$" and get true equations. Similarly, we can propose an infinite number of false propositions, but then negate them and make them true. On this account, since for any false proposition its negation (a true proposition) is also available, the probability of a depictor being true is .5. The latter case is how Plantinga looks at it. Even though the truth of a belief plays no role in the fitness of the organism, it still has a .5 chance of being true. But this is not enough. Under reductive materialism, beliefs are entirely dependent on (indeed, identical to) a neural pattern which is in place as an indicator because it played some role in our evolution. But since that indicator *has no bearing* on the belief's content, that belief's truth value is a crapshoot: it has a .5 chance of being true and a .5 chance of being false, which is no better than guessing.

Teleosemantic content

Derived content only has content by virtue of its relation to original content, so we cannot start with derived and build up to original content. Similarly, we cannot start with indicators, build up to depictors, and expect those depictors to be true or relevant. But according to some critics we cannot draw such a sharp distinction between indicators and depictors. Plantinga, it seems, "imagines that content can be assigned to a neural structure ... arbitrarily,"[15] but this fails to give materialism its due. Perhaps a given neural structure can only have one belief associated with it. If so, since neural structures are in place because they were selected by evolution and content is a materialistic property, then for a neural structure to have a different belief associated with it, we would have to posit a different evolutionary history along with it, one in which that different content was fitness-enhancing. But then that new belief with the new content would have the same strictures placed upon it that the old belief with the old content did. Regardless, by positing a different evolutionary history, it ceases to be a *nearby* possible world.

This has been argued by advocates of Ruth Millikan's teleosemantics,[16] which claims mental content is based on norms which are based on functions which are defined as an organ or organism's "powers or properties which account for its survival and proliferation. Hearts have proliferated because they pump blood, so pumping blood is the heart's function."[17] I think teleosemantic theories are the most promising materialistic prospect of keeping depictive content closely aligned to indicative accuracy and so avoiding the EAAN.

Brian Leahy argues that under teleosemantics, "The content of a signal is one of the environmental conditions that must obtain if the interpreter of the signal is to perform its functions in accord with a normal explanation," and that "The content of the belief is a consequence of [its] selectional history."[18] As such, it cannot vary as Plantinga suggests. Feng Ye presents an impressive atomistic theory of content which starts with map attributes, builds up to inner maps ("perceptual mental image[s] in one's memory"[19]), simple concepts, composite concepts, simple thoughts, and finally composite thoughts. Beliefs, then, are thoughts that the cognizer approves, or that he puts in his "belief box,"[20] and that beliefs (or thoughts in general) can have truth value.

However, Ye concedes that propositional content is incompatible with materialism, so obviously he does not see his teleosemantic system as meeting this definition. In fact, both Ye and Leahy seek to redefine content to make it accessible to materialism. Leahy explicitly refers to it as "teleosemantic content,"[21] while Ye argues that by using a concept of content that is incompatible with materialism Plantinga begs the question against it.[22]

Taking the last point first, Plantinga, as is his wont, is starting from the concept of content we already have and is reverse engineering it to see if materialism can account for it. We can certainly employ an alternative method, using only naturalistically acceptable terms and trying to build up towards content. But claiming this alternative method will not arrive at propositional content does not show this concept is not applicable or that Plantinga's method is not valid. Indeed, materialism's inability to accommodate propositional content is his *point*.

Plantinga's strategy is not only acceptable, it is one that materialists use. Ye points out how, for years, materialistic theories of content struggled to explain the possibility of misrepresentations, which teleosemantics happily provides.[23] But prior to the advent of Millikan's theory, no one thought that, since misrepresentation was apparently resistant to reduction, we should just define down our concept of misrepresentation in order to make it accessible to the materialistic theories then in vogue. Rather, we accepted that there are misrepresentations and then worked backwards to see how (or if) materialism could account for them.

Plantinga argues beliefs have *propositional* content. If someone wants to use a different concept and call it content, they are free to do so,[24] but then they are not addressing Plantinga's claims. And insofar as we are unable to produce propositional content with the tools and mortar naturalism provides, we are confirming the EAAN and agreeing that "Materialists ... should agree with eliminativists in thinking there aren't any beliefs."[25] When Ye claims, for example, that propositional content is incompatible with materialism, he is not advocating the *reduction* of such content but its *elimination*. Since he considers eliminativism implausible[26] this reveals a tension in his critique.

Ye objects that Plantinga assumes we can arbitrarily ascribe any content whatsoever to a neural configuration, without any control or limit.[27] As far as I understand him, yes, that is what Plantinga maintains. Perhaps we can limit this by noting our belief systems do not seem random and incoherent, but we cannot move from their appearance to their actuality, much less to the claim that they are mostly true.[28] Leahy and Ye argue we cannot ascribe a different content to a neural configuration than what it has because then we would have to posit a different evolutionary history. But this is only for their theories of teleosemantic content rather than propositional content. For the propositional content of a belief to be accessible to natural selection, we would have to solve the mind-body problem and show how the mind is a naturalistic semantic engine. If we define content down to indicative representation, we can make it accessible to natural selection, but this would not address the EAAN. Leahy's claims notwithstanding, we *can* posit possible worlds where different *propositional* content is associated with the same neural configuration, and these would be nearby possible worlds in terms of their physical history and make-up. So, we can deny the possibility of depictors and be eliminativists, or we can accept them and reject materialism. There is no third way.

Yet a question looms: why should we prefer Plantinga's propositional content over the teleosemantic content of Millikan, Ye, and Leahy? Propositional content is certainly a better match for our intuitive concept of content, but then why should we prefer our intuitive concept of propositional content over these materialistically reducible concepts of content?

Plantinga's answer: because it is only with propositional content that a belief can be true or false. If we want to abandon truth in order to avoid content, then we are, once again, advocating *eliminative* materialism, not reductive materialism. To be sure, Ye suggests his teleosemantic content "does seem to fit our intuitive understanding of truth,"[29] but does not explain how his version of indicative accuracy and inaccuracy is close enough to propositional truth and falsehood. To this reader at least, Ye's teleosemantic content only fits "our intuitive understanding of truth" when we treat his constructions as propositions—and since Ye denies that propositional content is compatible with materialism, treating his constructions propositionally is inadmissible. Regardless, if we are discarding one concept for another, the first is being eliminated, not reduced.

Now we can certainly consider the eliminativist option that "Truth, as currently conceived, might cease to be an aim of science."[30] But as we have seen, eliminative materialism is just as self-defeating as any other form of materialism, since without propositional content, the eliminativist's position can be neither expressed nor interpreted, much less accepted. Therefore, retreating to eliminativism is not a viable option.

A difficult dichotomy

The intuition behind these critiques is that there are natural connections between indicators and depictors and we cannot make such a sharp distinction between them. Plantinga, however, agrees, he is only arguing that naturalism cannot account for any connections between them. His proposal is not to embrace the disparity but to reject naturalism.

Ye and Leahy's objections try to establish a biological connection (roughly speaking) between indicators and depictors. Plantinga appeals to broadly logical possibility, arguing that virtually any depictor could be associated with any indicator. In other words, there are innumerable possible worlds, even nearby possible worlds (even *physically identical* possible worlds) in which the same neural configurations embody accurate indicators and false depictors. So, what if, instead of looking for a *biological* connection between indicators and depictors we look for a *logical* connection between the two?

Plantinga is assuming there is a distinction between indicators and depictors: having a reliable indicator says nothing about whether the depictor associated with it is true or even about the same situation that the indicator is responding to. But most depictors do not *only* depict; they also indicate. Take a depictor that has as its content, "There is a cheetah 200 meters to the left." This depictor depicts that there is a cheetah 200 meters to the left, but it also *indicates* that there is a cheetah 200 meters to the left. Of course, the depictor could be false, and the indicator inaccurate (or idiosyncratic). Nevertheless, the point remains: generally, one does not depict something about the world without also indicating something about it. A depictor is a type of indicator, one that, in addition to having indicative properties, also has depictive properties. The depictor and the indicator are the same thing looked at from two different angles, the depictor being a proposition built around what the indicator indicates. It's not as if the indicator and depictor are different entities that are haphazardly tied together—the depictor is not some free-floating object that may or may not be connected to a particular indicator. It is *the depictor itself* that is also an indicator. The statement "There is a cheetah 200 meters to the left" is a depictor because it has propositional content. But that statement is also an indicator that indicates the same thing. It is not something *else* that indicates it, it is the proposition itself that indicates it.

If we grant this point, many depictors are also indicators, and thus some indicators are depictors.[31] This would entail that there is a *logical, analytic* connection between such a depictor and an indicator. So, what is necessary for naturalism and materialism to go forward is for natural selection to select the indicator and the depictor will come with it, even though natural selection cannot "see" the depictive properties.

Unfortunately, we have switched the order. If we start with a true depictor and ask whether what it indicates is accurate, we will find that it does. This, again, is because the depictor, in addition to depicting something about the world, also indicates that same thing. But if we start with an indicator and posit that, somehow, depictive content arose and became "attached" to it, there is no reason to think it should happen to depict what the indicator indicates, that the depictor in question is that particular depictor that has an analytic attachment to that indicator. The indicator can be present without depicting something, and if content somehow arose, it could depict anything. If it just happened to depict what the indicator indicates it would be an incredible, mind-boggling coincidence, as if wine glasses only shattered when someone sang the word "shatter"; or as if the sun, wind, and rain had bleached rocks white and rolled them down a hill into the configuration "The British Railways welcomes you to Wales"—and it just happened to be adjacent to railroad tracks at the border of Wales;[32] "or as if, when I knocked out my pipe, the ashes arranged themselves into letters which read: 'We are the ashes of a knocked-out pipe.'"[33]

This creates problems, however. Say there is an indicator and a depictor is generated with it, but it is not the analytically corresponding depictor of that indicator. Yet this depictor also indicates what it depicts and so is also an indicator. So, the depictor would be associated with two indicators: one which is connected to it analytically and one which is connected to it biologically. The latter would be visible to natural selection but would have no logical bearing on the depictor's content. Moreover, an indicator could similarly be attached to two depictors, one analytically the other biologically.[34] Is this even remotely plausible?

Well, no, but "that's not a problem for thought; it's a problem for materialism."[35] It is the insistence that human beings are nothing more than their material components that leads to this scenario, since it requires the syntax to be the only causal component in behavior, with no role left over for semantics. The same problem remains: natural selection would only directly select the indicators and at best indirectly select the *biologically* associated depictors, not the *analytically* associated depictors. If we abandon materialism and naturalism, however, we can avoid the problem.

Perhaps we can take another tack. A depictor is an indicator since it indicates something as well as depicts something. Indicators are visible to natural selection. So why can't evolution see the indicative properties of this depictor and select it? Unfortunately, the answer has already been given: because the indicative properties do not require the depictive properties. Having the depictive properties entails having the indicative properties but having the indicative properties does not similarly entail having the depictive properties. We have to start with the depictor to get the necessary connection. We have to work top-down rather than bottom-up. We need a skyhook instead of a crane.[36]

But a top-down approach is incompatible with naturalism. Naturalism requires the evolutionary process that produced mentality to exclusively select indicative properties rather than depictive properties. This is a bottom-up process. If the foregoing analysis is correct, naturalism gives us a reason to deny that most of our beliefs are true, including evolution and, most poignantly, naturalism itself. To affirm naturalism as true, we must ultimately presuppose there is a top-down process at work which is incompatible with naturalism.

Plantinga's distinction between indicators and depictors is legitimate, and this leads to the problem that natural selection would only select beliefs or belief-forming properties by virtue of their indicative properties rather than their depictive properties. So, each of our hypothetical population's beliefs would have a .5 chance of being true (either it or its negation is true). But now we can broaden the scope to ask what is the probability that the preponderance of their beliefs are true?

Plantinga suggests a modest requirement for reliability would be two-thirds to three-fourths of beliefs being true.[37] If each belief has a .5 chance of being true, the probability that three-fourths of 100 independent beliefs are true is about .000001, or 1 percent of 1 percent of 1 percent. Of course, we have significantly more than 100 beliefs. If we take 1,000 independent beliefs the probability that three-fourths of them are true is less than 10^{-58}, or one chance in ten billion trillion trillion trillion, an unfathomable number.[38] Of course, this also applies to having three-fourths of beliefs be *false*. In most scenarios, about half would be true and half false. Regardless, a system where only half of the beliefs are true is no better than guessing.

This looks like a throwback to the first version of the EAAN. Once again, Plantinga argues that individual beliefs have a .5 chance of being true, and then adds them together to conclude that all our beliefs together would not meet a very modest requirement of reliability. This seems to make it subject to the same objection. He is ignoring the fact that our beliefs are not independent of each other: what we believe about one thing influences what we believe about many other things. We cannot simply take the conclusion about one belief and generalize it like this.

Although Plantinga does not address this objection in his "official and final version," his framing of the argument in terms of neurology points to its resolution. By phrasing it this way, he is not talking about the logical and rational connections between beliefs or even the nonrational psychological associations between beliefs. Rather, he is talking about the *neural, physical* connections between beliefs. This is as it should be since he is dealing with naturalism and materialism, where our beliefs are identical to (reductive materialism) or supervene on (nonreductive materialism) the neural processes involved in beliefs. One thousand "independent" beliefs does not refer to beliefs which are logically, rationally, or psychologically independent of each other; it refers to beliefs which are *neurologically* independent of each other, beliefs which do not use the same (numerically identical) neurons in their neuronal array as certain other beliefs.

So how many neurons does the human brain have? Plantinga answers:

> There are plenty of neurons to go around: a normal human brain contains some 100–200 billion neurons. These neurons, furthermore, are connected with other neurons via synapses; a single neuron, on the average, is connected with seven thousand other neurons. The total number of possible brain states, then, is absolutely enormous, much greater than the number of electrons in the universe.[39]

Given the number of neurons in the brain and the possible number of brain states, coming up with 100 or even 1,000 beliefs that are independent of each other in *this* sense would not be a problem.

Naturally, this is contentious. The premises and conclusion of an argument may have no neurological connections, but can we just ignore their logical connections? Of course not, but again, "that's ... a problem for materialism."[40] It is only by seeking to reduce beliefs to materialistic conditions that this problem arises. If we abandon that quest, the problem evaporates.

Still, can we just ignore these connections between beliefs? Even though we are examining the hypothetical population, they are supposed to be *like us*, and that would include their beliefs *seeming* to have logical and rational connections between them. Perhaps these connections are a problem for materialism, but we still have the bare phenomenon of the seeming. We (and thus the hypothetical population) do not *experience* our beliefs varying wildly with no rhyme or reason; we experience them being rationally ordered, or at least appearing to be rationally ordered. If you have not explained this experience you have not explained the mind. This will be dealt with in the following chapter, when we look at the conditionalization problem.

Truth and consequences

One more important point. Plantinga sets his argument entirely in terms of truth value but there is another way to consider reliability. Since an indicator could indicate one thing and the depictor biologically, physically, or psychologically associated with it could (and probably would) be about something entirely different under naturalism, how could we call this system reliable if it revealed *irrelevant* truths? Say an indicator indicates that there is a predator 200 meters away to my left while the associated depictor depicts that Saturn has more than twelve moons; a true proposition to be sure, but since it has nothing to do with the organism's immediate environment and the information its senses are relaying, since it has nothing to do with the indicator it is associated with, it could not be considered reliable. And here, we cannot negate some arbitrary false proposition and get a true one. We can certainly accept approximate answers as correct in many cases, but not irrelevant answers, even if they happen to be true. And the number of irrelevant answers in comparison to relevant ones would be enormous; perhaps infinite. This is a truly staggering species of unreliability.

Nonreductive materialism

If both eliminative and reductive materialism are problematic, we have to turn to nonreductive forms. In these views beliefs and other mental properties supervene on the neural patterns, events, and structures but cannot be reduced to them. For something to supervene on another means that the one does not vary independently of the other—that it is *determined* by the other, or both are determined by some third thing so that they covary together. The neurology of the brain determines the belief and its contents, but the belief and its contents cannot be reduced to the neurology. With nonreductive materialism, "You couldn't have a pair of structures—neuronal events, say—that had the same NP [neurophysiological] properties but different contents. Content is a *function* of NP properties."[41]

There are two forms of nonreductive materialism that Plantinga treats: strong and weak (or logical and nomic).[42] According to the strong form, "For any possible worlds

W and W* and any structures S and S*, if S has the same NP properties in W as S* has in W*, then S has the same content in W as S* has in W*."[43] So if someone believes a belief which is associated with a particular neural state, anyone else experiencing the same neural state *in any possible world* will also believe that belief. Since it applies across possible worlds this connection between the neural state and the belief is not contingent like physical laws. This is "broadly logical necessity: the sort of necessity enjoyed by, for example, true mathematical and logical propositions."[44]

This seems very promising. The difficulty with connecting indicators and depictors is that we need a logical, analytic connection between the two in order to avoid the EAAN. Logical supervenience supplies this with its connection between specific neural configurations and propositions. A particular neural configuration must have a particular propositional content by definition, in all possible worlds. So, the connections must be *a priori* and analytic.

But a neural state does not and cannot entail anything by necessity. Norman Malcolm demonstrates this by contrasting purposive explanations with neurological (or materialistic) explanations. He characterizes purposive explanations as follows:

> Whenever an organism O has goal G and believes that behavior B is required to bring about G, O will emit B.
> O had G and believed B was required of G.
> Therefore, O emitted B.[45]

If we add a *ceteris paribus* clause (understood as "provided there are not countervailing factors") to the first premise, it becomes an *a priori* proposition, not a contingent one. So, if a man's hat blows onto the roof and he wants it back and believes he must climb a ladder to do so, he will climb a ladder unless there is some countervailing factor (there's no ladder available; he's afraid of heights; etc.). But if there are no countervailing factors and the man does not climb a ladder, it means he did not really have the goal of retrieving his hat in the first place; he did not intend to do so. *By definition*, if he had such a goal or intention, then in the absence of countervailing factors, he would climb a ladder. That's what having a goal or intention *means*.

The parallel neurological (or mechanistic) explanation would be:

> Whenever an organism of structure S is in neurophysiological state q it will emit movement m.
> Organism O of structure S was in neurophysiological state q.
> Therefore, O emitted m.[46]

However, if we add a *ceteris paribus* clause to the first premise here, it does not result in an *a priori* proposition. A person in a particular neurological state will raise his arm *unless* there is some countervailing factor (his arm is broken or restrained in some way). Yet since a particular neurological state does not entail by definition the movement of the arm, this does not amount to an *a priori* proposition—if it did, we could deduce such a relation independent of all observations, which would effectively remove neurology from the sphere of the physical sciences which are by their very nature *a posteriori*. "There is no connection of meaning, explicit or implicit, between the description of any neural state and the description of any movement of the hand. No matter how many countervailing factors are excluded, the proposition will not lose the character of a contingent law."[47]

There are synthetic *a priori* truths—truths which must be assumed but which are not true by definition (such as causality)—but what is called for here are analytic *a posteriori* truths: true by definition but only discoverable via observation. Such truths would be anchored by rigid designators, terms that always and only refer to the same object in all possible worlds (or at least all possible worlds where the object exists). Saul Kripke proposes several possible analytic *a posteriori* propositions, including "water is H_2O" and "Hesperus (the evening star) is Phosphorus (the morning star)."[48] Water and H_2O are identical across all possible worlds, but we could not deduce water's chemical structure as H_2O apart from scientific observation, and throughout most of human history, people who knew perfectly well what water is would not have been able to rationally affirm that water is H_2O. Similarly, the morning star and the evening star are both the planet Venus, so they are identical, but it was only when astronomy advanced sufficiently with the Hellenistic Greeks that they were known to be the same thing.

But even if we accept there are rigid designators and analytic *a posteriori* truths (many philosophers do not), it does not give us the epistemic right to bestow that title on whatever we want in order to salvage our favorite theories. We need a *reason* to think something holds across all possible worlds but is only discoverable by observation—and "I really, really want naturalism to be true" doesn't qualify.

So, we have no reason to think there are analytic, logically necessary connections, holding across all possible worlds, between particular physical structures (neural or otherwise) and particular propositional contents, and plenty of reason to think there is not. It is only being proposed here to shield naturalism from the consequences of belief content being impotent in influencing action. We can easily imagine an identical physical structure that either lacks any propositional content or has different content than what it has in our experience.

If the physical structure itself logically entailed a particular propositional content, then why can we imagine it with a different content or none at all? For that matter, why aren't there similar logical connections between other physical structures and content? Why doesn't the particular series of physical marks that make up the word "location," for example, logically entail the content ascribed to it in English (a certain place) instead of the content ascribed to it in French ("rental")? Why doesn't "location" *require* the English meaning, so that it's impossible, *logically impossible*, to ascribe a different meaning to that sequence of marks, and any attempt to do so is simply an error (just as ascribing a different molecular structure to water is an error)? We have as much reason to think there is an analytic connection here as we do between belief contents and their subvenient neural properties.

But put all this to the side. Would strong nonreductive supervenience solve the problem of connecting the content of belief to appropriate action? Would it provide the necessary logical connection between depictors and indicators? If we grant broadly logical depictor-indicator connections spanning all possible worlds (or even most nearby possible worlds) this looks like a step in the right direction. There is an indicator that is selected by evolution; there is a depictor that supervenes on this indicator in all possible worlds (in no possible world does this depictor vary with respect to this indicator). Any creature in any possible world that has this indicator also has that depictor and thus believes that belief.

Yet the question remains the same: why think that belief is *true*? Perhaps the indicator indicates that there is a predator 200 meters to my left while the depictor depicts that my soup is cold. Or that the moon is made of green cheese. If the indicator is accurate it simply does not matter what the content of the belief is. Yes, there is a connection, even *ex hypothesi* a broadly logical connection, between the belief (the depictor) and the neural state (the indicator). But it is not between the belief's *content* and the neural state. It is only between the belief's *occurrence* and the neural state, and having a belief occur in association with a neural state does not say anything about whether that belief is true and relevant. We are still trying to construct a crane from the bottom-up rather than a skyhook from the top-down.

This leads to a bizarre scenario in which there is a connection between a physical structure and the content associated with it, a connection which, despite being naturalistic, transcends the accidental, contingent universe we find ourselves in. Yet this connection is not the logical, analytic connection discussed above. So, a depictor would have an indicator logically associated with it, but in all or nearly all possible worlds it would also have a *different* indicator associated with it, one which does not indicate what the depictor depicts, and natural selection only selects the latter. Certainly, it *can* select the former indicator, but that indicator is also associated with another depictor which does not depict what the indicator indicates. Even though the indicators would be mostly accurate (since indicators are visible to natural selection), the depictors associated with them would be false or irrelevant for the most part. Such a situation borders on incoherence, and the problem rests with the presupposition of naturalism.

So, strong nonreductive materialism is implausible and does not solve the problem. What about weak nonreductive materialism? This model does not apply to possible worlds, only to this world. Plantinga defines it as, "Necessarily, any structures that have the same NP [neurophysiological] properties have the same content."[49] where the necessity is not logical but nomological, "the sort of necessity enjoyed by natural laws."[50] However, if a logical connection is insufficient to connect the content of a belief with the neural state it supervenes on, it is difficult to see how a nomological connection would be. At most, as above, such a connection could hold between a belief's occurrence and a neural state, not between a belief's *content* and a neural state. But the latter is what is necessary to avoid the EAAN. Moreover, unlike the strong form, weak nonreductive materialism does not apply to other possible worlds. Connections between indicators and depictors are contingent: they could have been different than they are. This decreases weak nonreductive materialism's value dramatically.

Its only strength is that it doesn't posit as implausible a connection between beliefs and neural states as strong nonreductive materialism. It involves a kind of necessity, but the necessity is itself not a necessity. The laws of physics establish that things behave a certain way, all other things being equal, and any psycho-physical laws connecting beliefs with neural states would be similar (otherwise they would not be *laws*). But they all could have been different. There is no logical reason why the speed of light, say, or the strong nuclear force must have the precise values they have. Fortunately, on this point we do not have to rely solely on philosophers: it is generally acknowledged by physicists that the laws of nature and the cosmic initial conditions are contingent and could have been different.[51]

So eliminative materialism, reductive materialism, and nonreductive materialism are all problematic. It seems we've run out of materialisms. None of these theories of mind leave room for beliefs to influence actions by virtue of their contents. But such a scenario is precisely what is required in order to avoid the EAAN.

> We ordinarily think true belief leads to successful action because we also think that beliefs cause (part-cause) actions, and do so *by virtue of their content*. I want a beer; I believe there is one in the fridge, and this belief is a (part) cause of my going over to the fridge. We think it is by virtue of the *content* of that belief that it causes me to go over to the fridge; it is because this belief has as content that there is a beer in the fridge that it causes me to go to the fridge rather than, say, the washing machine.[52]

Any view that cannot account for belief contents influencing actions by virtue of their contents is susceptible to the EAAN or a similar argument.

Anti-materialistic atheism

Nagel and final causality

Most forms of atheism are materialistic and so have been dealt with at this point. However, there are atheists who do not accept materialism. Thomas Nagel, for example, has been arguing for decades that materialistic theories fail to account for some of the most rudimentary elements of the mind. He writes that the probability of creatures evolving with an ability for objective theorizing "is antecedently so improbable that the only possible explanation must be that it is in some way necessary. It is not the kind of thing that could be either a brute fact or an accident."[53] Yet he is also a staunch atheist and desperately wants to avoid appealing to God.

> I want atheism to be true and am made uneasy by the fact that some of the most intelligent and well-informed people I know are religious believers. It isn't just that I don't believe in God and, naturally, hope that I'm right in my belief. It's that I hope there is not a God! I don't want there to be a God; I don't want the universe to be like that. My guess is that this cosmic authority problem is not a rare condition and that it is responsible for much of the scientism and reductionism of our time.[54]

Nagel avoids theism by proposing teleological laws that are built into the universe, but no overarching mind behind them, a "teleology without intent."[55] This affirmation of teleology is not a denial of evolution, something he remains convinced of,[56] but of *materialistic* evolution. The insertion of teleology into the natural order would expand our concept of nature as well as science. It's an awkward position, however. To have causes directed towards an end without a mind to do the directing is difficult to hold together. The very concept of teleology implies a directing mind on some level, and the introduction of teleology into the natural order suggests a mind overarching the universe that is strikingly similar to the theism Nagel decries. Not to mention, teleology is not observable; it is a conceptual element of an explanation. Including it in science could make some heads explode.

Moreover, adding teleology to nature does not solve Nagel's problem unless it holds across all possible worlds. But there is no more reason to think this than there is to think a neural structure has the same belief associated with it in all possible worlds. If there are teleological laws built into the universe, they would be analogous to natural laws by being contingent, not logically necessary. But then they could have been different (or entirely absent for that matter), so we would need an explanation for why they are the case rather than not. If we are willing to grant that natural laws, while contingent, are not subject to change, then we could potentially say the same of Nagel's teleological laws. But if we want to know why any contingent law—natural or teleological—can be counted on to remain the same from one moment to the next, then we will ask it of both classes. Nagel seeks to resolve the problem as it applies to natural laws by appealing to teleological laws, but this just forces us to ask the same question of the latter. It seems that this backwards chain of contingency must terminate in a source that is not contingent, something that "is in some way necessary,"[57] but the mere presence of teleological laws does not provide that necessity.

Talbott and quasi-formal causality

William Talbott argues that while evolutionary forces would tend to select an ability for abductive reasoning or inference to the best explanation (IBE), it would only do so for local concerns, not global concerns. That is, it would select IBE as it applies to the specific environment our evolutionary ancestors actually inhabited but not for IBE as it applies universally. The local focus of our cognitive equipment is, in fact, one of the insights behind naturalized epistemology. But theoretical science is dependent on making global/universal inferences. Without them, we cannot justify the scientific evidence for the age of the earth or evolution itself, for example. While Talbott's strategy could potentially apply to all forms of IBE, including metaphysical reasoning (Plantinga's MR), he limits himself to theoretical science.

Of course, Talbott is not denying that science or biology or evolution are correct, he is looking for a way to validate them and finds this impossible within the limitations of naturalism.[58] His solution is to connect the contingent facts of the universe, as discovered by science, to metaphysically necessary truths which allow us to make the move from local to global concerns.

> If there were metaphysically necessary truths about IBE evidence relations that were true in all possible worlds, then by making the reasoning of our ancestors

probabilistically sensitive to local IBE evidence relations..., evolution could have indirectly made our ancestors probabilistically sensitive to IBE evidence relations in every domain, both local and non-local, because the same kind of reasoning would be rational in every domain.[59]

While Talbott distances himself from Plato's theory of forms, his suggestion can be seen as roughly similar to formal causality.[60] Note that these quasi-formal causes would not function as *efficient* causes—they are not the agencies that bring about the effect. They would function as, well, formal (or quasi-formal) causes. They're a sort of metaphysical anchor allowing the efficient and material (and perhaps final) causes to bring about the effect. Perhaps in many cases there is no need to appeal to these "metaphysically necessary truths about IBE evidence relations that were true in all possible worlds," but when it comes to justifying scientific inference, they are indispensable.

As with Nagel, Talbott is averse to embedding these metaphysically necessary truths in a metaphysically necessary *mind* such as God. His point is that the efficient and material causes of our explanatory hypotheses must be supplemented by quasi-formal causes to bridge the gap between local IBE sensitivities that evolution would select and global IBE sensitivities. Whether it is possible to have metaphysically necessary *anythings* without something like God is another question, as is how these metaphysically necessary truths would attach themselves as depictors to the indicators with which they are metaphysically (or logically) associated. Without a mind to bring them together, it seems any such association would be haphazard. And if we want to say that, these metaphysically necessary truths are also metaphysically necessarily attached to particular mental indicators, the hypothesis starts becoming impractically ad hoc.

Atheistic dualism

There are also atheists who embrace, or seem to embrace, some form of mind-body dualism.[61] Presumably, they would claim there is an immaterial component to the human being but while this component would be closely affiliated with the body, it is neither reducible to nor supervenient on it; it is free-floating. This immaterial component could avoid being determined by physical states of affairs, leaving it free to pursue logical states of affairs in following an argument from premises to conclusion (of course materialists would deny there is a dichotomy here). Perhaps this is even the central component of the human being—its soul or self.[62]

Yet we are also assuming this immaterial component is not produced by an agent who established specific psycho-physical connections between mind and body. This immaterial component emerged, somehow, from the neural processes in the brain. It is not *dependent* on them (logically or nomologically), still less *identical* to them, it just happened and whatever connections there are between the immaterial and the material are accidental or contingent. So, on this view, how probable is it that beliefs would be true?

We already know the answer. This corresponds to Plantinga's first two (of five) possibilities of the relationship between mind and body,[63] it is, essentially, epiphenomenalism. And in this case, the probability that most beliefs formed would be true is low. A free-floating consciousness has a belief that is associated with a neural state but not dependent on it: fine. Why think the content of that belief is true? Either there is a connection between a belief and a neural state or there is not. If there's no connection, then there's no connection. If there is a connection, it is between the belief as an *occurrence* and a neural state, not between the belief's *content* and a neural state. In either case, the probability of any given belief being true is .5. Even if we follow Talbott and posit a realm of metaphysically necessary truths that this immaterial self could theoretically come into contact with, there is no reason to think a soul/self/mind that emerged from the interplay of neurons would ever find a point of convergence with eternal forms of logic or mathematics or anything else, or that it would be capable of organizing its thoughts in accordance with them. As Nagel writes,

> Eventually the attempt to understand oneself in evolutionary, naturalistic terms must bottom out in something that is grasped as valid in itself—something without which the evolutionary understanding would not be possible. Thought moves us beyond appearance to something that we cannot regard merely as a biologically based disposition, whose reliability we can determine on other grounds. It is not enough to be able to think that *if* there are logical truths, natural selection might very well have given me the capacity to recognize them. That cannot be my ground for trusting my reason, because even that thought implicitly relies on reason in a prior way.[64]

Naturalism cannot account for our actions to be produced by beliefs and by virtue of their contents. Non-materialistic forms of atheism either do not solve the problem or appear unwieldy (at least more unwieldy than theism). The scenarios examined thus far have to posit ad hoc brute facts to salvage the theory, like teleological laws that meet just the right conditions we need for knowledge to be possible; or metaphysically necessary connections between local and global conditions; or analytic *a posteriori* truths requiring particular neural states to associate with particular belief contents. Theism, on the other hand, only involves one metaphysically necessary entity (God, in case you were wondering), and most theists would not consider this to be either a brute fact or ad hoc.

But what if we ignore all this and just grant the folk psychology view that belief contents are somehow capable of causing actions by virtue of their contents while also maintaining that this somehow arose from naturalistic evolution? Well, we can certainly just ignore everything discussed so far, but then a point from the initial version of the EAAN comes into play. Remember, what evolution selects for is *behavior* not belief. Even if we grant that belief content influences behavior, it is only the behavior that is "seen" and selected by evolution. Beliefs which result in identical behavior would be equally likely to be selected. Survival-enhancing behavior would be selected, even if the behavior was caused by false beliefs or unreliable belief-forming mechanisms. They would not be selected by virtue of their truth or reliability but by virtue of their usefulness, leaving more than enough room for false beliefs and unreliable belief-forming systems to be capable of promoting survival and so be selected in the evolutionary struggle.

So, the first premise of the EAAN holds: If naturalism is true, the probability the hypothetical population's cognitive faculties are reliable (especially those that produce metaphysical beliefs) is low. Since what is true of them is true of us, naturalism makes it improbable that our cognitive faculties are reliable as well—that is, P(R/N&E) is low. The question then becomes why this matters.

8

The Defeater Thesis

The opportunity to secure ourselves against defeat lies in our own hands.

Sun Tzu

P(R/N&E) is low, but why should this *defeat* R? Plenty of beliefs have low probabilities but we don't reject them on that account. If I'm playing poker and dealt a straight flush, the probability I would be dealt such a hand is astronomically low, but that doesn't defeat my belief that I have a straight flush. I see the cards, and this warrants believing it. The warrant it has by being perceived overwhelms any probability assessment (the same will hold the next day when it is not perception but memory that provides the belief with warrant). If I continue drawing excellent hands over and over, I may think the dealer is cheating in my favor and the low probabilities are not really being surmounted, but that doesn't defeat my belief that I have been dealt a straight flush. Therefore, the EAAN must move from R being improbable given naturalism to R being defeated given naturalism. This is the second premise of the EAAN, sometimes called the Defeater Thesis: "Anyone who accepts (believes) N&E and sees that P(R/N&E) is low has a defeater for R."[1]

Conditionalization

The EAAN is presented as a conditionalized probability assessment, where the probability of a belief being true (R in our case) is low when conditionalized on another (N&E). But we can make the same objection: many beliefs are improbable when conditionalized on others, but we do not reject them on this account. Take the beliefs (1) you own a Japanese car; (2) you own an old Nissan. The probability that (2) is true given (1) is low, since there are numerous other types of Japanese cars that you could own besides an old Nissan. Thus (2) is improbable when conditionalized upon (1). But (2) is not thereby defeated.

This is the conditionalization problem, to wit, what exactly a probability should be conditionalized on. For example, "the probability that ... Holland, Michigan, is thirty miles from Grand Rapids, given N&E" is low since N&E does not limit the number of possible locations (or existence) of these cities. Yet that does not suggest that N&E defeats the claim.[2] Clearly there are many cases where the improbability of one proposition given another does not defeat the first.

Yet just as clearly there are many cases where one proposition's improbability given another *is* thereby defeated. If a Freudian theist conditionalizes their belief in God on the idea that theistic beliefs are produced by wish fulfillment (which is unreliable), their belief in God is defeated. The realization that it is improbable their belief is true given its dubious provenance gives them a reason to stop believing it.

So, what's the difference between the scenarios where a low probability defeats a belief and where it does not, and which is more similar to belief in R given N? James Van Cleve mentions the "implicit premise thesis": "For any propositions A and B that I believe, if B is improbable or inscrutable with respect to A, then A is a defeater for B unless A derives its warrant from B."[3] So with the Japanese car, if the reason I believe you own a Japanese car is *because* I believe you own an old Nissan (since Nissans, old or otherwise, are Japanese cars), then the latter belief is not defeated by the former. The warrant for my belief that you own a Japanese car is derived from the warrant for my belief that you own an old Nissan.

But Van Cleve brought up the implicit premise thesis in order to rebut it: we do not have to consciously presuppose R to draw conclusions. A child does not knowingly assume the implicit premise that their cognitive faculties are trustworthy when they form beliefs; the idea has never occurred to them. Yet the child still has knowledge. So, both Van Cleve and Plantinga reject the implicit premise thesis: it's not necessary to consciously believe our cognitive faculties are functioning properly in order to accept their deliverances, since we may have never thought about it. We do not have to actively believe that our memory, for example, is reliable in order to have warranted memory beliefs.

The *converse*, however, is not true: if you thought your memory "is *not* reliable (in a certain range, say) *then* you have a defeater for any memory belief (in that range), provided there is no other source of warrant, for you, for the belief in question."[4] If the Freudian theist has no source for their belief in God other than wish-fulfillment, they have a defeater for their belief in God. The child who has never thought about the reliability of their cognitive faculties, however, can have genuine knowledge—not just because the implicit premise thesis is false, but because *they have no defeater for their beliefs*. Yes, the child is not appealing to R as an implicit premise to derive their knowledge claims from it, but this is because they've never reflected on it. It is a presupposition but not a *conscious* one; it does not function as a premise in an argument. Thus, the child does not have a defeater for R. The naturalist's position is distinct from this since they *have* reflected on it, and they *do* have a defeater for R.

Analogue devices

Plantinga argues for the second premise the same way he argues for the first: with analogies. His primary analogy for the first premise is the hypothetical population. For the remaining premises he gives several others, including some we have already encountered, such as the red widgets and the Freudian theist. In these analogies a source of information is unreliable, i.e., does not produce information that is probably true. Plantinga argues that in cases like these, we have a defeater for any belief solely produced by such sources.[5]

Another analogy is someone who believes they've ingested a drug, XX, which causes most people to form wildly false beliefs without any awareness they are doing so, but also knows that a small percentage of people who take it suffer no ill effects. This person's belief in the reliability of their own cognitive faculties—that is, R—has thus been defeated: they have a reason to think it does not hold for them. Or take a space explorer who discovers an alien device which seems to announce weather conditions on Earth in English. However, it could be relaying falsehoods or saying other propositions in some alien language since there is no connection between the device and the information it seems to be relaying. The explorer should withhold belief about the information's reliability, an undercutting defeater. Yet another case: I purchase a sphygmomanometer and assume it is reliable. Then I learn it was manufactured in a factory run by a rabid neo-Luddite, who wants to inject some chaos into society by making some unspecified percentage of his products inaccurate and unreliable. Since I cannot make an informed judgment about the reliability of my sphygmomanometer, I should withhold belief that it is reliable, and this gives me an undercutting defeater for the claim that it is reliable. Or take the standard example of someone driving through a countryside whose inhabitants have erected barn façades to make their community look more affluent. The driver sees what looks like a barn and comments on it. Their passenger, however, is more in the know and informs them about the façade situation. If the driver believes the passenger, they have a defeater for the belief that they are seeing a barn, even though they are looking right at it.[6]

In fact, this is on a level with traditional global skepticism, like the evil demon or brain-in-a-vat scenarios. Someone who genuinely believes this has a defeater for R. The commonality between the analogies is that a belief is found to be unreliably formed and, if there is no other source for it, it is defeated. The EAAN shows that R is improbable so any belief the naturalist forms obtains a defeater, including R, N, E, and N&E.

Some object that Plantinga's analogies are not sufficiently analogous. Timothy O'Connor, for example, argues that the Freudian theist case does not parallel the naturalist's, since the Freudian theist believes wish-fulfillment is untrustworthy because it has "an unreliable track record by more fundamentally established mechanisms."[7] Our belief in R, however, is not produced by processes with an established track record of unreliability. Therefore, the analogy does not hold.

In response, the reasons someone has for initially believing and then rejecting the reliability of a belief's source are irrelevant to the EAAN. True, there is an aspect of the Freudian theist case that is absent from the naturalist's, but there is bound to be since they are not identical but parallel: that's what makes them analogies. Plantinga is not comparing the *reasons* for accepting and then rejecting the reliability of some faculty, he is simply comparing someone whose belief B is produced by source S and then comes to reject S as a reliable source. They then have an undercutting defeater for B. It doesn't matter *why* they initially trusted S and no longer do, only *that* they initially trusted S and no longer do. Whether they were aware of their dependence on S, whether the problem is due to the external environment (as with the widgets) or their internal state (as with the drug XX)—all these considerations are irrelevant.[8]

Defeater-deflectors

Others have argued the analogies are not like the naturalist's situation. Why isn't naturalism closer to the cases where a belief conditionalized on another is improbable but is not defeated? "[T]he probability that I live in Michigan, given that the earth revolves around the sun, is low, and I believe that the earth revolves around the sun; this does not give me a defeater for my belief that I live in Michigan."[9] Maybe this is closer to the naturalist's situation.

The difference between this and Plantinga's analogies is a) the two beliefs are unrelated, whereas Plantinga's analogies deal with beliefs where one is about the source of the other; and b) we would conditionalize living in Michigan (or wherever) on many other, more relevant beliefs which would raise the probability to near certitude in most cases.

The naturalist cannot avoid a), as the analogies clearly parallel the EAAN by positing beliefs where one is about the other's source; b) is another question. Some philosophers argue that the naturalist could "add a bit"—add more beliefs to the equation so that their belief in R is not conditionalized solely on N&E. The naturalist, after all, does not *only* believe N, E, and R, they have many other beliefs which may be relevant to R. For that matter, they can use one of the beliefs just mentioned: perhaps they can conditionalize their belief in R on N, E, *and R itself*. That would raise the probability of R to 100 percent.[10] Or they could conditionalize on L, the belief that we won the evolutionary lottery and have reliable cognitive faculties by chance. They conditionalize R on N, E, and L, also raising the probability to 100 percent.[11] Or we can propose some unknown third proposition (O) that would render the probability high again. Conditionalizing on N, E, and O would make R probable.[12] So, sure, P(R/N&E) is low but P(R/N&E&(R∨L∨O)) is high. Plantinga calls these defeater-deflectors since they try to deflect the low probability of R/N&E from producing a defeater for R. Defeater deflectors are beliefs that make it impossible to rationally believe the defeater, or for it to function *as* a defeater.

There's a problem, however. If these suggestions can deflect N&E from defeating R, *they can deflect any defeater whatsoever*. Take a belief B and a defeater D. Now say we conditionalize B on D and B itself; that is, what is P(B/D&B)? Well, 100 percent. Or take L, that we won the belief lottery—that is, B, despite D, just happens to be true. What is P(B/D&L)? Also 100 percent. Or take O, some unknown belief that counterbalances D and renders B probable again. What is P(B/D&O)? High. If these strategies can deflect the EAAN, they can deflect any defeater of any belief at all. Since beliefs are sometimes defeated, these strategies are invalid.[13]

N.M.L. Nathan argues similarly but with an added twist. Rather than adding a proposition in an ad hoc manner to N&E, Nathan claims that there are other beliefs that the naturalist already has. It is not simply a matter of calculating the probability of R on N&E because we have other evidence for R. We have, for example, M, that we remember our belief-forming capacities being largely reliable in the past. If someone demands proof of M, "a vicious infinite regress may seem to loom: she will also need evidence for her evidence for M, and so on."[14] Thus, the equation becomes P/R(N&E&M), and with this, the naturalist is in a very different situation than Plantinga claims. "And if this is possible in the case of memory, why isn't something similar possible in the case of our other cognitive faculties?"[15]

The problem is that M cannot mean our memory beliefs of past events are true, since the reliability of our memory beliefs is called into question as soon as R is called into question. M is a subcategory of R, it stands or falls with it, so we cannot use it to prevent R from being defeated. Nathan's suggestion is more like a "withhold a bit" strategy than "add a bit." Perhaps he's just claiming our memory beliefs *seem* to be reliable and have seemed so in the past. But the question is not whether, given N, our cognitive faculties would seem to be reliable; it is whether they are *actually* reliable regardless of how they seem. To object that we remember (or seem to remember) that they have been reliable (or have seemed to be reliable) in the past just misses the argument.

So, can *anything* be added to or withheld from the process of forming beliefs besides our cognitive faculties? What about information that comes through our senses, or from other people? Are those not relevant? But this forgets what Plantinga means by "cognitive faculties": those faculties that produce *beliefs*—that is, mental depictors with propositional content—in us. Anything that produces beliefs is thus subsumed under the category of cognitive faculties. Of course, there are innumerable sources of information, but for that information to be converted into a mental depictor, it must go through the gatekeeper of our cognitive faculties, by definition. Our senses provide information, but this only entails that we would have accurate indicators, not true depictors. If we say our senses by themselves generate true beliefs—in addition to producing accurate depictors, they also produce true mental depictors—then we are incorporating them into the category of cognitive faculties and the EAAN comes into play.

Approaching the EAAN incrementally

William Talbott has pressed this "withhold a bit" objection in brilliant fashion.[16] He first argues that analogies challenging a particular faculty, like wish fulfillment, make fewer assumptions, and so should be preferable. Then he proposes an analogy similar to Plantinga's XX: a hallucinogen, H, which causes 95 percent of the people who take it to suffer from wild sensory hallucinations, but no other cognitive dysfunctions, within about an hour. But 5 percent of people have a genetic block making them immune to H. Talbott then presents three scenarios.

First, say someone takes H but has evidence he is one of the charmed 5 percent. Clearly it is rational for him to believe his sensory beliefs are not being caused by unreliable cognitive faculties. Second, say someone takes H but has no information whether he is one of the 5 percent. But about an hour after taking it, his doctor calls to say he does indeed have the genetic block. The phone call, however, could be a hallucination brought on by H. How is he to know? Well, Talbott argues, "he has not noticed much change in his perceptions,"[17] and memory is not affected by H. Moreover, H does not cause mundane hallucinations, like receiving a phone call, but dramatic ones, and he can recognize the difference since H also does not affect his ability to make such an assessment. Since he can compare his current sensory perceptions with those he remembers when his cognitive faculties were functioning properly and what kind of wild hallucinations he would expect H to produce, it is rational for him to believe that the phone call was veridical and that he is, in fact, among the 5 percent. Note that this is the case even though a significant part of the information he has is coming from his current sensory perceptions which are being challenged by the argument.

Third, someone takes H, but with the knowledge that it only has its deleterious effects for twenty-four hours. Within an hour, he begins to suffer wild hallucinations, but a friend takes him to a doctor who administers an antidote. His perceptions go back to normal. He did not anticipate being brought to a doctor, and was not even aware of an antidote, but based on his sensory experiences' seeming normality, he believes that he is no longer under the influence of H. Once again, he bases this belief on his sensory experiences, even though the claim is that his sensory beliefs may not be reliably formed.

In response, Plantinga suggests, and I agree, that Talbott's rephrasing of the argument so that only *some* cognitive faculties are unreliable is a "Trojan horse."[18] This allows Talbott to withhold some aspects of our faculties from the EAAN and establish R on the basis of the withheld aspects. But, as E.L. Mascall writes, such objections only work "so long as we exclude from the sphere of application of the naturalistic theory the examiner's conviction of the validity of his examination."[19] In Talbott's scenarios, the person can rely on his memories, his knowledge of H's effects, and his ability to rationally evaluate whether his present experiences are normal or abnormal. But if *all* our cognitive faculties are called into question, we cannot rely on our memories or evaluative assessments, since these are called into question along with everything else. The person in Talbott's scenarios can use his current sensory experiences as part of his assessment of whether he is under the influence of H even though H calls them into question, but he is only using them as raw data without presupposing their veridicality. Given these experiences, he can rationally evaluate whether they would be what H would produce—and he can rationally evaluate it because H does not impede his ability to rationally evaluate things.

The EAAN, however, argues that *all* our cognitive faculties would be unreliable. The belief that our experiences are or have been relatively coherent is something produced by our cognitive faculties, and their reliability is called into question by the EAAN. If we include in this sweeping annulment the claim that our memories may not be reliable and we may not be capable of recognizing the coherence of our past and present experiences—memory and recognition being cognitive functions, after all—we cannot rely on them to reestablish our cognitive faculties' reliability. The EAAN claims their *actual* reliability—not their *apparent* reliability, whether present or past—is called into question by naturalism.

Talbott also suggests a further wrinkle regarding the timing of the doctor's phone call. Switching back to XX, suppose someone knows it takes an hour to take effect, and receives word that they have the golden gene with five minutes to spare. Then they wouldn't have a defeater. But what if they receive word five minutes *after* the hour-mark is up? Then they would have a defeater, since the phone call is just as explicable as a hallucination brought on by XX. What if they receive word one minute after the hour-mark? Or just a few seconds? At what point do we grant that the exonerating phone call counts as a reason to think that they are not subject to the deleterious effects of XX? Any drug, after all, will have slightly different effects on different people: perhaps for some the effects don't kick in until one hour and two minutes and for others they start at fifty-seven minutes so that, even if the person receives the phone call at fifty-eight minutes, it would form a part of the hallucinations XX is causing. For that matter, say XX takes away any memory of taking the drug, or that it even exists, as well as the ability to recognize the coherence and ordinariness of one's cognitive faculties, currently and in the past. This, however, would apply to our present condition: we have no memory of such a drug existing much less of taking it, and we do not seem to observe our cognitive faculties fluctuating wildly.

Talbott's larger point is to challenge defeater-reasoning itself as being time-dependent. The person who has ingested XX should be able to bracket the skepticism and continue reasoning even after the hour-mark. I'll deal with this at the end of chapter 12, but for now I'll just say I think the EAAN requires the naturalist to bracket the skepticism and continue reasoning, otherwise it would be an argument against *rationality*, not *naturalism*. But I don't think we can discard defeater-reasoning.

Cognitive faculties, in Plantinga's sense, are those faculties that produce beliefs in us. This makes it a functional term, defined by its product rather than the processes which generate the product. Whatever processes produce beliefs in us are included in this definition. But there are many such processes: beliefs are multiply realizable. As long as the end-product is a mental depictor with propositional content, it's all good.

Given this multiple realizability, Talbott argues that challenging the reliability of *all* the various and sundry systems that produce beliefs is more ad hoc than challenging one or two of them.[20] Perceptual and memory beliefs in particular cannot be plausibly challenged. And if only some beliefs are being challenged, this could allow us to reestablish the reliability of our belief-forming processes through aspects that are not being challenged. This moves oppositely to Plantinga, who starts with the end-product and works backwards, asking how we acquire knowledge *given* that we have it. So whatever processes produce knowledge all fall under the same rubric. Talbott is arguing in the reverse direction (that is, the normal direction): perhaps the processes that generate some beliefs are unreliable, but we cannot assume this would hold for other processes and beliefs as well. Pointing out this divergence of approach does not rebut Talbott's objection, but it would apply beyond his intended target, and would concern other areas where Plantinga uses a similar approach.

However, I think this problem is resolvable. The conditions under which Plantinga suggests that our (or the hypothetical population's) cognitive faculties could be unreliable is not a matter of multiple conditions. Even though the faculties in question are diverse, they are unified in sharing a particular condition, and it is that condition that causes the same problem in all of them: naturalism. Naturalism is the poison pill that makes it enormously improbable to move from accurate indicators to true depictors, and it is only at the level of depictors that something achieves the status of belief and potentially knowledge. So, if the belief-producing processes are *naturalistic*, they create the problem Plantinga alleges. This is not ad hoc since it only appeals to one condition, and in fact one condition that the naturalist already accepts. Regardless of how diverse cognitive processes may be in other ways, if they are *naturalistic* processes, it renders P/R(N&E) low and R is thereby defeated.

Nevertheless, Talbott has a point in saying the EAAN is more palatable when directed at specific types of beliefs rather than all. In the introduction, I initially presented the argument this way, applying it first to religious beliefs, then metaphysical beliefs, then ethical, etc. But this is just an argumentative strategy. Suggesting that all our cognitive faculties are unreliable is a radical claim and we cannot seriously consider it as a possibility even if we wanted. Because of this, it is a wiser tactic to call a particular type of belief into question, especially a type of belief that is rejected by the naturalist, like religious beliefs. Upon doing so, however, we discover that the problem is with naturalism, and we can then explore whether the problem naturalism poses for religious beliefs poses a problem with other classes of beliefs, and whether there are some classes that are immune to it.

MR and SR

Ignoring all this though, the suggestion is if we only call some belief-producing attributes into question, we can use other attributes to save naturalism from the argument. But this is not necessarily the case. Really, all the EAAN must do is call into question the cognitive faculties responsible for belief in naturalism. So there are versions of the EAAN, or independent arguments, that seek to defeat naturalism more concisely without the difficulties that arise from calling R into question in general. Thus, we have Plantinga's suggestion to only apply the EAAN to the sources of *metaphysical* beliefs. The question then becomes whether these more narrowly defined faculties are reliable—MR rather than R.

This is not the same thing as Talbott's objection. In Talbott's scenario, one can use the cognitive faculties which are not being challenged to evaluate the reliability of those that are. In Plantinga's this is not possible, for the same reason we cannot add anything to the process of forming beliefs in addition to our cognitive faculties: anything that produces beliefs falls under the rubric of cognitive faculties already. If we found another source that produced beliefs, that source would be subsumed under the same rubric. There are plenty of sources of information, but for that information to be converted into a mental depictor (that is, a belief) it must go through the gatekeeper of our cognitive faculties.

The same goes when we substitute MR for R. Once the belief in question qualifies as a *metaphysical* belief, then those cognitive functions that produced it are those functions that fall under the cloud of suspicion that the EAAN produces. However, despite being more palatable, the argument's intuitive strength dissipates a bit here. If logic is reliable, then the application of logic to metaphysical issues is reliable—more specifically, if the cognitive faculties that produce logical beliefs in us are reliable, then those faculties are still reliable when they apply logic to metaphysical issues. Thought and reality are holistic, logical truths apply to metaphysical beliefs, scientific beliefs, ethical beliefs, etc. Divorcing one category from the overall structure would only seem viable if there was no point of connection, no overlap, of that category with any other. This is never the case.

But even though metaphysical beliefs are continuous with logical beliefs, they still go beyond them. Otherwise, metaphysical beliefs would just *be* logical beliefs. And the "beyond" parts are what are being called into question. Whatever makes metaphysical beliefs metaphysical is what is being challenged. Yes, there is continuity between them and beliefs that are not being challenged, but this continuity is nowhere near enough to ensure most of our metaphysical beliefs are true. The question is not whether evolution would select basic logical and mathematical acumen to ensure the survival of our evolutionary forebears on the plains of the Serengeti.

> The question is whether not only the physical but the mental capacity needed to make a stone axe automatically brings with it the capacity to take each of the steps that have led from there to the construction of the hydrogen bomb, or whether an enormous excess mental capacity, not explainable by natural selection, was responsible for the generation and spread of the sequence of intellectual instruments that has emerged over the last thirty thousand years.... I see absolutely no reason to believe that the truth lies with the first alternative.[21]

In fact, Talbott argues that naturalism cannot account for *scientific* beliefs, like evolution. Science depends upon "non-local evidence relations" but evolution could only make us sensitive to *local* evidence relations. Since naturalists consider evidence relations to be contingent, there is no way to move from the local to the non-local and have it remain reliable except by blind luck.

> I am saying that, other things being equal, evolution would have favored the most efficient reasoning that was locally reliable, and that the non-local applications of that kind of reasoning would be a spandrel, neither selected for nor selected against, because there would have been no significant evolutionary costs or benefits to the results of the non-local applications. If, as the evolutionary naturalist insists, evidence relations are contingent, then there would be no way for evolution to have made our belief in the non-local evidence relations involved in scientific inference probabilistically sensitive to the relevant contingent probabilities, except by sheer luck, and if the non-local application of this reasoning led to true beliefs in science, that, too, would be by sheer luck.[22]

This is Talbott's motivation to suggest a necessary relation between local and non-local evidence relations that bears a passing resemblance to formal causality, as we've seen. Without such a relation, we are unable to secure scientific evidence and cannot rationally affirm evolution (or the existence of DNA, the age of the universe, etc.); and without evolution, the motivation to accept naturalism in the first place decreases dramatically. So, although Talbott's argument differs from Plantinga's,[23] we can put it in Plantinga's terms: the reliability of our cognitive faculties that produce scientific beliefs is SR. The EAAN then becomes P(SR/N&E) is low, and this presents a defeater for N&E.

Abraham Graber and Luke Goleman make an even more austere argument.[24] They contend that scientific realism commits one to the principle of simplicity as a virtue in scientific theorizing, but naturalism removes any justification or warrant in accepting simplicity as a reflection of reality. Thus, scientific realism is precluded by naturalism.

If naturalism is true, science, including evolutionary theory, does not reveal "the real structure of the objective world."²⁵ P(SR/N&E) is low. And this removes any motivation for accepting naturalism. Like Talbott, Graber and Goleman think the argument needs to be applied to local skepticism rather than global skepticism, but that it is still possible to do so in a way that undermines naturalism. *Unlike* Talbott, they portray their argument as a reworking of Plantinga's, not as a distinct argument that draws similar conclusions.²⁶

Apparent and actual

So, again, the EAAN claims that our cognitive faculties' *actual* reliability (present or past) is called into question by naturalism, not their *apparent* reliability. This is an unusual claim, though: why should there be a dichotomy between how our cognitive faculties *seem* and how they *are*? But one could make this same objection to the singer breaking a glass. Why should there be a dichotomy between the content of the sentence the singer is singing and the resonance frequency of her voice that breaks the glass? The answer is that, to think there is an alignment here—that it is by virtue of the singer singing the words "shatter" or "break" that the glass breaks—is magical thinking. Once again, it would be "as if, when I knocked out my pipe, the ashes arranged themselves into letters which read: 'We are the ashes of a knocked-out pipe.'"²⁷ The EAAN argues that naturalism defeats the *actual* reliability of our cognitive faculties but doesn't address their apparent reliability except to say that our ability to evaluate how they seem to be would be defeated along with everything else.

Having said that, couldn't we follow Talbott in *some* regard? Can't we just use our experiences as raw data, without assuming their veridicality? This is an important point, and it will have some impact on the EAAN, precisely in what the objection is suggesting, that our experiences of our cognitive faculties as being relatively coherent should influence our assessment of whether they *are* in fact coherent.

Otte's EAAN

Richard Otte argues we can conditionalize on our experience—not its *veridicality*, just the bare fact of the experience as such-and-such. Otte reformulates the EAAN so that it bypasses implausible analogies of organisms believing in witch-clouds and the like. Since "Plantinga's argument *uses* conditional probabilities to argue for a philosophical conclusion,"²⁸ we should use four guidelines in assessing the probability of R:

1. "Where the obtaining of some proposition x is in question, you should only probabilize on information relevant" to whether x is generated or suppressed.²⁹ "In the case of the EAAN, N and E cover this ground exhaustively."³⁰

2. "What we conditionalize on must be limited to information accessible to us."³¹ This is because the EAAN only addresses whether the naturalist is internally rational as opposed to externally rational.

3. "We cannot conditionalize on anything that presupposes or is based upon that source being reliable" since this would beg the question.[32] Thus, we can neither "add a bit" by suggesting, for example, we won the evolutionary lottery, nor "withhold a bit" to reestablish the reliability of our cognitive faculties on the withheld elements.

4. "We must also conditionalize on all information we have that is independent of or not epistemically based on the source in question."[33] The source in question is R. Do we have independent evidence for R that is not epistemically based on it? Well, we have our experience, EXP, that our cognitive faculties seem relatively coherent. With the hypothetical population, this refers to the mere fact of their experience, not whether it's veridical. We do not conditionalize on whether their beliefs are *true*, only on their apparent coherence. Thus, the contents of their beliefs are irrelevant, beyond the mere fact that they *have* content (otherwise they would not be beliefs).

When we turn the focus to ourselves, however, we cannot avoid having beliefs about our own beliefs and experiences. They are pragmatically unavoidable. Nevertheless, being pragmatically necessary does not insulate them from defeat. Indeed, the charge of the EAAN is that, given N, they are defeated even though we cannot help but believe them, in the same way that the Freudian theist cannot just relinquish their belief in God even though it is defeated. Otte concludes, "we should conditionalize on naturalism, evolutionary theory, and a description of our beliefs and experience. We should not conditionalize on the truth of our beliefs, since this is what is being questioned."[34] Unfortunately for the naturalist, Otte argues that when we add this (EXP) to the equation—P(R/N&E&EXP)—R is still improbable and defeated.

This does rule out some possibilities though. William Hasker in presenting an argument similar to the EAAN, refers to "a possible world physically identical with the actual world, but in which mental properties are redistributed in as bizarre a fashion as one might wish."[35] Yet we do not experience our mental properties being random or chaotic like this. This does not necessarily mean that they are not, it merely means that *if* they are then we are not aware of it. Perhaps our mental properties flit to and fro constantly, but each change comes with an unshakable belief that it is coherent with the rest; or perhaps each moment comes with its own coherent backstory and previous moments are forgotten from one moment to the next; or perhaps there is a continuous yet unintelligible stream of experience but we impose an order onto it that is not there. (Or perhaps they are not random and chaotic at all, but are coherent and expansive, but nevertheless unreliable.) Otte's criterion of experience does not allow us to rule these out, but it at least allows us to rule out possibilities where our "mental properties are redistributed in as bizarre a fashion as one might wish"—and that we are *aware* of it. If we apply the argument to ourselves, then we have to take into account that our cognitive faculties seem to be relatively coherent and not chaotic; and since the hypothetical population is supposed to be like us in given respects, we therefore must posit that their mental lives seem modestly coherent to them. Again, this does not allow us to conditionalize on the claim that they are correct in so thinking, only that they do, in fact, think this. This is as it should be: an ability to recognize, be aware of, our mental properties being bizarre would mean that the part of our cognitive faculties involved in this ability are reliable—and per the EAAN such an ability should not be trusted under naturalism.

Partial defeat

Another possibility that Anthony Peressini and David Reiter suggest is that the EAAN only partially defeats N, requiring the naturalist to believe it less firmly, but not give it up.[36] If Plantinga's argument only provides a partial defeater of N it would certainly be interesting, but the naturalist could continue to rationally believe it.

However, since the claim is that N is *self*-defeating, it is difficult to see how it can fall short of complete defeat. If believing N leads to the conclusion that it is unwarranted or irrational to believe N, then it is not acceptable to continue believing but without the same degree of firmness. The naturalist's noetic structure is inconsistent, and the inconsistency is not produced by the *degree* to which they believe N, but by the mere *fact* that they believe it. In order to reobtain rationality, they must adjust their noetic structure so that consistency is achieved—and the only way to do so is to reject N.

> Plantinga has pointed out that the reflective naturalist is in a position that bears strong analogy to situations in which a probability thesis generates a defeater. Secondly, rational belief in situations such as these seems to demand at least getting the probability just mentioned up to or above .5. It seems that the naturalist has no way to pull this off. Consequently, the naturalist does not merely have a reason to hold R less firmly. They have a reason to abstain from the belief that R holds for them in the same way that they ought rationally not to believe the next flip of a coin will yield a heads; the agent should simply not have any mental state with respect to this proposition such that it would qualify as a belief. Hence, the naturalist faces a complete defeater for R. And from there, it is not hard to see that they have a complete defeater for all their beliefs.[37]

Peressini argues the EAAN only demonstrates that the conjunction of N&E&several-other-conditions is self-defeating. According to the Duhem-Quine thesis, contrary data does not necessarily disprove a theory since no theory can be tested in isolation. There will always be further assumptions being made, and it may be the case that one or more of these assumptions is what conflicts with the data. In fact, it may be the case that several assumptions have partial defeaters and combine to create a complete defeater; in which case, the appropriate response could be to continue holding the partially defeated assumptions less firmly rather than rejecting any of them. Their *conjunction* may have a complete defeater, but this does not necessarily mean any individual belief does.[38]

But Plantinga was excessively vigilant in only giving premises a naturalist would hold with *very* high confidence. He presented five exhaustive and mutually exclusive possible relationships between belief and behavior given N, arguing some of them, such as epiphenomenalism, are very probable, while others are low. This should not be contentious to naturalists, and in fact *is* not contentious since nearly all naturalists agree. Those who do not have to defend their disagreement. Plantinga goes on to argue that, at any rate, the likelihood of any of these scenarios resulting in reliable cognitive faculties that produce mostly true beliefs is low, less than or equal to .5. So, again, unless the naturalist counters Plantinga's assessments, he cannot point to the conjunction of his premises as a way out of the self-defeat (hence *complete* defeat) of N.

Can R be defeated?

Michael Bergmann argues that, even if P(R/N&E) is low, the naturalist can still be rational in believing R. He compares it to the purloined letter case, where a person has a great deal of objective evidence that they stole a letter but remembers taking a solitary walk when it was stolen and has no memory of taking the letter. Plantinga argues they should believe they are innocent because of their memory, even if all the objective evidence points to their guilt. Bergmann argues similarly that the naturalist's belief in R cannot be defeated by an argument showing it is improbable. In these cases, the individual has private (not publicly accessible), nonpropositional evidence that outweighs any other evidence proposed. This is not to say that R is undefeatable—the person who believes the evil demon scenario will have a defeater for R, for example—but having propositional evidence against a belief does not automatically defeat it.

Bergmann's point is not that the nonpropositional evidence defeats the defeater, allowing the naturalist to continue believing R; "Rather, the nonpropositional evidence for Z (i.e., for R) prevents the probabilistic inference from ever functioning as a defeater for Z in the first place."[39] Following Thomas Reid, he argues there are certain basic beliefs or first principles. Attempting to reject them brings forth "the emotion of ridicule. On the basis of this experience, we dismiss as absurd the contrary of the first principle and believe the first principle. In other words, we consider the contrary of a first principle and have an experience that prompts this sort of belief: 'That's absolutely nuts! It's ridiculous!'"[40]

If Bergmann were just arguing that we cannot help but believe R, that it is pragmatically necessary, then we could respond that being pragmatically necessary does not insulate a belief from defeat. But Bergmann is making a stronger and more interesting claim. Plantinga's whole epistemology, including his account of defeaters, is based on proper function. But proper function cannot require someone to give up belief in something as essential and fundamental as their own rationality. Anyone who did so would be malfunctioning rather spectacularly. Proper function itself dictates that we continue to believe we are rational in the face of an abstract argument to the contrary. We cannot reject the reliability of our own cognitive faculties and call it "proper function."

O'Connor argues similarly that R has so much warrant it would be incredible for it to be defeated. At least it would take much stronger evidence to defeat R.[41] He also brings up the purloined letter case and argues that in order for the naturalist to give up belief in R, there would have to be a design plan which "regulate[s] this belief strictly in accordance with our evidence for it."[42] But a design plan requiring us to give up belief in the reliability of our own cognitive faculties is incoherent.

> Strictly speaking, there *couldn't* be a defeater for R, for any creatures in any possible world. That would require a *design plan* which reliably aimed at truth in some circumstances, a part of which was that we ought to give up belief in R when we take note of certain of our beliefs about the world and about related conditional probabilities. But as that potential upshot would lead one to abandon the attempt to form true beliefs, it surely could not be part of a design plan with that very end.[43]

Therefore, there can be no proper function defeater of R. Note that this wouldn't just rule out the EAAN, it would rule out any kind of skepticism. The evil demon and brain-in-a-vat scenarios entail ~R, but this objection could be raised against them. Perhaps Bergmann and O'Connor don't have a problem with this, but others might.

Both Bergmann and O'Connor appeal to the purloined letter case as a close analogy to the naturalist presented with the EAAN. But the two cases do not seem analogous. Plantinga argues that the naturalist will initially believe R and N and then be shown that N defeats R. Of course, they will continue believing R regardless because it is pragmatically necessary, but, like Hume, they will realize in the quiet of their study that, as long as they believe N, they have a rationality defeater for R. With the purloined letter, a person is accused of stealing a letter, all the evidence points to them, and they had a strong motive for doing so, but their memory beliefs, which are properly basic, defeat this evidence. The defeaters in the two cases are N (for belief in R) and the circumstantial evidence (for belief in the reliability of one's memories). But the naturalist believes N *initially* whereas the accused thief does not initially believe the circumstantial evidence against them. Indeed, the accused thief should *reject* the evidence, deny that it proves their guilt, because it conflicts with their basic belief that they were somewhere else when the crime took place. If this analogy proves anything it proves that the naturalist should similarly reject that which defeats their belief in R, namely N.

The purloined letter case is disanalogous to the EAAN in other respects. The former does not present us with a case of someone who discovers that a belief *they themselves hold* conflicts with a properly basic belief, while the latter does. When a conflict like this arises, the person in question must do something to maintain rationality. Simply continuing to believe the two conflicting propositions is not acceptable in most situations, and the cases where it is do not parallel the naturalist's situation.[44] Moreover, the relationship between the defeater and the defeatee is not the same. With the EAAN, the naturalist's belief in N (the defeater) *is produced by their cognitive faculties* (the defeatee). With the purloined letter, the circumstantial evidence (the defeater) is not produced by the accused thief's trust in their memories (the defeatee); the two have no relation to one another except for their conflict.

Nevertheless, the larger claim that proper function cannot require us to give up belief in our own rationality is a strong objection. In one sense at least, someone would be drastically malfunctioning if they tried to deny that R holds for themselves, even if they have taken the drug XX with its severe cognitive consequences. However, if the EAAN is sound thus far, they also have a good reason to deny R. As Plantinga writes,

> one wants to say that in *some* way she really *does* have a defeater for R specified to her case. She believes that R no longer holds for the vast majority of those who take this drug; she knows of nothing that distinguishes her case from theirs; someone who was thinking straight would certainly no longer (without additional evidence) believe R for someone *else* she thought had ingested XX; so doesn't rationality dictate that she cease believing R in her own case?[45]

So, yes, proper function requires us to continue believing R, but it *also* requires us to follow the logic of arguments, even when the conclusions are intolerable and impracticable. As we are essentially in the same situation as Hume, this is a Humean rationality defeater. But since the proper function of one aspect of our cognitive faculties is to follow arguments to their conclusions, and since the defeater is produced by these properly functioning cognitive faculties, it is also a proper function rationality defeater. So, in response to the proper function *objection* to the EAAN, we can point to this proper function *version* of the EAAN. To be sure, this does not refute the objection, it just shows that proper function, and rationality in general, pulls us in two directions at once. Rationality requires us to follow the logic of arguments to their conclusion, but it also requires us to retain belief in R in the face of a defeater for it.

However, another response to the Bergmann/O'Connor objection is that we can bypass rationality defeaters in favor of *warrant* defeaters. These are not asking whether a property is functioning properly but what its function is, what is the goal or purpose or aim of the design plan governing the cognitive faculties that produced the belief in question. Will the continued belief in R in the face of an argument to the contrary be produced by cognitive faculties *aimed at producing true beliefs?* A warrant defeater says no. They may be functioning properly, doing what they're supposed to do, but their function is not to produce true beliefs. So, one may continue believing something, but it would be unwarranted and would not qualify as knowledge.

The Bergmann/O'Connor objection argues that rationality cannot require us to relinquish belief in our own rationality. But this would only show a proper function defeater cannot defeat R (if that); if the individual's cognitive faculties are functioning properly, they will not relinquish their belief in R even if it is defeated because properly functioning cognitive faculties will produce belief in R regardless. Yet this does nothing against a warrant defeater. Certainly, the naturalist will continue believing R, but *why* will they continue believing it? Not because the relevant cognitive faculties are aimed at truth; if they were, they would relinquish belief in R. Other functions may compel them to continue believing R, but the question is, will this belief have warrant for them? In the light of the undercutting defeater Plantinga presents, they will not, since their continued belief will not be produced by cognitive faculties aimed at the production of true beliefs.

> [I]f only our truth-aimed processes were at work in these situations, she *would* have a defeater. Some of the processes governing the maintenance of R are aimed not directly at truth but rather at the ability to carry on our cognitive life. And our design plan is such that if those processes—the processes that govern the maintenance of R but are not directly aimed at truth—were excised, she *would* have an ordinary rationality defeater. This becomes evident when we reflect on what we would think about the reliability of *someone else* who had ingested XX.[46]

Similarly, proper function may dictate that someone with a usually fatal disease will believe they will survive. This belief is produced by properly functioning faculties, optimistic overriders, but the faculties are not aimed at forming true beliefs, they are aimed at forming beliefs that comfort or relieve anxiety. If these overriders were not operating, the patient would have a proper function rationality defeater for their belief that they will survive; but even if they *are* operating, the patient still has a warrant defeater for the belief. Similarly, the naturalist who is apprised of the EAAN will continue believing R because an optimistic overrider will dictate that they continue believing R (at least while they are out living their lives and not alone in their study). But the faculties involved in producing and sustaining the belief are not aimed at forming true beliefs. Therefore, their continued belief in R will not be warranted.

> The strength of Plantinga's reply here is that it runs parallel to the comments of David Hume on the same topic. Hume was aware that no person could force themselves to give up the beliefs skeptical arguments seemed to require them to give up. Furthermore, it would ... be irrational to give up these beliefs. But the skeptical arguments are not thereby undermined. Therefore, it seems that any reply to Plantinga which attacks his appeal to [warrant] defeat must be strong enough to demolish the arguments of Hume with regards to skepticism and that is an unenviable task in the extreme. Furthermore, if one grants Plantinga the defeat concept but attempts to make a case that such defeat is uninteresting, they will have to account for why Hume's arguments receive such universal applause.[47]

We can go further: if someone has a rationality defeater for a belief—Humean or proper function—then they will also have a warrant defeater for that belief. If they come to realize that a belief was produced by malfunctioning cognitive processes, they will also realize that if those processes were aimed at truth, the malfunction prevents it from achieving that end (at least in the proper way). So, a rationality defeater also serves as a warrant defeater. If someone's belief B is not rational, it is also not knowledge.

Does this go the other way? Are warrant defeaters also rationality defeaters? Initially it would seem not. Someone's belief B could be produced by properly functioning cognitive faculties but if the function in question is not to produce true beliefs, they would have a warrant defeater but not a rationality defeater. This is precisely the point of an optimistic overrider. However, there is an important qualification: if someone *realizes* their belief B is produced by cognitive faculties not aimed at producing true beliefs, then even if those faculties were functioning properly, their awareness that their function is other than the formation of true beliefs would make it irrational to continue believing B. It would mean they realize they do not believe B *because it is true*. And if a belief's truth is irrelevant to why they believe it—if they would believe it even if it were false—the belief would no longer be rational. Indeed, it would seem to be incoherent: they would continue to believe B is true even if they come to believe that the truth of B is irrelevant to their belief in B. Remember the Freudian theist: even if the "wish-fulfillment" faculty is functioning properly in producing belief in God, it would be irrational for them to continue believing theism. In sum: rationality defeaters automatically produce warrant defeaters, but the converse is not the case—unless, that is, someone is *aware* of a warrant defeater. In that case, "then (typically) you also have a rationality defeater."[48]

What the proper function objection of Bergmann and O'Connor boils down to is that some of our beliefs and belief-forming processes do not appear unreliable, and some we cannot seriously question. This is especially so for acts of reasoning. Properly constructed logical syllogisms seem to lead inescapably from premises to conclusion. The problem here is that while the EAAN is significantly different from standard global skeptical arguments, it still functions as a global skeptical argument. One cannot object to brain-in-a-vat skepticism by saying their experiences seem veridical. The brain-in-a-vat explanation applies just as much to their experiences' seeming veracity. As Nagel puts it, "finding something self-evident is no guarantee that it is necessarily true, or true at all—since the disposition to find it self-evident could have been an evolutionary adaptation to its being only approximately, and contingently, true."[49]

If the EAAN is successful, we have a reason for thinking our experiences would not be veridical, regardless of how they seem—namely, because they were produced by cognitive faculties aimed at something other than producing true beliefs. It is not merely that we don't have a reason to affirm R, we *do* have a reason to deny it. Once that reason is in place, it applies to everything. Just as some philosophers seek to explain away religious or moral beliefs as evolutionary hangovers which helped our progenitors to survive, so the EAAN shows that this would apply to *all* beliefs, including scientific beliefs (and thus E) and metaphysical beliefs (and thus N).

The main point is that, in other skeptical scenarios which evoke Bergmann's "emotion of ridicule," such as the evil demon and brain-in-a-vat suggestions, the response is (and should be) not only to reject the absurdities, but to reject anything that unavoidably leads to them. If theism inevitably led to the evil demon scenario, the response should not only be to reject the evil demon and continue believing we are rational, but to reject theism as well. Similarly, if N leads us to think that P(R/N&E) is low and R is thereby defeated, the response should not be merely to continue to affirm R, but to reject N.

Alston's EAAN

William Alston accepts the EAAN but reformulates it so that R defeats N&E instead of N&E defeating R. Plantinga has shown that the set of beliefs R, N, and E are inconsistent, they fail to be internally rational. But this does not tell us which of the three beliefs should be excised from our noetic structure.

> ... the considerations that support that result [P(R/N&E) ≤ .5] equally support a low value for the reverse relation, P(N&E/R). For if the naturalistic evolutionary story of the development of human cognitive faculties makes it unlikely that they are reliable, then, by the same token, it [sic] they are reliable that makes it unlikely that they arose in the naturalistic evolutionary way. If certain meteorological conditions make a thunderstorm unlikely, then if a thunderstorm occurs it is unlikely, in the absence of other relevant information, that those meteorological conditions prevailed.[50]

Generally, in these cases we rid ourselves of the belief that enjoys the least warrant; and since R has a great deal of warrant, N has significantly less, and rejecting E would not resolve the inconsistency, we should reject N.

Essentially, Alston has created a twin of Plantinga's EAAN going the other way. Both say, "one who insists on holding on to N&E cannot preserve internal rationality except by giving up R."[51] In either case, one cannot believe in naturalism and remain rational. This is not incompatible with Plantinga's EAAN, it is simply the other side of the coin. Plantinga is arguing the modus ponens that the naturalist, *as a naturalist*, should give up their belief in their own rationality: N → ~R; N; ∴ ~R. Alston is arguing the modus tollens that the naturalist, *as a rational agent*, should give up their belief in naturalism: N → ~R; R; ∴ ~N. As Bergmann writes, Plantinga is addressing the warrant or "justificational status" of R in the face of a defeater, whereas Alston is addressing how someone should change their beliefs in light of it. In other words, Plantinga is focusing on internal rationality, which is "downstream from experience,"[52] while Alston is focusing on external rationality, what "*perfect* rationality would require."[53] If the naturalist chooses to follow Alston in this, Plantinga is no longer addressing his argument to them. It's not as if, after telling the naturalist that they are committed to accepting ~R, Plantinga is commending them to remain in such a lamentable condition. It's called the Evolutionary Argument against *Naturalism*, not the Evolutionary Argument against *Rationality*.

Alston's EAAN further answers the Bergmann/O'Connor objection that R is not defeatable. Even if presented with a reason to think R is not true, we could not give it up. Proper function allows nothing less, since a properly functioning individual would not give up belief in R in the face of an abstract argument. Plantinga's response is twofold: first, the EAAN parallels Hume's skepticism in which someone accepts R in their daily life but recognizes in their more philosophical moments that they should not. Thus, while proper function would require us to retain belief in R, it would also require us to relinquish it. This functions as a rationality defeater (both proper function and Humean). Second, the EAAN can also be framed as a warrant defeater for R rather than a rationality defeater, and once the naturalist becomes aware of the fact that their belief in R is not produced by processes aimed at producing true beliefs, this produces another rationality defeater for R.

However, granting the Bergmann/O'Connor objection for the sake of argument, Alston steps into the gap to argue that an EAAN can still be constructed going the other way. Once we realize that N and R are incompatible with each other, and since we cannot give up R, we should preserve rationality by giving up N. Again, if a specific metaphysical position leads to an intolerable scenario that evokes Bergmann's "emotion of ridicule," we should not only reject the intolerable scenario; we should also reject the metaphysical position that leads to it. N is just such a metaphysical position. Therefore, according to Alston's EAAN, it should be abandoned.

So Plantinga's second premise is successful: the person who sees that P(R/N&E) is low has a defeater for their belief in R. They have a reason to withhold belief in R.

9

The End of the Argument

Fallacious and misleading arguments are most easily detected if set out in correct syllogistic form.

Immanuel Kant

The second-and-a-half premise

There is an important detail left out of Plantinga's syllogism, although he addresses it in his exposition of the EAAN: the defeater for R is ultimately undefeated (or unresolved). The low probability of R/N&E defeats R but defeaters can often be defeated themselves, and this is the case for some of Plantinga's analogies. The widgets case is the best illustration. The widgets look red and an observer believes they are red. Then someone tells them they are irradiated by a red light when they emerge from the machine: now the observer has a defeater for their belief they are red. Then the manager tells them the person who said that is a compulsive liar: now they have a defeater-defeater. Then several employees tell them that the manager is a practical joker: now they have a defeater-defeater-defeater. Then they overhear those employees laughing about how they believed them; then they observe a red light above the conveyer belt illuminating the widgets; etc. At each stage a new defeater can be introduced, but only if the *source* of the new defeater is not what has been challenged by the old defeater—otherwise we would be relying on a source that has been called into question, and such circularity is invalid.

With other defeaters and other analogies, this is not the case. Someone who takes XX, or thinks they're being deceived by an evil demon or that they're just a brain in a vat has a reason to distrust *everything* their cognitive faculties relay to them. They cannot reestablish confidence in their cognitive faculties because any method would require trusting their (supposedly) unreliable cognitive faculties. So, some defeaters cannot be defeated themselves,[1] and these analogies are the ones which most closely resemble the naturalist's situation, since both call a source of all of our beliefs into question.

A defeater for R will be ultimately undefeated or unresolved since, to counter it, we would need a reason, a *good* reason (one that actually entails its conclusion) that R is true. But to get a good reason we would have to rely on our cognitive faculties and so presuppose their reliability—which is just R. We could only obtain a reason for trusting

R by trusting R, and this is blatantly circular. This may be fine for epistemic circularity, but it cannot "restore lost confidence" in the trustworthiness of a faculty that has been called into question.[2] "Trying to prove that our reason is not deceptive by any kind of reasoning is absurd in the same way as trying to settle whether a man is honest or not by asking him."[3] So if R is defeated, that defeater cannot be defeated itself; it is either an ultimately undefeated or unresolved defeater. Any argument to reestablish R will proceed via premises to a conclusion, and we have the same reason to doubt any premise (as well as its connection to the other premises and the conclusion) as we do for R: namely, an undefeated or unresolved undercutting defeater.[4]

The third premise

The third premise of the EAAN is "Anyone who has a defeater for R has a defeater for any other belief she thinks she has, including N&E itself."[5] Once we have lost trust in our cognitive faculties' reliability, reestablishing it would have to proceed via our cognitive faculties which, per the argument, are not trustworthy. Other beliefs produced by our cognitive faculties cannot help us determine whether our cognitive faculties are reliable unless we begin by presupposing they are reliable, and the EAAN does not allow such a move.

But this means that all those other beliefs, regardless of whether they would help reestablish R, are no longer trustworthy. If we have a reason to distrust the reliability of our cognitive faculties, we have a reason to distrust any belief *produced* by our cognitive faculties—which would be all of them. This has already been demonstrated: given N&E, any given belief would only have a .5 probability of being true, which is no better than guessing. So, if we have a defeater for R, we have a defeater for any and every belief we have. The naturalist is thus faced with a form of global skepticism.

This is not a problem for Plantinga: R is properly basic and does not require evidence or a reason or an argument to be warranted. But properly basic beliefs can still be defeated, and the EAAN alleges to do this for R—but only for the naturalist. The naturalist can only trust their cognitive faculties if they already trust them, and the EAAN takes away that trust.

Back to analogies

Many of the analogies Plantinga uses to establish the second premise can also be used to establish the third. Plantinga suggests these analogies illustrate a rough-and-ready formula which effectively establishes the third premise: "In general, if you have considered the question whether a given source of information or belief is reliable, and have an undefeated defeater for the belief that it is, then you have a defeater for any belief such that you think it originates (solely) from that source."[6] So the person who thinks they have taken the drug XX, which causes most people to hold wildly false beliefs without realizing it, has a defeater for R and hence for any belief solely produced by R, which, again, is all of them. The same holds for someone who believes they are under the control of an evil demon, or that they are a brain in a vat. In both cases, they have a defeater for R, and thus a defeater for every other belief. Since the EAAN calls *all* the naturalist's beliefs into question, it is an argument for global skepticism.

Other analogies illustrate the rough-and-ready formula but do not carry over as directly to the third premise. The Freudian theist will become skeptical of the (alleged) source of their belief in God, viz. wish-fulfillment. But this just means that they have a defeater for beliefs they think are entirely produced this way. It does not lead to global skepticism unless they think all their beliefs are produced by wish-fulfillment,[7] which is not very likely. Rather, this is a textbook case of *local* skepticism, skepticism about a particular source or set of beliefs but not all.[8]

Regardless, someone who thinks they have taken XX, or that they are being deceived by an evil demon, or who believes N, has a defeater for their belief that their cognitive faculties are reliable (R), and thus a defeater for all their beliefs, since they are all produced by their unreliable cognitive faculties. There is no stopping the rot once it has started. When the naturalist sees the validity of the EAAN,

> things get real bad, real fast, cognitively speaking. For apparently we (or, rather, those hapless evolutionary naturalists among us) now have come to have reason to withhold belief in the reliability of our cognitive faculties. But so long as *that* remains the case, the light of reason tells me (as a last bit of illumination, before the power shuts off completely) that I similarly have reason to be agnostic with respect to any of my beliefs.[9]

"Add a bit" revisited

Once R is called into question, we cannot "go to the MIT cognitive-reliability laboratory for a check-up,"[10] since we could only know we are at MIT, that they have such a laboratory, that their methods of determining the reliability of one's cognitive faculties are trustworthy, etc., if our cognitive faculties are reliable. But whether our cognitive faculties are reliable is precisely what is being challenged. We cannot appeal to R to establish R once we have a reason to reject it.

Paul Churchland, however, suggests that having a defeater for R does not entail having a defeater for every belief, because our beliefs are not *solely* produced by our cognitive faculties. They are also produced by "superadded mechanisms [that] lie mostly outside the biological brain."[11] These mechanisms weed out false beliefs and make it much more plausible that the preponderance of our beliefs are correct—at least our scientific beliefs. This last point is important because it prevents Plantinga from arguing that naturalism defeats the scientific theory of evolution.

The most relevant superadded mechanism is the larger scientific community and their techniques for verifying whether a claim stands up to empirical scrutiny. While our cognitive faculties are only designed (by evolution) to enable the organism to survive, the scientific community can consciously pursue truth and so correct any deviation from truth on the part of one person's unreliable cognitive faculties. They can use the scientific techniques developed throughout the history of science for evaluating how well a (scientific) belief accords with experimental results, how well it accords with the broader scientific view of the world (earlier discoveries and how well they cohere with each other), as well as "techniques for avoiding 'cherrypicking' and other forms of experimenter bias, techniques such as 'double blind' procedures,"[12] etc. Thus,

> the cognitive engine of the Collective Scientific Community can supply rational warrant—both positive and negative—far beyond what can be supplied by a single individual with his native smarts and sensory equipment. In particular, it can supply warrant for the weave of naturalistic claims and explanations that constitute modern evolutionary theory. And it can do so even if we all *agree* that an individual brain "designed" by natural selection has no significant claim to be a "truth tracker."[13]

Although it goes unmentioned in his article, Churchland is approaching this from an eliminativist position, according to which there are no beliefs, no cognitive elements that have propositional content. He has specifically used this to argue that "Truth, as currently conceived, might cease to be an aim of science."[14] So in the present article, when he refers to truth, he is probably not referring to depictive (propositional) truth but to indicative accuracy; and so, when he refers to rationality, he is probably not using this term as it relates to forming true, depictive beliefs. This is significant because the EAAN does not challenge whether evolution would select accurate indicators; it challenges whether this would lead to true depictors or a capacity to form them. We can accept everything he says here about superadded mechanisms weeding out false scientific beliefs, because "beliefs" for him do not have propositional content, and it is only with such content that they are true or false. Of course, it's possible he is granting Plantinga's definition of beliefs as mental depictors, but he does not say so, and that would be a pretty significant detail to leave out.

Churchland's scenario sounds like another "add a bit" strategy discussed in the previous chapter, where we can conditionalize the probability of R on more than just N&E and thereby avoid a defeater for R. But Churchland is not arguing at that stage: he is granting that the individual cognizer has a defeater for R with respect to themselves,[15] but that "the cognitive engine of the Collective Scientific Community" has no such defeater, and it is this collective that supplies us with most of our beliefs—or at least, that supplies the more enlightened of us with most of our scientific beliefs. So, while the individual has a defeater for R, the collective can overcome it by pooling their resources and avoid having a defeater for all our other beliefs. Thus, Churchland's objection applies to the third premise of the EAAN not the second.

In any case, the response should be obvious. Churchland's beliefs that the methods of the larger scientific community are reliably aimed at truth and that there even *is* a larger scientific community would only be trustworthy if his individual cognitive faculties are reliable. But the EAAN gives him a defeater for this claim, and thus for the beliefs about the larger scientific community. Churchland seems to think we can take a reading of what our own brains tell us and then compare it with what other people's brains tell *them*. But of course, one could only know what other people's brains tell them if one's own brain is functioning reliably enough to produce true beliefs about them. But that's just R, the very proposition that, by Churchland's admission, has been defeated.

> If you think about it, the inside of your own mind is the only thing you can be sure of. Whatever you believe—whether it's about the sun, moon, and stars, the house and neighborhood in which you live, history, science, other people, even the existence of your own body—is based on your experiences and thoughts, feelings, and sense impressions. That's all you have to go on directly, whether you see the book in your hands, or feel the floor beneath your feet, or remember that George Washington was the first president of the United States. ... Everything else is farther away from you than your inner experiences and thoughts, and reaches you only through them.[16]

Churchland's appeal to a broader community as a source of knowledge is a clear reference to social epistemology, where knowledge (or some forms of knowledge) is seen as a collective enterprise rather than an individual one. Social epistemology is one of the great insights in recent epistemological studies, but Churchland's use of it is problematic: he argues that, while our cognitive faculties may be unreliable *individually*, they can be reliable *collectively*. But I don't think he can make this work. The question here is the order of dependence: if our individual rationality is dependent on the broader community, then the whole scenario falls apart for the reason already given: how do you know those other people exist—that what they seem to be saying is what they're actually saying—that the methods they've developed are reliable—unless you *already* trust your cognitive faculties on an individual level to reveal these truths to you?

In Plantinga's epistemology, there's plenty of room for beliefs that are not basic to have more warrant than beliefs that are, and even for nonbasic beliefs to *defeat* basic beliefs.[17] But not if the warrant and veridicality of the nonbasic belief is dependent on the warrant and veridicality of the basic belief. If it is only through something that is directly perceived that we can rationally believe an object of knowledge that is indirectly perceived, we cannot use the latter to verify or falsify the former.

Plantinga and Aaron Segal responded to Churchland, abbreviating his claim "that when our cognitive faculties are operating in special circumstances that include the use of 'artificial mechanisms for theory-creation and theory-evaluation embodied in the complex institutions and procedures of modern science,' ('laboratory circumstances' for short), we form mostly true beliefs" as R+.[18] Churchland's argument, then, is:

1. Although P/R(N&E) is low, P/R+(N&E) is not.
2. Although the low probability means N&E defeats R, N&E does not defeat R+.
3. Since N&E is included within R+, the naturalist can rationally believe N&E.

We have already seen that the first premise is incorrect, and Segal and Plantinga agree: sources independent of our cognitive faculties can only be known by us via our cognitive faculties, so if R does not hold, we cannot bolster it up with these extra sources. The second premise fares no better, since R+ refers to beliefs produced in "laboratory circumstances" with all the bells and whistles that Churchland posits in his collective scientific community. This would obviously include most scientific beliefs. But of course it would not include numerous other beliefs, such as logical and mathematical beliefs (which are apprehended a priori and so do not rely on feedback from others); beliefs about what other people are thinking and feeling (which would include the thoughts of other scientists in laboratory circumstances, the exclusion of which immediately sabotages Churchland's scenario); beliefs that God exists, doesn't exist, or cannot be known to exist; or even that P/R+(N&E) is high.

Churchland's conclusion, apart from being based on false premises, is problematic for another reason. Belief in evolution would be produced in "laboratory circumstances" and so would belong to that charmed corpus of beliefs that are warranted and rational. But Churchland thinks since this is the case for E it would be the case for N&E as well. Naturalism, however, is a metaphysical belief that is *not* produced in laboratory circumstances, and so is not eligible for membership in Churchland's club. Again, it is not *evolution* that Plantinga is contesting, it is *naturalism*. His point of putting them together as N&E is not intended to suggest they stand or fall together; it is intended to take what the naturalist perceives as their greatest weapon and use it against them. The Evolutionary Argument *against Naturalism* claims that we cannot rationally accept both naturalism and evolution but must choose one or the other.

In other words, the point of the third premise is more than that *all* the naturalist's beliefs are defeated, it is that a *particular* belief is defeated: N&E. The naturalist's belief in E would be defeated, since it is, after all, a belief they have which is produced by unreliable cognitive faculties. They cannot find some further evidence for E because their beliefs that such evidence a) exists and b) supports E are just more beliefs produced by their unreliable cognitive faculties. Again, Plantinga doesn't target E to call it into question, but because naturalists typically see it as the linchpin establishing their position. Plantinga is pointing out that it works the other way: we cannot accept N *and* E. And regardless, rejecting E *would not resolve the problem:* the naturalist has a defeater for all their beliefs, including E, so they reject E. Now what? They still have a defeater for all their other beliefs.

Churchland argues that Plantinga's scenario would not affect scientific beliefs such as E because such beliefs are not solely produced by our cognitive faculties. But the claim is not that our cognitive faculties are the only source of information, but that they are the source of *beliefs*—depictive mental representations. Our cognitive faculties are the gatekeeper through which information must go to be converted into a belief. Churchland tries to exclude scientific beliefs from these circumstances, but his attempt to do so can only get underway if R holds, which is precisely what the EAAN challenges. And ignoring that, recall Talbott's point that scientific inference requires "non-local evidence relations," but E could only select local evidence relations.[19] Even if scientific beliefs were immune to the EAAN, the naturalist would still face Talbott's defeater of scientific beliefs because N does not provide the necessary connection between local and non-local evidence relations.

If N is true, the naturalist has a reason to reject E: their cognitive faculties would be unreliable, so their belief in E would not be reliably produced. On the other hand, if our belief in E is veracious, then our cognitive faculties *are* reliable in producing this belief, and if our cognitive faculties are reliable it means N is not true. Either naturalism is true or evolution is true. Not both.

So, belief in N defeats every other belief, including E. But obviously it would defeat belief in N too, since it is just one more belief. If N entails that no belief is reliably produced, it would mean that belief in *N* is not reliably produced. And if not being reliably produced provides a defeater for a belief it means that belief in N provides a defeater for belief in N. Believing N gives one a reason for withholding belief in N. It defeats itself.

Loops and infinite regresses

Yet there is a problem looming. If we have a defeater for R we have a defeater for all our beliefs, and if we have a defeater for all our beliefs, we no longer have a reason for believing N. But then we no longer have a reason for believing we have a *defeater* for N either. The defeater undercuts all the naturalist's beliefs, *including belief in the defeater itself*. Surely this should make us skeptical of the argument.[20]

Plantinga originally proposed the EAAN as a diachronic Humean loop.[21] If someone accepts N, then they have a defeater for all their beliefs; thus they have a defeater for their belief in N; thus they have a defeater for the *defeater* for their belief in N, since that defeater is itself a belief and has been defeated; thus they no longer have a defeater for all their beliefs, including N; thus they accept N—and then they have a defeater for all their beliefs again, including N; and on it goes. This is not particular to the EAAN, it is the structure of many forms of global skepticism. The skeptical scenario is completely dependent on reason—it could only be valid if we accept reason's general reliability. But then the skepticism calls reason into question. There are plenty of cognitive faculties that are "non-separable" such as memory, perception, and rational inference:[22] any assessment of the reliability of these faculties could only get underway by using them and thus presupposing their reliability. So, Hume argues, we recognize the valid reasoning behind the skeptical argument, and thus reject reason; but having rejected reason, we can no longer accept reason's dictates to accept the skeptical conclusion, since that conclusion was reached, after all, by reasoning. So, we reject the skepticism and accept reason again, but once we do the reasoning for the skeptical conclusion immediately comes back into play, and so forth.[23] The presupposition of the reliability of one's reasoning faculties and the conclusion denying that reliability does not mean that the argument is contradictory but that the skepticism is unstable. The only way to stop the loop is to not start it in the first place by rejecting what leads to it, which, in our case, is N. "The point remains, therefore: one who accepts N&E (and is apprised of the present argument) has a defeater for N&E, a defeater that cannot be defeated by an ultimately undefeated defeater. And isn't it irrational to accept a belief for which you know you have an ultimately undefeated defeater?"[24]

However, if we are wavering back and forth between N&E being defeated and then not being defeated, this would constitute an ultimately *unresolved* defeater, not an ultimately *undefeated* defeater. We are alternately presented with a defeater for N&E and then a defeater for the defeater. This takes away the defeater, so N&E can be believed again, whereupon we immediately obtain a defeater for N&E again. At no point in the loop is there an undefeated defeater for N&E. In the same way, someone who takes the drug XX has a defeater for R and for every other belief they have—including their beliefs that they took XX and that XX causes most people's cognitive faculties to become unreliable. But if they have a defeater for *those* beliefs, they no longer have a defeater for R. They can trust their cognitive faculties again. But then their cognitive faculties tell them that they took XX and that XX has its deleterious effects, so they have a defeater for R again, etc. I leave it as an exercise for the reader to apply this to the evil demon and brain-in-a-vat forms of skepticism.

Peressini notes this and asks why the naturalist should focus on the step where N&E obtains a defeater. Why can't they focus on the step where the defeater-defeater allows them to accept N&E again? Certainly, one could be a pessimist and focus on the fact that N&E cannot be accepted without also acquiring a defeater for it, but one could be an optimist instead and focus on the fact that there is no undefeated defeater of N&E. What we have here is "two mutually contradictory (contrary) claims," and any reason for choosing one over the other is arbitrary. He compares it to the problem of counting to infinity, given an infinite amount of time.

> Could I count to infinity if I were to live indefinitely? On one hand we might answer in the affirmative, since for any natural number you can name there will be a time at which I count it; but on the other hand we might be inclined to deny this, because there is no time at which all the (natural) numbers have been counted. The problem is the same: we have no clear, non-arbitrary way to decide between two contrary but well-supported answers to the question.[25]

But Peressini has not avoided the problem. The Humean loop is not simply an indefinite continuation, it is an indefinite *circular* continuation. As Troy Nunley points out, the appropriate parallel is not whether someone who were to live indefinitely could count to infinity but whether someone who were to live indefinitely could count to infinity *if they restarted whenever they reached the number two*.[26] Therefore, the Humean loop is an ultimately unresolved defeater, since one can see it is an irresoluble scenario involving defeat. When we see an irresoluble scenario like this, the rational response is to avoid it and deny whatever leads to it.

Moreover, in response to this objection, Plantinga reformulates the nature of the defeater. Rather than seeing it function diachronically as a Humean loop, he sees it synchronically as an infinite regress. The naturalist who realizes they have a defeater for R will then believe ~R at level 0. But on level 1 they realize that ~R defeats all their beliefs, including ~R itself; it is a defeater-defeater. Therefore, they believe ~~R. However, we can't stop here: the defeater for all their beliefs on level 1 is ~R, and the claim here is that it defeats itself, namely their belief ~R. But it does not *only* defeat itself; ~R *also defeats* R. Since any belief B is defeated by its negation ~B, R is defeated by ~R.

This may seem obvious, but part of John Pollock's original definition of defeaters is that the defeater must be logically compatible with what it defeats.[27] If it were not then we would just be left with two contradictory premises but no clue which one we should accept. We could just reject the defeater and continue believing the belief, thereby retaining rationality since we no longer accept two premises that are logically incompatible.

So, in saying that ~R defeats R I seem to be going against this. Obviously, R and ~R are logically incompatible. But two issues serve to resolve any difficulty. First, the

EAAN is dealing with internal rationality not external rationality. This means that the question being asked is whether a defeater can do its work *given* that an individual accepts it. Second, when we are dealing with self-defeat, there is no question of whether one can reject the defeater and continue believing what it would defeat, since the defeater and what it defeats *are the same thing*.[28]

We are justified, therefore, in saying that, while ~R defeats ~R (it is self-defeating), ~R also defeats R. So again, on level 0, the naturalist has a defeater for their belief R and accepts ~R. On level 1, ~R defeats level 0 (~R) so they believe its negation: ~~R, which is just R. But ~R also defeats R, so they *also* believe its negation on level 1: ~R. In other words, on level 1, they accept both R and ~R. On level 2 ~R defeats level 1 (~~R) and so they believe its negation: ~~~R (or ~R). But again, ~R still defeats R, so they also believe ~R via a less circuitous route. So, on level 2 they believe ~R and ~~~R. Etc. Plantinga formulates it as follows, where ~R(p) means that the proposition of level p is defeated:

level 0: ~R
level 1: ~R and ~R(0) (i.e., ~R(~R)) (which is a potential defeater for level 0, i.e., ~R)
level 2: ~R and ~R(1) (which is a potential defeater for level 1 and a potential defeater-defeater for level 0)
level 3: ~R and ~R(2) (which is a potential defeater for level 2 and a potential (defeater-defeater)-defeater for level 0)
...
level n: ~R and ~R(n-1) (which is a potential defeater for level n-1)[29]

The point being that, unlike other cases of defeater-defeaters, *~R is present at each level*.

> This is extraordinary: in the more usual case, if one acquires a defeater-defeater for a belief B, that is, a defeater for a defeater of B, one no longer has that defeater for B—or else its defeating power is neutralized. But not so here. The difference is that here the original defeatee shows up at every subsequent level. When that happens—when, roughly speaking, every potential defeater in the series is really the potential defeatee plus a bit—the defeater-defeater doesn't nullify the defeater. The defeater gets defeated, all right, but the defeatee remains defeated too, as will happen whenever a defeater is a universal defeater. Accordingly, any time at which the skeptic believes ~R, he has a defeater for ~R, even if he also has, at that time, a defeater for that defeater. Skepticism of this kind, then, really is self-defeating, even if it is also the case that the skeptic has a defeater for his defeater.[30]

Therefore, Peressini's objection does not obviate the EAAN and Plantinga's third premise is established. The naturalist who realizes P(R/N&E) is low acquires a defeater for R, and so acquires a defeater for every one of their beliefs including N&E itself. The defeater can be taken as a Humean loop and an ultimately unresolved defeater, or as an infinite regress and an ultimately undefeated defeater

The story so far

Let's run over how far we've come with the EAAN.

(1) P(R/N&E) is low.

In order to avoid this, a belief would have to cause action by virtue of its propositional content not by virtue of its material or physical properties, as naturalism claims. To get the necessary connection, we would have to solve the mind-body problem. In fact, we would have to do more, since having a connection between belief content and action would not help the naturalist unless the beliefs in question were a) true and b) relevant.

Of course, N could allow for our indicators to be accurate but not for our depictors to be true and relevant. We naturally tend to think that if a depictor arose it would depict what its associated indicator indicates. But if N is true, there would be no control on what a depictor would depict. If content somehow arose, it could depict anything. So, the probability that the preponderance of beliefs are true, given N, is low.

All of this was argued with respect to the hypothetical population that evolved by naturalistic processes and is relevantly like us in that they have beliefs with propositional content. Plantinga never specifies when we should switch from them to us; it seems to me we can do so at any point from the end of the first premise to the conclusion.

(2) Anyone who accepts (believes) N&E and sees that P(R/N&E) is low has a defeater for R.

This is because we are conditionalizing the probability on only R, N, E, and, as Otte points out, EXP, the experience that our beliefs (or the hypothetical population's) seem relatively coherent and not haphazard or chaotic—again, not that they *are* coherent, just that they *seem* to be.[31] Attempts to add other elements in order to avoid the defeater would be applicable to virtually any defeater. Since some beliefs are occasionally defeated, such moves are invalid.

Plantinga argues for the second premise by appealing to numerous analogies, such as the person who takes XX. These analogies show that if a source of information is unreliable, then we have a reason to withhold belief in any belief we think is exclusively produced by this source.[32] Couldn't someone find another source after the fact though? Can't we follow Wittgenstein and throw away the ladder once we have climbed it?[33] Not in this case: any alternative source for verifying the reliability of our cognitive faculties must go through the gatekeeper of our cognitive faculties, and this is what the EAAN has called into question. Therefore, the low probability of R/N&E provides a defeater for R.

(3) Anyone who has a defeater for R has a defeater for any other belief she thinks she has, including N&E itself.

Since all our beliefs are produced by our cognitive faculties, and since belief in N defeats our cognitive faculties' reliability, the naturalist cannot treat their cognitive faculties as a reliable source. Any attempt to find another source for our beliefs cannot succeed, since this other source must proceed via our cognitive faculties. So, the naturalist has a defeater for virtually every belief they hold, and this includes N&E. So, N defeats R, and in so doing defeats E as well as N. To reiterate, E (evolution) is not the target of Plantinga's argument, N (naturalism) is.

Fourth premise and conclusion

(4) If one who accepts N&E thereby acquires a defeater for N&E, N&E is self-defeating and can't rationally be accepted.[34]

This premise can be subdivided into several: a) a belief that provides a defeater for itself is self-defeating. This is just the definition of self-defeat. b) N&E provides a defeater for itself. This follows from the previous premises. c) Therefore, N&E is self-defeating. This follows from a) and b). Finally, d) self-defeating beliefs can't rationally be accepted. Plantinga does not argue this, he simply presents it, but it's pretty easy to defend: if belief in N&E gives one a reason to withhold belief in N&E, continuing to belief N&E would either involve believing it and simultaneously not believing it or believing it and simultaneously recognizing that one has a reason to not believe it and can have no reason to believe it. (In the latter case, the naturalist avoids drawing the conclusion and does not withhold belief in N&E.) Regardless, in either case, continued belief in N&E is irrational by every definition of rationality there is. One cannot rationally believe a proposition while simultaneously believing its denial or while simultaneously recognizing that one has an undefeatable defeater for it. Since N&E is self-defeating and self-defeating beliefs can't rationally be accepted, we are led to the end of the argument:

N&E can't rationally be accepted.[35]
Quod erat arguendum.

Part Four

Objections

10

Analogies, Coherence, and Evolution

Nothing will ever be attempted if all possible objections must be first overcome.
Samuel Johnson

Many objections to the EAAN have been dealt with in our treatment of the argument itself. Nevertheless, plenty remain and some of those brought up only received a cursory response. In the remainder of this book, we will look at the many and varied objections to the EAAN and the vistas they open.

There's something about analogies

On general principles

We have seen some critics object to using analogies, such as analogies where a low probability of R generates a defeater of R. *Sometimes* low probabilities have this effect, but often they do not. Plantinga's analogies are cases where they do, but what is it about them that makes them so? What is the difference between scenarios where a low probability defeats a belief and those where it does not, and which is more like the EAAN? What these critics are pushing for is a general principle of when defeat occurs.[1] Plantinga declines the challenge: "I don't know of any general principle here that will do the job. (Finding such general principles is always a pretty tall order.) But why would I need such a principle? Indeed, wouldn't the right procedure for here be broadly inductive; shouldn't we, at least in this specific sort of case, follow Chisholm, in being particularists?"[2] So, arguing by analogy is perfectly appropriate if the analogies in question are sufficiently similar to the naturalist's position and clearly lead to defeat. He is willing to provide the rough-and-ready formula these analogies illustrate: "In general, if you have considered the question whether a given source of information or belief is reliable, and have an undefeated defeater for the belief that it is, then you have a defeater for any belief such that you think it originates (solely) from that source."[3] But he is unwilling to develop this into a general principle, instead letting the analogies do the dirty work.

There is a good reason to argue via analogies rather than a general principle. As J.R. Lucas writes, potential explanations must meet a logical requirement, but only in a weak sense, not in the strong sense of instantiating a general principle.

All that rationality, claimed by the use of the word 'because', requires is a weak principle of universalizability, not the strong. That is, if I offer an explanation to a questioner, and he produces a *prima facie* parallel case for which the explanation will not work, I must be able to show what the difference between the two cases is: but I do not have to be able to specify exactly in advance the features of the event to be explained and the proffered cause, and an exactly specified universal hypothetical statement connecting them.[4]

What does this mean for the EAAN? The naturalist is offering an explanation (namely, naturalism), and Plantinga is providing *prima facie* parallel cases (his analogies) for which the explanation will not work. In these parallel cases, the low probability of a source of information's reliability leads to its defeat, and thereby the defeat of all beliefs solely produced by that source. Insofar as they really parallel the naturalist's situation, they serve to establish the second and third premises of the EAAN: that anyone who believes N&E and sees that P(R/N&E) is low has a defeater for R, and therefore for all their beliefs including N&E.

So Plantinga is well within his epistemic rights to argue by analogies rather than a general principle of when defeat occurs.[5] Note too how well this harmonizes with his epistemological method: rather than specifying beforehand what conditions must be met for beliefs to qualify as knowledge, we grant that we know many things and reverse engineer it to see what must be the case for this to be true. Similarly, we don't need to specify in advance what conditions must be met for something to be defeated (by positing a general principle), and so fail to qualify as knowledge. We look at cases where beliefs are clearly defeated, and if they are like the naturalist's situation, the EAAN is successful.

Certainly, it would be nice to have a general principle of when defeat occurs, so philosophers who request one are sympathetic figures. Jonathan Kvanvig, for example, sees Plantinga's account as "The best-developed account of a back-door theory" of defeat (or propositionalism), but what is needed for a full epistemology is a front-door account (or doxasticism).[6] Michael Rea proposes a general principle, but pulls his punches acknowledging that it makes an assumption that "no doubt ... is false; but making it will simplify the following discussion without substantially affecting the argument or its conclusion."[7] Similarly, Otte reformulates the EAAN to not require Plantinga's unusual analogies of a hypothetical population believing everything is a witch.[8] Unfortunately, by requesting a principle of defeat, they are also requesting a principle of knowledge, which places the doubting of R before any probability conditionalization—they must *begin* by looking for evidence to establish R. This is problematic. Applying this to the red widgets example means we should doubt whether they are red and look for evidence one way or the other before we are told that they are irradiated by a red light. *We should doubt they are red before having any reason to doubt it.* This transforms the EAAN into a standard global skeptical argument, such as Descartes's evil demon, where we should doubt everything until we get to some bedrock-level belief that is indubitable. This problem touches all attempts to formulate a general principle of defeat.

Regardless, Plantinga's analogies are sufficient to make his case, and in fact he does go further by giving the rough-and-ready formula that when a source of belief is found to be unreliable, this defeats any belief based solely on that source. He even goes further than this, suggesting some traits a general principle should have:

> If a principle is wanted, I'd suggest starting with something pretty limited, something about beliefs specifying the origin and provenance of cognitive faculties. The antecedent of such a principle would capture what is in common to situations in which (a) I believe that I have taken XX, or am a brain in a vat, or a victim of a Cartesian evil genius, and (b) I also believe that the probability of R on the condition in question is low or inscrutable; the consequent would say that in those situations I have a Humean rationality defeater for R. And the claim would be that the antecedent of such a principle applies to the naturalist who accepts the Probability Thesis.[9]

Are the analogies analogous?

Instead of objecting to Plantinga's use of analogies in general, some object to the specific analogies, arguing they are not analogous to the naturalist's situation. O'Connor, for example, argues that in the red widget case the person recognizes an "inconsistency of output," where their senses tell them one thing, and an authority tells them something else.[10] The problem is not one of a belief-forming mechanism, it is a problem with the external world such that the relevant belief-forming mechanisms are inapplicable. He argues that the wish-fulfillment case is dissimilar as well: we think wish-fulfillment is unreliable because it has been shown to be unreliable by other sources. But this is not the case for R. Therefore, in both cases, Plantinga's analogies do not parallel the naturalist's situation.

The response here is the same as before: the analogies are not comparing *why* someone initially trusted a source and no longer does, only *that* someone trusted a source and no longer does. The reasons for accepting and then rejecting the source are irrelevant. So, yes, the analogies are not as analogous as O'Connor wants them to be, but that does not detract from the argument at all. All they are doing is illustrating the rough-and-ready formula where someone has a belief B produced by source S, and then comes to believe that S is unreliable. The person thus obtains a defeater for any belief entirely produced by S, including B.

Moreover, O'Connor's response to the red widget scenario implies the person has direct evidence against (a rebutting defeater for) their belief that the widgets are red, another disanalogy.[11] But this is incorrect. The individual does not have a reason for thinking the widgets are *not* red, they merely no longer have a reason for thinking they *are*. They could still be red, but their reason for thinking so is obviated. This is not a rebutting defeater it is an undercutting defeater, and thus is analogous to the naturalist's situation.

While O'Conner attacks the analogies addressing the second and third premises, Erik Wielenberg attacks the analogy addressing the first, namely the hypothetical population.[12] He argues that to make this scenario parallel to our own we would have to add that the hypothetical population *know* that their cognitive faculties are reliable.

But then we would think the probability of most of their beliefs being true would be high rather than low.

However, the reason why the naturalist has knowledge before being apprised of the EAAN is that they have no defeater for their beliefs. When we add that element to the hypothetical population—that they initially have no defeater for their beliefs—it doesn't mean that they cannot ever obtain such a defeater. Perhaps the claim is that if either we or the hypothetical population *know* that our (or their) cognitive faculties are reliable, then it entails that whatever metaphysical conditions are necessary for knowledge have been met, and this raises the probability that these metaphysical conditions have been met to certainty. But this leads to the same problem as the "add a bit" strategy: if we're just allowed to assert that our cognitive faculties, or the hypothetical population's, are reliable, then this strategy could be used to deflect any defeater whatsoever. It would preclude the possibility of any belief ever being defeated. Since some beliefs are and can be defeated, this option is unacceptable.

Are there better analogies?

Talbott has presented a close analogy he thinks does not lead one to affirm ~R.[13] Instead of the drug XX, he suggests the drug ZZ which is present in every fetus and makes it probable they will not generate reliable cognitive faculties. However, there is also an antidote given to every fetus before it's born which renders these deleterious consequences ineffective. On his twentieth birthday, a man learns about ZZ but argues that since his cognitive faculties seem reliable and he has the memory of living a moderately coherent life, he should conclude that, despite ZZ, something prevented it from taking effect. Later he learns there was an antidote administered to everyone so that the deleterious effects of ZZ never took place.

But again, if ZZ defeats R, the man cannot use his memories and ability to evaluate his cognitive faculties' reliability because their reliability is challenged once R is. Recall that the question isn't whether we can *actually* give up belief in R but whether R is defeated. Recall also that Talbott wants to withhold some cognitive faculties from the effects of the EAAN because, he argues, to call *all* our cognitive faculties into question is more ad hoc than one particular faculty. But this doesn't stop the argument from applying to all cognitive faculties. Again: the condition that prevents a faculty from being reliable is N, and it does so intrinsically. In fact, the ZZ analogy (sans the antidote) is similar to the evil demon scenario. I disagree it is more ad hoc to call all our cognitive faculties into question, but even if it were, an evil demon that only renders an aspect of one's cognitive faculties suspect—say, the ability to reliably form metaphysical beliefs—rather than all of them, would not prevent the traditional argument from working because the reason why one faculty is unreliable (the evil demon's machinations) would also be a reason why every *other* faculty is unreliable. In fact, applying the evil demon thesis to one faculty and not others is more ad hoc and contrived.

Interestingly, Talbott proposes another analogy: the *malicious* demon. Here, it is exactly the same as the evil demon, but includes the detail that the demon lets his victim know that he is in control of his faculties and demonstrates it.[14] In this case, Talbott thinks the person *would* conclude that his cognitive faculties are not reliable.

But this still seems very close to the ZZ analogy *sans* antidote: a person has a reason to accept ~R and no reason to counter it, since any such reason would only have force if ~R were false. So, I don't think the malicious demon scenario is sufficiently different from that of ZZ. In both cases, one has a strong reason to think their cognitive faculties are not reliable, and this reason prevents any other reason from counteracting it. The difference is that in one case we have a non-intentional cause (ZZ) rendering our cognitive faculties unreliable while in the other we have an intentional agent doing so—and the former case, the one which Talbott thinks would not produce a defeater, is the stricter analogue to the naturalist's situation. However, I think one *does* have a defeater for R in the ZZ case and thus in the N case as well. The difference between ZZ and the malicious demon, at best, would be the psychological effect of whether someone is really able to hold before their mind, constantly and consistently, the idea that their cognitive faculties are unreliable. Plantinga thinks a person in either situation would still believe R because they just could not help it, whereas Talbott thinks they would continue believing R in the ZZ case but not in the malicious demon case.[15] But this does nothing to blunt the defeater for R given ZZ.

Do the analogies prove anything?

Trenton Merricks accepts the analogies as valid to a point but suggests nothing follows from them. He alters the evil demon scenario so that it is only very probable the demon wants to deceive us. He counters that if you believe this of someone else, but then see them functioning well—indeed of evincing no apparent cognitive dysfunction whatsoever—you would conclude they somehow beat the odds. And if the charge is we are *all* under the revised demon hypothesis, you would conclude that, since others seem to have reliable cognitive faculties, so must you. Similarly, even if Plantinga's analogies are valid, we can conclude, after observing others, that R *does* hold for them, and that we therefore must have beaten the odds.

Merricks thinks the hypothetical population analogy is misleading, since we do not think R has warrant for them initially, while in our own case we do. But again, we can grant that their beliefs have no defeaters initially and are thus warranted. And if the claim is that if their beliefs have warrant then the metaphysical conditions necessary for warrant must have been met, this just falls into the "add a bit" strategy which could be used to deflect any defeater whatsoever. Or perhaps he thinks a belief that is properly basic, and thus initially warranted, is not defeatable by evidentiary concerns.[16] But in Plantinga's epistemology properly basic beliefs *are* potentially defeatable: it is a fallibilist foundationalist theory of knowledge.

Merricks objects to the claim that, "If P(R specified to someone else/revised demon hypothesis) is low or inscrutable, then one who believes the revised demon hypothesis about someone else has a defeater for R specified to that other person."[17] In a sense, this is suggesting the hypothetical population is not sufficiently analogous, but the disanalogy is simply the move from the third-person perspective to the first-person perspective.[18] As such, we cannot apply any conclusions we draw regarding the hypothetical population to ourselves, and can never conclude that our cognitive faculties are unreliable just because theirs would be.

If we apply this standard, however, it would undermine the entire scientific enterprise. Contemporary science describes phenomena from a third-person objective perspective rather than a first-person subjective perspective, at least partially because subjective impressions are not as easily falsifiable. Obviously, science is much more complex than this; my point is merely that if we are not allowed to apply conclusions made from a third-person perspective to ourselves it would subvert the whole scientific approach.

In Merricks's revised evil demon hypothesis we can objectively investigate whether another person is manifesting indications of cognitive dysfunction. This other person can be taken as a member of Plantinga's hypothetical population, substituting the evil demon for naturalistic evolution. We would conclude it is improbable their cognitive faculties are reliable, but since the hypothetical population shows no sign of cognitive malfunction as they go about surviving, procreating, and whatever else there may be to life (I forget now), we would conclude that they must have beat the odds. And we can analyze this from a third-person perspective because we are not positing that *we* are also under the domination of the evil demon. All this would show, though, is that they have reliable *indicators* not reliable *depictors*. They are able to survive because their indicative representations are accurate; but their depictive representations, their *beliefs*, need not be true or relevant—and the idea that true depictors and accurate indicators just naturally correlate is as plausible as the specific words a singer sings (like "break" or "shatter") naturally correlating with her voice's resonance frequency so that they shatter a wine glass.

Since we can only examine *external* signs as to whether the other person is experiencing cognitive dysfunction, we would have to presuppose that the content of belief causes behavior, and this is enormously improbable under naturalism. So, the other person showing no external signs of cognitive dysfunction would not justify us in believing that R holds for them. We can even offer a revised-revised evil demon hypothesis where the evil demon only renders the cognitive faculties of 95 percent of us unreliable, and then tells us that we are in the charmed 5 percent. Would you trust the evil demon? Even if we assume that we are not under the influence of this demon, and so can rely on R holding for *us*, it doesn't mean that we can extrapolate from other people's outward behavior that their beliefs are true and relevant.

Plantinga's first analogy of the hypothetical population is from a third-person perspective. Since it is from this perspective, there will obviously be some differences between it and a first-person perspective. But we can just specify that R is properly basic or initially warranted for the hypothetical population—they are supposed to be relevantly like us, after all. But properly basic beliefs can still be defeated, even by non-properly basic beliefs.[19] They are innocent until proven guilty, and we can say the hypothetical population's belief in their own rationality is properly basic for them, even though it may not be properly basic for us as we hypothesize them. When we turn from them to ourselves, our belief in R is properly basic and this means it is pragmatically necessary to believe it, we can't really make ourselves withhold belief in R. But none of this means R can't be defeated.

It seems Merricks is arguing that when we apply the EAAN to someone else (third-person perspective), we see it is not the same as applying it to ourselves (first-person), so saying R may not hold for them does not say whether it would hold for us. But then he argues that if they show no external sign of cognitive dysfunction, we can assume their depictors line up with their indicators just as we assume ours do. So, he excludes the third-person perspective from the consequences of the EAAN by assuming whatever holds from the first-person holds for the third, and then uses that to argue that this would hold of the first-person as well. This is obviously a circular argument; in fact, it's strikingly similar to the Cartesian Circle. Regardless, Plantinga's second set of analogies, such as the drug XX, are from a first-person perspective and cover Merricks's objections.

Van Cleve and Reiter argue that if the hypothetical population is not warranted in their belief in R, then they could have no propositional knowledge whatsoever. Any proposition, having been produced by their cognitive faculties, would have an undefeated defeater. But then it would follow that neither they nor the naturalist can know anything, including rudimentary beliefs like 2 + 3 = 5. Something must be wrong with the argument if it leads to such absurd conclusions, even if the analogies hold.[20]

This is a reductio ad absurdum: if N is true, then the naturalist does not know anything. Plantinga, it seems, endorses this, since the point of the EAAN is that the naturalist cannot know N is true because they cannot know *anything* is true. Note that the claim is not that the naturalist's beliefs are *false* but that they no longer qualify as knowledge, and that they cannot rationally believe them anymore once they are apprised of the EAAN: "many who don't believe in God know much. But that is only because they don't accurately think through the consequences of this rejection. Once they do, they will lose their knowledge; here, therefore, is another of those cases where, by learning more, one comes to know less."[21]

It is certainly counterintuitive to claim naturalists do not even know elementary truths like 2 + 3 = 5. The naturalist and the supernaturalist have access to the same information, and go through the same cognitive processes in forming and maintaining this belief, so how could one be defeated and fail to be knowledge, while the other is undefeated and known? The answer is because the EAAN is operating in *internal rationality*. The claim is that the naturalist has other beliefs that affect their claims to knowledge. If I believed, "No belief is rational, no, not one," this would give me a reason to think any belief I had—including "2 + 3 = 5" and "No belief is rational"—is not rational. Someone who didn't believe that no belief is rational would not have a problem. I must either reject that belief or embrace the irrationality. If the EAAN is successful, belief in naturalism has the same consequences, but not as obviously.

Coherence

Another analogy of Plantinga's raises different issues, although I have not seen anyone make the point. He imagines a space explorer being the first human being to land on a planet. To his amazement, he discovers an artifact that speaks in English, giving current weather conditions on Earth. However, Plantinga argues, since the explorer has no knowledge of what the machine's purpose is, he has no reason to think that what appear to be English descriptions are not some alien language saying something else.

But we *do* have a reason for thinking the artifact is designed to report (truly or falsely) weather conditions in English: the fact that its output coheres with the English language system. How likely is it that there is another language exactly like English but the sentences mean something totally different and yet perfectly meaningful?[22]

Essentially, this is an appeal to coherence, where a belief's intelligibility, plausibility, rationality, or truth comes from its connections to other beliefs in our noetic net. An example often given is that of someone doing a jigsaw puzzle with all the pieces turned over. If, when finished, they turn the puzzle over and see that it makes a beautiful picture, it would be strange to say this does not count as some sort of evidence or reason to think the pieces are put in the right place.

One does not have to adopt anything like a full-blown coherentist epistemology or theory of truth to see that coherence can count as evidence, at least in some cases. In presenting her foundherentist theory of knowledge,[23] Susan Haack compares it to a crossword puzzle: certainly the clues for 23-across play a large role in determining what the word is, but the letters already in place from 17- and 21-down are surely relevant in deciding whether a potential word is correct. The word for 23-across must *cohere* with the words from 17- and 21-down if we expect to solve the puzzle. Remember how Dennett lists himself, Quine, Putnam, Shoemaker, and Davidson as among those who find it obvious that any coherent and expansive system of beliefs must be composed of true beliefs for the most part.[24] Even Descartes, that arch-foundationalist, gives a nod to coherence:

> You are trying to read a document written in Latin but encoded; you guess that every "a" should be a "b", every "b" a "c", and so on through the alphabet, and when you decode the document on that basis it makes good sense. You won't doubt that you have detected the code and understood the letter—you'll be morally certain of that. But it is possible that you are wrong, and that the document involves some other code and means something different from what your decoding made it mean. *Possible*, but hardly *credible*—especially if the document is long.[25]

But doesn't this rebut Plantinga's analogy, and thus the EAAN? If we encounter an alien device seeming to communicate propositions in English, it would be "possible, but hardly credible" to think it was actually saying something different in an alien language. We would not have to know the device's provenance or purpose in order to recognize that what it seems to be claiming is what it is actually claiming.[26] Similarly, our webs of belief are, by and large, coherent, as well as expansive. Since a lengthy, coherent system gives Descartes a reason to think a system is relaying what it seems to be relaying, so the expansiveness and coherence of our systems of beliefs give us a reason to make the same inference. Notice though that this does not entail that the claims of Descartes's encoded letter or Plantinga's alien artifact are *true*, just that what they seem to be claiming is probably what they are actually claiming. The constructors of the artifact could have made it to relay falsehoods, after all.

But the response has already been given. This would only apply to our depictors and we have no guarantee they will be true and relevant. At most, we have to add EXP to the equation P(R/N&E), which only refers to our experience of our cognitive faculties' apparent reliability, not their actual reliability—and this does not raise the probability up for the naturalist to avoid the EAAN.

Principles of rationality and omniscient interpreters

We can explore this by considering the views of Donald Davidson, who makes up part of Dennett's pro-true-belief coterie. Davidson argues that to understand an agent we have to understand their acts; and to understand their acts, we must presuppose they understand their environment the same way we do: "belief is in its nature veridical."[27] J. Wesley Robbins thinks this rebuts the EAAN,[28] since "the content of a belief is not so far removed from the means by which we come to ascribe beliefs to other epistemic agents in our environment.... Whatever propositional content the mental state of an agent has, we simply ascribe this to an agent in the course of making sense of their transactions with the external world."[29] Therefore, the very concept of belief entails that an agent must have mostly true beliefs, and it is impossible for an agent to have mostly false beliefs. We must assess others via "principles of humanity" or "principles of rationality": to have knowledge of other people, we must make assumptions about them. Davidson demonstrates this by positing a hypothetical omniscient interpreter who understands our acts perfectly. For this to be possible, the omniscient interpreter must presuppose most of our beliefs are correct; and since this interpreter is omniscient, this presupposition must be correct.[30]

There are several problems with this: for example, it overlooks the possibility that we all share the same misunderstandings of our environment, that we all think incorrectly in the same way. But most importantly, Plantinga had already dealt with Davidson's claims, as had Richards Foley and Fumerton.[31] Ultimately, Davidson has not shown there cannot be creatures with mostly false beliefs, just that we could not *understand* creatures that held mostly false beliefs (although this is arguable). But that doesn't mean they could not exist—"and a fortiori it doesn't follow that my own beliefs are mainly true."[32] Davidson and Robbins assume that since a person's behavior shows they have reliable indicators, they must also have most true depictors. Of course, we *do* assume this and we're right to do so, but N gives us a reason to think otherwise.

Davidson posits his hypothetical omniscient interpreter to bridge the gap between creatures with mostly false beliefs being unintelligible to us to their being ontologically impossible. But this assumes an omniscient interpreter could only understand other persons by interpreting their actions. An omniscient interpreter, however, would not *need* to interpret because it would already know all true propositions. It would not have to deduce items of knowledge about other persons since it would already know them.

Moreover, Davidson seems to argue from (1) "If there were an omniscient interpreter using Davidson's methods of interpretation, he would believe that most of what S believes is true," to (2) "Most of what S believes is true." But this is only if there were such an omniscient being. If there is not—if N is correct—there is no such interpreter, and no reason to accept (2). Foley and Fumerton think Davidson is relying on another premise, (3) that if an omniscient being *would* believe a proposition, that proposition must be true.[33]

They then point out that (3) is surely true if indeed there *is* an omniscient being, but need not be true if there isn't. Here they are right. Indeed, more can be said; as they point out, (3) is *necessary* for the proposition that there is an omniscient being, but in fact it is also *sufficient*. Clearly (and necessarily) one proposition any omniscient being worth its salt would believe is that there is an omniscient being. Hence Davidson's premises for his conclusion that most human beliefs are true also entail, as an unexpected bonus, that there is an omniscient being. This conclusion won't much disturb a theist, but there will be those (and possibly Davidson is among them) who may find it unsettling.[34]

So even if Davidson's scenario allowed us to reject the EAAN, which it doesn't, it could only do so by presupposing that God exists and thus that N is false.

Evolutionary concerns

Evolution and Plantinga's first EAAN

The issue of coherence is behind the objections to Plantinga's initial version of the EAAN. He had proposed a scenario where any belief could be false, since evolution would only select for behavior rather than belief content, and he illustrates this with, for example, a hominid who runs away from a bear because he thinks it signals the start of a ten-kilometer race. But this strategy doesn't let us challenge *most* of the hominid's beliefs. Evan Fales challenges Plantinga "or anyone else" who thinks this scenario is plausible to provide a more comprehensive account.

> Construct *in detail* an account according to which a monkey, presented, say, with a fruit-bearing tree, forms (obeying some information-processing algorithm, we must assume) a false belief (*which* false belief?) such that it meets the following conditions: (1) combined with other present false beliefs and/or destructive desires, it leads (with good probability) to felicitous action; (2) when combined on other occasions with yet *other* false beliefs/bad desires, it *still* is likely to produce correct action; and (3) if destructive desires are invoked, a plausible Darwinian story can be told about how they evolved from the action-guiding desires of the pre-rational ancestors of the monkey, or in some other way. Now construct a system of algorithms that will achieve this for the monkey's beliefs generally. I say it can't be done.[35]

The challenge is to construct a coherent and expansive system of mostly false beliefs in ad hoc fashion. Start with the hominid-bear scenario, add a bizarre belief or desire that would produce the correct survival behavior. Then the hominid encounters other dangers requiring a response, so add further bizarre beliefs or desires *that do not conflict with each other* and allow the hominid to survive. Continue this procedure until you have produced the hominid's lifelong itinerary of all the dangers it ever encounters. This may not be strictly impossible—perhaps someone could write a computer program to accomplish something like this³⁶—but it is certainly beyond our ken.

However, I don't think Plantinga has any obligation to construct a complete, detailed system like this for the first version of his argument to be acceptable, any more than an evolutionary biologist has to provide a complete, detailed system of how mutations and the struggle for survival led to complex, conscious life forms to evolve from simple, single-celled life forms in order for evolution to be acceptable. Each mutation would have to alter an organism's morphology in such a way that it does not hinder its ability to survive and procreate, and they all have to integrate with each other in such a way that extremely complicated and diverse organs and structures evolve. Biologists have not offered anything even approaching this, because (at least in part) it is such a gargantuan task. Yet the biologist does not have to "construct in detail" such an account before accepting Neo-Darwinism. In fact, Plantinga has less obligation to produce such a system than the biologist does, since he is just suggesting hypothetical possibilities while the biologist would be trying to construct an actual history that really took place.

Even ignoring all this, we can further point out that this objection only relates to the level of indicators, not of depictors. The difficulty in imagining an expansive, coherent system of false beliefs is in finding such a system that would not put the hominid's life in danger. But absent a naturalistic solution to the mind-body problem, a belief system does not have to be connected to the hominid's actions at all, much less connected so that beliefs cause action by virtue of their content.

Evolution and Plantinga's second EAAN

Even ignoring *this*, we can turn to Plantinga's second version of the EAAN to respond to Fales's challenge to "construct in detail" a scenario wherein our population of hominids form an expansive and coherent system of beliefs that are mostly false and which do not put them in harm's way. Plantinga responds by piggybacking on the system of beliefs we already have and adding a false belief at the definitional level that touches all other beliefs, such as that everything is a witch. So instead of thinking "that rock is smooth" they think "that witch-rock is smooth." Since there are no such things as witches, most or all their beliefs would be false.

William Ramsey responds that, in order to maintain this position, Plantinga must be assuming that "If you suffer from a deep misconception of some subject, then all (or most) of your beliefs about that subject are false," where "deep misconceptions" means "false beliefs about what might be considered essential or definitional properties, as opposed to merely contingent features."³⁷ This position, however, is inconsistent with externalism, the view that Ramsey holds and that Plantinga claims to, according to which "our concepts of natural objects ... are determined by the actual object of which they are a concept."³⁸

Plantinga counters that we can ascribe "witch-ness" to the hypothetical population's predicates instead of (or in addition to) their objects. "They think everything is a witch; perhaps, then, their analogue of property ascriptions involves ascribing certain sorts of *witches* (rather than properties). (One of these witches, for example, is such that, as *we* would put it, if a thing *has* it, then that thing is red.)"³⁹ The progression is: if we take the belief "that rock is smooth," the members of Plantinga's hypothetical population, thinking everything is a witch, believe "that witch-rock is smooth." Ramsey counters that such a "deep misconception" would only render this belief false if we abandon externalism, since the object, whatever one wants to call it, *is* smooth. Our conception of the rock and their conception of the witch-rock are both caused by an object in the external world, and it is *this* relationship that bestows truth upon the beliefs. Plantinga responds that they could refer to smoothness the same way:[40] "that witch-rock is witch-smooth." Then all their beliefs would be false since witches do not exist.

To avoid this, one must say the predicates are caused the same way the objects are: just as the rock causes us to form the conception of a rock and the hypothetical population to form the conception of a witch-rock, so its smoothness causes us to form the predicate "smooth" and the hypothetical population to form the predicate "witch-smooth." But then, Plantinga argues, *no one could ever hold a false belief*. If the objects *and* the predicates cause someone to hold the beliefs they do, they could never be wrong about anything, since any ascription of a predicate to an object would be covered by the relation between the predicate (smoothness in our example) and its object, and this is all that matters to an externalist.[41] Obviously this is unacceptable. People can disagree, and only one of them is right. For that matter, given the enormous complexity of our noetic faculties, someone could easily have incompatible beliefs without realizing they are incompatible.[42]

Evolutionary epistemology

One objection critics often raise is that evolution selects belief-forming processes, attributes, or strategies that produce survival-enhancing behavior, not individual beliefs. Beliefs are the *product* of such attributes. Evolution would only select the attributes, not the product—just as it selects opposing thumbs but not the products of manual labor.[43] Michael Ruse argues that basic logic and mathematics would be selected in the evolutionary struggle, simply because lacking them would not be survivable.

> A tiger is seen entering a cave that you and your family usually use for sleeping. No one has seen the tiger emerge. How else does one achieve a happy end to this story, other than by an application of those laws of logic that we try to uncover for our students in elementary logic classes? Analogously for mathematics. Two tigers were seen going into the cave. Only one came out. Is the cave now safe?[44]

Ruse is not referring to logical and mathematical *beliefs* but logical and mathematical *reasoning*. Certainly, such strategies could have associated beliefs—logical reasoning would be associated with beliefs about the laws of logic—but we cannot simply equate the two. One is a tool, the other is a description of the tool. He even argues that this would hold for less strict forms of reasoning, such as inference to the best explanation.

> One hominid arrives at the water-hole, finding tiger-like footprints at the edge, blood-stains on the ground, growls and snarls and shrieks in the nearby undergrowth, and no other animals in sight. She reasons: "Tigers! Beware!" And

she flees. The second hominid arrives at the water, notices all of the signs, but concludes that since all of the evidence is circumstantial nothing can be proven. "Tigers are just a theory, not a fact." He settles down for a good long drink. Which of these two hominids was your ancestor?[45]

Feng Ye, on the other hand, suggests evolution may directly select certain neural configurations by virtue of their inherent production of very simple beliefs about the environment but not complex, composite beliefs.[46] If beliefs are reducible to or supervenient on particular neural configurations, evolution could select a configuration, along with the belief associated with it, as long as it is simple enough and enhances the organism's survivability. What it comes down to is whether simple individual beliefs are more analogous to opposable thumbs (which evolution would select)[47] or the products that opposable thumbs make possible (which it would not).

There is a deep question here regarding evolutionary epistemology. As a descriptive account of our cognitive faculties and their origin, evolutionary epistemology falls squarely into the category of naturalized epistemology, although it predates Quine's theory.[48] It does not just seek to explain the origin of our cognitive mechanisms, it also recognizes a strong parallel between the evolutionary process and how we test our beliefs against one another. Scientific theories (and beliefs in general) can be seen in evolutionary terms, complete with the survival of the "fittest"—i.e., the better theories being accepted and the inferior theories being discarded.

Originally these two parts of evolutionary epistemology were treated as continuous with each another, the one being an extension of the other, although they have since been distinguished. Sometimes "evolutionary epistemology" is reserved for the application of evolution to the origin of our cognitive mechanisms, although some call it evolutionary epistemology of mechanisms (EEM) while applying it to our theories and beliefs and how they compete with one another for cognitive space is called evolutionary philosophy of science or evolutionary epistemology of theories (EET).[49] The latter applies Darwinian concepts such as "survival" and "propagation" analogically rather than literally (i.e. to a domain other than the biological).

There is a strong case that EEM and EET are not merely two sides of the same coin.[50] If so, the issue whether evolution would select particular beliefs seems to apply EEM to the categories of EET. According to EET, our beliefs (theories) compete for their own survival, not the survival of the organism. To say evolution directly selects beliefs says that some beliefs compete for the survival of the *organism*. Stephen Toulmin calls the idea that evolution would directly select beliefs Mach's fallacy, after Ernst Mach.[51]

So, since Plantinga appeals to the propositional content of beliefs, it looks like he may be committing Mach's fallacy: he is assuming that evolutionary forces would literally (not metaphorically) select particular beliefs. But even if we grant this on the level of very simple beliefs, it is absurd to suggest that my belief about what I had for lunch last Tuesday was selected for in my evolutionary forebears' struggle for survival. Evolution selects mechanisms that produce true beliefs, not beliefs themselves.

Fortunately, however, the EAAN makes no such claim, so it does not commit Mach's fallacy. If anything, it goes the other way: Plantinga places the evolutionary process a step even further removed from the content of beliefs since the mechanisms that would be selected in the struggle for survival would be *indicator*-producing mechanisms. Any depictors or depictor-producing mechanisms would not go through the evolutionary mill so as to make the mechanisms more conducive to survival, let alone so that they tend to produce true beliefs.

Probability and inscrutability

Some object that Plantinga's probability assessments are "extremely imprecise and poorly grounded,"[52] and all we can claim is P/R(N&E) is inscrutable, not improbable. For example, Alston suggests Plantinga has not sufficiently demonstrated the low probabilities he assigns to R/N&E because he used a parochial probability rather than a global probability.

> Suppose I ask, "If all you know about a woman is that her favorite novelist is Proust, what level of education would you suppose she has attained?" I am asking for the parochial probability of 'She has attained level n' on 'Her favorite novelist is Proust' (where the latter, of course, takes into account what Proust's novels are like). But when we make explicit probability judgments, they are almost always more global. Thus if we say something like "Given the meteorological conditions in the vicinity, the probability of rain in the next twenty-four hours is very high", we mean the basis to include not only the particular conditions in this vicinity now, but also some relevant body of general meteorological knowledge and hypotheses.[53]

Since Plantinga only provides parochial (i.e., local) probabilities in the EAAN, all we can claim is that R is inscrutable on N, not improbable.[54]

Plantinga responds that Alston has only looked at the probability of our beliefs being mostly true on N. He has not looked at the probability that our beliefs have no causal efficacy (~C) on our behavior on N. This latter probability is high: it is very likely, given N, that the contents of our beliefs would not influence our behavior by virtue of their content. When this is added to the equation, it allows Plantinga to proceed with his "low or inscrutable" formula.[55] Regardless, for both Plantinga and Alston, the EAAN is still successful: if a belief's truth is inscrutable, one has a reason to withhold belief in it, an undercutting, complete defeater for it. This would be the case for R, N, E, and N&E.

Fitelson and Sober argue that the EAAN assumes all possible variants were available to natural selection but evolution can only select among those variants with which it is presented. There is no reason to think Plantinga's examples of witch-rocks would have even been available to our evolutionary ancestors or those of the hypothetical population.

> Plantinga's mistake here is that he ignores the fact that the probability of a trait's evolving depends not just on its fitness, but on its *availability*. The reason zebras don't have machine guns with which to repel lion attacks is not that firing machine

guns would have been less adaptive than simply running away; the trait didn't evolve because it was not available as a variation on which selection could act ancestrally.... Plantinga, in effect assumes that natural selection acts on the set of *conceivable* variants. This it does not do; it acts on the set of *actual* variants.[56]

Therefore, we simply have no basis for assessing how likely false beliefs are, and this would hold for any population. This is an attempt to prevent the EAAN from getting started.

Similarly, Wielenberg argues we are simply ignorant of the original inputs, the specific mutations, that were present to our evolutionary ancestors. He adds that, additionally, we are ignorant of the specific mechanisms which weeded them out—not that we are ignorant of natural selection, but of the specific environmental conditions which selected one mutation over another in a particular circumstance.[57]

This objection, however, ignores the fact that Plantinga addresses this issue in his first presentation of the argument,[58] and quotes a passage from Stich to illustrate it which has a strikingly similar theme to Fitelson and Sober's.

Modern technology builds prosthetic limbs out of space age alloys and communications systems that transmit messages with the speed of light. It seems very likely indeed that certain organisms would have a real competitive edge if they were born with such limbs, or with nerves that conduct impulses at the speed of light. The fact that there are no such creatures surely does not indicate that the imagined changes would not enhance fitness. Rather, we can be pretty confident natural selection never had the chance to evaluate organisms that utilize such materials.[59]

Plantinga doesn't need to assume all possible variants were available, he only has to claim that false beliefs (or false belief forming mechanisms) are just as likely to be produced by the evolutionary process as true beliefs (or true belief forming mechanisms). The objection assumes that, since we are ignorant of the actual variants available to our evolutionary ancestors, the only way to fill in the blanks is by assuming *all* possible variants were. But all Plantinga has to say in response is that whenever a true belief is available, its denial, a false belief, is available as well.[60] Moreover, none of this addresses whether the beliefs that an organism produced by evolution has is likely to have any influence on its behavior; if so whether the beliefs are adaptive; if so whether the beliefs in question are true; if so whether the beliefs are relevant. Given N&E, all these steps are extremely improbable.

It's true, of course, that we are ignorant of the specific building blocks and processes available to our evolutionary ancestors. But N&E informs us of at least one relevant thing about them: the evolutionary processes would not have been directly aimed at producing cognitive faculties that yield mostly true beliefs. Surely this is germane. Under naturalism, the building blocks produced by the random variation of mutation would have no goal or design plan, either metaphorically or literally. As for natural selection, the only goal or design plan it can be said to have "is to get the body parts where they should be in order that the organism may survive" and procreate.[61] As long as this design plan is distinct from the design plan of producing true beliefs—and if I remember my undergraduate days correctly, the drive to procreate is not usually credited with seeing things as they truly are—then our beliefs do not have warrant and the EAAN comes into play.

At any rate, the most these points would prove is that we cannot assess the probabilities involved as low and so they must remain inscrutable. Other than Alston these critics believe that inscrutable probabilities are beyond our ken, and as such, no argument can be based off them. But, with certain qualifications I'll go over in chapter 12, this is false. To say a probability is inscrutable is to say that we have no basis for considering it probable ($> .5$) or improbable ($< .5$). However, this just leads us to neither believe nor disbelieve, but to *withhold* belief. Yes, we should be open to further information if it becomes available and revise our probability assessments appropriately, but the question is, in the *absence* of further information, how should we proceed? And the answer is, by withholding belief. Admittedly, this is the same procedure if one thinks one *can* assign a specific probability, namely .5, but so what? The *reason* for withholding belief may differ, but the fact of withholding belief does not. And to withhold belief in a proposition is a form of not believing it (disbelieving it, actively thinking it is false, is another form). Once again, if we assess P/R(N&E) as inscrutable, we have an undercutting, believed, *complete* defeater for R, and that is all that is necessary for the EAAN to proceed.

11

Expanding the Target

There is no philosophy without the art of ignoring objections.
Joseph-Marie de Maistre

One interesting type of objection suggests that, despite having a defeater for R, the naturalist can rationally continue believing N because the alternative is worse. One example comes from Nathan: he argues we generally cannot choose our beliefs—I cannot just decide to believe I had a bowl of corn flakes for breakfast this morning—so the naturalist cannot give up their belief in N. If they believe N, then to reject it would be to reject something they believe is true. This is an incoherent scenario; "to hold that one's opinion is false is the same thing as not to hold it."[1] Rather than introduce this level of irrationality into their noetic structure, they should prefer to accept the, presumably lesser, irrationality with which the EAAN presents them.

> N, as we are supposing, is indeed something that you believe. So if you ask yourself whether, were you to go on believing N, you would be believing the truth then of course your answer will be affirmative. A negative answer would be evidence that, contrary to our supposition, N isn't something that you believe. ... But if you actually start from the position of believing that N, you can hardly deny that to destroy your belief that N would be to destroy a true belief, and this may well console you for the irrationality by which with Plantinga's help you see yourself to be afflicted.[2]

Epistemic voluntarism claims we choose to believe what we want, but I agree with Nathan (as does Plantinga) that we cannot, for the most part, do so.[3] However, we do sometimes change our beliefs (or, passively, they are sometimes changed) due to the recognition of valid arguments or evidence against them. The scenario Nathan envisages would be one in which no one could ever change their mind about anything, since such a change would be to reject something that they have, up until that point, believed. Besides which, the consolation he offers is weak; indeed, it's difficult to see how it would qualify as consolation at all. "Cognitive inflexibility of this sort should render the opposite of comfort. In this context paradoxes are not allowed to do the one thing for which they are intended, that is, to tease the mind into thought."[4]

Applying the EAAN to everyone

Some philosophers, in contrast with attempts to *limit* the EAAN's applicability to, for example, religious or metaphysical beliefs, object that we can expand its applicability so that it doesn't uniquely indict N. For example, Van Cleve argues that even if the naturalist abandons N, for all they know N is true and R has a low probability. Therefore, abandoning N doesn't accomplish anything since the problem will still be present.[5] However, this objection would only work if we impute the implicit premise thesis to Plantinga, and Van Cleve predicted (correctly) that Plantinga "does not subscribe to that thesis."[6]

By making the skepticism apply to all agents merely because "for all they know" N might be true after all, Van Cleve is transforming the EAAN into a standard global skeptical argument.[7] In these cases, if we cannot be 100 percent certain R is true, we cannot rule out the possibility it is not, and so we cannot have knowledge of anything. It's *possible* that we're being deceived by an evil demon, even if we don't believe we are. Van Cleve's suggestion tries to bypass the EAAN by claiming it applies to everyone equally. Yes, the low probabilities of R on N do constitute a defeater for N, but they also constitute a defeater for every other view, and so the naturalist is not obliged to abandon N in favor of these other views. In other words, N may be defeated, but since there's nowhere else to go, the naturalist can remain a naturalist.[8]

Yet this is not how the EAAN argues. In other global skeptical scenarios we have no reason to think they are true, they're just bare possibilities. We have no reason to think we are under the control of an evil demon or are just brains in vats. In contrast, the EAAN, by appealing to the actual worldview of the naturalist, *gives the naturalist a reason to accept the skepticism*. It is not merely *possible* that the naturalist's cognitive faculties are unreliable, it is *probable*. And this does not apply to everyone equally but only to those who accept N.

The EAAN and global skepticism

I have argued that Plantinga's argument constitutes a type of global skepticism, but there are some significant differences. This leads some to deny the EAAN should be taken as a form of skepticism,[9] but this is just a terminological issue: if we define skepticism as requiring those elements it does not share with the EAAN, obviously the EAAN fails to qualify. If we don't include those elements as necessary, then it does.

A first difference, as just noted, is that many traditional forms indict everyone equally. The EAAN, however, only applies to the naturalist; it is only if one believes N that the argument can go forward. A second difference, as a very interesting corollary, is that unlike other skepticisms, Plantinga's provides a *way out*: by rejecting N. This is a vital point. Other forms of skepticism apply to everything and everyone at all times. It is left to us to find some way to void the skeptical conclusions. But Plantinga's skepticism provides a way within itself to void these conclusions. Simply deny N and you're home free.

To be clear, this would allow us to *avoid* the skepticism when we see it approaching, but not to *escape* it if we are already enmired within it. The proposition that rejecting

N would obviate the skepticism is, after all, one more belief, and once someone accepts the skepticism, they have as much reason to withhold belief in this proposition as any other. However, while someone couldn't really reason or argue their way out of the skepticism, they could potentially *recover* from it by recognizing how mind-blowingly insane it is and rejecting it. Furthermore, this could be a rational move on their part, since rejecting insane positions is generally a rational thing to do.[10]

Third, many traditional forms of skepticism (not all) are only introduced for hypothetical or methodological purposes. We are not expected to genuinely consider the evil demon or brain-in-a-vat scenarios,[11] they're just too bizarre to take seriously. The naturalist, however, really believes N, so they are in the position of someone who really believes they're under the control of an evil demon or that they're a brain in a vat.[12] The naturalist is not proposing N as a method to explore ideas but genuinely accepts it as an account of reality.[13]

Fourth, traditional global skepticism *begins* in doubt. It asks, "Why should I believe this?" and for every answer, asks the same question of it. In Plantinga's naturalized epistemology, however, there are properly basic beliefs that don't need to be defended by reference to some other belief or experience. They are beliefs that are "not accepted on the evidential basis of other propositions," and, as such, are "starting points for thought."[14] Properly basic beliefs are innocent until proven guilty: they automatically have warrant and do not require further justification—but they can be overturned by evidence that has greater warrant than the basic belief.

So Plantinga's skepticism begins by accepting R as a properly basic belief. We do not have to hunt around for some reason to believe it; it comes with its own warrant and qualifies as knowledge (if it is true). But the EAAN provides the naturalist with a defeater for it. The doubting of R is not the EAAN's starting point but its conclusion. The naturalist can trust the reliability of their cognitive faculties up until the point where they realize they have a defeater for it.

A fifth difference is that standard global skepticisms are primarily a problem for internalist epistemologies. Externalist and naturalized epistemologies arose in part to provide theories of knowledge not subject to these skepticisms. With the evil demon and brain-in-a-vat hypotheses our internal experiences would be the same as if they were veridical. Thus, there is no internal criterion by which one could rule out these skeptical cases. In externalist epistemologies the warrant or justification a belief has is connected with its objective reality: hence, you do not necessarily have to rule out the internalist skepticisms in order to have knowledge, you do not have to know that you know something in order to know it.

As such, part of Plantinga's genius is that the EAAN is a global skeptical argument that arises *within* naturalized epistemology and externalism. The standard ways of avoiding such arguments do not work here. It is not enough to say R does not need to be justified before we accept it—Plantinga agrees. But once the naturalist sees that R is improbable and defeated, they have a reason to not believe it, and this defeater cannot itself be defeated. The EAAN demonstrates that externalists and naturalized epistemologists do not escape the threat of global skepticism—but only so long as they are wedded to naturalism.

Naturalized skepticism

In fact, this is one of the most momentous consequences of the EAAN: it applies even to naturalized epistemology, a theory of knowledge specifically formulated to avoid the skeptical questions that plague other theories. Quine wasn't asking how we justify our beliefs but how our beliefs hang together and connect with our sensory experiences. As such, his epistemology is usually taken as a form of coherentism except it focuses on descriptive connections instead of prescriptive connections. This lets him use any information available to examine these connections, including the science that is their output. Naturalized epistemology uses our scientific theories—our beliefs—to observe how the external world impacts on our senses, and how our senses produce the beliefs by which we examine the whole process in the first place. This, again, is epistemic circularity, where we use a rule in its own testing. This is permissible but limited; really, all it can show is that a system is internally coherent, not that it is consistent with external factors.

Hookway argues that, under naturalized epistemology, knowledge is based on our intuitions which are passive and tend toward simpler, conservative explanations (we take new information into our web of belief in the simplest and most conservative way).[15] Simplicity and conservativeness play a huge role in scientific thinking, and our intuitive acceptance of them would have been selected for in the struggle for survival since they allow the organism to process information with the least amount of energy output. Our cognitive faculties and evaluative traits are simply given, they do not need to be defended, we do not need a reason to trust them before trusting them. Moreover, simplicity and conservativeness were only selected for in the evolutionary struggle to address local issues, namely, the particular environment our evolutionary forebears found themselves in. Applying them to global issues is inappropriate, and this is what allows naturalized epistemology to sidestep global skepticism. Unless we have a reason to be suspicious of our passive acceptance of simplicity and conservativeness, we are rational in accepting them.[16] "To refute Quine's position, one would need to show that this standpoint is internally incoherent..."[17]

The response should be obvious. Hookway argues that our cognitive faculties' reliability are innocent until proven guilty. Plantinga, however, agrees. We do not *begin* by questioning their reliability, we begin by assuming they are reliable. Belief in their reliability is properly basic and comes with its own warrant—but it is not undefeatable. The EAAN takes our cognitive faculties' reliability as given, and then shows that if they are entirely explicable by naturalistic evolution, we have a defeater for believing they are reliable. Traditional global skeptical arguments work differently: they begin by questioning our cognitive faculties or some aspect of them and then searching for something independent of whatever aspects are being questioned that could validate or justify them. Naturalized epistemology avoids the latter type of global skepticism but does not touch Plantinga's.

Therefore, Hookway's claims fail. He argues we do not need to question our cognitive faculties until we have reason to do so. But Plantinga has *provided* a reason for doing so: the EAAN. This is truly remarkable. Hookway's response to Plantinga's argument is to challenge him to provide precisely what the argument provides. Similarly, Hookway argues the burden of proof is on the one who challenges our cognitive faculties' reliability. But Plantinga *accepts* the burden of proof: the naturalist can trust their cognitive faculties until they have a defeater, which the EAAN provides. Hookway argues we would have to show Quine's position is internally incoherent to refute it. But that is precisely what the EAAN does: it purports to show that naturalism is *self-defeating*, it gives the naturalist a reason to not believe naturalism that cannot be overruled by other considerations. Of course, we can still embrace naturalized epistemology without the naturalism, and this is exactly what Plantinga does: "naturalistic epistemology flourishes best in the garden of supernaturalistic metaphysics."[18]

What about the claim that naturalized epistemology was devised to avoid skepticism? It examines the connection between sense experiences and belief formation, not trying (or needing) to rule out evil demons or brains in vats. Such scenarios afflict internalist theories of knowledge because our inner experiences and awareness would be identical to what they would be if these skeptical scenarios were true. There is no test by which one could see whether their experiences are real or whether they are being produced by the evil demon since any test could make up part of the demon's illusion. Naturalized epistemology, however, is not interested in such inner experiences, it is just examining—scientifically, in non-epistemic terms—how we get "from stimulus to science."[19]

But the EAAN does not require any internalist component. The naturalized epistemologist, at least if they are also a naturalist, has a *defeater*, a reason to withhold belief, for any belief they have. This immediately cuts the legs out from any attempted examination of how our beliefs are connected to our sensory experiences. Before we can even ask if the beliefs in question are true, the EAAN gives us a defeater for the initial beliefs about our sensory experiences and the effect they have on belief production. It's not a matter of whether their internal experiences would be the same as with other skepticisms. We cannot begin the naturalized epistemology project because we have a defeater for every step of the analysis. So, the EAAN applies to naturalized, externalist, and internalist epistemologies.

If this is the case, why wouldn't the traditional skeptical problems apply to naturalized epistemology as well? Because these problems present the bare possibility of unreliable cognitive faculties; the EAAN presents the naturalist with the *probability* of unreliable cognitive faculties, and this then leads to a defeater for R and hence N. The evil demon and brain-in-a-vat hypotheses don't make it probable that one's cognitive faculties are not reliable since we are given no reason to accept the scenarios they envisage. Indeed, the scenarios they envisage are outrageous. But Plantinga's argument takes something the naturalist actually believes and demonstrates that it makes it probable their cognitive faculties are unreliable.

Perhaps someone could object that Plantinga's definition of belief (a mental depictor with propositional content) is inherently epistemic, and so is not consistent with naturalized epistemology's endeavor to provide a theory of knowledge in non-epistemic terms. But Quine and naturalized epistemologists in general do not eschew beliefs—that is the charge of eliminativists. And, as we have seen, eliminativism is just as self-defeating as naturalism is. So rejecting the possibility of beliefs with propositional content, for whatever reason, simply leads to self-defeat. If the objection is that the affirmation of beliefs or normativity render something epistemic (which is certainly debatable), thus making it inconsistent with the naturalized epistemologist's goal to explain knowledge in non-epistemic terms, then the response would be that no one has ever produced a true naturalized epistemology, since all forms of it, even Quine's initial proposal, include normative elements.

The naturalized epistemologist may counter that all they are doing is observing how sensory stimuli eventually lead to beliefs, ignoring the questions of whether the resulting beliefs and their beliefs about how the stimuli produce them are true. The EAAN gives them a reason to think that the beliefs are not reliably formed, but that's not the question they're asking. However, the EAAN gives them a reason to think that their beliefs about the science they are using to observe the connections are not reliable, as well as the beliefs that undergird their motives for wanting to pursue naturalized epistemology in the first place. They have a reason to distrust their beliefs (a defeater) about how the input of sensory information leads to the formation of beliefs.

If they argue that their sensory experiences, which are indicators, are veridical (since evolution would "see" indicators and tend to select the more accurate ones), that's fine, but this does nothing to insulate them from the EAAN. On the one hand, if they are rejecting beliefs, they are endorsing eliminativism, which is self-defeating. On the other hand, if they are arguing they can make these observations and formulate theories and explanations without entering into the realm of beliefs (not necessarily denying them per se), I would point out that theories have propositional content. On the gripping hand, if they are suggesting accurate indicators will tend to produce true depictors, I would say N gives us a reason to think they would not.

But the whole point of naturalized epistemology, one might argue, is that our cognitive faculties are not in place to address global issues. They arose via evolution due to the *local* environment of the organisms. So how could a global skeptical argument get any purchase on an epistemology that only asks local questions?

In response, firstly, the skepticism is global because it attaches to every belief the naturalized epistemologist has. If the only beliefs they have are local, that doesn't rebut the charge: they still have a defeater for all these local beliefs. So, it's global in the sense that it applies to every belief, be it local or global.

Secondly, while the naturalized epistemologist is only *asking* about local issues,[20] it doesn't mean global issues will not impact the answers. More specifically, the question being asked is, how probable is it under naturalism that the input of our local environment impacting itself on our senses would produce mostly true beliefs? How probable is it that the preponderance of our beliefs, our mental depictors, are true if the entire process is naturalistic, moving from sensory perceptions to beliefs and scientific hypotheses? If the answer to this question is "not very," then when we add the defeater thesis to it, it entails global skepticism. We cannot avoid this by saying we do not want to address global issues: regardless of what we want or ask, the answer has global repercussions. Again, this is Plantinga's genius, a global skepticism arising from local queries.

The implications of this are far-reaching. It means we cannot bracket global issues and only address local ones because the global issues will insert themselves into our local concerns and questions. Any form of epistemological relativism, subjectivism, or perspectivalism is not only false, it is self-defeating. This may not come as news to many: an obvious question to ask when someone says all knowledge is relative or subjective is whether that is the case for that person's belief that all knowledge is relative or subjective. If it is, then it allows for other people's beliefs (and even the relativist's other beliefs) to be neither relative nor subjective but objective and global. It does not even rule out the possibility that relativism and subjectivism are objectively false. "But then it does not call for a reply, since it is just a report of what the subjectivist finds it agreeable to say."[21] If, however, the claims about relativism or subjectivism are intended to communicate the way things really are then they are self-defeating, because they are saying *sub*jectivism is *ob*jectively true. They are making a global claim, and as such are providing a counterexample to themselves.

So, the EAAN is a naturalized skepticism, a form of global skepticism that applies to naturalized epistemology. But of course, it does not *only* apply to naturalized epistemology. The issues involved (naturalism and the reliability of our cognitive faculties) are not particular to any system of knowledge,[22] and so one cannot avoid the argument by rejecting Plantinga's epistemology. They apply across the board to any theory of knowledge.

Et tu quoque?

Rather than expand the application of the EAAN to everyone, the more common method is to only expand it to theists by formulating a similar argument against theism or Christianity. If valid, the naturalist cannot be obliged to abandon naturalism in favor of theism, since the same problem presents itself. Naturally, this leaves open the possibility of adopting a third position that avoids the self-defeat of both naturalism and (allegedly) theism, like anti-realism,[23] Nagel's "teleology without intent,"[24] or Talbott's "metaphysically necessary truths" that anchor local observations to global truths.[25] But Plantinga, somewhat brazenly, suggests the two primary competitors in the worldview Olympics are naturalism and theism, so the rejection of one effectively implies the other.

Plantinga argues that theism—at least Judeo-Christian theism—renders it *probable* our cognitive faculties would be reliable. But why? The theist must be adding something since the bare existence of God does not tell us anything about his intentions and whether he would have created our cognitive faculties to be reliably aimed at the production of true beliefs. It looks like the theist is cheating, and the naturalist is not being allowed to cheat in the same way. As Carl Ginet puts it,

> Now how is it that the theist is allowed to build into her metaphysical hypothesis something that entails R or a high probability for R but the naturalist isn't? Why isn't it just as reasonable for the naturalist to take it as one of the tenets of naturalism that our cognitive systems are on the whole reliable (especially since it seems to be in our nature to have it as a basic belief)? If it is cheating to include such a thing in naturalism, for the purposes of deciding whether it is reasonable to believe naturalism, then why isn't it cheating to include the corresponding thing in theism, for purposes of deciding whether it is reasonable to accept it?[26]

The *sensus divinitatis*

The answer comes from Plantinga's religious epistemology. Recall that for a true belief to be an item of knowledge in his general epistemology, it must a) be produced by properly functioning cognitive faculties that are b) reliably c) aimed at producing true beliefs d) in an appropriate epistemic environment. He then proposes his A/C (Aquinas/Calvin) model: if Christianity is true, God would have created us with an innate disposition to form beliefs about him, the *sensus divinitatis*. Since this would be one of "those faculties, or powers, or processes that produce beliefs or knowledge in us,"[27] the *sensus divinitatis* would qualify as a cognitive faculty. And since God put it in place in order for it produce true beliefs about him in us, that means the beliefs it produces are (or can be) produced by properly functioning cognitive faculties that are reliably aimed at producing true beliefs in an appropriate epistemic environment. So, if Christianity is true, belief in God and the tenets of Christianity would meet all the conditions necessary for warrant, and so would qualify as knowledge. In fact, belief in God would be properly basic, one of Plantinga's "starting points for thought."[28] This doesn't mean it cannot be defeated, but that, in the absence of a defeater, theism is warranted and does not need to be defended. It is innocent until proven guilty.

Of course, this is only *if* Christianity is true.[29] If it is not, belief in God would not be rational or warranted and so wouldn't be knowledge. But this has a very interesting consequence: we cannot argue that Christianity (or theism generally) is irrational or unwarranted without also arguing it is *false*. We cannot address the epistemological (*de jure*) question of whether belief in God is rational or justified or warranted independently of addressing the ontological (*de facto*) question of whether God exists. This is significant because many arguments against theism claim there is insufficient evidence or reason to believe in God, so even if he *does* exist, it would not be rational or warranted. But the A/C model argues that, if God exists, belief in God would probably be warranted because there would be something like the *sensus divinitatis* so that we appropriately form beliefs in God and the truths of Christianity in certain circumstances.[30] As such, it is very unlikely that belief in God would be unwarranted *if God exists*. In order to argue belief in God is unwarranted or irrational, therefore, one must first demonstrate that God does not exist: the *de jure* issue cannot be answered independent of the *de facto* issue. "This fact by itself invalidates an enormous amount of recent and contemporary atheology; for much of that atheology is devoted to *de jure* complaints that are allegedly independent of the *de facto* question."[31]

De jure objections are harder to pin down than *de facto* objections because it is not always clear what they are claiming. Is it that theism is irrational? Unjustified? Unwarranted? These lead to different answers and so it is incumbent upon these critics to specify what they are claiming. Ultimately, Plantinga argues *de jure* objections would only work if they claim theism is unwarranted.[32] Regardless, *de jure* objections cannot work independently of *de facto* objections. We need a reason for thinking theism is *false* before we can address whether it is *warranted*.

> There is no sensible challenge to the rationality or rational justification or warrant of Christian belief that is not also a challenge to its *truth*. That is, there is no *de jure*

challenge that is independent of a *de facto* challenge. That means that a particularly popular way of criticizing Christian belief—to be found in the evidentialist objection, in the F&M [Freud and Marx] complaint, in many versions of the argument from evil, and in still other objections—is not viable.[33]

This is the opposite of how things stand with naturalism: the whole point of the EAAN is that the naturalist has a total undercutting defeater for N, and as such, belief in N is irrational and unwarranted. If N is true, we have a reason to reject N. So, we *can* answer the *de jure* question independently of the *de facto* question for naturalism.[34] If N's truth entails its own defeat (and hence its irrationality), this effectively divorces its truth from its rationality.

Thus, to formulate an EAAN-type argument against theism flies in the face of Plantinga's religious epistemology. This does not give us a reason to reject *tu quoque* arguments out of hand, but it makes their acceptance more problematic. If the *tu quoques* are successful, it would also rebut Plantinga's religious epistemology. But then we would have to explain why, if the Judeo-Christian God exists, he probably would *not* give us reliable cognitive faculties. We will see how this plays out below.

T+ and N+

To further examine the *tu quoque* objections we must make a distinction between what I'll call bare theism and broad theism. Bare theism refers to the unadorned claim that God, a perfect being, exists and created human beings. I propose abbreviating this as T. In contrast, broad theism refers to the more detailed claims of God common to Judaism and Christianity. Since this supplements T with more detail, I propose abbreviating it as T+. The idea is that T does not say anything about whether our cognitive faculties are reliable in general, much less when they produce beliefs in God. We must add to T the propositions common to T+ that God created us with reliable cognitive faculties, particularly when they produce beliefs in God.[35]

So, the *tu quoque* argument is: if the theist can supplement T to make T+, why can't the naturalist supplement N to make N+, where the "+" adds to naturalism whatever conditions must be met in order to make R probable? Conversely, if the naturalist cannot do this, neither can the theist. So either both N and T have a defeater for R or neither do; in either case, the naturalist is not obligated to reject N in favor of T.

The problem is that the relationship between N, N+, and R is not the same as the relationship between T, T+, and R.[36] The theist who believes T+ also believes T: they believe the bare proposition that God exists, and much else besides. But this belief is directly derived from their belief in T+. They believe in God because they believe in the *Judeo-Christian* God. They do not begin with T and then supplement it to reach T+; they begin with T+ and see that it entails T. This, again, is due to Plantinga's religious epistemology: the *sensus divinitatis* tells us not only that God exists but that some specific doctrines (such as that he loves us, that he is trustworthy, that he wants us to know him, etc.) are true. If a God like the God of the Bible exists, he would want us to come to know him, and so would probably endow us with a propensity to believe in him and the "great things of the gospel,"[37] and these beliefs would be rational and warranted—in a word, knowledge.

So, the broad theist moves from T+ to T, not from T to T+, and if their belief in T+ is warranted (and per the A/C model, it will be if T+ is true), then their belief in T is warranted as well. What about their belief in R, that their cognitive faculties are reliable? T+ renders R probable since it claims God is the ground of rationality, perfectly loving and trustworthy, and created us to be rational agents. However, the broad theist does not *derive* R from T+ since R is a properly basic belief. But since they also believe T+ the broad theist does not have a *defeater*, a *reason to withhold belief* in R, since T+ entails the truth of R. The broad theist has no reason to doubt the reliability of their cognitive faculties, no reason to think they are not reliably aimed at producing true beliefs. Like the naturalist, they cannot *argue* for R, since any such argument would have to presuppose R.[38] But unlike the naturalist, they have no need to argue for it because their worldview does not call it into question. The theist's belief in R is properly basic, as is the naturalist's, but the theist has no defeater which calls R into question, since T+ entails R.

So, we (or rather the broad theists among us) are starting with two properly basic beliefs: T+ and R, neither being derived from the other, and between which there is no conflict (and even support, with T+ making R probable), and then we derive T from T+. To parallel the naturalist's case, the naturalist would have to be starting with N+ and R, and then derive N from N+. But this is not the case. Their belief in N is not derived from their belief in N+. Instead, the "+" was added in order to shore up the difficulties in N that the EAAN presents. Since the relationship between N and N+ is not the same as the relationship between T and T+, the naturalist's belief in N is self-defeating, but the broad theist's belief in T is not. Since the naturalist cannot appeal to N+, they cannot view R in light of N+. They must view R in light of N, and this produces a defeater for their belief in R. So again, the broad theist does not obtain a defeater for their belief in R, but the naturalist does.

Could the naturalist start with N or even N+ as a properly basic belief? Quine tried something like that with his "revolutionary step, naturalism self-applied ... not based on anything else."[39] But N is not an immediate, intuitive belief. If evolution had deigned to provide us with a *sensus naturalis* by which we spontaneously form belief in the nonexistence of God and the truth of N, we would not have similar grounds to trust it as we do with the *sensus divinitatis*. First, belief in N cannot remotely be connected with survivability, so there is no reason for N&E to select a propensity to believe it. Second, if it somehow had been connected, evolution would have selected it for its usefulness not for its tendency to produce true beliefs. Thus, we would have no reason to trust such a propensity *even if it were true*. Third, this glosses over the distinction between indicators and depictors. N&E would select a propensity to produce accurate indicators but not to produce true depictors. Fourth, we have empirical evidence that people intuitively believe in God.[40] We do not have evidence that people intuitively disbelieve in God or believe in N. So, we do have something like a *sensus divinitatis* but not a *sensus naturalis*. Most naturalists would acknowledge this: they do not claim N is an immediate, intuitive belief but rather a conclusion derived from evidence and argument. For naturalism to parallel the broad theism scenario, N+ would have to be properly basic, and then the naturalist would have to infer N from it. But the naturalist goes in the opposite direction, inferring N from evidence and argument and then inferring N+ from N. Even if N *were* properly basic, the naturalist would still have a defeater for R and hence N, N+, N&E, etc.

Some object that the naturalist's belief in N *is* derived from their belief in N+, since N+ is simply N + R and the naturalist already believes N and R. If the naturalist did not believe R, they would not rationally believe N or anything else. So, their belief in N is derived from their belief in R, and since they believe N and R they believe N+. But this is too simple. It is not enough for one belief to presuppose another, otherwise belief in R would validate all possible beliefs, since any belief presupposes R. Instead, the first belief must be *inferred* from the other; and naturalists do not infer N from the bare fact that they can think rationally.

R and the imago Dei

To examine this further, we must dig a little into general theology and comparative religion. Part of the concept of T+ (Judeo-Christian theism) is that God is unwilling or unable to deceive, in which case he would not create us with unreliable cognitive faculties. This is the traditional view of God in Judaism and Christianity; and while there are Bible passages that suggest God can deceive (e.g., 1 Kgs. 22:19–23; Jer. 4:10; 20:7; 2 Thess. 2:11), there are more explicit and universal biblical statements to the contrary (e.g., Num. 23:19; 1 Sam. 15:29; Tit. 1:1–2; Heb. 6:13–20), and the doctrines of these religions reflect the more explicit claims and affirm that God does not or even cannot deceive, and that the seemingly contrary passages must be understood in consideration of that fact.

Interestingly, it is *not* a part of traditional Islamic theology: suggesting God cannot deceive denies his omnipotence. Moreover, the Qur'anic passages that seem to support the idea that God can (and does) deceive are much more blatant than the biblical passages (3:54; 7:99; 8:30; 13:52).[41] This shouldn't be surprising, since the Judeo-Christian idea that we are created as rational creatures comes through the doctrine that we are created in the image of God (*imago Dei*), and God is conceived as the ultimate intellect—Jesus of Nazareth, who Christians believe is God incarnate, is explicitly identified as the universal *logos*, the incarnated cosmic principle of rationality (Jn. 1:1–18). We are rational agents because we are created by and in the image of the ground of rationality.

The doctrine of *imago Dei* is absent from Islamic theology. Claiming there can be an image of God at all is usually considered blasphemous in Islam, so obviously human beings cannot be created in his image. Three hadith do state that God created Adam in his image,[42] but this is usually understood to mean God created Adam in the image *which he had in mind* not in the image which God himself *bears*. Having said that, Muslim theologians and philosophers don't deny that God created human beings as rational agents, they just don't use the *imago Dei* doctrine to secure it, and they affirm that God can and does deceive.

What about the doctrine common to Judaism and Christianity that human beings have fallen into sin, degrading the image of God and thus the reliability of our cognitive faculties?[43] The answer here is threefold: first, the fall does not necessarily entail that our cognitive faculties are unreliable *in general*, but only (or at least primarily) with regards to belief in God.⁴⁴ Therefore, it does not present the broad theist with a defeater for R. Second, the fall did not erase the image of God in human beings: the Bible explicitly states that people still bear God's image after the fall (Gen. 9:6; Jms. 3:9–10) and nowhere denies it. Third, Judaism and Christianity also claim God *repairs* the results of the fall in human beings so we *can* form reliable beliefs (about God and whatever else was poisoned by the fall). The broad theist does not believe the doctrine of the fall in isolation from the doctrines of *imago Dei*, regeneration, and redemption; they come as a complete package. They are what comprise T+ and they have the same basis for all of them: the *sensus divinitatis*.⁴⁵ This, again, is from Plantinga's A/C model. If that model is possible, the fall of humankind does not present the broad theist with a defeater for R.⁴⁶

Another objection is that "the image of God" is an obscure phrase and does not give us much to go on in constructing a basis for accepting R.⁴⁷ Of course, the image of God has been conceived as involving many issues (some more controversial than others), but Christians have always thought it involved rationality. Aquinas even argued that rationality is the *primary aspect* of what it means to be created in the image of God.⁴⁸ So appealing to it here is not contrived or ad hoc. Plantinga isn't trying to protect Christian theism from defeat by interpreting *imago Dei* in a new and innovative way, he's taking the traditional interpretation which was in place long before any thought of R being defeated was in the margins.

Given Judeo-Christian theism, it is probable God would construct our cognitive faculties so that we could form true beliefs. This is because a) the Judeo-Christian God wants human beings to have communion with him, so it is likely he would construct us so that we can; and b) the Judeo-Christian God is perfectly loving and trustworthy, perfectly rational and knowledgeable, unable or unwilling to deceive, and is responsible for the creation of our cognitive faculties (perhaps via the evolutionary process). It follows from this that he would not create our cognitive faculties so that they generally deceive us. If it is objected that *imago Dei* still does not guarantee R, we can respond that it doesn't need to guarantee it. It is enough that it doesn't produce a *defeater* for it.

The *tu quoques* and the problem of evil

One interesting perspective is taking the *tu quoques* against theism as a form of the problem of evil.⁴⁹ If God allows evil in the world, why wouldn't he allow the particular evil of creating agents with unreliable cognitive faculties? Logical arguments from evil aren't defended much anymore (although they are still sometimes *asserted*),⁵⁰ largely because of Plantinga's free will defense,⁵¹ so contemporary arguments from evil are probabilistic or inductive. Regardless, if the *tu quoques* work, then the problem of evil applies to our knowledge and rationality. Conversely, if we say God would not tolerate ~R, it means his allowance of evil extends to atrocities like the Reign of Terror, the Holocaust, and the Great Purge, but not to our cognitive faculties being unreliable. That seems an unusual place to draw the line. Additionally, many theodicies (theories to accommodate evil within theism) would allow ~R. Perhaps God only allows evil when he can bring an even greater good out of it, but then why couldn't a greater good come from allowing ~R?⁵²

The problem of evil is a huge subject and we can only make a pass at it here. T+ says God is the greatest good, and the greatest thing for human beings is to know him. So, God does not allow ~R because it would prevent our greatest good and preventing that good would be the greatest evil. The general problem of evil does not parallel this: while experiencing evil leads some people to reject God, ironically it also leads many to accept him. The philosophical problem of evil is most prominent in the first world; in the third world evil is a fact of daily experience, and God is often seen as the *solution* to it.

But is this acceptable? Is not knowing God worse than the Holocaust? Well, if T+ is true, not knowing God results in eternal privation from him, to be forever separated from the source of goodness, love, meaning, and joy. As unimaginably horrific as the Holocaust was, it was finite. Comparing nonquantifiable concerns is pretty risky, and using the Holocaust to make a philosophical point will always be incredibly callous; nevertheless, when dealing with the problem of evil it is necessary to discuss horrific evils.[53] If the critic considers it implausible that not knowing God is the greatest evil, we can respond that it is not implausible *if T+ is true*. The critic needs another reason for thinking T+ is false, independent of the problem of evil, before denying that knowing God is the greatest good. This is another occasion where the *de jure* question cannot be resolved independently of the *de facto* question.

If we take the concept of a perfect being in isolation, we would probably predict it would allow neither evil *nor* ~R, but we have two specific reasons for acknowledging the reality of evil that do not apply to ~R. First, we perceive evil but we do not perceive ~R. We *could* not perceive ~R since to do so would require our cognitive faculties to be reliable. Second, theistic religions are often *responses* to evil. Positing that a perfect being (one that is maximally loving, moral, powerful, and knowledgeable) which created us and our cognitive faculties gives us a positive reason to think R is true, and this is strengthened by the doctrine that we are created by and in the image of the ground of rationality. So ~R would come as a surprise to the broad theist, but the occurrence of evil does not. It's not as if no one noticed there was evil in the world until after the Bible was written and then we had to scramble to find some ad hoc explanation of it. The Bible was written within a context of frequent and great evils. Biblical scholars claim the book of Job—which is about God allowing a righteous man, who did not deserve to suffer, to suffer horribly—was the first book of the Bible written.

We do not have similar reasons for thinking God would allow ~R as we do for thinking he would allow evil (or *other kinds* of evil if we grant that ~R would be a type of evil, as I am inclined to do). Whatever evil takes place, evil that prevents us from knowing God will not be allowed. This isn't special pleading since we have specific reasons for affirming the reality of evil that do not apply to ~R, and those reasons form a part of T+. Nor is this the only kind of evil the God of the Bible disallows (1 Cor. 10:13).

To all of this, however, is a strong counterargument: someone may not be able to observe R does not hold for themselves, since any assessment they make could only work if it does. But we can observe other people who clearly do *not* have reliable cognitive faculties. Paranoid schizophrenics, Alzheimer's patients, people with severe mental handicaps or dementia, have unreliable cognitive faculties. So, if God exists he *does* allow the great evil of allowing ~R.[54]

In response, first, this assumes the folk psychology view that beliefs cause actions by virtue of their propositional content, which is very difficult to reconcile with naturalism. Without this assumption we cannot link someone's actions to their beliefs, and so we cannot assume that displaying apparent cognitive malfunction indicates a propensity to form false beliefs. To make this objection, the naturalist must first rebut the EAAN and show how our depictors line up with our indicators under naturalism.

Second, it is not immediately clear that most of the beliefs of people suffering from these illnesses are incorrect. Yes, they have more false beliefs than most, but, as Plantinga writes, this is all against a background of countless Moorean beliefs that are true.[55] An Alzheimer's patient may falsely believe the person visiting her is her brother rather than her son, and this will compromise some of her other beliefs about these two relatives (such as their ages, whether one of them is still alive, etc.), but she still has numerous true beliefs about them, and the world, that are not compromised. Remember, in Plantinga's epistemology, knowledge and rationality attach to beliefs individually: "the rationality of my belief that China is a large country is not compromised by the fact that I harbor irrational beliefs about my neighbor's dog."[56] This could even be the case if someone can no longer comprehend what's going on around her (cannot move information from the world to her mind) and can no longer speak (cannot move information from her mind to the world).

I don't mean to minimize the severity or horrendousness of these conditions at all. My point is just that the critic will have to demonstrate more clearly that R does not hold for such people, meaning their beliefs are not usually true. Nor am I arguing R *does* hold for such people. Frankly, I suspect it does not. If Plantinga's definition of cognitive reliability (having cognitive faculties that produce a preponderance of true beliefs) allows them to be treated so that R holds for them then I would argue his definition is too lenient. (Of course, this makes the EAAN stronger since it argues that N does not even allow for this lenient definition of R to be the case.)

In fact, Plantinga presents a thought experiment that is very apropos here. A man climbing a mountain "is struck by a wayward burst of high-energy cosmic radiation" so that "his beliefs become fixed, no longer responsive to changes in experience."[57] Despite whatever sensory experiences he has from there on out, he still believes he is on a mountain ledge looking at the scenery. Plantinga's target here is coherentism, and he is arguing the cognitively inflexible climber does not have reliable cognitive faculties despite having a coherent belief system. But couldn't we say the same thing about an Alzheimer's patient who can no longer take in new information? Even if we do not adopt a coherentist epistemology, we need a definition of reliable cognitive faculties that would not include the cognitively inflexible climber or the Alzheimer's patient. Since the inflexible climber example comes from Plantinga, he may think so himself.

Third, the aspect of rationality supposedly affected by the fall of humankind is our ability and willingness to know and love God, and God offers corrections for it we can accept or reject. R will be an important element in our ability to know God since, without reliable cognitive faculties, it would be difficult to have warranted true beliefs about *anything*, much less God. Difficult, but not necessarily impossible. Again, rationality attaches to beliefs individually in Plantinga's epistemology, not collectively. Take someone who is severely mentally handicapped for their whole life, and so (ignoring the second point above), R does not hold for them. We can also say their *sensus divinitatis* does not function properly, but this is not due to their mental handicap but the fall of humankind. God corrects their *sensus divinitatis* so that they *can* form warranted true beliefs about God. If it is objected that their diminished mental capacity prevents them from accepting God's offer to repair this, the response is a) there is no particular reason to think this, and b) even if it were true, God could certainly give someone the ability, even if it is temporary, to respond to his offer of grace. In fact, this is pretty much the definition of prevenient grace in Arminian, and especially Wesleyan theology, wherein God overcomes our inability to accept him by buoying us up so that we *can* accept him (although we can still reject him).

But if God can repair one's *sensus divinitatis* without repairing R for people with these mental conditions, why bother giving anyone reliable cognitive faculties if they don't need them to affirm T+? But this is like asking, why bother inspiring a holy book if we don't need one for God to communicate to us? I mean, he is God, after all. He can (and does according to T+) communicate with people on an individual level. So why add this unnecessary complication of inspired writings? The answer goes back to the claim that humanity is *fallen* and we are willing to go to great extremes to avoid acknowledging God on his terms, both consciously and subconsciously, even when he directly speaks to us. Just because God infallibly speaks does not mean that we infallibly hear.[58] In this case, we are predisposed to twist individual revelations to mean what we want them to mean, and without an objective criterion against which to evaluate them, we will be less likely to come to God on his terms.

Of course, the history of religion demonstrates we're pretty good at twisting inspired writings too—if we are fallen, we are predisposed to do so; and at any rate, language is fallible. But at least it makes it more *difficult* to make a message mean what we want it to, since other people will receive the identical message and will have different motivations. And if there is a perfectly loving God who communicates with us collectively in inspired writings, that does not suggest he would not communicate with us individually as well.

Similarly, God gives us reliable cognitive faculties even though we only need one aspect of them, the *sensus divinitatis*, to form warranted true beliefs in him. This allows us to use other aspects of our cognitive faculties to evaluate what the *sensus divinitatis* seems to be telling us. Rationality and intellect are holistic: our different cognitive faculties have significant overlap with each other, even if, per Plantinga, we are only evaluating the rationality of beliefs individually. So while some aspects of our cognitive faculties might be less reliable than others, R is still a basic belief and is innocent until proven guilty. T+ does not give us grounds for questioning it, but N does. Not to mention that if we are created in the image of the ground of rationality, it would be odd to suggest we are generally *not* rational.

But then, what about the claim that T+ implies R? After all, the claim here is that, in a theistic world, there are people for whom R does not hold (dementia sufferers, for example), but this does not prevent them from accepting T+. Doesn't this mean T+ does *not* imply R? But this would entail that having exceptions to a general rule means there is no rule at all: either the rule covers all cases or no cases. Obviously, this is not correct. For the theist to avoid a defeater for R, it is enough to say T+ implies R. We do not have to say it *logically entails* R. This does not mean we derive R from T+ since this would be circular: attempting to prove R must presuppose R; plus, R is a properly basic belief, not derived from others. The claim that a perfectly loving, rational, and powerful being created our cognitive faculties implies R, but it does not and need not give us absolute assurance. It is enough that it does not produce a defeater for R like N does. Otherwise, we slip into more traditional forms of global skepticism where, if we cannot absolutely prove there is no evil demon or whatever, we cannot know anything.

Moving from T to T+

A final objection: perhaps someone who begins from T+ can avoid a defeater for R, but what about someone who only believes T, the bare proposition that God exists? Say someone comes to believe that a teleological argument successfully demonstrates the existence of a cosmic designer.[59] But since teleological arguments do not even try to argue this cause is a perfect being or the ground of morality, etc., this person becomes a bare theist, accepting T, but not by way of accepting T+. Since their belief T is not derived from T+, they aren't starting from a position that entails R, as T+ does. Isn't R defeated the same way for them as for the naturalist? If so, someone could not come to believe T and then later T+ without first going through atheism. Plantinga seems willing to concede this,[60] but there are other things to consider.

The problem with N is that it posits that there is only one kind of force responsible for the production of our cognitive faculties, and that kind of force provides *a known, competing function* for our cognitive faculties other than the formation of true beliefs. Our beliefs are not produced *in order to* believe truths but in order to allow us (or our evolutionary forebears) to survive and produce progeny. Even if we are reticent to ascribe any kind of functionality within a naturalistic framework, we can still ascribe it metaphorically so that the point holds: our cognitive faculties were not selected in the struggle for survival to produce true beliefs but to promote our ancestors' survival. While a propensity to form reliable indicators would almost certainly be selected in the evolutionary struggle a propensity to form true depictors would not because, absent a naturalistic solution to the mind-body problem, belief content is irrelevant to action and survival.

T does not posit something similar: not only does it allow for more than one kind of force to produce our cognitive faculties, one of those forces could very well have produced them so that they are aimed at the production of true beliefs (at least, sometimes). The bare theist can think their cognitive faculties were produced by God, perhaps via natural processes, in such a way that R holds for us. Unless we posit a form of theism where the processes that do not directly aim our cognitive faculties at true beliefs (i.e., natural processes) supersede those that do, no problem arises. This leads to further questions, such as whether God is responsible for natural processes or whether they are independent of him. But does the bare theist need to have a position on this? It seems they could just say God is one of the forces involved in the production of their cognitive faculties and other forces do not prevent him from accomplishing his goals.

We're not out of the woods yet, though. On N the only forces responsible for producing our cognitive faculties provide either a known, competing function or no function at all, and this gives the naturalist a defeater for R. On T there could be multiple forces, and one of them *could* have endowed our cognitive faculties with the function of producing true beliefs. But is this enough? The bare theist may not have a positive reason to think R is false, but they have no positive reason to think R is true either. If the bare theist has no basis for making a judgment about whether God created their cognitive faculties to be reliable, then the probability of R for them is *inscrutable*. But if a belief's truth is inscrutable it has a complete undercutting defeater. So, while the broad theist does not have a defeater for R, the bare theist, at least by this assessment, does have a defeater for R, just as the naturalist does.[61] In fact, it looks like the only thing that *could* lift us out of defeat is Descartes's project. Unless we have a positive reason to think the forces responsible for creating our cognitive faculties chose to make them reliable, it will be inscrutable that they *are* reliable. And if it is inscrutable, we supposedly obtain a defeater for R and hence all our beliefs.

By way of response, I do not necessarily object (at least not without further analysis) to lowering the threshold of when a metaphysical account of our cognitive faculties' origins defeats their reliability. Just because someone does not see how such an account entails R, a reasonable person could still be reticent to say R is defeated. There is (or should be) room for one to not understand how their beliefs regarding the origins of their cognitive faculties entail R (or rather, *don't* entail ~R) without immediately acquiring a defeater. Having said that, I do not think we can lower the threshold for defeat so far as the naturalist wants since we *do* see how N entails ~R: as long as there is only a known, competing function of our cognitive faculties, or none at all, this provides us with a reason for withholding belief in R.

Anyway, it is Descartes's *conclusion* that lifts one out of defeat, not the methodology he uses to reach it. It is the proposition that a rational and benevolent God exists that shields R from defeat. If someone starts with T+ because of the proper functioning of their *sensus divinitatis*, they have no reason to challenge their belief in R because R is probable, not inscrutable, given T+.

This still leaves us in the unusual position where someone who believes T cannot move from there to T+. As I said, Plantinga seems willing to accept this, but this leads to a further response: T+ obviously ascribes more attributes to God than does T. Some concepts of God are just of a supernatural being, not perfect, not particularly moral, with some superhuman powers. I suspect some of Plantinga's critics are assuming an evolutionary account of religion which starts with animism, moves on to an inchoate sense of something beyond nature, and over time adds attributes, enhances them, bakes them at 375°, and after a good long while out comes your friendly neighborhood monotheism.[62] But such theories have been out of vogue for decades among scholars in the relevant fields,[63] and regardless, any theory about the origin and early development of religion is bound to be extraordinarily speculative due to the paucity of evidence regarding prehistoric religious beliefs. Plus, thinking this might constitute an objection to T+ would commit the genetic fallacy.

The real problem arises when we ask which properties of T+ can we remove and still call the result "God"? This may delve too greedily and too deep into theories of reference, but I would argue that any concept of God granted to T must at least be of a being that is *worthy of worship*. This leads to further difficulties since there are numerous religions whose adherents worship small-g gods, not conceiving them as perfect but as amoral or immoral and having greatly limited powers. Call this T−. Such gods may be worshipped but they would not be *worthy* of worship—in fact, the "worship" offered to them seems more like the homage and fealty offered to a feudal baron.

For any God to be worthy of worship, it must be, in some sense, *ultimate*, it must be the supreme, absolute authority. In both T and T+, God is a perfect being; that is why he is worthy of worship. We do not have to develop this into a full-blown perfect being theology, we just have to say that any being that is perfect and worthy of worship would be the paramount authority, at least with regards to such things as morality and rationality. It must be the absolute authority on morality, the final arbiter on whether something is moral or immoral. It must be the absolute authority on rationality, the final arbiter on whether something is rational or irrational, true or false. And this leads directly to the claim that the God of T is maximally moral and maximally rational.

But if these concepts attach to T, bare theism, there is no longer a specter of inscrutability that attaches to R. A being that is perfectly rational, moral, loving, and powerful would more probably create minds that are trustworthy, reliable, and rational than minds that are not. In this case, *T already implies R*. It may not secure it as firmly as T+ does by grounding it in the doctrine of *imago Dei*, but since the concept of God in T is that of a perfect being who is worthy of worship, it includes God's perfect rationality and morality. While this is certainly a less robust claim than that human beings are created by and in the image of the ground of rationality and morality, it does make R probable—at least more probable than not, allowing the bare theist to avoid a defeater for R. So, the bare theist does not have a reason to withhold belief in R as the naturalist does, nor are they left in inscrutability.

What about other religions which go beyond T, different forms of T+ than the Judeo-Christian tradition?[64] Since they entail T, can't the same thing be said for them? Here it would be incumbent on these religions' doctrines to not *conflict* with T, that there is a perfect being that is worthy of worship. We have already seen with Islam, for example, that it portrays God as a deceiver;[65] it also portrays God as only loving *some* people (namely, Muslims) and not loving others (everyone else) (Qur'an 3:32; 30:45). This suggests, to some people at least, that such a God would not be a perfect being.

Of course, one could try to make a similar case about the Judeo-Christian God, and many atheistic arguments are attempts to do so: some arguments from evil focus on specific biblical claims to show that the Judeo-Christian God does not love everyone (Mal. 1:3; Rom. 9:13) or is morally culpable for some evils (Josh. 10:30–32; 40–42)[66] and thus is not morally perfect and not worthy of worship. This does not deny that the Bible defines God as morally perfect but suggests instead that this concept does not line up with the biblical account of some of his actions. And the response is the same as before: Christian doctrine affirms the explicit claim that God is morally perfect and loves everyone, so the passages that seem to conflict with this must be understood in light of it. But then this response may be available to the Muslim as well. If the Qur'an and Hadith clearly define God as morally perfect and omnibenevolent, the Muslim exegete could argue that the seemingly contrary passages must be understood in light of the clearer passages. Traditionally, however, Muslims have not taken the Qur'an and Hadith this way. The clearer passages seem to affirm that God is a deceiver, does not love everyone, and is morally culpable for evils (at least, events we would consider evil). At any rate, the more common method with arguments from evil is not to argue from specific holy books or doctrines, but from the presence of evil in the world to the claim that it precludes the existence of a perfectly loving, moral, and powerful being. But that's a tome for another time.

We are still left with the person who accepts, for example, a teleological argument and concludes there is a designer of the universe. This conclusion would not justify that this designer is trustworthy, maximally rational and moral, or even rational or moral at all. We cannot argue this designer is a perfect being, worthy of worship, or the ultimate anything. What do we do here? There are two ways of looking at this. First, someone could accept only the bare minimum that the argument they accept demonstrates. In this case, however, their position would be a form of T–, and R, for them, would be inscrutable and defeated.

There is a second way to look at it though: as noted above, we have empirical evidence that human beings tend to intuitively believe in God—a perfect being, maximally powerful, rational, moral, loving, and worthy of worship. Regardless of whether someone actually accepts the existence of God, the concept seems to be hardwired into us. A successful theistic argument (other than an ontological argument) would only demonstrate a being with some of those characteristics, not all. But since we already have the idea of a perfect being, a theistic argument does not need to demonstrate everything about it in one fell swoop, only that we have an argument pointing in that direction. Establishing certain narrow points can effectively confirm a broader theory without establishing every single possible element and consequence of that theory.

In effect, I'm appealing to confirmation theory. I'm not suggesting T and T+ constitute theories per se, but that it may be suitable to treat them as theories in this instance. Of course, this is a hazardous method: perhaps there is a different theory that shares the same established data points. Moreover, in this case, the concept of a perfect being and widespread belief in it would be both datum and explanation. Nevertheless, recognizing an argument that establishes specific elements of a broader concept can at least be taken as a reason for accepting the broader concept, and this could be the case for successful theistic arguments, if any there be.

Obviously more rigorous analysis must be done to establish this, but I think that the bare theist will already have the building blocks necessary to avoid having a defeater for R. The naturalist, however, does not. The EAAN still stands.

12

Loose Ends

"... you shall burn the remainder with fire ..."

Exodus 29:34

There are, of course, many objections to the EAAN. In the previous chapters I have addressed some of the most common ones, but there are plenty more, some strong, others not so much. In this final chapter I will go over those I've encountered. I have organized them into some rough categories, but plenty of them fit in more than one, and others do not really fit in any. I realize I must have missed some, probably some very obvious ones—in these cases, I apologize. Such is life.

Fallacies and bad reasoning

Objection: Plantinga begs the question. To make his argument he presupposes that R holds for *him*, at least, so he cannot argue that it does not.[1]

Plantinga assumes R holds for everyone, not just himself, since it is a properly basic belief. N, however, gives the naturalist a defeater for it. Those who do not accept N (like theists) do not obtain a defeater. There is nothing question begging here.

Objection: Plantinga begs the question. Since he concludes that N and R are incompatible, and since he accepts R, he must be presupposing that N is false, perhaps even that T (theism) is true.[2]

The answer here is similar. Saying the naturalist has a defeater for R while others do not is the *conclusion* of the argument, not a presupposition. He's not assuming at the outset that N and R are incompatible, he's *arguing* that N and R are incompatible.

Objection: Plantinga begs the question since his conception of R must be R + ~N.[3] But this is no better than the vitalist who assumes that life involves having a vital spirit, so any denial of vitalism entails that one is not alive and so cannot be valid.[4] If we can take E neat, without tying it to any particular metaphysic, why can't we take R the same way?

Well, Plantinga *is* just taking R neat and demonstrating that it is incompatible with N. R is the claim that our cognitive faculties are reliable, and reliability is parsed as entailing that most of our beliefs are true. Can someone redefine R? Sure. It is one of those concepts where no one can seem to agree on the definition (so is philosophy by the way; and science; and religion). But then it would mean our cognitive faculties' ultimate function is not to produce true belief, and this would lead to self-defeat. What if we just redefine R to be R + N? In that case, we are assuming a definition of R that is consonant with N right out of the gate. But this leads to the same problem: if we define R so that it does not require that the ultimate function of our cognitive faculties is to produce true belief, then we end in self-defeat. There's a *reason* why Plantinga defines R the way he does; it's not arbitrary, it's the bare minimum that allows us to avoid self-defeat. Certainly, there is more to rationality than this, but not less.

Objection: Epiphenomenalism and emergentism involve entities with no causal powers. Ockham's Razor should remove them, so Plantinga should not appeal to them in his five possibilities of the relation between mind and body given N.[5]

Ockham's Razor says a quantitatively or numerically simpler explanation is preferable to more complex explanation, all other things being equal. But epiphenomenalism and emergentism are not part of an explanatory hypothesis in the EAAN, they are the *consequences* of an explanatory hypothesis, namely, N. It does not contradict the Razor to analyze how probable certain consequences are under a hypothesis. Plantinga intends the five possibilities to be mutually exclusive and *exhaustive*. If he just ignored two possibilities—specifically possibilities that are "widely popular among those enthusiastic about the 'scientific' study of human beings"[6]—his analysis would be incomplete.

Objection: Ockham's Razor makes it implausible that depictors would not be about what their indicators indicate.[7]

We could make the same objection to the opera singer shattering a wineglass. The present objection is that Ockham's Razor makes it implausible that the words she's singing would not be about the glass shattering. We should expect the resonance frequency and the words to line up so that she can only sing at that frequency when singing words like "shatter" or "break." But this is magical thinking, and the same would hold for the indicator-depictor dichotomy under naturalism.

Again, all other things being equal (which is rarely the case), the fewer entities we posit in formulating an explanatory hypothesis the better. But the EAAN is not positing more entities by making a distinction between indicators and depictors—or, more accurately, between indicative and depictive *properties* of a single representation. Since it is not multiplying the number of representations but rather their qualities, it is not quantitatively less simple but qualitatively less simple. Ockham's Razor has no bearing on this. Plus, if we did apply the Razor here, we would remove one of the properties and just affirm the other. But we cannot remove the indicative properties and keep the depictive properties because a depictor is a *type* of indicator. The only option would be to remove the depictive properties and keep the indicative ones. But there's a reason for affirming depictors: we directly experience them. We have beliefs and are aware of it. So, all other things are *not* equal and Ockham's Razor is overruled (assuming it applied in the first place). At any rate, if we remove depictors we are back in eliminativism, and this is self-defeating as well.

Objection: The EAAN commits the genetic fallacy and the circumstantial ad hominem fallacy. It argues that if N is true, our belief forming capacities either have no function or a function other than believing truth. But we cannot determine a belief's truth value based on how the cognizer came to believe it, or because they have ulterior motives for it. We must distinguish between how we come to believe something and whether the belief is true.

Yes, of course. Fortunately, the EAAN is addressing whether our beliefs would be rational and warranted so the genetic and circumstantial ad hominem fallacies do not apply. An *accidentally* true belief is not warranted and so is not knowledge. And once someone realizes they do not believe something because it is true but for another reason—that they would continue believing it to be true even if they realized it was not true—then that belief is no longer rational for them to hold.[8]

Perhaps the objection is to the Probability Thesis, that if N is true, the probability our cognitive faculties reliably produce true beliefs is low. This uses beliefs' origins as a reason to think they are not true. But this forgets that the EAAN is working in internal rationality. It isn't asking whether a belief is objectively false but whether the individual has other beliefs that make it inappropriate to continue thinking the first belief is true. Remember the case of the Freudian theist who comes to believe that belief in God is always the product of wishful thinking and that wishful thinking does not reliably produce true beliefs. The question here is not whether theism is objectively true but whether the Freudian theist is rational (or justified or warranted) in believing it *in light of other beliefs they hold*. Given those other beliefs, the Freudian theist has a reason for withholding belief in theism.

Objection: To say warrant defeaters usually produce rationality defeaters commits the genetic and circumstantial ad hominem fallacies. If someone realizes they do not believe B because B is true, they have a warrant defeater. Once they see this, they will also have a rationality defeater, since they would realize that the truth of B is irrelevant to their believing it. But to criticize someone for having the wrong reason for a belief does not address the truth value of that belief.

No, it doesn't. But it *does* bear on whether that belief is warranted, justified, and rational. If someone realized they don't believe something because it's true but for some other reason, then if they continue to believe it—believe it to be *true*—they would not be rational.

Epistemological issues

Objection: Rebutting Plantinga's epistemology effectively rebuts the EAAN since we no longer have to appeal to proper function or a design plan.[9]

This objection, I presume, is based on how Plantinga initially derives the argument from his overall epistemology. After defending a naturalized epistemology based on proper function, he argues that proper function cannot be accounted for in naturalistic terms,[10] and then presents the EAAN.[11] However, the issue is the reliability of our cognitive faculties under N, and no theory of knowledge is immune to it.[12] So refuting his epistemology does not refute the EAAN.

A similar objection is that Plantinga's is not a true naturalized epistemology since it invokes elements that have not yet been shown to be naturalistically reducible, like truth, beliefs, intentionality, *functions*, etc. So, it may be possible to avoid the EAAN by adopting a purer form of naturalized epistemology.[13] But every naturalized epistemology suggested, even Quine's original proposal, includes beliefs, truth, as well as some form of normativity like functions. So, this objection appeals to an idealized naturalized epistemology which has never actually been formulated[14] and which lies in the opposite direction from how naturalized epistemology has evolved.[15] Plus, if we reject truth and belief we are back in eliminativism with its own version of self-defeat. If naturalizing our epistemology requires us to go down that road, we already know where it ends.

Objection: Plantinga argues that either all our beliefs are reliably formed or none are. This leads to the "Foundationalist fallacy," that the foundations of our knowledge must be infallible.[16]

The one correct thing in this objection is that Plantinga is arguing that there are scenarios which entail that none of our beliefs are reliably formed—namely, *skeptical* scenarios like the evil demon or brain-in-a-vat proposals. These have played an enormous role in philosophical history. But Plantinga is not suggesting we embrace skepticism. He is arguing that N leads to a global skeptical scenario where none of our beliefs are reliably formed including N, and so it should be rejected.

The other side of this, however, is not true. Plantinga has never said or even implied that rejecting N makes everything everyone believes warranted, rational, reliably formed, or whatever. He's contrasting having *some* knowledge with having *none*. Skepticism is in the latter category and at least some forms of it are self-defeating. These skepticisms—and any position that leads to them—are unacceptable.

As for the "Foundationalist Fallacy" (that an epistemic foundation must be infallible): Infallibilism certainly has its problems but it has been very influential in epistemology, and it is more than a little strange to call a major epistemological position a fallacy. More importantly, though, *Plantinga explicitly rejects infallibilism*. That is a central part of his theory of knowledge, that properly basic (foundational) beliefs can be defeated, even by beliefs that are not properly basic. Criticizing Plantinga for being an infallibilist is like criticizing Descartes for being a coherentist. You have to find out what someone is saying before you criticize them for saying it.

Objection: Plantinga sometimes addresses his argument towards propositional content and sometimes towards truth value. These lead to different situations: the belief "that mushroom is not poisonous" has content, but its truth value depends on what mushroom someone is looking at. Even if it has identical neurophysical properties in different occasions, its truth value would change based on the external environment. The connection between truth and action is not the same as that between truth and adaptiveness. Relational properties, like truth, are potentially selectable by evolutionary processes since truth influences survivability.[17]

Of course, the truth of a belief varies in different circumstances, where those circumstances dictate whether or not the belief is true. But the EAAN does not challenge this. It just argues that if a belief's content does not influence behavior by virtue of its content, then the truth value of that belief is invisible to natural selection. Certainly, *truth* influences survivability but the question is whether *true beliefs* do. The truth that eating a particular mushroom will kill you is very relevant to whether you live or die, but if belief content has no influence on behavior then whether you *believe* a mushroom will kill you has no bearing on whether or not you eat it.[18]

Objection: The EAAN is more plausible when applied to a subset of our beliefs, like metaphysical beliefs or evaluative judgments. It is not as plausible when applied to sensory beliefs (like "there's a tiger in front of me") or scientific beliefs (like "evolution is true").

Well, if this just means calling something we cannot help but believe into question is not credible, then sure. We cannot take a challenge to our entire cognitive systems seriously so an argument that does that is at a disadvantage—a *rhetorical* disadvantage, not a philosophical or logical one. That may be a good enough reason to only apply the argument to metaphysical beliefs (Plantinga), scientific beliefs (Talbott), or normative reasons (Street), and thereby show that naturalism is self-defeating. Then again, it may not.

However, the Evolutionary Argument against Naturalism is, again, an argument against *naturalism*. The reliability of our cognitive faculties comes into play because Plantinga is arguing that naturalism leads to an absurd conclusion. Making the conclusion less absurd by only applying it to, for example, metaphysical beliefs makes the argument less forceful: the greater the absurdity, the more forceful the argument is that N leads to that absurdity. Any position that leads to a conclusion like ~R is not rational and should not be accepted. Yes, Plantinga modifies it to only apply to our metaphysical beliefs, as have others, but as an accommodation, not a concession, in order to obviate the rhetorical implausibility of calling all our beliefs into question.

However, if the claim is there are philosophical grounds (not just rhetorical grounds) for thinking certain categories of belief, like sensory or scientific beliefs,[19] are not susceptible to the EAAN, I disagree. Plantinga's argument is about *belief content* and its invisibility to natural selection. If this is the case, then it applies across the board whether we want it to or not. We automatically associate our belief contents with our experiences, as we should, but the EAAN argues that N does not allow us to do so.

Objection: It is impossible to call all our beliefs or cognitive faculties into question, since any such attempt must presuppose the truth of some beliefs or the reliability of some cognitive faculties.

Correct: as I pointed out in chapter 1, to use Descartes's evil demon hypothesis to doubt all our beliefs, we must accept one belief, namely, the evil demon hypothesis itself. It is impossible to call all our beliefs or the reliability of all our cognitive faculties into question. Fortunately, no one is suggesting we should. Instead, we should reject any belief that entails it.

But how could we ever reach ~R as a conclusion? Well, if we start from the premise ~R, obviously we would conclude ~R. But what if we start from some belief, X, that immediately and self-evidently entails ~R? Couldn't we say that entailment is challenged by ~R? X immediately entails ~R, sure, but X and its entailment of R could be illusions wrought upon us by our unreliable cognitive faculties. Yet this just leads to the Humean loop or Plantingian regress. How about another belief, Z, that leads to ~R but only via extended reasoning? This is in the same situation as X: believing Z and the reasoning involved to derive ~R from Z is challenged by ~R, but that just leads to the loop or regress. The difference is only that Z does not entail ~R as self-evidently as X does. But that does not challenge the claim Z → ~R. This latter situation is the case for N.

Probability and defeat

Objection: Plantinga's probabilities are too indefinite, we need more specific calculations. Plantinga only provides estimates that are "both extremely imprecise and poorly grounded."[20]

Plantinga acknowledges "the very idea of a calculation (suggesting, as it does, the assignment of specific real numbers to these various probabilities) is laughable. The best we can do are vague estimates." However, he also says, "that will suffice for the argument."[21] Why? Because his only concern is whether P(R/N&E) is low or not. He does not have to provide specific calculations, he only has to provide estimates demonstrating that P(R/N&E) ≤ .5. If I am arguing that two factors are less probable than .5 each—if I have a reason for thinking neither of them are more probable than not—I have a reason for thinking the two of them together are not more probable than .5. I do not need to provide more specific probabilities. Approximations "will suffice for the argument."

Objection: If a probability is just inscrutable—if we are ignorant as to how probable it is—it does not provide us with a defeater. Lots of probabilities are inscrutable but we do not suspend belief because of them.[22] It is an error to think that "ignorance of probabilities is a guide to belief."[23]

There is some truth here, but it cannot rescue naturalism from the EAAN. Say you believe a process is relevant to our cognitive faculties' origins, but you know nothing about the process—whether it will be truth-conducive, reliable, etc. You also believe, as a properly basic belief, that your cognitive faculties are reliable. I do not think it is unreasonable to infer that the process must reliably produce true beliefs, given the two data points that R holds for you and the process is responsible for the production of your cognitive faculties.

However, that is not the naturalist's situation. The naturalist has a reason for thinking the process is *not* truth-conducive: N provides a known, competing function. Given this, why say P(R/N&E) is low *or inscrutable*? The inscrutability was only an option if beliefs cause actions by virtue of their contents and are not maladaptive (the fifth possibility), but there is still a difference. Even if the processes allow our faculties to be reliable, they would only do so *accidentally*. They would be producing our cognitive faculties to pursue a function other than forming true beliefs, but this other function (allegedly) often *coincides* with the production of true beliefs. This is not enough for knowledge, however. Even if the processes that produce our beliefs are generally reliable, they would only be, at best, *accidentally* reliable, and accidentally true beliefs are not knowledge.[24] A cognizer wouldn't believe belief B because B is true but for some other reason or none at all. This gives them a warrant defeater, and if they realize that they do not believe B because B actually is true—if they realize they would continue believing B is true even if they understood that it is not true—they then obtain a rationality defeater.

So, in one sense, yes: if we think it is inscrutable that the forces that produce our cognitive faculties would have made them truth conducive, this does not necessarily provide one with a defeater. However, if the only possibility of inscrutability applies to forces that would have allowed our cognitive faculties to be reliable as a side-effect or by-product of what they are *actually* aimed at, then the inscrutability produces a defeater.

Objection: We need direct evidence and specific information to call R into question and Plantinga just provides general concerns (i.e., naturalism) and vague probabilities. An undercutting defeater isn't enough, we need a rebutting defeater.[25]

All we need in order to show that N is self-defeating is sufficient evidence that produces an undercutting defeater, because this entails that the naturalist has a reason to withhold belief in N, and no compensating reason to accept it. The sufficient evidence is N: given N, we have a reason to think that our belief contents and reasoning cannot influence our behavior so that R holds. Note that it is not just that we have no reason to think there is an influence, we *have* a reason to think there is *not* an influence. Once again, N is the poison pill.

Objection: The EAAN is arguing from "naturalism does not give us a reason to think R holds for us" to the conclusion "naturalism gives us a reason to think R does not hold for us."[26] This is not a logically valid move.

That's not the argument. The claim is, for knowledge to be possible, our cognitive faculties' ultimate function must be to have true beliefs. If N is true, either their ultimate function would be "to get the body parts where they should be in order that the organism may survive,"[27] or they would have no function at all. In either case, we have a reason to think that our cognitive faculties do not have the ultimate function of forming true beliefs. This does not merely imply that we do not have a reason for R but that we have a reason for ~R. This provides the naturalist with both warrant and rationality defeaters.

Objection: Even if R is defeated, the EAAN does not show that a non-negligible minority of our beliefs are true, and so it does not follow that every belief is thereby defeated.[28]

The EAAN shows that if R is defeated, we have a reason to think our beliefs do not line up with their apparent objects. As such, whether a particular belief is true or false is no better than flipping a coin: either the belief or its negation is true. The objection is that this means about half of our beliefs would be true under naturalism, not a minority of our beliefs, so we have a reason for *trusting* our beliefs to some extent. But, as Plantinga responds, if I do not know *which* of my beliefs are true I have a defeater for all of them,[29] specifically an undercutting total defeater. This is important: the defeater does not give us a reason to think a belief is false, it just gives us a reason to withhold belief in it. But it is still a *total defeater*—it does not merely give us a reason to believe less firmly but to not believe at all.

Objection: Plantinga must be presupposing a general principle regarding probability and the coherence of sets of beliefs, and this makes the EAAN a "close relative" of the lottery paradox.[30]

If a lottery or raffle has a million tickets and only one ticket will win, the probability of ticket one winning is one in a million, so the rational response would be to believe ticket one will not win. But of course, this is true of ticket two, three, etc., and the same rational response will be to believe tickets two, three, etc., will not win—in fact, *none* of the tickets will win. But we also know one of those tickets *will* win. So, the rational thing is to believe ticket one won't win, ticket two won't win . . . and so on up to ticket one million won't win; and also that one of the tickets between one and one million will win. This is an inconsistent set, there is no possible world where it is true that each individual ticket will lose and one of them will win.

But this does not parallel the EAAN. The analogies Plantinga gives all have a source of information being called into question in light of other beliefs an agent has. There is no such element in the lottery paradox. Besides which, Plantinga is *not* relying on a general principle, he is arguing from analogy. Thus the lottery paradox and similar scenarios[31] do not constitute a rebuttal to Plantinga's EAAN.

Objection: A perfect being would be logically necessary, not contingent (otherwise it wouldn't be perfect). So, theism (T) is either necessarily true (if God exists) or necessarily false (if he does not), and since naturalism entails God's non-existence, its probability would covary with it. But then for P(E/T) and P(E/N) the probability would have to be 1.0 for one and 0.0 for the other. But in Plantinga's equations they are not.

This and the following two objections are based on Tyler Wunder's criticisms of Plantinga's response to Paul Draper's argument from evil.[32] As a bonus, Wunder notes that his criticisms also have relevance for the EAAN. Here, I will just point out that saying something is necessarily the case (or necessarily not the case) does not mean every argument about it must *demonstrate* that it is necessarily the case. If someone argued that the Platonic forms, if they exist, would exist necessarily, it does not mean they cannot present arguments that Platonism is more probable than not. Saying something has a modal property does not require every argument about it to refer to or prove it has that modal property. The issues involved are "meta-logical rather than truth-functional,"[33] and, as such, we cannot use the necessary truth or falsehood of T to object to the use of probabilities of N.

Wunder seems to be assuming a principle like, "For all propositions p, if p is necessarily false, then there can be no conditional probability on p."[34] There is certainly an intuitive plausibility here, but it must be defended not just assumed. Karl Popper argues to the contrary,[35] and it is nowhere near a settled issue.

Moreover, as Perry Hendricks has pointed out, we can change the target from N to D, which he defines as "God, or anything at all like him, did not intervene (or order the world from the beginning) to ensure that his creatures' cognitive faculties are reliable."[36]

Since the claim that God intervened in this way is not logically necessary, Wunder's objection would not apply to it.

While Hendrick's suggestion significantly changes the argument—it is no longer addressed to N, after all—there are responses to make. First, while Plantinga usually defines N as entailing God's nonexistence, he sometimes defines it as entailing God's nonexistence *or inaction*.[37] Second, this amendment has the benefit of greatly expanding the applicability of the argument, since it would apply to many worldviews other than naturalism as it is usually defined; "N entails D, but D does not entail N."[38] This lets the argument apply to deism, pantheism, and other explicitly religious concepts.[39] Its weakness is that it makes the first premise harder to defend: the reason why P(R/N&E) is low is because N says something specific about the origins of our cognitive faculties and their truth-directedness. Deism and pantheism do not assert—or do not need to assert—that same thing. I am not saying Hendricks's amendment is not a significant contribution, I think it is, but it comes with its own problems.

Objection: If God exists necessarily we cannot formulate P(R), so Plantinga is not able to include such an assessment in his equations.

Wunder argues that if T is necessarily true, P(R/T) would equal P(R). But, as Plantinga notes, we cannot formulate P(R). In response to Fitelson and Sober's objection to his initial Bayesian argument, Plantinga writes,

> if we are thinking of the *absolute* probability of R (conditioned only on necessary truths), then I cannot claim (as I did) that P(R) is high: how would I know what proportion of the space of possible worlds is occupied by worlds in which R is true? In particular, the fact that R is true *in fact* is no reason for assigning it a high absolute (logical) probability.[40]

So, if P(R) is incalculable, and if P(R) = P(R/T), then P(R/T) is incalculable as well—and this is relevant to Plantinga's *general* argument not just his Bayesian one.[41]

I think the answer here is the same as above: saying P(R/T) is high doesn't require us to refer to the fact that if T is true it is true by necessity. We are not, in this equation, addressing the modal properties of God but what the probability is that a maximally rational, powerful, moral, and loving God—*if* he exists—would create creatures with reliable cognitive faculties. Yes, if he exists, then he exists necessarily, but that is not the question being addressed in the EAAN, and it does not need to include it for the argument to go through.

Objection: If we cannot formulate the absolute probability of R, then we cannot formulate the objective probabilities Plantinga uses in the EAAN.

Wunder put this question to Plantinga, and Plantinga responded to him via email, acknowledging that there are certain difficulties in formulating the argument in objective probabilistic terms.[42] Rather than resolve these difficulties, however, Plantinga just suggests, as he has from the beginning, to reformulate the argument in epistemic probabilistic terms.[43] But, Wunder points out, no one has actually done so, and it is not immediately clear that such a reformulation would be successful or even possible.[44]

The first point in response is that this objection would have much broader application than the EAAN; it would affect any move from objective to epistemic probability, something generally thought to be relatively unproblematic—unproblematic, that is, except for the enormous problems regarding probability theory in general. Regardless, epistemic and objective probability are closely related so they tend to correlate with each other: as Alston points out, "epistemic probabilities give us our best access to objective probabilities."[45]

Nevertheless, there *are* huge problems in probability theory, and while we have an intuitive sense of objective probability—Michael Rea considers it "an unanalyzed primitive"—it is difficult to transfer this intuition into a strict definition (as is often the case). Rea suggests replacing it with "rational degree of confidence" which he thinks we have "a clear[er] grasp of" than objective probability.[46] Moreover, this would also respond to the "add a bit" objection. Even if there were a belief we could add to N&E to raise the probability, it couldn't raise our rational degree of confidence.

Wunder does point out that Plantinga's presentation of the EAAN in *Warranted Christian Belief*, "arguably ... is not explicitly presented in terms of objective probability."[47] But this fact by itself does not amount to putting the EAAN in terms of *epistemic* probability, although it may pave the way for such an exercise. As far as I know, Wunder's challenge to reformulate the EAAN in epistemic probabilistic terms has gone unanswered, but this doesn't constitute an objection per se. I am not going to attempt to do so here, but I would certainly like to see someone try it.

Evolutionary issues

Objection: Since we are ignorant of the exact events and processes in our evolutionary history, we are not able to calculate any kind of probability regarding the reliability of our cognitive faculties. Ignorance of our origins does not produce a defeater.

This last point is correct: this is precisely why I made a distinction above about how some beliefs that render R inscrutable may not produce a defeater for R. But this is not the case for N. Certainly, most of the specific steps in the descent of man are unknown to us, but the EAAN is not arguing from what we *don't* know. It's arguing from what we *do* know. Specifically that, under N, the steps in our evolutionary development would have been guided exclusively by natural processes, and these processes would be oriented towards the survival of the organism. So, again, our cognitive faculties would not be in place to produce true beliefs but for another reason. And even if that other reason tended to coincide with the production of true beliefs, then we could only ever have accidentally true beliefs, not knowledge. So, yes, it is true that ignorance of our origins does not produce a defeater. But *awareness* of our origins and their lack of being essentially truth-oriented (under naturalism) does.

Objection: Naturalistic evolution provides a better explanation than theism for why some of our reasoning processes are unreliable. We would expect some beliefs and reasonings to be misleading on naturalism, but not on theism.[48]

This strikes me as a close relative of the argument from evil. From the existence of a perfectly loving, perfectly good, omnipotent God we would predict there would be no evil, and from N we would predict a great deal of evil (or suffering or however we want to unpack it). It also strikes me as similar to objections to certain teleological arguments that point to "poor" design plans in living creatures, like the panda's thumb.[49] I do not want to enter into these larger discussions (I'm trying to finish a book not start another one), but for now I will make two points.

First, Plantinga's epistemology, with its treatment of "trade-offs and compromises"[50] explains why we would have some unreliability just as well as naturalistic evolution does. Perhaps that is a more particular answer than is wanted, since the question is how *theism* explains this not how *Plantinga* explains it. But theism has never suggested that, since God is perfect, the world, his creation, must also be perfect. To the contrary, theism has always affirmed that God alone is perfect and the universe and its elements are radically limited and imperfect. Plantinga's trade-offs and compromises simply puts this theistic claim into the context of the reliability of our cognitive faculties. God is perfect, we are not; therefore, neither is our capacity for rationality.

Second, it is more likely on theism than on N that there would be natural laws at all, including those governing evolution. If there is nothing beyond the physical world there is no reason to think the way it has behaved in the past will be the way it will continue to behave. Thinking it *will* continue the same way is more rational if we think something not subject to change is keeping the natural laws in operation and can be trusted to continue doing so into the future. Yes, this is the problem of induction, and no, I'm not trying to make it into a theistic argument.[51] I'm just sayin'.

> *Objection*: Certainly, some creatures can survive without beliefs, just as some creatures can survive without wings. But it does not follow that those creatures who *do* have wings won't have *reliable* wings.[52] True beliefs may not be necessary for survival, but they can still be useful.[53] Moreover, beliefs are costly in terms of energy expenditure, and evolution is not in the habit of producing useless and prohibitively expensive faculties. "The hypotheses that belief has no effect on behavior, or that having beliefs reduces fitness, are completely absurd. If this were the case then there would be strong selection for not having beliefs, as beliefs are very costly to acquire and maintain."[54]

The first point, obviously, is true. Wings evolved because they were evolutionarily useful. So, while animals do not need wings to survive, those that have wings have them because they played a positive role in survival. And just as obviously, this is not parallel to beliefs and the EAAN. To keep this short (well, shorter), I'll only address the claim that beliefs have "no effect on behavior," not that they could reduce fitness, although that is addressed elsewhere in the present work.[55]

The suggestion that the brain and its neural processes may not influence behavior but still somehow avoided the evolutionary chopping block is indeed completely absurd. But the claim is whether *beliefs* could have, since they would have "no effect on behavior," where "beliefs" are defined as mental properties that have propositional content (depictive mental representations). The EAAN is not asking whether the brain would connect to behavior under naturalism but whether beliefs would—not by virtue of their neurological properties but by virtue of the truth and relevance of their propositional contents. And it is not obvious that having propositional content supervening on neurological processes changes the energy expenditure or evolutionary cost that the neurological processes alone have, much less by making it prohibitively expensive. If these processes were present without any propositional content, they would still use the same amount of energy and would have gone through the same evolutionary processes as they would have if they did have propositional content. This is just the issue of indicators and depictors all over again.

Moreover, the reason for suggesting that, under N&E, beliefs would have no effect on behavior is because there is no naturalistic pathway to allow such a connection. Evolution would select for behavior, not propositional content. Depictors are effectively invisible to natural selection. Remember, the mind-body problem just tries to find *any* connection between mind and body. The EAAN requires a much more particular connection, whereby beliefs influence behavior by virtue of the truth and relevance of their propositional contents. We can't wave this away when we can't even provide a naturalistic solution to the mind-body problem.

Objection: Naturalistic evolution (N&E) is a scientific hypothesis and scientific progress would be stultified if we abandoned hypotheses immediately upon some of their elements being defeated. Much of Copernicus's and Galileo's defenses of heliocentrism were erroneous and the evidence was still inconclusive long after their deaths.[56] So is it "*ever* alethically rational for a proponent of a scientific research program to continue to hold that the research program is viable in the face of empirical disconfirmation or explanatory inadequacy?"[57]

Evolution (E) is a scientific hypothesis. *Naturalism* (N) is a metaphysical hypothesis. As such, naturalistic evolution (N&E) is both—and the part that is being challenged by the EAAN is the metaphysical part. If naturalism falls (by being self-defeating) then naturalistic evolution falls with it. But evolution *simpliciter* does not, and it could potentially be combined with other metaphysical hypotheses that are not subject to the failings of naturalism.

The other question in this objection asks about the nature of scientific hypotheses or research programs in the face of apparent contravening evidence. Well, if we take any position as a research program (or method for that matter) we can continue indefinitely. Perhaps those who want to continue with the naturalist program are doing so because they really believe it is true, but this is irrelevant to the continuing of a research program, just as it is irrelevant whether Descartes really doubted that he had a body. He *could* have—he may have been motivated by an irrational disbelief in his body—but that has no bearing on whether using doubt as a research project is appropriate.

...and the rest

Objection: If Plantinga can select the possible world where God creates us so that R holds (by selecting the worlds where God creates us to have reliable cognitive faculties), the naturalist can select the possible world where R holds despite N being true.[58]

The problem with this is similar to the problem with reliabilism: a system can be *accidentally* reliable. This is precisely why Plantinga includes the design plan in his epistemology: beliefs produced by a process that is reliable but is "pathologically out of accord" with the design plans of our cognitive faculties are not warranted.[59] In the same way, in the naturalistic possible worlds where R would still hold for us despite all of the issues discussed thus far, it would be a happy accident, they would only be accidentally reliable. Conversely, in the *theistic* possible worlds where R would hold for us, it would be because our cognitive faculties were designed (perhaps through the evolutionary process) in order to be reliable—in which case, their reliability would *not* be mere accident or luck.[60]

Objection: Plantinga's distinctions between truth and falsity, between R and ~R, are too simplistic. "[C]ognitive disaster, and the avoidance of cognitive disaster, cannot be simply parsed in terms of the proportion of one's beliefs which are true or false."[61]

Plantinga gives specific definitions for what he means by "belief" and "reliability." No one has to accept those definitions as authoritative, but that is irrelevant. Using those concepts Plantinga constructs an argument to show that N defeats R which in turn defeats N, thus making N self-defeating. We cannot avoid this by saying we prefer different definitions for beliefs and reliability in general. We can just substitute other terms or constants for Plantinga's definitions and use them to demonstrate that N is self-defeating.

If the objection is that truth and falsity, reliability and unreliability, do not capture the complexity of our cognitive processes, then of course that is true, but it is also irrelevant to the argument. Our brains are more than belief forming faculties, but they are not *less* than that either, and since they have those properties, the EAAN comes into play. As for "cognitive disaster," it will depend on how we define *that* term. I think it is reasonable to define it so that it applies to positions that produce defeaters for themselves. And if one doesn't want to define it that way, so what? These positions are still self-defeating. Believing them gives us a reason to withhold belief in them.

Objection: The EAAN is too complex. Most people do not know enough about probability theory and evolutionary biology to have a warranted belief about P/R(N&E). This leads to a sort of "epistemic elitism."[62]

Plenty of philosophical arguments are too complex for the uninitiated to follow but we don't reject them on those grounds. In any case, I don't think the EAAN is beyond the ken of the average person. While it's complex in some ways, the basic ideas undergirding it are easily understandable. The Lucas-Penrose Argument is enormously complicated, based as it is on Gödel's incompleteness theorems, but Lucas himself says it is also based on the same intuition as C.S. Lewis's argument from reason, which is a very accessible commonsense argument.[63]

Objection: The EAAN is too simple. We cannot prove the existence of God so quickly and easily.[64]

First, the EAAN isn't an argument for the existence of God as such, it's an argument against naturalism. Plenty of nontheists reject naturalism, and some have even produced arguments similar to Plantinga's, like Talbott. Second, as above, this isn't really an objection. If an argument is sound, then it's sound regardless of whether it's simple or complex. At best one might argue that an argument that seems overly simple is a red flag, but that just means we should reevaluate it; and if it still appears sound, so be it.

> *Objection*: The evil demon case does not parallel the role of naturalism in the EAAN. In the former we have an intentional agent deceiving us, one who has a motive for doing so. Naturalistic processes are mechanical or automatic and do not involve this. So, while someone who believes there really is an evil demon manipulating their thoughts obtains a defeater for R, this does not translate over to N. "While it may be alethically irrational to give much or even any weight to one's evidence for the reliability of one's faculties in the Evil Demon Scenario, it is not alethically irrational to give at least some weight to such evidence in the machine cases."[65]

This is an unusual objection. Can we now say that we can determine if something is designed, whether for good or evil? Because that opens doors the critic may not want to open. The EAAN can be taken as a design argument after all.[66] The primary objection to design arguments is that mechanistic natural processes can produce the same effects as an intentional agent—more specifically, they can produce the same effects as a *good* intentional agent. But then they can also produce the same effects as a *bad* intentional agent (like the evil demon).

> *Objection*: The EAAN shows that *belief* in naturalism is self-defeating, where "belief" is defined as a mental depictive representation. But if we take naturalism as a *stance* instead of as a belief, the argument cannot take hold.[67] Or, in a similar vein, we can take naturalism as a research project.[68] As long as we do not move from a naturalist stance or naturalist research project to actually believing that naturalism is true, no problem arises.

I have no problem with taking N as a stance or a research project. I have no problem with methodological naturalism either, any more than I have a problem with Descartes's methodological doubt. Remember, he was not trying to actually doubt he has a body or that 2 + 3 = 5, he was just using doubt as a tool to explore the concept of knowledge. One could also use doubting as a stance (doubting claims when you hear them in a procedural sense but fully accepting many of them right out of the gate) or a research project (which would be pretty close to what Descartes did). This is like fictionalism, where we take concepts that we know are not true and use them to explore reality. We use fictions in nearly all fields of thought, including science (ideal gases), mathematics (imaginary numbers), philosophy (possible worlds), politics (social contracts), and elsewhere. In the same way, we can use N as a fiction to explore the natural world.

Some may say we have no reason to take N as a fiction. We do not encounter any limits or boundaries to it when we use it. But a) the whole point of the present work is that we *do*: N cannot account for knowledge or rationality and ends up being self-defeating; and b) so what? Not encountering a limit or boundary does not automatically make it rational to convert a methodology into a metaphysical position. Methodological naturalism has been a very helpful tool in the development of science but taking N as a worldview because of this is unwarranted and will inevitably create enormous problems.

So, in general, I have no objections to taking N as a stance, research project, methodology, form of fictionalism, or whatever. But as soon as one tries to take it as an accurate account of reality, as soon as one believes N is actually *true*, the EAAN comes into play. If someone wants to say N is still unacceptable in these other forms, they are free to do so. Michael Rea, for example, has argued persuasively against taking N as a research project.[69] But that goes beyond my purpose here.

Objection: If we can take ideal gases and imaginary numbers as fictions, tools we use without any confusion about their objective reality, why can't we take Plantinga's *functions* this way? If we do, that not only damages his epistemology, but the EAAN.

Saying our cognitive faculties have no function leads to the same problem as saying they have a different, competing function to the production of true beliefs. In either case, P(R/N&E) is low, R is defeated, and thus, so is N, making the latter self-defeating.

Plantinga addresses taking functionalism as fictionalism right before presenting his initial version of the EAAN.[70] Ultimately, if functions are not real, there is no qualitative distinction between a functioning heart and a malfunctioning one; between a healthy organism and a sick one; between a living animal and a dead one. We can try to really believe this, but I don't see any reason why we should, and I doubt we would be successful. As far as I can tell, the only reason to deny functionalism is if you think we can only make sense of functions if N is false and you really, really want N to be true. That may give one a *motive* to reject functionalism, but not a *reason*. We don't get to reject concepts because they lead to consequences that we wish weren't true.

Objection: It is not enough to say we have no reason to think our indicators would line up with our depictors or that it is improbable they would. We need a specific reason for thinking they do not.[71]

No, we don't. Saying it is improbable is enough, in the same way that it is enough to say it is improbable that the voice singing at the resonance frequency that breaks the wineglass also happens to be singing a word like "break" or "shatter." We do not need to have a specific reason for thinking the singer was not singing that word. Given how improbable it is that she would just happen to be singing a word like that, the critic must provide a reason for thinking that she was.

Objection: Beliefs cannot be distinguished and counted the way Plantinga envisions since any given belief is connected to many other beliefs. "Tom says he has an older brother living in Cleveland *and* that he is an only child. What does he *really* believe?"[72]

The kernel of truth here is that beliefs are more than their propositional content. But they are not *less* than their content either, and this allows us to distinguish and count them. It is also true that beliefs are not free standing, they are connected to numerous other beliefs by being logically related, psychologically associated, or neurologically linked with them. But for naturalism, the logical relation is irrelevant. Yes, if a man believes he is an only child and that he has an older brother, there is a *logical* inconsistency between the two beliefs. We may also say there is a psychological inconsistency, because consciously holding two contradictory beliefs at the same time would not be possible (although *unconsciously* holding them is a matter of common experience—just ask Frege). But of course, the reason we do not associate two contradictory beliefs like that is precisely because they are logically inconsistent, so this just reverts to logical inconsistency. For naturalism, however, the only thing that matters is the neurological connection between beliefs—and for these connections to also correspond to logical connections between the contents of beliefs would be an incredibly fortuitous coincidence. But this means that the connections between beliefs do not detract from the EAAN: beliefs *can* be distinguished and counted the way the argument does.

Objection: Skeptical theism entails that the bare theist is not justified in moving from a perfectly knowledgeable, perfectly moral, perfectly loving being to the conclusion that this God would not allow certain evils, including the evil that our cognitive faculties may not be reliable. We simply do not know enough to say anything about what God would do in order to accomplish his goals. We need to have the *imago Dei* doctrine as an anchor, since this entails that we share in God's knowledge and reasoning by virtue of being created in his image.

This is an objection against bare theism (T) not broad theism (T+), so it means someone who just believes in a perfect being would have to go through atheism to get to the Judeo-Christian set of beliefs. This is odd, since the bare theist, by virtue of believing in a perfect being, would be more open to consider further claims about this being, such as that he created us in his image, than the atheist would. In fact, it would mean rationality requires that someone can only jump into a fully-fledged Judaism or Christianity in one go rather than incrementally, which excludes the experience of many people who have come into these religious traditions. Indeed, the incremental process is how classical apologetics have been done in Christianity through the ages.

I would argue that if we are just working from the isolated idea of a perfectly moral, perfectly loving, perfectly powerful Creator and Sustainer of the universe, then it's reasonable to think events will reflect this being's love unless we have reason to think otherwise. And of course, we *do* have reason to think otherwise: we live in a world saturated with evil. But we do not and cannot have a similar reason to believe ~R, since we could only become cognizant of such a belief if R is true. So, while we can take ~R as a type of evil, it is a unique type. Note how well this fits with Plantinga's epistemology: R is properly basic, and all properly basic beliefs are innocent until proven guilty.

I'm actually a fan of skeptical theism, although I'm not sure if this is because it's good philosophy or because I'm a pessimist. My natural state is to expect things to go badly, and for expectations and beliefs to be wrong, so I am not drawn to this "innocent until proven guilty" position by my inclinations.

Objection: Plantinga follows Hume in defining rationality so that belief in the reliability of our cognitive faculties can be defeated. This is too rigid—too closed to further information—to be called rationality. We must allow for a more liberal type of circularity to accommodate this.[73]

This is Talbott's objection to the EAAN. He rejects defeater-reasoning (at least as used by Hume, Plantinga, and their ilk) because it's quasi-inferential and time-dependent. If a person who has taken XX obtains a defeater for R an hour later, then nothing after that point can break them out of their lamentable situation. Talbott argues, however, that rationality must be holistic and *not* time-dependent so that the person can continue reasoning at any point. Basically, we can always bracket the skeptical situation and start reasoning again, even if we have a defeater for R which would call any conclusion we reach into question.

I'm inclined to agree with this up to a point. The EAAN does leave the naturalist in a position where they have a defeater for any and every belief they hold, so in a sense they are unable to rationally argue themselves out of it. But that's not the whole story since they will be unable—literally unable—to maintain this skepticism about their cognitive faculties once they take their mind off it. So not only can they bracket the skepticism, they can't *not* bracket it. This inability is not irrational on their part, nor is it a mere brute fact: it is the product of the proper functioning of their cognitive faculties. After they draw their skeptical conclusions, they will later have a moment of clarity where they trust their cognitive faculties again and are aware of it. Once this happens, they can run through the argument again, and if they accept it, they will be led back into defeat—and then at some point their rationality will reestablish their trust in their cognitive faculties again, back and forth. Eventually, after one of these moments of clarity, they will break out of the loop by refusing to give up their rationality and then rejecting whatever leads to the skepticism, which in this case is N. So, the naturalist *can* argue during one of those moments of clarity, and the reasoning they employ can be trusted and can lead them out of the skepticism.

The point where I stop agreeing with Talbott is his rejection of defeater-reasoning. Granted, if a person believes R but has no idea whether the processes that produced his cognitive faculties made them truth-conducive, they don't have a defeater because they don't have a reason to reject R, they just have no reason to affirm it. But if they believe the processes were *not* truth-conducive—by being directly aimed at something else like survival or nothing at all—then they *would* have a defeater for R, and this is the case for the naturalist. We cannot use circularity to "restore lost confidence" in a source's trustworthiness, any more than we can "settle whether a man is honest or not by asking him."[74] Bracketing the problem and continuing to reason is not the same thing as epistemic circularity.

So, I think Talbott is right that we can continue reasoning after R is defeated, but I don't think this calls defeater-reasoning into question or justifies circular reasoning. At any rate, the EAAN *requires* the naturalist to continue reasoning. The naturalist accepts N, sees that N defeats R, and concludes they are rationally obligated to accept ~R. *But they don't*. Instead, they affirm R and continue reasoning. If they can't find a loophole to the claim that N defeats R, they conclude they are rationally obligated to reject N. That's why it's an argument against naturalism, not rationality. Basically, they start with Plantinga's modus ponens and end with Alston's modus tollens. So, I don't think this leads to some kind of rigidity that is completely closed off as Talbott fears.[75]

Conclusions

In his debate with Plantinga, Dennett compared the evolution of minds to calculators:

> Arithmetical truth, whatever it is, definitely takes the hindmost, when it comes to what happens inside a hand calculator. For instance, it would be easy enough to design a bogus hand calculator that usually, or always, got its arithmetical answers wrong. Such a device is just as physically possible as a highly reliable calculator. But for obvious reasons, such devices have not been made. For the same sorts of reasons, unreliable empirical-belief calculators have not been generated by evolution.[1]

This, however, opens the door to an obvious response by Plantinga:

> Calculators, of course, are designed and created by intelligent beings, namely us human beings. Calculators track the truth, and do so precisely because they are *designed* to do so.... If we want to put EAAN into the context of Dennett's analogy, we would suppose that calculators reproduce themselves with occasional copy errors leading to different electronic designs. Some of these designs would be somehow adaptive with respect to their reproducing themselves. Furthermore, let's suppose these calculators produce shapes on a screen, as in fact they do, and finally, let's suppose these machines were not planned or designed by any intelligent beings at all. What would be the probability, on these suppositions, that the shapes on their screens are English sentences that express truths?[2]

Dennett's analogy would be salvageable if those "shapes on a screen" had propositional content, and those contents were what made the calculators adaptive to their environments. People build calculators so that the shapes on the screen mean something, and those meanings are the motive for people to use them, thus ensuring that the calculators survive and multiply (ha!). Unfortunately, this option is not available for Dennett and his ideological confrères. The calculators operate according to their inner mechanical processes and *these* are what would make the calculators more or less adaptive to their environments under N. Propositional content has no role to play; "truth takes the hindmost." This is Dennett's distinction between syntactic and semantic engines. The former is entirely explicable by the physical processes involved, while the latter imagines an engine run in accordance with propositional content—something as physically absurd as a perpetual motion machine.[3]

Can we avoid this by rejecting Dennett's metaphysic? After all, he admits that his is "a 'radical' position, which in lonely and implausible fashion declares that much of the work at the presumed cutting edge is beyond salvage," thereby shutting himself out of many traditional and contemporary philosophical concerns and discussions.[4] Unfortunately, while most naturalistic philosophers of mind do not embrace a position as extreme as Dennett's, they still tend to deny that belief contents can influence behavior[5]—which, in the calculator analogy would translate into the meaning of the shapes on the screen having no influence on behavior, leading to the same conundrum as Dennett's.

Even if we say the shapes on the calculator screen have causal power, it is not enough. We must say they have causal power *by virtue of their propositional contents*. Yet even this is not enough: we naturally assume that if such a scenario were made actual, the content would cause behavior in accordance with the content's *meaning*, but this is not given. The content of the belief "My handkerchief is neon orange" could cause the organism that has it to run away and hide from potential dangers. To think the content will just line up with the behavior it causes is magical thinking. I've mentioned the voice shattering the glass because of the resonance frequency, not because it was singing the word "shatter." But even if the content of the word did cause it to shatter, there is no reason the word in question would be "shatter." Maybe the glass shatters when the singer sings the word "kumquat." So, it is not just that the belief (or shapes on the calculator screen) must have causal power by virtue of its propositional content, it has to have causal power by virtue of the *truth and relevance* of its propositional content. And naturalism precludes this scenario.

Problems and solutions

Someone who believes N has a reason to think there cannot be depictive mental representations, i.e., beliefs. They don't just lack a reason for them, N gives them a reason to reject them. Ignoring that, N gives them a reason to think their beliefs are not true for the most part. Ignoring *that*, N gives them a reason to think their beliefs are not relevant to their actual circumstances.

I believe the EAAN succeeds in showing N is self-defeating. I also believe the reason some people express such incredulity towards it is not because the argument miscarries but because it bases itself on ideas we can't take seriously. The response is that the EAAN is not defending these scenarios as plausible: indeed, it is trading on the fact that they are immensely implausible and can't be taken seriously. The point is that *N leads to these scenarios*. Their implausibility is what ultimately leads to N's self-defeat.

For example, ~R is about as counterintuitive as anything can be. Even though it is logically possible, someone could only ever consider it in the quiet of their study, not when they are out playing backgammon with their friends. But the EAAN argues that, as implausible as this is, it would be probable (not just possible) under N. Similarly, we can't take the distinction between indicators and depictors seriously: *of course*, the depictive contents of our beliefs line up with what they indicate. But N leads to a situation in which it is probable that they would not line up. Plus, the argument challenges a worldview that many philosophers and academics have an intellectual and emotional attachment to—and denying it opens the door to other worldviews they find repugnant.

In the preface, I showed that the EAAN is an evolutionary debunking argument. Additionally, it is a transcendental argument. Immanuel Kant discusses transcendental deductions, arguments, or proofs, which argue that skepticism regarding certain claims, like that the physical universe is real, can only be made by undercutting the very conditions that make the skepticism possible. Transcendental arguments were very popular a few decades ago but have since been regarded with suspicion because they presuppose premises one could rationally deny.[6]

The EAAN is a transcendental argument but its presuppositions can only be denied on pain of irrationality—that is, denying them gives us a reason to stop denying them, it gives us an undefeatable defeater for the belief that those presuppositions are not true. Even if we deny the possibility of beliefs in general, this only renders the claim uninterpretable and incomprehensible, and so we are led to self-defeat just the same. The objections to other transcendental arguments do not apply to the EAAN.

Beyond the veil

If N is self-defeating, we must posit something beyond the natural world that anchors our cognitive faculties to objective reality so that R is the case. Here, we can briefly speculate how to accomplish this. I have already mentioned a few attempts. Nagel's "teleology without intent" is a notable example, although he wants to include it within N. This adds purposes or goals to the world but without adding an intentional agent who wants to accomplish them. There is also Talbott's metaphysically necessary truths that function, vaguely, like formal causes. The problem with these suggestions is that merely positing such causes—which do not function as *efficient* causes, that is, "causes" in Modern and scientific language—does not explain why or how they hook up with the physical world (including our brains) so that the world responds in accordance with them. Granting the existence of such conditions, we are still left with the question *why* the universe acts in accordance with them.[7] We would have to posit something else, an *efficient* cause, to explain this alignment. No such cause has been suggested in these cases, but even if they were, they would be an addition to the final and formal explanations and so would be more ad hoc. Can we posit that the universe is such that it automatically aligns itself in accordance with these final and formal causes? We certainly could, but then since we would be adding a feature to the universe that was not previously considered a part of it—since we would be adding this feature solely in order to shore up the theory's weak spot—then such an addition would be ad hoc.

What if we posit a mechanistic or automatic supernatural force to avoid the EAAN? In this case we could have an efficient cause that could create the universe so that it has the properties it does and causes minds to exist so that they have the properties they do without being a mind itself. It's just an impersonal force. But then there is nothing about *this* concept that would involve final or formal causes, much less the arrangement of the universe in accordance with them. Once again, we must add ad hoc elements in order to make the case.

So, let's take a theistic idea, that there is a *personal* agent that transcends the universe (and so is not naturalistic), which has goals and intentions (and so has final causes in itself), and which is the ground of those metaphysically necessary truths (and so has formal causes in itself). This may be in a better position than the theories mentioned thus far, but there is still an enormous problem: what if this personal cause is uninterested or positively hostile to us? What if it wants to deceive us? In fact, this sounds a lot like Descartes's evil demon.

The problem with all these cases is that they are, understandably, starting at the beginning and working towards the end. Plantinga, however, is starting from the end and working toward the beginning. This is his pattern: "warrant," for example, is whatever must be added to true belief to make it knowledge. Since we have knowledge, Plantinga reverse engineers how these cases differ from mere true beliefs. He is not starting with true belief (the beginning) and working towards knowledge (the end), he is starting with knowledge and working backwards to true belief to see what the former has that the latter lacks.[8]

Similarly, Plantinga starts with the Judeo-Christian God and argues that it explains all the difficulties raised by the EAAN. This is not ad hoc because the concept of God in Judaism and Christianity just naturally accounts for these issues. God is the ground of rationality, the ground of morality, and has created human beings in his image. This gives us a reason to think that he would create us to be knowers and would want to do so. This option would be available to other forms of theism that share the relevant traits with Christianity as well, since they could also reverse engineer their theologies to show how the reliability of our cognitive faculties follows from them.

Intellect and will in God's nature

We're not done yet though. Within Christianity there is a debate regarding which properties of God are logically prior to others, and the relevant issue is whether God's intellect or his will is prior. Plantinga comments on this with regards to scientific knowledge specifically, but it applies *mutatis mutandis* to knowledge in general, or at least to those areas of knowledge that the EAAN calls into question if one is reticent to apply it so broadly.

> ... if *intellect* is primary in God, then God's actions will be predictable, orderly, conforming to a plan—a plan we can partially fathom. On the other hand, if it is *will* that is primary in God, then his actions would involve much more by way of caprice and arbitrary choice and much less predictability. If it is intellect that is prior in God, then his actions will be rational—rational in something like the way that we are rational; if it is will that is prior, then one can't expect as much by way of rationality.[9]

We can explore the issue here via a classical philosophical problem: the Euthyphro dilemma. In a debate with Socrates, Euthyphro argues that the gods are beyond good and evil in that they create the moral laws. But this means moral laws are not *intrinsically* good; if the gods had commanded hatred instead of love then hatred would be the moral good and love would be evil. Socrates disagrees with this: if the gods could have

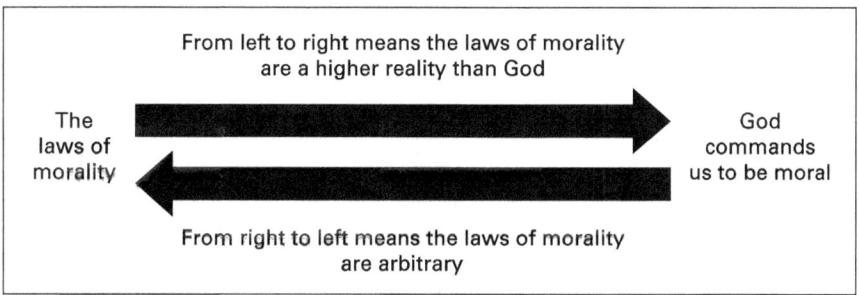

Figure 1 The Euthyphro dilemma.

made the laws of morality different, then they are arbitrary. In this case there would not *be* any real, ultimate good or evil, right or wrong. Besides which, what would we mean when we say the gods are good if "good" just means "whatever the gods do"?

But moral laws and the good, Socrates argues, are *not* arbitrary. However, this would mean that they are a higher reality than the gods, and the gods command us to obey them because they must align themselves with it just as much as we do. Any such gods would not be ultimate, would not be perfect, and would not be worthy of worship—they would not be capital-g God. So either the moral laws are dependent on God's commands (and thus are arbitrary) or God's commands are dependent on the moral law (and thus God is not the ultimate reality). Neither option is acceptable.

Traditionally, Christianity has split the horns of this dilemma. The moral laws are intrinsically good, they are not arbitrary. But their goodness is not something *outside* of God, they are expressions of God's intrinsically good nature. The error of the Euthyphro dilemma is that it tries to put the two concepts—the goodness of certain acts and God's command of them—into a dependence relationship. If the goodness of these acts explains why God commands them, then they are a higher reality than he. But if his commanding them explains why they are good, they are arbitrary. Neither, however, is the case: these two concepts are both dependent on a third thing: God's nature. In other words, the ground of reality is identical to the ground of morality.[10]

What goes for morality also goes for rationality. If will is prior to intellect in God (the intellect being the conduit of rationality) then God could have made the laws of rationality different. He could have made the universe so that it was not consistent or open to our understanding. Or he could have made us so that we could not access the universe even if it *was* consistent. But this is the same binary pattern of the Euthyphro dilemma, substituting rational laws for moral laws. Either rational laws are intrinsically rational, and God commands them because they are a higher reality than he, or his command is what makes them rational, and they are arbitrary. But neither is true. Rational laws are intrinsically rational, not arbitrary, because they are expressions of God's inherently rational nature. Whatever he creates will reflect this rationality. And we, being created in his image, will be able to rationally explore reality. If intellect is prior to will in God, then he *grounds* the laws of rationality and morality, he doesn't just cause or create them, and so they could not have been different than they are. The ground of reality, morality, and rationality all converge in the single entity that is God.

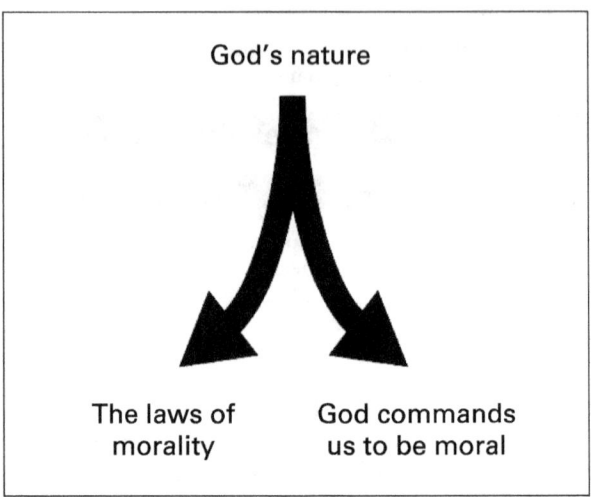

Figure 2 The traditional Christian resolution to the Euthyphro dilemma.

So, the possibility of knowledge naturally follows from a God in whom intellect is prior to will. To be sure it does not *guarantee* it. That is to move from beginning to end instead of from end to beginning. But it does not need to guarantee it, it just needs to not defeat it. The logical priority of intellect over will in God's nature is the majority view in the history of Christian thought, but there have been plenty of Christian thinkers on the other side. Descartes even suggested God could have made the laws of logic different had he wanted, or at least that he could have made them not necessary.[11] As important as these voices and the arguments they present are, they do not represent mainstream Christian thought on this issue.

Regardless, the point is that a God in whom will is prior to intellect *would* present a defeater for knowledge. His will would not be constrained by his intellect or anything else; if it were then his will would not be prior to them. He must be free to do something his intellect perceives as irrational. This takes away any motive for thinking his creation is rational and comprehensible by rational beings, or that we are rational beings in the first place. And if we're created in God's image, our intellects would take backseat to our wills since God's intellect takes a backseat to his. This presents the same problems that allow the EAAN to take force.

So, in order for us to know anything, there must be a God who grounds rationality so that his intellect is logically prior to his will. But now, can't we go back to consider a mindless, cosmic *force* that grounds rationality? Why couldn't there be a cosmogonic principle of rationality that is *just* a principle, not a person? But this still has the same problems as above. A mind that grounds rationality can and would choose to organize reality accordingly. It would structure what it creates (efficient cause) to meet some end-goal (final cause) in accordance with its own inherently rational nature (formal cause). A mindless force could potentially produce a universe, but it would do so blindly, taking away any confidence we might have that its universe would be in accordance with its own internal nature (*pace* Talbott) or would have some end-goal (*pace* Nagel). Plus, how could intellect be prior to will in a mindless force? A mindless force would not have an intellect in the first place, and thus no conduit for rationality. How could rationality be grounded in something inherently mindless? Minds are the arena where rationality takes place.[12]

We can also ask about philosophical idealism or anti-realism.[13] The relevant issue here is the claim that we impose structure onto the universe to understand it. However, if the one who imposes structure onto the universe is not the nexus where existence, morality, and rationality are grounded, we would have a defeater for knowledge for the same reasons already given.

What about bare theism which posits a perfect being without adding all the rigmarole of saying we are created in its image? It depends on how we unpack the concept of a perfect being, whether intellect would be prior to will or vice-versa. I would argue that a being in which will is prior to intellect would not be perfect: it would not be perfectly or maximally rational if rational laws were just arbitrary decisions, subject to its will, just as it would not be perfectly or maximally moral if moral laws were arbitrary decisions. Those Christian theologies which make will prior to intellect in God would not be presenting a perfect being. However, if God tells me I'm wrong when I go before him, I won't press the point.

What about Islam? Interestingly, in Islam, the priority of will over intellect in God is all but the universal position throughout Islamic history—universal among Islamic philosophers and theologians, that is, not necessarily among your average Muslims in the street. This is a misleading way to put it though since it asks which of these two elements are prior in God's *nature*, and Islam denies that God has a nature. If he did, this would restrict what he could do, and God must have no limits placed on his power, else he would not be God—no rational restrictions, no moral restrictions, etc. To be sure, some Christian thinkers have argued this as well, but again, they are in the minority.

All of this is preliminary and speculative and should not be mistaken for resolved claims. They are starting points for further research, not settled conclusions.

Points of contention

This book has been supportive of Plantinga and the EAAN, but I do have areas where I disagree with him. Most notable is that I don't accept his epistemology. I have also mentioned my concern about inscrutability and whether someone could continue rationally trusting their cognitive faculties if they have no idea whether the forces that produced them would tend to be truth conducive. Short answer: it depends.

Another issue I have with Plantinga is his challenging of R instead of MR or SR or normativity. This is a purely rhetorical issue, not a philosophical one. I do not agree with Talbott that challenging one aspect of our cognitive faculties is less ad hoc than challenging all of them,[14] but I do think it makes it more palatable. There will be plenty of people, philosophers included, who will simply tune out when they hear that a popular philosophical position entails ~R. Hearing instead that it leads to the rejection of normativity, or scientific knowledge, or metaphysical knowledge, won't have the same effect—*fewer* people will tune out, at least. Challenging the reliability of all our cognitive faculties is a heavy-handed move: it shows that N defeats itself by defeating virtually every belief we have. Challenging a subset of our cognitive faculties allows N to still be defeated without such an extreme move. Again, this is not a philosophical objection: arguing that true depictors or a propensity to form them are invisible to naturalistic evolution applies to all our cognitive faculties, not just some of them.

However, limiting the argument like this takes away some of its force. It allows for the possible objection that we can shore up the problems of the unreliable cognitive faculties with those that are still reliable. By saying N challenges R, Plantinga is preventing that objection from being made by incorporating the response to it into the structure of the argument itself. Which of the two strategies is more likely to convince others is an open question.

A fourth area of dispute follows the same pattern as the third: I do not think it is necessary to bring evolution into the argument at all. We could easily just say

$N \rightarrow \sim R$
$\sim R \rightarrow \sim N$
$\therefore N \rightarrow \sim N$

Thus, naturalism is self-defeating. If it's true, then it's false. Instead, Plantinga argues

$N \rightarrow \sim R$
$\sim R \rightarrow \sim E$
$\therefore (N \rightarrow \sim E) \lor (E \rightarrow \sim N)$

If naturalism is true, then evolution is false—or, conversely, if evolution is true, then naturalism is false.

Certainly, if we went with the first argument, many naturalists would immediately appeal to E to challenge the first premise, and we could then present them with the second argument. By just presenting the second argument, Plantinga undercuts the appeal to E by not only defeating N but doing so in a way that precludes the immediate objection most critics will make—just as arguing that N defeats R (rather than MR or SR) precludes the objection that we might be able to use those aspects of our cognitive faculties that are not defeated to reinforce those that are.

My objection is twofold: first, since the target of the argument is N, not E, it is more concise to only bring in those issues necessary for the argument to establish its conclusion. The first argument is more efficient in this sense since it includes fewer variables and establishes its conclusion more immediately and forcefully. The second argument, however, is more efficient in another sense, since it takes out N as well as forestalling the primary objection to the EAAN all in one go.

Second, E brings so much more emotion into the discussion that people who are already outraged at the idea of N being defeated are just going to blow a gasket. This not only impedes objective evaluations of the argument, it impedes *comprehension* of the argument. The number of brilliant people who think the Evolutionary Argument *against Naturalism* is an argument *against evolution* is distressing. Of course, they could just be equating E with N&E, but since one of the main points of the EAAN is to distinguish N&E from E, this must be defended, and usually we do not get anything close. Often the identity of E with N&E is not even asserted, it is just assumed and goes unmentioned.

So, rhetorically, I think including E in the argument is a mistake. Evolution is a cultural flashpoint, and many people will immediately marginalize the argument as belonging to one side of the culture wars and not give it any more thought. Of course, it is incredibly clever of Plantinga to formulate it as he does, and it fits in with his general pattern of being a philosophical provocateur, but I think the effect is to produce more heat than light.

The EAAN argues that N is self-defeating and that, therefore, we must presuppose (unknowingly in many cases) that it is false in order for any kind of knowledge or reasoning to be possible. By using E in the structure of the argument, Plantinga is showing that *scientific* knowledge and reasoning in particular cannot be valid if N is true. Science presupposes that N is false. If we are going to trust science, we must come to terms with the fact that the natural world does not exhaust reality. And we *should* trust science, since the alternative is irrationality and self-defeat.

Notes

Preface

1. A.E. Taylor, "Freedom and Personality," *Philosophy* 14/55 (1939): 259–80; "Freedom and Personality Again," *Philosophy* 17/65 (1942): 26–37.
2. Taylor, "Freedom and Personality Again," 26.
3. Cyril Bailey, ed. and trans., *Epicurus: The Extant Remains* (Oxford: Clarendon, 1926; New York: Georg Olms, 1970), 112–13 (fragment XL).
4. Jim Slagle, *The Epistemological Skyhook: Determinism, Naturalism, and Self-Defeat* (New York: Routledge, 2016).
5. There is a huge literature on this I am not equipped to summarize. You could do worse than to look at Joseph Bulbulia, "The Evolution of Religion," in *The Oxford Handbook of Evolutionary Psychology*, eds. Robin Dunbar and Louise Barret (New York: Oxford University Press, 2007), 621–36, and Russell Powell and Steve Clarke, "Religion as an Evolutionary Byproduct: A Critique of the Standard Model," *The British Journal for the Philosophy of Science* 63/3 (2012): 457–86.
6. Guy Kahane, "Evolutionary Debunking Arguments," *Nous* 45/1 (2011): 103–25; David Enoch, "The Epistemological Challenge to Metanormative Realism: How Best to Understand it, and How to Cope with It," *Philosophical Studies* 148/3 (2010): 413–38.
7. John S. Wilkins and Paul E. Griffiths, "Evolutionary Debunking Arguments in Three Domains," in *A New Science of Religion*, eds. Gregory W. Dawes and James Maclaurin (London: Routledge, 2012), 133–46.
8. Alvin Plantinga, "Two (Or More) Kinds of Scripture Scholarship," *Modern Theology* 14/2 (1998): 243–78; *Warranted Christian Belief* (New York: Oxford University Press, 2000), 374–421; *Where the Conflict Really Lies: Science, Religion, and Naturalism* (New York: Oxford University Press, 2011), 152–61.
9. David Diekema and Patrick McDonald, "In Defense of Simonian Science," *Faith and Philosophy* 33/1 (2016): 74–93.
10. E.g. David Hume, *Enquiry Concerning Human Understanding* (1748), Jonathan Bennett (ed.) (2017), available online: http://earlymoderntexts.com/assets/pdfs/hume1748.pdf (accessed January 28, 2021), 85.
11. For example, Thomas Nagel, *Mind and Cosmos: Why the Materialist Neo-Darwinian Conception of Nature Is Almost Certainly False* (New York: Oxford University Press, 2012), 97–126.
12. David Hume, *A Treatise of Human Nature* (1739–40), Jonathan Bennett (ed.) (2017), available online: http://earlymoderntexts.com/assets/pdfs/hume1740book3_1.pdf (accessed January 28, 2021), 242.
13. Sharon Street, "A Darwinian Dilemma for Realist Theories of Value," *Philosophical Studies* 127/1 (2006): 109–66.
14. Nagel, *Mind and Cosmos*, 109.

15 Sharon Street, "Evolution and the Normativity of Epistemic Reasons," *Canadian Journal of Philosophy* 39/supplement 1 (2009): 213–48.
16 Nagel, *Mind and Cosmos*, 125n17.
17 Michael Williams, *Problems of Knowledge: A Critical Introduction to Epistemology* (New York: Oxford University Press, 2001), 33.
18 Although see Jaegwon Kim, "What Is 'Naturalized Epistemology'?" in *Supervenience and Mind: Selected Philosophical Essays* (Cambridge: Cambridge University Press, 1995), 228, and Donald Davidson, "A Coherence View of Truth and Knowledge," in *Epistemology: An Anthology*, eds. Ernest Sosa and Jaegwon Kim (Oxford: Blackwell, 2000), 154–63.
19 Not to mention that the statement "science is the only pathway to knowledge" is not ascertainable by science.
20 William J. Talbott, "A New Reliability Defeater for Evolutionary Naturalism," *Philosophy and Phenomenological Research* 113/3 (2016): 538–64.
21 May God have mercy on your soul if so.

Chapter 1: The Cartesian Dream

1 A.N. Whitehead, *Process and Reality: An Essay in Cosmology* (New York: Macmillan, 1929), 39.
2 Bernard Williams, Introductory essay to René Descartes, *Meditations on First Philosophy: with Selections from the Objections and Replies* (1641), John Cottingham (ed. and trans.) (Cambridge: Cambridge University Press, 1996), viii–ix.
3 René Descartes, *Meditations on First Philosophy* (1641), Jonathan Bennett (ed.) (2017), available online: http://earlymoderntexts.com/assets/pdfs/descartes1641.pdf (accessed January 28, 2021), 1.
4 G.E. Moore, "Proof of an External World," *Proceedings of the British Academy* 25 (1939): 273–300. Although Moore is not arguing the same thing as Descartes, whether it is *possible* to doubt this hand I am holding up is my hand.
5 René Descartes, *Objections to the Meditations and Descartes's Replies* (1642), Jonathan Bennett (ed.) (2017), available online: http://earlymoderntexts.com/assets/pdfs/descartes1642.pdf (accessed January 28, 2021), 25.
6 Descartes, *Meditations*, 4.
7 Ibid., 5.
8 Ibid.
9 Ibid., 8.
10 Ibid., 9. Traditionally, "clarus et distinctus" is translated "clearly and distinctly" rather than "vividly and clearly."
11 Howard Robinson, "Substance," in *The Stanford Encyclopedia of Philosophy* (2018), ed. Edward N. Zalta, available online: https://plato.stanford.edu/entries/substance/ (accessed January 28, 2021).
12 Descartes, *Meditations*, 12.
13 Ibid., 14.
14 Ibid., 16.
15 Descartes, *Objections*, 75.
16 Hume, *Treatise of Human Nature*, 50–4.
17 Bas van Fraassen, *Laws and Symmetry* (New York: Oxford University Press, 1989), 142–3.

18 This option is usually bifurcated into two: one where the foundational belief is justified, and one where it is not. Since there is no theory of knowledge based on the second alternative that I am aware of, I will not treat it here.
19 Victor Reppert, "Eliminative Materialism, Cognitive Suicide, and Begging the Question," *Metaphilosophy* 23/4 (1992): 386.
20 For some examples, see Nicholas Rescher, *The Coherence Theory of Truth* (New York: Oxford University Press, 1973); Laurence BonJour, *The Structure of Empirical Knowledge* (Cambridge, MA: Harvard University Press, 1985); and Keith Lehrer, *Theory of Knowledge*, 2nd ed. (Boulder, CO: Westview, 2000). BonJour has since rejected this view.
21 Most notably Peter Klein. See his "Human Knowledge and the Infinite Regress of Reasons," *Philosophical Perspectives* 13 (1999): 297–325; "When Infinite Regresses Are Not Vicious," *Philosophy and Phenomenological Research* 66/3 (2003): 719–29; and John Turri and Peter Klein, eds., *Ad Infinitum: New Essays on Epistemological Infinitism* (New York: Oxford University Press, 2014).
22 Laurence BonJour, *Epistemology: Classic Problems and Contemporary Responses*, 2nd ed. (Lanham, MD: Rowman & Littlefield, 2010), 205.
23 E.g. William Alston, "An Internalist Externalism," *Synthese* 74/3 (1988): 265–83.
24 Daniel Howard-Snyder, Frances Howard-Snyder, and Neil Feit, "Infallibilism and Gettier's Legacy," *Philosophy and Phenomenological Research* 66/2 (2003): 304–27.
25 Edmund Gettier, "Is Justified True Belief Knowledge?" *Analysis* 23/6 (1963): 121–3.
26 Kim, "What Is 'Naturalized Epistemology'?" 219.
27 Alvin Plantinga, "Reason and Belief in God," in *Faith and Rationality: Reason and Belief in God*, eds. Alvin Plantinga and Nicholas Wolterstorff (Notre Dame, IN: University of Notre Dame Press, 1983), 60–1.
28 This pre-Gettier example is from Bertrand Russell, *Problems of Philosophy* (Oxford: Oxford University Press, 1912), 132, cited in Alvin Plantinga, *Warrant and Proper Function* (New York: Oxford University Press, 1993), 33.
29 Plantinga, *Warrant and Proper Function*, 36. On the definition of warrant see chapter 3.

Chapter 2: Quinean Tonic

1 Willard V.O. Quine, "Epistemology Naturalized," in *Ontological Relativity and Other Essays* (New York; London: Columbia University Press, 1969), 75.
2 Willard V.O. Quine, "Two Dogmas of Empiricism," in *From a Logical Point of View*, 2nd ed. (New York: Harper & Row, 1961), 20–46.
3 C.S. Lewis, *Miracles: A Preliminary Study*, 2nd ed. (London: Collins, 1960), 24.
4 Hilary Putnam, "'Two Dogmas' Revisited," in *Realism and Reason: Philosophical Papers, vol. 3* (Cambridge: Cambridge University Press, 1983), 87–97.
5 Plantinga, *Warrant and Proper Function*, 15.
6 Konrad Lorenz, "Kant's Doctrine of the A Priori in the Light of Contemporary Biology," Donald Campbell, ed., Charlotte Ghurye, trans., in *Konrad Lorenz: The Man and His Ideas*, by Richard I. Evans (New York: Harcourt Brace Jovanovich, 1975), 181–217. Originally published as "Kants Lehre vom Apriorischen im Lichte gegenwärtiger Biologie," *Blätter für Deutsche Philosophie* 15 (1941): 94–125.
7 Although not necessarily with atheism, as Plantinga notes. See Alvin Plantinga, "Against Naturalism," in *Knowledge of God*, by Alvin Plantinga and Michael Tooley (Malden, MA: Blackwell, 2008), 19.

8   Peter Hylton, "Willard van Orman Quine," in *The Stanford Encyclopedia of Philosophy* (2014), ed. Edward N. Zalta, available online: http://plato.stanford.edu/archives/win2014/entries/quine/ (accessed January 28, 2021).
9   Willard V.O. Quine, *Theories and Things* (Cambridge, MA: Harvard University Press, 1981), 21.
10 By "objective norms" I mean norms that should be followed regardless of whether anyone actually does or thinks we should.
11 Quine, "Epistemology Naturalized," 75.
12 Ibid., 83.
13 Quine, "Two Dogmas of Empiricism."
14 Willard V.O. Quine and Joseph S. Ullian, *The Web of Belief* (New York: Random House, 1970).
15 Quine, "Epistemology Naturalized," 76.
16 Hylton, "W.V.O. Quine."
17 Thomas Reid, *Essays on the Intellectual Powers of Man* (1785), Jonathan Bennett (ed.), (2017), available online: http://earlymoderntexts.com/assets/pdfs/reid1785essay6.pdf (accessed January 28, 2021), 259.
18 Troy M. Nunley, "A Defense of Alvin Plantinga's Evolutionary Argument against Naturalism" (Ph.D. diss., University of Missouri-Columbia, 2005), 224.
19 Michael Bergmann, "Commonsense Naturalism," in *Naturalism Defeated? Essays on Plantinga's Evolutionary Argument against Naturalism*, ed. James Beilby (Ithaca, NY: Cornell University Press, 2002), 77–8.
20 Donald Davidson, "Quine's Externalism," *Grazer Philosophische Studien* 66/1 (2003): 281–97.
21 Robert Sinclair, "Why Quine Is Not an Externalist," *Journal of Philosophical Research* 34 (2009): 279–304.
22 Christopher Hookway, "Naturalized Epistemology and Epistemic Evaluation," *Inquiry* 37/4 (1994): 465–86.
23 Quine, "Epistemology Naturalized."
24 Hookway, "Naturalized Epistemology and Epistemic Evaluation," 470.
25 Nunley, "Defense of Plantinga's EAAN," 76.
26 Hookway, "Naturalized Epistemology and Epistemic Evaluation," 479.
27 Stephen Stich, "Could Man Be an Irrational Animal? Some Notes on the Epistemology of Irrationality," in *Naturalizing Epistemology*, ed. Hilary Kornblith (Cambridge, MA: MIT Press, 1985), 256–60; *The Fragmentation of Reason: Preface to a Pragmatic Theory of Cognitive Evaluation* (Cambridge, MA: MIT Press, 1990), 55–74; but see John Macnamara, *A Border Dispute: The Place of Logic in Psychology* (Cambridge, MA: MIT Press, 1986), 182–5.
28 Willard V.O. Quine, "The Nature of Natural Knowledge," in *Mind and Language*, ed. Samuel Guttenplan (Oxford: Clarendon, 1975), 70.
29 Willard V.O. Quine, "Natural Kinds," in *Ontological Relativity*, 126.
30 Stich (*Fragmentation of Reason*, 55–6) suggests this is often assumed rather than argued.
31 Chris Buskes, *The Genealogy of Knowledge: A Darwinian Approach to Epistemology and Philosophy of Science* (Tilburg: Tilburg University Press, 1998), 19–21.
32 Lorenz, "Kant's Doctrine of the A Priori."
33 Hylton, "W.V.O. Quine."
34 Richard Fumerton, *Metaepistemology and Skepticism* (Savage, MD: Rowman & Littlefield, 1995), 177–8.

35 Kim, "What Is 'Naturalized Epistemology'?" 222.
36 It's the only way to be sure.
37 Kim, "What Is 'Naturalized Epistemology'?" 227.
38 Stephen Stich, "Naturalizing Epistemology: Quine, Simon and the Prospects for Pragmatism," in *Philosophy and Cognitive Science*, eds. Christopher Hookway and Donald Peterson (Cambridge: Cambridge University Press, 1993), 2–3.
39 Willard V.O. Quine, *Pursuit of Truth*, rev. ed. (Cambridge, MA: Harvard University Press, 1992), 19.
40 Willard V.O. Quine, "Reply to Morton White," in *The Philosophy of W.V. Quine*, 2nd ed., eds. Lewis Edwin Hahn and Paul Arthur Schlip (Chicago: Open Court, 1998), 664–5.
41 Cf. Hilary Kornblith, "Epistemic Normativity," *Synthese* 94/3 (1993): 357–76.
42 Joseph M. Boyle, Germain Grisez, and Olaf Tollefsen, *Free Choice: A Self-Referential Argument* (Notre Dame, IN: University of Notre Dame Press, 1976), 160.
43 Lynne Rudder Baker, *Saving Belief: A Critique of Physicalism* (Princeton, NJ: Princeton University Press, 1987), 134–48; "Cognitive Suicide," in *Contents of Thought*, eds. Robert H. Grimm and Daniel D. Merill (Tucson: University of Arizona Press, 1988), 1–30. See chapter 6.
44 Hilary Putnam, "Why Reason Can't Be Naturalized," in *Realism and Reason*, 246.
45 Peter Geach, *The Virtues* (Cambridge: Cambridge University Press, 1977), 28.
46 Ibid., 51.

Chapter 3: Naturalized Epistemology Reformed

1   Alvin Plantinga, *Warrant: The Current Debate* (New York: Oxford University Press, 1993), 3–29.
2   Plantinga, *Warrant and Proper Function*, 176–93. He calls his epistemology "Reidian foundationalism" after Thomas Reid (ibid., 183–5).
3   Plantinga, *Warrant: The Current Debate*, 79–80. On the other hand, we could argue that foundationalism is a form of coherentism, since the derived beliefs must be related in appropriate ways to the basic beliefs—and being "related in appropriate ways" is just another way of saying that they must *cohere* with them in some way.
4   Plantinga, "Reason and Belief in God," 80.
5   Plantinga, *Warrant: The Current Debate*, v.
6   Plantinga, *Warrant and Proper Function*, 36.
7   Ibid., 44; cf. ibid, 99–101.
8   Plantinga, "Reason and Belief in God," 50.
9   Plantinga, *Warranted Christian Belief*, 344. For an example, see Maarten Boudry and Michael Vlerick, "Natural Selection Does Care about Truth," *International Studies in the Philosophy of Science* 28/1 (2014): 65–77.
10 Plantinga, *Warrant and Proper Function*, 33.
11 See, for example, Keith Lehrer and Thomas Paxson, Jr., "Knowledge: Undefeated Justified True Belief," *The Journal of Philosophy* 66/8 (1969): 225–37.
12 Or *almost* unified. See Crispin Sartwell, "Knowledge Is Merely True Belief," *American Philosophical Quarterly* 28/2 (1991): 157–65; "Why Knowledge Is Merely True Belief," *The Journal of Philosophy* 89/4 (1992): 167–80.

13 James Beilby, *Epistemology as Theology: An Evaluation of Alvin Plantinga's Religious Epistemology* (Burlington, VT: Ashgate, 2006), 74.
14 Memory beliefs are properly basic while testimonial beliefs are not. Moreover, "a belief can easily change status from nonbasic to basic and vice versa" (Plantinga, "Reason and Belief in God," 50). As such, a belief that is properly basic in one set of circumstances "may *not* be properly basic in other circumstances" (ibid., 74).
15 Plantinga, *Warrant and Proper Function*, 4, 5.
16 Peter Melander, *Analyzing Functions: An Essay on a Fundamental Notion in Biology* (Stockholm: Almqvist & Wiskell, 1997); Lowell Nissen, *Teleological Language in the Life Sciences* (Lanham, MD: Rowman & Littlefield, 1997).
17 Plantinga, *Warrant and Proper Function*, 6.
18 Ernst Mayr, "How to Carry Out the Adaptationist Program?" *The American Naturalist* 121/3 (1983): 328; George C. Williams, *Plan and Purpose in Nature: The Limits of Darwinian Evolution* (London: Phoenix, 1996), 22.
19 Alvin Plantinga, "Naturalism Defeated," (1994), available online: https://web.archive.org/web/20090930150703/http://www.calvin.edu/academic/philosophy/virtual_library/articles/plantinga_alvin/naturalism_defeated.pdf (accessed January 28, 2021), 21.
20 Plantinga, *Warrant and Proper Function*, 11.
21 Ibid., 16.
22 Plantinga considers intentional design as literal and unintentional design as metaphorical because the former make up our paradigms of what "being designed" means.
23 Daniel C. Dennett, "Intentional Systems," in *Brainstorms: Philosophical Essays on Mind and Psychology* (Cambridge, MA: MIT Press, 1978), 12; Plantinga, *Warrant and Proper Function*, 13.
24 Plantinga, *Warrant and Proper Function*, 13–14.
25 Ibid., 14.
26 Ibid., 216–17.
27 Plantinga, *Warranted Christian Belief*, 197.
28 Plantinga, *Warrant and Proper Function*, 40.
29 Ibid., 17–18.
30 Ibid., 19. Note here a fundamental aspect of naturalized epistemology: the way we should form beliefs is the way we do.
31 Ibid., 22.
32 Ibid.
33 Ibid., 23.
34 Ibid., 25.
35 Peter Klein, "Warrant, Proper Function, Reliabilism, and Defeasibility," in *Warrant in Contemporary Epistemology: Essays in Honor of Plantinga's Theory of Knowledge*, ed. Jonathan L. Kvanvig (Lanham, MD: Rowman & Littlefield, 1996), 105; cf. Richard Feldman, "Plantinga, Gettier, and Warrant," in ibid., 209–19; Robert Shope, "Gettier Problems," in *Routledge Encyclopedia of Philosophy*, vol. 4, gen. ed., Edward Craig (New York: Routledge, 1998), 57–8.
36 Alvin Plantinga, "Respondeo," in *Warrant in Contemporary Epistemology*, ed. Kvanvig, 313.
37 Ibid., 316; cf. Plantinga *Warranted Christian Belief*, 156–61.
38 Plantinga, *Warranted Christian Belief*, 171n5, 175.

39 Alvin Plantinga, *God and Other Minds: A Study of the Rational Justification of Belief in God* (Ithaca, NY: Cornell University Press, 1967).
40 Plantinga, *Warranted Christian Belief*, 259.
41 Ibid., 286–9, 326–42.
42 Ibid., 175; cf. Plantinga, "Reason and Belief in God," 17.
43 Plantinga, *Warranted Christian Belief*, 175–6.
44 This is a point Plantinga has defended throughout his philosophical career. See his *God and Other Minds*, 187–271; "Is Belief in God Properly Basic?" *Nous* 15/1 (1981): 41–52; "Reason and Belief in God," 65ff; etc.
45 Plantinga, *Warrant and Proper Function*, 19.
46 "Biologists must constantly keep in mind that what they see was not designed, but rather evolved" (Francis Crick, *What Mad Pursuit: A Personal View of Scientific Discovery* [New York: Basic Books, 1988], 138); "Biology is the study of complicated things that give the appearance of having been designed for a purpose" (Richard Dawkins, *The Blind Watchmaker: Why the Evidence of Evolution Reveals a Universe without Design* [New York: W.W. Norton & Co., 1987] 1). Note that both authors take evolution to be incompatible with literal design, something that I (and Plantinga) deny.
47 The only full-length book on this I know of is Erik Baldwin and Tyler Dalton McNabb, *Plantingian Religious Epistemology and World Religions: Prospects and Problems* (Lanham, MD: Lexington, 2019). Other movements in this direction include Erik Baldwin, "On the Prospects of an Islamic Externalist Account of Warrant," in *Classic Issues in Islamic Philosophy and Theology Today: Islamic Philosophy and Occidental Phenomenology in Dialogue*, eds. A.-T. Tymieniecka and N. Muhtaroglu (Dordrecht: Springer, 2010), 19–44; Rose Ann Christian, "Plantinga, Epistemic Permissiveness, and Metaphysical Pluralism," *Religious Studies* 28/4 (1992): 553–73; Tyler Dalton McNabb, "Closing Pandora's Box: A Defence of Alvin Plantinga's Epistemology of Religious Belief. (Ph.D. diss., University of Glasgow, 2016); Tyler Dalton McNabb and Erik Baldwin, "Reformed Epistemology and the Pandora's Box Objection: The *Vaiśeṣika* and Mormon Traditions," *Philosophia Christi* 18/2 (2016): 451–65; David W. Tien, "Warranted Neo-Confucian Belief: Religious Pluralism and the Affections in the Epistemologies of Wang Yangming (1472–1529) and Alvin Plantinga," *International Journal for Philosophy of Religion* 55/1 (2004): 31–55; Julian Willard, "Plantinga's Epistemology of Religious Belief and the Problem of Religious Diversity," *Heythrop Journal* 44/3 (2003): 275–93.
48 Plantinga, "Reason and Belief in God," 74–8; *Warranted Christian Belief*, 342–51; cf. Michael Rea, *World without Design: The Ontological Consequences of Naturalism* (Oxford: Clarendon, 2002), 221–5.
49 Plantinga, *Warrant and Proper Function*, 6.
50 Ibid., 46, 210–11.
51 Ibid., 194–215; Plantinga, "Against Naturalism," 20–30.
52 For the conditions that a norm must meet to qualify as a categorical imperative, see Slagle, *Epistemological Skyhook*, 102–8.
53 Earl Conee, "Plantinga's Naturalism," in *Warrant in Contemporary Epistemology*, ed. Kvanvig. To be fair, this is just his opening salvo; he goes on to argue that Plantinga's epistemology does not meet the criteria for naturalized epistemology. For Plantinga's response, see his "Respondeo," 352–7.
54 Plantinga, *Warrant and Proper Function*, 237.

Chapter 4: Terms of Engagement

1. Plantinga, *Where the Conflict Really Lies*, 310n4.
2. Ibid., 344–5.
3. Plantinga, *Warrant and Proper Function*, 161–4; *Where the Conflict Really Lies*, 332. For the difference between epistemic and objective probability, see *Warrant and Proper Function*, 139–42.
4. Plantinga, *Warrant and Proper Function*, 142–58; Emmett F. Mashburn, "On Alvin Plantinga's Evolutionary Argument against Naturalism" (Ph.D. diss., University of Tennessee, Knoxville, 2010), 153–9. It may also be possible to formulate the EAAN with Bayesian or Kyburgian probability, but I'm unaware of anyone who has tried to do so.
5. Alvin Plantinga, "The Evolutionary Argument against Naturalism: An Initial Statement of the Argument," in *Naturalism Defeated?* ed. Beilby, 1. As Bas van Fraassen points out, this could not suffice as a definition, since it would be circular: "naturalism" would just mean "anti-supernaturalism," leaving the initial concept undefined ("Science, Materialism, and False Consciousness," in *Warrant in Contemporary Epistemology*, ed. Kvanvig, 172).
6. Plantinga, *Where the Conflict Really Lies*, 318.
7. Materialism, physicalism, and naturalism are often used interchangeably. Sometimes, however, they have stricter definitions (J.R. Lucas, *The Freedom of the Will* [Oxford: Clarendon, 1970], 101–2; Slagle, *Epistemological Skyhook*, 29–34).
8. Plantinga, *Where the Conflict Really Lies*, 311.
9. Plantinga, *Warrant and Proper Function*, 223.
10. Plantinga, *Where the Conflict Really Lies*, 313, 332–3.
11. Plantinga, *Warrant and Proper Function*, 217.
12. Plantinga, *Where the Conflict Really Lies*, 335–6.
13. Ibid., 8–9.
14. Ibid., 10.
15. Ibid., 11; cf. Plantinga, "Naturalism Defeated," 3n7.
16. Elliot Sober, "Evolution without Naturalism," in *Oxford Studies in Philosophy of Religion*, vol. 3, ed. Jonathan L. Kvanvig (New York: Oxford University Press, 2011), 192. I do not think this is an acceptable definition. Physical mechanisms function as efficient causes. Foreseeing which mutations would be beneficial would be to function as a final cause. Saying efficient causes are not final causes is pretty underwhelming.
17. Daniel C. Dennett, "Truths That Miss Their Mark: Naturalism Unscathed," in *Science and Religion: Are They Compatible?* by Daniel C. Dennett and Alvin Plantinga (New York: Oxford University Press, 2011), 27). This comes from a longer quote from Daniel C. Dennett, "The Interpretation of Texts, People and Other Artifacts," *Philosophy and Phenomenological Research* 50(supplement) (1990): 189–90, which he also articulates in Daniel C. Dennett, *Darwin's Dangerous Idea: Evolution and the Meanings of Life* (New York: Simon & Schuster, 1995), 318.
18. Jaegwon Kim, "Mechanism, Purpose, and Explanatory Exclusion," in *Supervenience and Mind*, 251.
19. Ibid., 252.
20. In fact, most of these possibilities would be acceptable within theism, although different traditions may make more specific claims. The first possibility would mean God's usual intentions or actions just are the laws of nature. With the second, the laws of nature could supervene on or be reducible to God's actions. However, the reverse (that God's actions

supervene on the laws of nature) would not be consistent with traditional theism, since it makes God contingent, dependent on something more fundamental than he. With the third, God could create the laws of nature to be distinct from (yet completely dependent upon) himself, and then intend to accomplish something via these laws, making both God and the laws partial causes, so that neither God's intention (specifically, the intention to produce the effect *by way of other causes*) nor the laws of nature would have produced the effect by themselves. (Of course, if God intends to simply produce the effect, not by way of something distinct from him, that intention would be sufficient for the effect's production.) Or God could be the overarching cause of which all the partial causes are part. But if the laws of nature are the overarching cause and God is merely a partial cause there is an inconsistency with traditional theism, for the same reason as above: it makes God contingent. With the fourth possibility, God and the laws of nature could be different links in the same causal chain, God, once again, choosing to accomplish something via the laws of nature. Only if the laws of nature (or anything else) come before God in the chain does it become inconsistent with traditional theism.

21 Plantinga, *Where the Conflict Really Lies*, 265–303.
22 Daniel C. Dennett, "Habits of Imagination and Their Effect on Incredulity: Reply to Plantinga," in *Science and Religion*, by Dennett and Plantinga, 49.
23 Plantinga, *Where the Conflict Really Lies*, 142.
24 Alvin Plantinga, "Science and Religion: Where the Conflict Really Lies," in *Science and Religion*, by Dennett and Plantinga, 16; "Evolution versus Naturalism," in *The Nature of Nature: Examining the Role of Naturalism in Science*, eds. Bruce Gordon and William Dembski (Wilmington, DE: ISI Books, 2011), 137–8.
25 Plantinga, *Where the Conflict Really Lies*, 311.
26 Hylton, "W.V.O. Quine." See above, pp. 20–1.
27 Plantinga, "Evolution versus Naturalism," 138.
28 Alvin Plantinga, "When Faith and Reason Clash: Evolution and the Bible," *Christian Scholar's Review* 21/1 (1991): 8–33; "Naturalism Defeated," 2–3n7; "Evolutionary Argument against Naturalism," 1; *Where the Conflict Really Lies*, 3–63.
29 See below, pp. 23–4.
30 John Pollock, *Contemporary Theories of Knowledge* (Totowa, NJ: Rowman and Littlefield, 1986), 38; Plantinga, *Warrant and Proper Function*, 230–1.
31 That is, that the widgets are painted red or are made of red material; that they would appear red under normal lighting conditions.
32 Setting the belief/nonbelief threshold at .5 is standard but doesn't seem correct. If you thought something only had a .51 probability of being true, you probably would *not* believe it, even though you would necessarily be putting the probability it is false at .49. Plantinga (*Warranted Christian Belief*, 271n56) concurs: "I take it that belief that p is more probable than not is nowhere nearly sufficient for belief that p. (I am about the throw an ordinary die: I believe it is more likely than not that it won't come up showing face 2 or 3, but I certainly don't *believe* that it won't; what I actually believe on this head is only that it will come up showing one of faces 1 through 6 (and not, for example, wind up delicately balanced on one of its points or edges).)"
33 Daniel Crow, "A Plantingian Pickle for a Darwinian Dilemma: Evolutionary Arguments against Atheism and Normative Realism," *Ratio* 29/2 (2016): 145.
34 In earlier versions of the EAAN, Plantinga referred to warrant defeaters as purely alethic or epistemic defeaters.
35 Plantinga, *Warrant: The Current Debate*, 115, 131, 132, 212; *Warrant and Proper Function*, vii, 126; "Naturalism Defeated," 21; *Warranted Christian Belief*, 109, 132.

36 Specifically a Humean defeater. Plantinga, *Warrant and Proper Function*, 42.
37 Plantinga, *Where the Conflict Really Lies*, 166–7.
38 Michael Bergmann, *Justification without Awareness: A Defense of Epistemic Externalism* (Oxford: Clarendon, 2005), 161.
39 Descartes, *Meditations*, 1; Plantinga, *Warranted Christian Belief*, 133. Descartes doesn't actually mention the football helmet.
40 Alvin Plantinga, "Reply to Beilby's Cohorts," in *Naturalism Defeated?* ed. Beilby, 274.
41 On this, see Bergmann, *Justification without Awareness*, 154.
42 Plantinga, *Warrant and Proper Function*, 143; cf. *Warrant: The Current Debate*, 114–61.
43 For example, in addressing Plantinga's argument, Donald Palmer seems incredulous that accepting a belief could give one a reason to not accept it (*Does the Center Hold? An Introduction to Western Philosophy*, 6th ed. [New York: McGraw-Hill, 2014], 192).
44 Jim Slagle, "Self-Refutation and Self-Defeat," *Logique et Analyse* 56/222 (2013): 157–64.
45 Also a mental state defeater, which I will not go into here (Bergmann, *Justification without Awareness*, 154–9).
46 Hume, *Treatise of Human Nature*, 96.
47 Jim Slagle, "Plantinga's Skepticism," *Philosophia* 43/4 (2015): 1139–42.

Chapter 5: The Evolution of the Evolutionary Argument

1 Alvin Plantinga, "An Evolutionary Argument against Naturalism," *Logos: Philosophic Issues in Christian Perspective* 12 (1991): 27–49, republished in Elizabeth S. Radcliffe and Carol J. White (eds.), *Faith in Theory and Practice: Essays on Justifying Religious Belief* (Chicago: Open Court, 1993), 35–65; *Warrant and Proper Function*, 216–37. *Warrant: The Current Debate* and *Warrant and Proper Function* were presented as Gifford Lectures in 1987–8 and presumably the latter would have included the EAAN. I won't go into whether he presented it *viva voce* in other venues before publishing it.
2 Plantinga, "Naturalism Defeated"; *Warranted Christian Belief*, 227–40, 281–5; Beilby, ed., *Naturalism Defeated?*
3 Paul Draper and Alvin Plantinga, *God or Blind Nature? Section 2: Evil and Evolution* (2007), available online: http://infidels.org/library/modern/paul_draper/intro2.html (accessed January 28, 2021); Plantinga and Tooley, *Knowledge of God*; Dennett and Plantinga, *Science and Religion*.
4 Plantinga, *Where the Conflict Really Lies*, 310n4. This book was also presented as a series of Gifford Lectures in 2005.
5 Actually, P isn't a constant, it indicates a mathematical function; thanks to an anonymous reviewer for pointing this out. Also, in Plantinga's first argument, he includes another constant C, "a complex proposition whose precise formulation is both difficult and unnecessary, but which states what cognitive faculties we have—memory, perception, reason, Reid's sympathy—and what sorts of beliefs they produce" (Plantinga, *Warrant and Proper Function*, 220). However, since his analogy of the hypothetical population (below) includes the claim that their cognitive faculties are relevantly like ours, C is "dispensable," and in his later formulations he drops it (*Warranted Christian Belief*, 229).
6 Plantinga, "Evolutionary Argument against Naturalism," 11.
7 Plantinga, *Where the Conflict Really Lies*, 310.
8 Plantinga, *Warrant and Proper Function*, 218–22; *Where the Conflict Really Lies*, 314–16)

9   Patricia S. Churchland, "Epistemology in the Age of Neuroscience," *The Journal of Philosophy* 84/10 (1987): 548–9.
10 William Graham, *The Creed of Science: Religious, Moral, and Social* (London: Kegan Paul, 1881).
11 Charles Darwin, *The Life and Letters of Charles Darwin, Including an Autobiographical Chapter: Vol. 1*, ed. Francis Darwin (London: John Murray, 1887), 316.
12 This phrase has since been taken over by some critics of evolution to refer to problematic steps in the evolutionary story. Neither the present work nor the EAAN challenges evolution and they should not be taken as such.
13 Darwin, *Life and Letters*, 316, italics mine.
14 Cf. Evan Fales, "Plantinga's Case against Naturalistic Epistemology," *Philosophy of Science* 63/3 (1996): 436n6.
15 Darwin, *Life and Letters*, 316n; George Douglas Campbell (Duke of Argyll), "What Is Science?" in *Good Words for 1885* (vol. 26), ed. Donald MacLeod (London: Isbester & Co., 1885), 244; cf. idem, *What Is Science?* (Edinburgh: David Douglas 1898), 62–3.
16 And let's just ignore that elephant in the room: within the last year of his life Darwin was telling people, in correspondence and conversation, that he had an inward and sporadically overwhelming conviction that the universe is not the product of chance but of mind. This supports the claim that he was a "muddled theist" rather than an agnostic or atheist. See David N. Livingstone, "Re-placing Darwinism and Christianity," in *When Science and Christianity Meet*, eds. David C. Lindberg and Ronald L. Numbers (Chicago: The University of Chicago Press, 2003), 184–9.
17 Stich, *Fragmentation of Reason*, 56; Plantinga, *Warrant and Proper Function*, 220–1.
18 Moreover, even if it has the opportunity to select a characteristic, natural selection is not the only force involved in evolution. Random genetic drift, for example, can eliminate the fitter characteristics from a population.
19 Cf. William Ramsey, "Naturalism Defended," in *Naturalism Defeated?* ed. Beilby, 24.
20 Plantinga, *Warrant and Proper Function*, 227.
21 Ibid., 222–3.
22 Ibid., 224.
23 Dennett, "Truths That Miss Their Mark," 35; *Intuition Pumps and Other Tools for Thinking* (New York: W.W. Norton & Co., 2013), 178–9.
24 Plantinga, *Warrant and Proper Function*, 225.
25 See Calum Miller, "Response to Stephen Law on the Evolutionary Argument against Naturalism," *Philosophia* 43/1 (2015): 151.
26 Plantinga, *Warrant and Proper Function*, 226.
27 Plantinga, *Warranted Christian Belief*, 232.
28 Ibid., 234.
29 Cf. Ibid., 161–2, 194; Victor Reppert, *C.S. Lewis's Dangerous Idea: In Defense of the Argument from Reason* (Downers Grove, IL: InterVarsity, 2003), 64–5.
30 Plantinga, *Warrant and Proper Function*, 228–9.
31 Plantinga, *Warranted Christian Belief*, 230.
32 Branden Fitelson and Elliot Sober, "Plantinga's Probability Arguments against Evolutionary Naturalism," *Pacific Philosophical Quarterly* 79/2 (1998): 115–29.
33 See chapter 8.
34 Although this is highly contentious. See below, pp. 165–77.
35 Plantinga, *Warranted Christian Belief*, 231.
36 Plantinga, *Warrant and Proper Function*, 228–9; *Warranted Christian Belief*, 229–31). In addition to Fitelson and Sober, Richard Otte ("Conditional Probabilities in

Plantinga's Argument," in *Naturalism Defeated?* ed. Beilby, 136–41) also addressed Plantinga's initial argument, although not until after Plantinga reworked it.
37   Plantinga, *Warrant and Proper Function*, 229–30.
38   Ibid., 231. This little caveat is significant. It is impossible, practically, to believe some belief B while also believing B is irrational. It is almost as preposterous as believing B while also believing B is false. To believe B is irrational, to think the probability that B is true is less than or equal to .5, just means to not believe B. To continue believing B covertly assumes that something raises the probability back up to an appropriate level.
39   Plantinga, *Where the Conflict Really Lies*, 311.
40   Plantinga, *Warrant and Proper Function*, 231.
41   Stephen Law, "Plantinga's Belief-cum-Desire Argument Refuted," *Religious Studies* 47/2 (2011): 252.
42   Ibid., 255.
43   Talbott, "New Reliability Defeater for Evolutionary Naturalism," 559.
44   Daniel C. Dennett, "True Believers," in *The Intentional Stance* (Cambridge, MA: MIT Press, 1987), 19n1.
45   Ibid.
46   According to which, "'The tallest man in Boston is wise', for example, abbreviates 'There is exactly one tallest man in Boston, and it is wise'" (Plantinga, "Reply to Beilby's Cohorts," 260).
47   Plantinga, *Warranted Christian Belief*, 235.
48   Plantinga, "Reply to Beilby's Cohorts," 260–2.
49   I have received exactly this response at philosophy conferences when presenting Plantinga's claims.
50   James Henry Collin, "Semantic Inferentialism and the Evolutionary Argument against Naturalism," *Philosophy Compass* 8/9 (2013): 854.
51   Jerry Fodor, "Is Science Biologically Possible?" in *Naturalism Defeated?* ed. Beilby, 39.
52   Frank Herbert, *Dune* (New York: Chilton, 1965), 40.
53   Konrad Lorenz, *Behind the Mirror: A Search for a Natural History of Human Knowledge*, Ronald Taylor (trans.) (London: Methuen, 1977), 7.
54   Konrad Lorenz, Geleitwort, in Gerhard Vollmer, *Was können wir wissen? Band 1. Die Natur der Erkenntnis* (Stuttgart: Hirzel, 1985), XIV. The translation comes from Peter Janich, *Euclid's Heritage: Is Space Three-Dimensional?* trans. David Zook (Kluwer: Dordrecht, 1992), 102.
55   There are issues here about how, and whether, two-dimensional beings could function (Stephen Hawking, *A Brief History of Time: From the Big Bang to Black Holes* [New York: Bantam, 1988], 174–5), but we could add that evolution has also given these creatures the inclination to think two-dimensional beings are not plausible, and this strengthens their belief that they are three-dimensional.
56   Richard Foley, "Knowledge Is Accurate and Comprehensive Enough True Belief," in *Warrant in Contemporary Epistemology*, ed. Kvanvig, 87–95.

Chapter 6: Elimination Game

1   That is, propositional truth, as exemplified in a belief.
2   He does say that the acceptance of beliefs "isn't essential" to establishing that P/R(N&E) is low, but, infuriatingly, he never explains how (Plantinga, "Science and Religion," 17).

3   Plantinga, *Warrant and Proper Function*, 223.
4   Plantinga, "Against Naturalism," 31.
5   Gottfried Leibniz, *The Principles of Philosophy known as Monadology* (1714), Jonathan Bennett (ed.), (2017), available online: http://earlymoderntexts.com/assets/pdfs/leibniz1714b.pdf (accessed January 28, 2021), 3.
6   Hume, *Treatise of Human Nature*, 242.
7   Plantinga, "Against Naturalism," 54.
8   Michael Tooley, "Reply to Plantinga's Opening Statement," in *Knowledge of God*, by Plantinga and Tooley, 196.
9   Alvin Plantinga, "Can Robots Think? Reply to Tooley's Second Statement," in *Knowledge of God*, by Plantinga and Tooley, 222n2.
10 Plantinga, "Against Naturalism," 52.
11 Ibid., 59.
12 Arthur Stanley Eddington, *Science and the Unseen World* (New York: Macmillan, 1929), 63–7.
13 Richard Taylor, *Metaphysics*, rev. ed. (Englewood Cliffs, NJ: Prentice-Hall, 1974), 114–19. Plantinga (*Warrant and Proper Function*, 237n28) cites this as a predecessor to the EAAN.
14 Plantinga, "Against Naturalism," 55. Of course, Plantinga is not the first to make this distinction: see, for example, Daniel C. Dennett, "Evolution, Error, and Intentionality," in *Intentional Stance*, 287–321.
15 Thus my appellation of these kinds of arguments as Epistemological Skyhooks.
16 Dawkins, *Blind Watchmaker*, 43–4.
17 On the other hand, they indicate *to* someone. If there is no mind present to receive them, it is debatable whether they *actually* indicate something or just *potentially* indicate something. Intuitions may vary on this question.
18 Jim Slagle, "Yes, Eliminative Materialism Is Self-Defeating," *Philosophical Investigations* 43/3 (2020): 199–213.
19 William Hasker, *The Emergent Self* (Ithaca, NY: Cornell University Press, 1999), 7–8.
20 See Lucas, *Freedom of the Will*, 155–7; cf. ibid., 18.
21 Nicholas Denyer, *Time, Action and Necessity: A Proof of Free Will* (London: Duckworth, 1981), 64 (§43). I have substituted eliminativism for the determinism Denyer is addressing, since his claims apply to eliminativism just as well if not better.
22 Lucas, *Freedom of the Will*, 22; Boyle, Grisez, and Tollefsen, *Free Choice*, 109.
23 Hasker, *Emergent Self*, 7.
24 Ibid., 15.
25 They are not the first to resort to such tactics: in its heyday Behaviorism was often defended with similar rhetoric. J.B. Watson, for example, argued that behaviorism ignores mental states "in the same sense that chemistry ignores alchemy and astronomy ignores horoscopy. The behaviorist does not concern himself with them because, as the stream of his science broadens and deepens, such older concepts are sucked under never to reappear" ("Is Thinking Merely the Action of Language Mechanisms?" *The British Journal of Psychology* 11/1 [1920]: 94; cf. Paul M. Churchland, *Matter and Consciousness: A Contemporary Introduction to the Philosophy of Mind*, [Cambridge, MA: MIT Press, 1984], 47–8). On the Epistemological Skyhook applied to behaviorism, see Arthur Lovejoy, "The Paradox of the Thinking Behaviorist," *The Philosophical Review* 31/2 (1922): 135–47, and Slagle, *Epistemological Skyhook*, 167–9.

26 Patricia S. Churchland, *Neurophilosophy: Toward a Unified Science of the Mind–Brain* (Cambridge, MA: The MIT Press, 1986), 398–9; *Touching a Nerve: Our Brains, Our Selves* (New York: W.W. Norton & Co., 2013), 13–18.
27 On the "exalted" claim, see Jim Slagle, "The Myth of Mortification: The Cosmic Insignificance of Humanity and the Rhetoric of 'Copernican Revolutions,'" *Theology and Science* 11/3 (2013): 289–303.
28 See, for example, Ronald L. Numbers, ed., *Galileo Goes to Jail and Other Myths about Science and Religion* (Cambridge, MA: Harvard University Press, 2009). References could be multiplied.
29 Patricia Churchland, "Epistemology in the Age of Neuroscience," 548–9.
30 Paul M. Churchland, *A Neurocomputational Perspective: The Nature of Mind and the Structure of Science* (Cambridge, MA: MIT Press, 1989), 150.
31 Hasker, *Emergent Self*, 15.
32 See the discussion of Wittgenstein's Ladder below.
33 Hasker, *Emergent Self*, 18–19.
34 Hilary Putnam, "Brains in a Vat," in *Reason, Truth, and History: Philosophical Papers, vol. 2* (Cambridge: Cambridge University Press, 1981), 1–21.
35 Rod Bertolet, "Saving Eliminativism," *Philosophical Psychology* 7/1 (1994): 87–100; Patricia S. Churchland, "Is Determinism Self-refuting?" *Mind* 90/357 (1981): 99–101; *Neurophilosophy*, 397–9; Paul Churchland, *Matter and Consciousness*, 47–8; *Neurocomputational Perspective*, 21–2; Andrew D. Cling, "Eliminative Materialism and Self-Referential Inconsistency," *Philosophical Studies* 56/1 (1989): 53–75.
36 Reppert, "Eliminative Materialism, Cognitive Suicide, and Begging the Question," 389.
37 Ibid., 390.
38 Baker, *Saving Belief*, 134–48.
39 William Ramsey, "Where Does the Self-Refutation Objection Take Us?" *Inquiry* 33/4 (1990): 457.
40 Boyle, Grisez, and Tollefsen, *Free Choice*, 133–8.
41 Ramsey, "Where Does the Self-Refutation Objection Take Us?" 460.
42 Ibid.
43 Ibid., 461.
44 Ibid., 461–2.
45 Victor Reppert, "Ramsey on Eliminativism and Self-refutation," *Inquiry* 34/4 (1991): 503.
46 Ludwig Wittgenstein, *Tractatus Logico-Philosophicus*, trans. C.K. Ogden (1922; New York: Barnes & Noble, 2003), 157 (6.54).
47 For example, at the end of a debate in which Alex Rosenberg presented his eliminative case, they take questions from the audience, and the final questioner asks—very politely—how Rosenberg avoids self-defeat. Without answering the question, Rosenberg responds with incredulity that he could be accused of overlooking such an obvious error: "It's not as if I haven't figured out that this is an issue. . . . I ain't so stupid that I would contradict myself in the puerile way you're suggesting." (online: https://www.youtube.com/watch?v=bhfkhq-CM84&feature=youtu.be&t=2h40m43s (accessed January 28, 2021).
48 Although Hasker (*Emergent Self*, 17–20) points out that many philosophers who are not eliminativists seem very reticent to accuse eliminativism of self-defeat. He suggests they foresee certain consequences of eliminativism being self-defeating that they want to avoid.
49 Plantinga, "Against Naturalism," 52.

Chapter 7: The Probability Thesis

1. Plantinga, *Where the Conflict Really Lies*, 310n4.
2. Ibid., 344–5.
3. Jim Slagle, "Indicators and Depictors," *The Philosophical Forum* 48/1 (2017): 91–107.
4. Plantinga, "Reply to Beilby's Cohorts," 264.
5. Ibid., 259.
6. Ibid., 264.
7. Anthony O'Hear, *Beyond Evolution: Human Nature and the Limits of Evolutionary Explanation* (Oxford: Clarendon, 1997), 40–1.
8. There are various forms of reductive materialism, but we do not need to express that diversity for our purposes.
9. Plantinga, *Where the Conflict Really Lies*, 334.
10. Alvin Plantinga, "Content and Natural Selection," *Philosophy and Phenomenological Research* 83/2 (2011): 447; *Where the Conflict Really Lies*, 329.
11. Of course, accuracy is not necessarily selected. An organism that is less accurate in the form of overgeneralizations may have a better chance of surviving than a more accurate organism in certain environments. See above p. 63.
12. Plantinga, *Warranted Christian Belief*, 232; *Warrant and Proper Function*, 224n14.
13. Dennett, "Truths That Miss Their Mark," 35.
14. This is apparently what fueled Popper's views on evolutionary philosophy of science. See Nicholas Rescher, *A Useful Inheritance: Evolutionary Aspects of the Theory of Knowledge* (Savage, MD: Rowman & Littlefield, 1990), 18.
15. Feng Ye, "Naturalized Truth and Plantinga's Evolutionary Argument against Naturalism," *International Journal for Philosophy of Religion* 70/1 (2011): 35.
16. Ruth Millikan, *Language, Thought, and Other Biological Categories* (Cambridge, MA: MIT Press, 1984).
17. Peter Godfrey-Smith, Review of *Language, Thought, and Other Biological Categories* by Ruth Millikan, *Australasian Journal of Philosophy* 66/4 (1988): 556.
18. Brian Leahy, "Can Teleosemantics Deflect the EAAN?" *Philosophia* 41/1 (2013): 229, 233.
19. Ye, "Naturalized Truth and Plantinga's EAAN," 38.
20. Ibid., 39.
21. Leahy, "Can Teleosemantics Deflect the EAAN?" 228.
22. Ye, "Naturalized Truth and Plantinga's EAAN," 31–4.
23. Ibid., 36–7.
24. Plantinga, *Warrant and Proper Function*, 223.
25. Plantinga, "Against Naturalism," 52.
26. Ye, "Naturalized Truth and Plantinga's EAAN," 29.
27. Ibid., 35.
28. Otte, "Conditional Probabilities in Plantinga's Argument," 142–9. See below, pp. 120–1.
29. Ye, "Naturalized Truth and Plantinga's EAAN," 42.
30. Paul Churchland, *Neurocomputational Perspective*, 150.
31. I will not address here the possibility of depictors that do not indicate anything (perhaps because they depict nonexistent states of affairs) and depictors which indicate something other than what they depict (e.g., a spy whispering into a microphone "The crow flies at midnight" to indicate that they are being followed).
32. Taylor, *Metaphysics*, 114–19.

33 C.S. Lewis, "*De Futilitate*," in *Christian Reflections*, ed. Walter Hooper (Grand Rapids, MI: Eerdmans, 1977), 64–5.
34 Remembering, though, that the indicator can be present without any depictor whatever.
35 Plantinga, "Against Naturalism," 59.
36 Dennett, *Darwin's Dangerous Idea*, 74–6; Slagle, *Epistemological Skyhook*, 4–6.
37 Plantinga, *Where the Conflict Really Lies*, 313, 332–3.
38 Ibid., 333.
39 Ibid., 320–1.
40 Plantinga, "Against Naturalism," 59.
41 Ibid., 36.
42 As with reductive materialism, nonreductive materialism is diverse and the number of forms it takes could be multiplied.
43 Plantinga, "Against Naturalism," 36.
44 Plantinga, *Where the Conflict Really Lies*, 324n21.
45 Norman Malcolm, "The Conceivability of Mechanism," *The Philosophical Review* 77/1 (1968): 47.
46 Ibid.
47 Ibid., 49.
48 Saul Kripke, *Naming and Necessity* (Cambridge, MA: Harvard University Press, 1980), 97–105, 108–10, 128–34. He calls them "necessary" rather than "analytic," which is a subtle distinction we do not need to address here.
49 Plantinga, "Against Naturalism," 36.
50 Plantinga, *Where the Conflict Really Lies*, 324n21.
51 Paul Davies, *The Mind of God: Science and the Search for Ultimate Meaning* (New York: Simon & Schuster, 1992), 168–9.
52 Plantinga, *Where the Conflict Really Lies*, 336.
53 Thomas Nagel, *The View from Nowhere* (New York: Oxford University Press, 1986), 81.
54 Thomas Nagel, *The Last Word* (New York: Oxford University Press 1997), 130–1.
55 Nagel, *Mind and Cosmos*, 93.
56 Ibid., 30.
57 Nagel, *View from Nowhere*, 81.
58 While Nagel rejects materialism but not naturalism, Talbott rejects both.
59 Talbott, "New Reliability Defeater for Evolutionary Naturalism," 550.
60 Ibid., 543. I should point out that he states, "I myself would reject the metaphysics of formal (or quasi-formal) causes" (personal communication), so you should probably read his essay and draw your own conclusions.
61 Plantinga ("Against Naturalism," 49n66) lists Bertrand Russell, C.D. Broad, and "possibly" G.E. Moore.
62 Ibid., 49–51.
63 Plantinga, *Warrant and Proper Function*, 227. See above, pp. 63–6.
64 Nagel, *Mind and Cosmos*, 81.

Chapter 8: The Defeater Thesis

1 Plantinga, *Where the Conflict Really Lies*, 344–5.
2 Plantinga, "Naturalism Defeated," 39–40.

3   James Van Cleve, "Can Atheists Know Anything?" in *Naturalism Defeated?* ed. Beilby, 118.
4   Plantinga, "Reply to Beilby's Cohorts," 241.
5   Ibid., 241.
6   Contrast this with the straight flush case above.
7   Timothy O'Connor, "An Evolutionary Argument against Naturalism?" *Canadian Journal of Philosophy* 24/4 (1994): 537.
8   This is different from the Japanese car case since it's not about deriving a belief from a reason but a belief's source, which we don't have to be aware of to be rational.
9   Plantinga, *Where the Conflict Really Lies*, 342–3.
10 Carl Ginet, "Comments on Plantinga's Two-Volume Work on Warrant," *Philosophy and Phenomenological Research* 55/2 (1995): 407.
11 Plantinga ("Reply to Beilby's Cohorts," 221) ascribes this suggestion to John Perry in personal conversation.
12 O'Connor, "Evolutionary Argument against Naturalism?" 535–6.
13 Plantinga, "Reply to Beilby's Cohorts," 222–4; Otte, "Conditional Probabilities in Plantinga's Argument," 137–41.
14 N.M.L. Nathan, "Naturalism and Self-Defeat: Plantinga's Version," *Religious Studies* 33/2 (1997): 138.
15 Ibid.
16 William Talbott, "The Illusion of Defeat," in *Naturalism Defeated?* ed. Beilby, 153–64; "More on the Illusion of Defeat," in *The Nature of Nature: Examining the Role of Naturalism in Science*, eds. Bruce Gordon and William Dembski (Wilmington, DE: ISI Books, 2011), 152–65; "Is Epistemic Circularity a Fallacy?" *Philosophical Studies* 177/8 (2020): 2277–98; Alvin Plantinga and William Talbott, "Evolutionary Naturalism: Epistemically Unseated or Illusorily Defeated?" in *The Nature of Nature*, eds. Gordon and Dembski, 166–78.
17 Talbott, "Illusion of Defeat," 160.
18 Plantinga, "Reply to Beilby's Cohorts," 227.
19 E.L. Mascall, *Christian Theology and Natural Science: Some Questions in Their Relations* (London: Longmans, Green & Co., 1957), 215.
20 Talbott also points out that, by calling his suggestion a "Trojan horse," Plantinga acknowledges that it is less ad hoc, since the whole idea of a Trojan horse is that it is attractive enough to trick you into bringing it inside the walls (Talbott, "More on the Illusion of Defeat," 156).
21 Nagel, *View from Nowhere*, 80–1. Cf. Geach, *Virtues*, 51; see above, p. 27.
22 Talbott, "New Reliability Defeater for Evolutionary Naturalism," 551.
23 Ibid., 558–9.
24 Abraham Graber and Luke Goleman, "Plantinga Redux: Is the Scientific Realist Committed to the Rejection of Naturalism?" *Sophia* 59/3 (2020) 395–412. Cf. Jeffrey Koperski, "Theism, Naturalism, and Scientific Realism," *Epistemology and Philosophy of Science* 53/3 (2017): 152–66.
25 Hasker, *Emergent Self*, 15.
26 Graber and Goleman's argument is pretty much the same as the second "false start" against eliminativism (see above, pp. 80–1), but applied to naturalism. Talbott's argument may very well meet the necessary conditions to turn that false start into a valid charge of self-defeat if we add the further premise that eliminativism presupposes IBE.
27 Lewis, "*De Futilitate*," 64–5.

28 Otte, "Conditional Probabilities in Plantinga's Argument," 142.
29 Ibid., 142–3.
30 Nunley, "Defense of Plantinga's EAAN," 176; Otte, "Conditional Probabilities in Plantinga's Argument," 142.
31 Otte, "Conditional Probabilities in Plantinga's Argument," 142–3.
32 Ibid.
33 Ibid.
34 Ibid., 147.
35 Hasker, *Emergent Self*, 71.
36 Anthony Peressini, "Naturalism, Evolution and Self-Defeat," *International Journal for Philosophy of Religion* 44/1 (1998): 43–5; David Reiter, "Plantinga on the Epistemic Implications of Naturalism," *Journal of Philosophical Research* 25 (2000): 141–7.
37 Nunley, "Defense of Plantinga's EAAN," 256.
38 Peressini, "Naturalism, Evolution and Self-Defeat," 48–9.
39 Bergmann, "Commonsense Naturalism," 74.
40 Ibid., 67. This makes it a defeater-deflector rather than a defeater-defeater.
41 O'Connor, "Evolutionary Argument against Naturalism?" 536.
42 Timothy O'Connor, "A House Divided Against Itself Cannot Stand," in *Naturalism Defeated?* ed. Beilby, 131.
43 Ibid. Perhaps the evil demon could create creatures who are completely irrational except in the moment they realize it, but this is a completely ad hoc scenario. Although, the evil demon hypothesis by itself is already pretty ad hoc.
44 Such as the Lottery Paradox; see below, p. 186.
45 Plantinga, "Reply to Beilby's Cohorts," 206–7.
46 Ibid., 208.
47 Nunley, Defense of Plantinga's EAAN," 61–2. I have replaced "purely alethic defeat" with "warrant defeat," as the former was one of Plantinga's earlier terms for it.
48 Plantinga, *Where the Conflict Really Lies*, 166–7.
49 Nagel, *Last Word*, 134.
50 William Alston, "Plantinga, Naturalism, and Defeat," in *Naturalism Defeated?* ed. Beilby, 195–6.
51 Ibid., 202.
52 Plantinga, "Reply to Beilby's Cohorts," 274.
53 Bergmann, *Justification without Awareness*, 164–5.

Chapter 9: The End of the Argument

1 Plantinga, *Warrant and Proper Function*, 235.
2 Bergmann, "Commonsense Naturalism," 77–8.
3 Reid, *Essays on the Intellectual Powers of Man*, 259.
4 This cuts both ways; the other way will be addressed in the following chapter.
5 Plantinga, *Where the Conflict Really Lies*, 344–5.
6 Plantinga, "Reply to Beilby's Cohorts," 241.
7 By this light, we could perhaps argue that the brain-in-a-vat scenario is not global skepticism either, because it is usually framed as calling our sensory beliefs about the world into question, but not necessarily all beliefs. I think it *could* be made into global skepticism if we grant the experimenters the same powers as the evil demon, but short

of that, someone could still trust that they feel pain, that 2 + 3 = 5, that a proposition and its denial cannot both be true, etc.
8   Cf. Talbott, "Illusion of Defeat," 154.
9   O'Connor, "Evolutionary Argument against Naturalism?" 533.
10 Plantinga, *Where the Conflict Really Lies*, 345.
11 Paul M. Churchland, "Is Evolutionary Naturalism Epistemologically Self-Defeating?" *Philo* 12/2 (2009): 137.
12 Ibid.
13 Ibid., 138
14 Paul Churchland, *Neurocomputational Perspective*, 150.
15 This, despite the fact that he begins "Is Evolutionary Naturalism Epistemologically Self-Defeating?" by answering the titular question with "Not in the slightest" (135). But if he accepts that N defeats R with respect to the individual person, and it is only in a scientific community forged in the Modern age that we can correct this lamentable condition, then naturalism is at least *slightly* self-defeating.
16 Thomas Nagel, *What Does It All Mean? A Very Short Introduction to Philosophy* (New York: Oxford University Press, 1987), 8. Cf. Richard Fumerton, *Knowledge, Thought, and the Case for Dualism* (Cambridge: Cambridge University Press, 2013), 143.
17 Plantinga, "Reason and Belief in God," 50; *Warranted Christian Belief*, 344.
18 Aaron Segal and Alvin Plantinga, "Response to Churchland," *Philo* 13/2 (2010): 202.
19 Talbott, "New Reliability Defeater for Evolutionary Naturalism," 551.
20 Thomas McHugh Reed, "Evolutionary Skepticism," *International Journal for Philosophy of Religion* 42/2 (1997): 84; Peressini, "Naturalism, Evolution, and Self-Defeat," 46–7. Donald Palmer (*Does the Center Hold?* 192) suggests that Plantinga never addresses this issue, but in fact, Plantinga addressed it in his initial statement of the argument (*Warrant and Proper Function*, 234–5) and many times since.
21 Plantinga, *Warrant and Proper Function*, 234.
22 Talbott, "More on the Illusion of Defeat," 154–6; Plantinga and Talbott, "Evolutionary Naturalism," 173.
23 Hume, *Treatise of Human Nature*, 96.
24 Plantinga, *Warrant and Proper Function*, 235.
25 Peressini, "Naturalism, Evolution, and Self-Defeat," 46–7.
26 Nunley, "Defense of Plantinga's EAAN," 247.
27 Pollock, *Contemporary Theories of Knowledge*, 38; "Defeasible Reasoning," *Cognitive Science* 11/4 (1987): 484.
28 Slagle, "Self-Refutation and Self-Defeat," 159–60.
29 Plantinga, "Naturalism Defeated," 56; "Reply to Beilby's Cohorts," 269–70.
30 Plantinga, "Reply to Beilby's Cohorts," 270.
31 Otte, "Conditional Probabilities in Plantinga's Argument," 143–4.
32 Plantinga, "Reply to Beilby's Cohorts," 241.
33 Wittgenstein, *Tractatus Logico-Philosophicus*, 6.54.
34 Plantinga, *Where the Conflict Really Lies*, 345.
35 Ibid.

Chapter 10: Analogies, Coherence, and Evolution

1   Van Cleve, "Can Atheists Know Anything?" 121–3; Trenton Merricks, "Conditional Probability and Defeat," in *Naturalism Defeated?* ed. Beilby, 175; David Silver,

"Evolutionary Naturalism and the Reliability of Our Cognitive Faculties," *Faith and Philosophy* 20/1 (2003): 59–62.
2. Plantinga, "Reply to Beilby's Cohorts," 239–40.
3. Ibid., 241. As stated, this formula is meant to illustrate the third premise, which moves from a defeater for a source of information to a defeater for all beliefs produced by that source.
4. Lucas, *Freedom of the Will*, 38–40.
5. Perhaps one could argue *Plantinga* is offering an explanation. Then the naturalist would have to provide analogies where a source of information is unreliable, we have no other source for the information, and yet we do *not* obtain a defeater for it. Then Plantinga would have to show how those analogies are not really analogous to the EAAN.
6. Jonathan L. Kvanvig, *Rationality and Reflection: How to Think about What to Think* (New York: Oxford University Press, 2014), 32. Kvanvig's front door account is the same as Talbott's "top-down approach" ("More on the Illusion of Defeat," 152–3).
7. Rea, *World without Design*, 186.
8. Otte, "Conditional Probabilities in Plantinga's Argument," 142–3.
9. Plantinga, "Reply to Beilby's Cohorts," 240. When critics began proposing *tu quoque* arguments against theism in response to the EAAN (see chapter 11), Plantinga responded by giving three principles of defeat to show that the *tu quoques* are not successful. These are not principles for when defeat takes place but for when defeat does *not* take place. The three principles are (1) "If S rationally believes that the warrant a belief B has for him is derivative from the warrant a belief A has for him, then B is not a defeater, for him, of A"; (2) "If S rationally believes that the warrant, for him, of a belief B is derivative from that of a belief A, then B won't be a defeater, for him, for any belief C unless he rationally believes that A is a defeater for C"; and (3) "If D is a defeater of B for S, then for any belief B^* of S, if S rationally believes that the warrant B^* has for her is derivative (wholly or partly) from the warrant B has for her, then B^* is not a defeater-defeater, for S, of D" (Plantinga, "Naturalism Defeated," 41, 45, 51).
10. O'Connor, "Evolutionary Argument against Naturalism?" 538.
11. Nunley, "Defense of Plantinga's EAAN," 213.
12. Erik Wielenberg, "How to Be an Alethically Rational Naturalist," *Synthese* 131/1 (2002): 81–98.
13. Talbott, "More on the Illusion of Defeat," 161–2.
14. One objection is that the demon may be *lying*: he may only have limited power over one's cognitive faculties, or only occasional power once every decade or so, but wants to manipulate the victim into thinking he is in complete control. Assuming the victim believes that the demon exists (they could just think they're having a nervous breakdown), they wouldn't have to conclude that their life is one big illusion or that R does not hold for them in general. We can apply this to the brain-in-a-vat situation too.
15. He also thinks that, upon realizing this, most people would commit suicide. At the very least, people wouldn't engage in the same activities as when they believed reality is what it seems to be, such as donating to charity, helping others, studying philosophy, etc. However, there are real people who believe, or claim to believe, that we are living in a computer simulation who, nevertheless, don't seem to live lives of hedonism and ignorance culminating in suicide. I suspect people who come to believe their experiences are not veridical would deceive themselves, refusing to think about it, and would continue to live their lives as if everything were as it seemed—only occasionally having flashes of horror when they remember that their whole lives are illusory before stuffing it back down into their subconscious.

16 Merricks, "Conditional Probability and Defeat," 169.
17 Ibid., 173.
18 Cf. Wielenberg, "How to Be an Alethically Rational Naturalist."
19 Plantinga, "Reason and Belief in God," 50; *Warranted Christian Belief*, 344.
20 Van Cleve, "Can Atheists Know Anything?"; Reiter, "Plantinga on the Epistemic Implications of Naturalism," 146.
21 Plantinga, *Warranted Christian Belief*, 240.
22 There's a Simpsons episode where the eponymous family is abducted by aliens. When they ask one of the aliens how they came to speak English, he responds, "I am actually speaking Rigelian. By an astonishing coincidence both of our languages are exactly the same."
23 Susan Haack, "A Foundherentist Theory of Empirical Justification," in *Epistemology*, eds. Sosa and Kim, 232–4.
24 Dennett, "True Believers," 19n1.
25 René Descartes, *Principles of Philosophy* (1644), Jonathan Bennett (ed.) (2017), available online: http://earlymoderntexts.com/assets/pdfs/descartes1644.pdf (January 28, 2021), 71–2.
26 Note how closely this parallels William Paley's watchmaker argument for the existence of God (*Natural Theology: or, Evidences of the Existence and Attributes of the Deity, Collected from the Appearances of Nature* [London: R. Faulder, 1802], 1–8).
27 Davidson, "Coherence View of Truth and Knowledge," 159; cf. Kim, "What Is 'Naturalized Epistemology'?" 228.
28 J. Wesley Robbins, "Is Naturalism Irrational?" *Faith and Philosophy* 11/2 (1994): 255–9.
29 Nunley, "Defense of Plantinga's EAAN," 108, 109–10.
30 Davidson, "Coherence View of Truth and Knowledge," 161.
31 Plantinga, *Warrant and Proper Function*, 80–1; "Naturalism Defeated," 5–6n12; Richard Foley and Richard Fumerton, "Davidson's Theism?" *Philosophical Studies* 48/1 (1985): 83–90.
32 Plantinga, "Naturalism Defeated," 6n12.
33 Foley and Fumerton, "Davidson's Theism?"
34 Plantinga, *Warrant and Proper Function*, 81.
35 Fales, "Darwin's Doubt, Calvin's Calvary," in *Naturalism Defeated?* ed. Beilby, 51–2; cf. Ramsey, "Naturalism Defended," 20–5.
36 Or perhaps an omniscient being could construct such a system, but hopefully an omniscient being would have better things to do.
37 Ramsey, "Naturalism Defended," 26.
38 Nunley, "Defense of Plantinga's EAAN," 123.
39 Plantinga, *Warranted Christian Belief*, 235n52.
40 Specifically that they reference by means of definite description.
41 Similar points can be made regarding Putnam's causal theory of reference.
42 For example, Frege's beliefs that there are sets and that there is a property of being non-self-membered.
43 Buskes, *Genealogy of Knowledge*, 52.
44 Michael Ruse, *Taking Darwin Seriously: A Naturalistic Approach to Philosophy*, 2nd ed. (Amherst, NY: Prometheus, 1998), 162.
45 Ibid., 163.
46 Ye, "Naturalized Truth and Plantinga's EAAN," 35–8.
47 Ignoring the rather large issue that evolution would not select a depictor-producing mechanisms by virtue of the propositional contents produced but only by virtue of its indicative properties.

48 Lorenz, "Kant's Doctrine of the A Priori in the Light of Contemporary Biology"; Buskes, *Genealogy of Knowledge*, 19–21.
49 Michael Bradie, "Assessing Evolutionary Epistemology," *Biology and Philosophy* 1/4 (1986): 401–59.
50 O'Hear, *Beyond Evolution*, 51–7.
51 Stephen Toulmin, *Human Understanding: The Collective Use and Evolution of Concepts* (Oxford: Clarendon, 1972), 320–1; cf. Buskes, *Genealogy of Knowledge*, 30–61.
52 Peressini, "Naturalism, Evolution, and Self-Defeat," 229; cf. Douglas V. Henry, "Correspondence Theories, Natural Selective Truth, and Unsurmounted Skepticism," *Philosophia Christi* 5/1 (2003): 96n9.
53 Alston, "Plantinga, Naturalism, and Defeat," 179.
54 Ibid., 182–3.
55 Plantinga, "Reply to Beilby's Cohorts," 272.
56 Fitelson and Sober, "Plantinga's Probability Arguments against Evolutionary Naturalism," 120–1.
57 Wielenberg, "How to Be an Alethically Rational Naturalist."
58 Plantinga, *Warrant and Proper Function*, 221.
59 Stich, *Fragmentation of Reason*, 65; Plantinga, *Warrant and Proper Function*, 221n11.
60 Alvin Plantinga, "Probability and Defeaters," *Pacific Philosophical Quarterly* 84/3 (2003): 291–8.
61 Patricia Churchland, "Epistemology in the Age of Neuroscience," 548–9.

Chapter 11: Expanding the Target

1 Nunley, "Defense of Plantinga's EAAN," 238.
2 Nathan, "Naturalism and Self-Defeat," 139.
3 Plantinga, *Warrant and Proper Function*, 23–4.
4 Nunley, "Defense of Plantinga's EAAN," 241.
5 Van Cleve, "Can Atheists Know Anything?" 123–4.
6 Ibid., 124.
7 Slagle, "Plantinga's Skepticism."
8 Although it's not clear why one can't just be agnostic, not believing naturalism, theism, or any other -ism in the general area.
9 Mashburn, "On Plantinga's EAAN," 145–6.
10 Plantinga, "Reply to Beilby's Cohorts," 229. This is like the proper function objection to the EAAN (see above, pp. 123–5) but in the latter case the recognition of the absurdity takes place *before* one descends into skepticism. And of course, if N leads to a position one recognizes as absurd, the rational response is to reject N.
11 This is because the naturalist accepts ontological naturalism as a true account of reality. Methodological naturalism only uses naturalism as a tool, like Descartes used the evil demon. The EAAN is only concerned with ontological naturalism.
12 Of course, there are further differences between these scenarios as well, but they do not mitigate the point.
13 See below, pp. 192–3.
14 Plantinga, *Warranted Christian Belief*, 175–6.
15 Hookway, "Naturalized Epistemology and Epistemic Evaluation."
16 Ibid., 479.
17 Ibid., 482.

18 Plantinga, *Warrant and Proper Function*, 237.
19 Willard V.O. Quine, *From Stimulus to Science*, rev. ed. (Cambridge, MA: Harvard University Press, 1998).
20 Or *claims* to only be asking about local issues. If Talbott ("New Reliability Defeater for Evolutionary Naturalism") is right, science is utterly dependent on inference to the best explanation, and this requires us to ask global questions. Insofar as naturalized epistemology accepts (indeed tries to base itself upon) science, naturalized epistemology has to ask global questions to ground inference to the best explanation.
21 Nagel, *Last Word*, 15.
22 Plantinga, "Reply to Beilby's Cohorts," 205n2.
23 Plantinga, "Against Naturalism," 15.
24 Nagel, *Mind and Cosmos*, 93.
25 Talbott, "New Reliability Defeater for Evolutionary Naturalism," 550.
26 Ginet, "Comments on Plantinga's Two-Volume Work on Warrant," 407.
27 Plantinga, *Where the Conflict Really Lies*, 311.
28 Plantinga, *Warranted Christian Belief*, 175–6.
29 Also, *if* Plantinga is right. He has been accused of fideism on this point by other Christian philosophers.
30 This does not mean that one must accept the A/C model in all its detail. One could accept something moderately similar that would still have the same results.
31 Plantinga, *Warranted Christian Belief*, 191.
32 Ibid., part II.
33 Ibid., 169.
34 Plantinga's initial foray where he argues N is false is a *de facto* argument; see above, pp. 66–7.
35 Plantinga and others have made similar distinctions with similar abbreviations. There are subtle differences between them, so the reader is warned not to read others' definitions into mine or vice-versa.
36 Plantinga, "Naturalism Defeated," 47.
37 Plantinga, *Warranted Christian Belief*, 80.
38 Ibid., 236.
39 Hylton, "W.V.O. Quine."
40 Pascal Boyer, "Religion: Bound to Believe?" *Nature* 455/7216) (October 23, 2008): 1038–9; University of Oxford, "Humans 'Predisposed' to Believe in Gods and the Afterlife," *ScienceDaily* (July 14, 2011), available online: http://sciencedaily.com/releases/2011/07/110714103828.htm (accessed January 28, 2021).
41 Cf. Erik Baldwin and Tyler McNabb, "An Epistemic Defeater for Islamic Belief?" *International Journal of Philosophy and Theology* 76/4 (2015): 352–67. The Qur'anic passages listed state that God deceives and even that he is the greatest deceiver (from the root mekr). Contrast this with Jer. 4:10 and 20:7 in the Bible where the author accuses God of having deceived him or the Israelites. In the latter case, Jeremiah is ranting against God, while in the Qur'anic passages God's role as a deceiver is stated by the angel revealing the contents of the Qur'an to Muhammad.
42 Al-Bukhaari 6227; Muslim 2612; Muslim 2841.
43 Keith Lehrer, "Proper Function versus Systematic Coherence," in *Warrant in Contemporary Epistemology*, ed. Kvanvig, 29–30.
44 Granted, some Christian thinkers and Christian traditions extend this to R more generally, but it is difficult to see how they can avoid the same kind of self-defeat the EAAN engenders for N.

45 Plantinga, *Warranted Christian Belief*, 282–4.
46 Plantinga, "Respondeo," 336–7.
47 Fales, "Darwin's Doubt, Calvin's Calvary," 53–6.
48 *Summa Theologica* 1.93.4; 1.93.6. Specifically, he refers to intellect which is the vehicle for rationality.
49 Lehrer, "Proper Function versus Systematic Coherence," 28–30; D. Blake Roeber, "Does the Theist Have an Epistemic Advantage Over the Atheist?" *Journal of Philosophical Research* 34 (2009): 305–28.
50 E.g. David Lewis, "Divine Evil," in *Philosophers without Gods: Meditations on Atheism and the Secular Life*, ed. Louise Anthony (New York: Oxford University Press, 2004), 231; Galen Strawson, Georges Rey, and Thomas Nagel, "What Can Be Proved about God?" *New York Review of Books*, December 6, 2012, available online: http://nybooks.com/articles/2012/12/06/what-can-be-proved-about-god/ (accessed January 28, 2021), specifically Strawson's contribution.
51 Plantinga, *God and Other Minds*, 131–55; *The Nature of Necessity* (Oxford: Clarendon, 1974), 164–95; *God, Freedom, and Evil* (Grand Rapids, MI: Eerdmans, 1977), 30–55; *Warranted Christian Belief*, 461–2.
52 Fales, "Darwin's Doubt, Calvin's Calvary," 55–7.
53 See, for example, Marilyn McCord Adams, *Horrendous Evils and the Goodness of God* (Ithaca, NY: Cornell University Press, 1999).
54 This is the flip side of Merricks's ("Conditional Probability and Defeat") revised evil demon hypothesis; see above, pp. 147–9.
55 Plantinga, *Warrant and Proper Function*, 217.
56 Plantinga, "Naturalism Defeated," 21.
57 Plantinga, *Warrant: The Current Debate*, 82.
58 Dallas Willard, *Hearing God: Developing a Conversational Relationship with God* (Downers Grove, IL: InterVarsity, 1999), 196.
59 Antony Flew seems to have experienced something like this. See Antony Flew with Roy Abraham Varghese, *There Is a God: How the World's Most Notorious Atheist Changed His Mind* (New York: HarperCollins, 2007).
60 Plantinga, "Naturalism Defeated," 44.
61 Contrast this with the case of the dualistic atheist (above, pp. 107–8).
62 Darwin himself suggested religion started with animism, which developed into fetishism, polytheism, and eventually monotheism (*The Descent of Man and Selection in Relation to Sex* [Princeton, NJ: Princeton University Press, 1871], 68).
63 E.E. Evans-Pritchard, *Theories of Primitive Religion* (New York: Oxford University Press, 1965), 104–5 and *passim*.
64 See chapter 3 note 48 for some references.
65 Baldwin and McNabb, "An Epistemic Defeater for Islamic Belief?"
66 C.S. Cowles, Eugene H. Merrill, Daniel L. Gard, and Tremper Longman III, *Show Them No Mercy: Four Views on the Canaanite Genocide* (Grand Rapids, MI: Zondervan, 2003).

Chapter 12: Loose Ends

1 Ramsey, "Naturalism Defended," 22.
2 James Beilby, "Is Evolutionary Naturalism Self-Defeating?" *International Journal for Philosophy of Religion* 42/2 (1997): 69–78.
3 Ye, "Naturalized Truth and Plantinga's EAAN," 30.

4 See above, pp. 83–5.
5 Daniel D. Novotný, "How to Save Naturalism from Plantinga?" *Organon F: Medzinárodný Časopis Pre Analytickú Filozofiu* 14/1 (2007): 32–48.
6 Plantinga, *Warranted Christian Belief*, 232.
7 Michael Levin, "Plantinga on Functions and the Theory of Evolution," *Australasian Journal of Philosophy* 75/1 (1997): 95.
8 Slagle, *Epistemological Skyhook*, 118–21.
9 Marshall Swain, "Warrant versus Indefeasible Justification," in *Warrant in Contemporary Epistemology*, ed. Kvanvig, 132, 134, 145.
10 Plantinga, *Warrant and Proper Function*, ch. 11.
11 Ibid., ch. 12.
12 Plantinga, "Reply to Beilby's Cohorts," 205n2.
13 Conee, "Plantinga's Naturalism"; Novotný, "How to Save Naturalism from Plantinga?"
14 Plantinga, "Respondeo," 352–7.
15 Stich, "Naturalizing Epistemology," 2–3.
16 Boudry and Vlerick, "Natural Selection Does Care about Truth," 71–2.
17 Ibid.; Bernardo Cantens, "Cognitive Faculties and Evolutionary Naturalism," *Proceedings of the American Catholic Philosophical Association* 80 (2007): 201–8.; Robbins, "Is Naturalism Irrational?"; Ramsey, "Naturalism Defended," 16–19.
18 Nunley, "Defense of Plantinga's EAAN," 117; Mashburn, "On Plantinga's EAAN," 55–60.
19 Boudry and Vlerick, "Natural Selection Does Care about Truth," 71–2; Paul Churchland, "Is Evolutionary Naturalism Epistemologically Self-Defeating?"
20 Novotný, "How to Save Naturalism from Plantinga?"; Henry, "Correspondence Theories, Natural Selective Truth, and Unsurmounted Skepticism," 96n9.
21 Plantinga, "Evolutionary Argument against Naturalism," 9.
22 Omar Mirza, "A User's Guide to the Evolutionary Argument Against Naturalism," *Philosophical Studies* 141/2 (2008): 125–46. Mirza reconfigures the EAAN so that it is still viable.
23 Fitelson and Sober, "Plantinga's Probability Arguments against Evolutionary Naturalism," 124.
24 Recall the trade-offs or compromises in Plantinga's epistemology: "a belief has warrant for you only if the segment of the design plan governing its production is *directly* rather than indirectly aimed at the production of true beliefs" (*Warrant and Proper Function*, 40). If it is a by-product of some other goal then the belief fails to have warrant.
25 Wielenberg, "How to Be an Alethically Rational Naturalist," 91–3; O'Connor, "Evolutionary Argument against Naturalism?" 536; Nunley, "Defense of Plantinga's EAAN," 207–9.
26 Lehrer, "Proper Function versus Systematic Coherence," 27.
27 Patricia Churchland, "Epistemology in the Age of Neuroscience," 548–9.
28 Fitelson and Sober, "Plantinga's Probability Arguments against Evolutionary Naturalism," 126.
29 Plantinga, "Probabilities and Defeaters," 295.
30 Fitelson and Sober, "Plantinga's Probability Arguments against Evolutionary Naturalism," 126.
31 Such as the preface paradox (Plantinga, *Warrant and Proper Function*, 43; *Warranted Christian Belief*, 23n25).
32 Tyler A. Wunder, "Alvin Plantinga on Paul Draper's Evolutionary Atheology: Implications of Theism's Noncontingency," *International Journal for Philosophy of*

Religion 74/1 (2013): 67–75; "The Modality of Theism and Probabilistic Natural Theology: A Tension in Alvin Plantinga's Philosophy," *Religious Studies* 51/3 (2015): 391–9.
33 Richard Bosse, "Wunder's Probability Objection," *International Journal for Philosophy of Religion* 84/1 (2018): 139.
34 Ibid., 136.
35 Karl Popper, *The Logic of Scientific Discovery* (New York: Harper & Row, 1968), 349–86. Bosse ("Wunder's Probability Objection," 137–8) cites this from a later edition with slightly different pagination, noting specifically p. 353n1 in Popper and the account of how theorem (33′) is derived.
36 Perry Hendricks, "Response to Wunder: Objective Probability, Non-Contingent Theism, and the EAAN," *Religious Studies* 56/2 (2020): 294.
37 "Say that metaphysical naturalism (call it 'N') is the idea, roughly, that there is no such person as God or anything at all like God—or if there is, this being plays no causal role in the world's transactions" (Plantinga, "Content and Natural Selection," 435).
38 Hendricks, "Response to Wunder," 3.
39 See Baldwin and McNabb, *Plantingian Religious Epistemology and World Religions*.
40 Plantinga, *Warranted Christian Belief*, 230.
41 Wunder, "Alvin Plantinga on Paul Draper's Evolutionary Atheology," 73–4.
42 Wunder, "Modality of Theism and Probabilistic Natural Theology," 394.
43 Plantinga, *Warrant and Proper Function*, 161–4; *Where the Conflict Really Lies*, 332.
44 Wunder, "Modality of Theism and Probabilistic Natural Theology," 394–6.
45 Alston, "Plantinga, Naturalism, and Defeat," 179.
46 Rea, *World without Design*, 179–80, 186.
47 Wunder, "Modality of Theism and Probabilistic Natural Theology," 398n14.
48 Petteri Nieminen, Maarten Boudry, Esko Ryökäs, and Anne-Mari Mustonen, "Biblical and Theistic Arguments against the Evolutionary Argument against Naturalism," *Zygon* 52/1 (2017): 10; Ramsey, "Naturalism Defended," 28–9; Fales, "Darwin's Doubt, Calvin's Calvary," 57–8. Descartes devoted a significant amount of the *Meditations* to answering this question.
49 Stephen Jay Gould, *The Panda's Thumb: More Reflections in Natural History* (New York: W.W. Norton & Co., 1980).
50 Plantinga, *Warrant and Proper Function*, 38–40.
51 Although see Alvin Plantinga, "Two Dozen (or so) Theistic Arguments," in *Alvin Plantinga*, ed. Deane-Peter Baker (Cambridge: Cambridge University Press, 2007), 220.
52 Boudry and Vlerick, "Natural Selection Does Care about Truth," 68–9.
53 Lehrer, "Proper Function versus Systematic Coherence," 27.
54 Paul E. Griffiths and John S. Wilkins, "Crossing the Milvian Bridge: When Do Evolutionary Explanations of Belief Debunk Belief?" in *Darwin in the Twenty-First Century: Nature, Humanity, and God*, eds. Phillip R. Sloan, Gerald McKenny, and Kathleen Eggleson (Notre Dame, IN: University of Notre Dame Press, 2015), 208. Evan Fales also makes this point in "Plantinga's Case against Naturalistic Epistemology," 440–1 and "Darwin's Doubt, Calvin's Calvary," 48–9.
55 See above, pp. 64–5. Moreover, as also already noted, Plantinga is giving an exhaustive account, where all possibilities are addressed. He could not have ignored the possibility that beliefs are detrimental to survival and still called his account "exhaustive."
56 James Beilby, "Alvin Plantinga's Pox on Metaphysical Naturalism," *Philosophia Christi* 5/1 (2003): 131–42; "Plantinga's Pox on Naturalism Revisited: A Reply to Michael Thune," *Philosophia Christi* 7/2 (2005): 169–76. On the evidence being inconclusive,

see Christopher M. Graney, *Setting Aside All Authority: Giovanni Battista Riccioli and the Science against Copernicus in the Age of Galileo* (Notre Dame, IN: University of Notre Dame Press, 2015).
57 Beilby, "Plantinga's Pox on Naturalism Revisited," 173.
58 Matthew Tedesco, "Theism, Naturalistic Evolution and the Probability of Reliable Cognitive Faculties: A Response to Plantinga," *Philo* 5/2 (2002): 235–41.
59 Plantinga, *Warrant and Proper Function*, 14. For examples, see ibid., 197–208.
60 Ignoring, again, that if God exists, he exists in all possible worlds and has the same properties in all possible worlds.
61 Collin, "Semantic Inferentialism and the EAAN," 854; Boudry and Vlerick, "Natural Selection Does Care about Truth," 66–7; Ramsey, "Naturalism Defended," 25.
62 Crow, "Plantingian Pickle for a Darwinian Dilemma," 144–7.
63 J.R. Lucas, "The Restoration of Man," *Theology* 98/786 (1995): 453–5. On the Lucas-Penrose argument, see Lucas, *Freedom of the Will* and Slagle, *Epistemological Skyhook*, 52–60. On Lewis's argument from reason, see ibid., 110–23 and Reppert, *C.S. Lewis's Dangerous Idea*. These books will point the interested reader towards further references. I am not defending these arguments here, but they are of the same family as the EAAN.
64 Reed, "Evolutionary Skepticism," 91–2.
65 Wielenberg, "How to Be an Alethically Rational Naturalist," 92; Ramsey, "Naturalism Defended," 28.
66 Plantinga, *Warrant and Proper Function*, 214–15; cf. Slagle, *Epistemological Skyhook*, 221–3.
67 van Fraassen, "Science, Materialism, and False Consciousness."
68 Beilby, "Alvin Plantinga's Pox on Metaphysical Naturalism"; "Plantinga's Pox on Naturalism Revisited"; Michael Thune, "Plantinga Untouched: A Response to Beilby on the Evolutionary Argument Against Naturalism," *Philosophia Christi* 7/1 (2005): 157–68.
69 Rea, *World without Design*.
70 Plantinga, *Warrant and Proper Function*, 211–15.
71 Fodor, "Is Science Biologically Possible?" 40.
72 Daniel C. Dennett, "Self-Portrait," in *Brainchildren: Essays on Designing Minds* (Cambridge, MA: MIT Press, 1998), 362.
73 William Talbott, "Is Epistemic Circularity a Fallacy?" *Philosophical Studies* 177/8 (2020): 2277–98.
74 Bergmann, "Commonsense Naturalism," 77–8; Reid, *Essays on the Intellectual Powers of Man*, 259.
75 Talbott's objection actually goes much deeper than this. See his *Learning from Our Mistakes: Epistemology for the Real World* (New York: Oxford University Press, forthcoming), which is nothing less than a complete overhaul of our concepts of reasoning and rationality.

Conclusions

1 Dennett, "Truths That Miss Their Mark," 35–6.
2 Alvin Plantinga, "Superman vs. God?" in Dennett and Plantinga, *Science and Religion*, 43.
3 Dennett, "Truths That Miss Their Mark," 35.

4 Dennett, "Self-Portrait," 366.
5 Plantinga, *Warrant and Proper Function*, 224n14.
6 Robert Stern, "Transcendental Arguments," in *The Stanford Encyclopedia of Philosophy* (2019), ed. Edward N. Zalta, available online: https://plato.stanford.edu/archives/sum2019/entries/transcendental-arguments/ (accessed January 28, 2021).
7 This parallels the problem of how the propositional content of a belief lines up with the neural, physical substrate on which it supervenes.
8 Plantinga, *Warrant and Proper Function*, v.
9 Plantinga, *Where the Conflict Really Lies*, 273.
10 As noted, this is the traditional Christian resolution to the Euthyphro dilemma through the centuries, from Augustine to Aquinas to Alston. It always amazes me how so many brilliant philosophers seem to be completely unaware of it. They bring up the Euthyphro dilemma as a silver bullet against theism, as if no one has ever thought of a response to it over the last 2,500 years.
11 Descartes, *Objections*, 153–4; 156–7; Peter Geach, *Providence and Evil* (Cambridge: Cambridge University Press, 1977), 10–11; Alvin Plantinga, *Does God Have a Nature?* (Milwaukee: Marquette University Press, 1980), 95–109.
12 Not to mention that anything created in the image of a mindless force would be a mindless force itself.
13 Plantinga ("Against Naturalism," 15–17) addresses this, distinguishing between "creative anti-realism" and "postmodern anti-realism." He rejects both but for reasons other than the EAAN.
14 Talbott, "Illusion of Defeat," 154; "More on the Illusion of Defeat," 156.

Bibliography of the EAAN

The following list contains all the references I have found on Alvin Plantinga's Evolutionary Argument against Naturalism. If only a part of a citation addresses the argument, the relevant page numbers are in brackets following its entry. I only include references that interact with the argument, not those that just mention it or signal their agreement or disagreement with it. I include Doctoral dissertations, some book reviews, and a few scholarly online sources, but I do not include references that focus solely on Plantinga's claim that proper function is incompatible with naturalism. Even though this is the initial foray into the argument and its consequences, I believe that it would be misleading to include them unless they go on to engage directly with the EAAN. As must be the case, I'm sure there are references I have missed, so if the reader knows of any that did not make it into this bibliography, they are invited to contact me.

Alston, William. "Plantinga, Naturalism, and Defeat." In *Naturalism Defeated? Essays on Plantinga's Evolutionary Argument against Naturalism*, edited by James Beilby, 176–203. Ithaca, NY: Cornell University Press, 2002.

Anderson, James. "If Knowledge Then God: The Epistemological Theistic Arguments of Plantinga and Van Til." *Calvin Theological Journal* 40/1 (2005): 49–75.

Arnold, Alexander. "The Argument from the Confluence of Proper Function and Reliability." In *Two Dozen (or so) Arguments for God: The Plantinga Project*, edited by Jerry Walls and Trent Dougherty, 170–83. New York: Oxford University Press, 2018.

Atalay, Sare Levin and Caner Taslaman. "Natüralizm ve Teizm Açısından Akıl Delilinin Değerlendirilmesi (An Evaluation of the Argument from Reason with Regard to Naturalism and Theism)." *Kader* 15/2 (2017): 362–89. [371–4]

Attfield, Robin. "Darwin's Doubt, Non-Deterministic Darwinism and the Cognitive Science of Religion." *Philosophy* 85/4 (2010): 465–83. [470–2, 480–3]

Baldwin, Erik and Tyler Dalton McNabb. "An Epistemic Defeater for Islamic Belief?" *International Journal of Philosophy and Theology* 76/4 (2015): 352–67.

Baldwin, Erik and Tyler Dalton McNabb. *Plantingian Religious Epistemology and World Religions: Prospects and Problems*. Lanham, MD: Lexington, 2019. [41–54]

Beilby, James. "Is Evolutionary Naturalism Self-Defeating?" *International Journal for Philosophy of Religion* 42/2 (1997): 69–78.

Beilby, James., ed. *Naturalism Defeated? Essays on Plantinga's Evolutionary Argument against Naturalism*. Ithaca, NY: Cornell University Press, 2002.

Beilby, James. "Alvin Plantinga's Pox on Metaphysical Naturalism." *Philosophia Christi* 5/1 (2003): 131–42.

Beilby, James. "Plantinga's Pox on Naturalism Revisited: A Reply to Michael Thune." *Philosophia Christi* 7/2 (2005): 169–76.

Bergmann, Michael. "Commonsense Naturalism." In *Naturalism Defeated? Essays on Plantinga's Evolutionary Argument against Naturalism*, edited by James Beilby, 61–90. Ithaca, NY: Cornell University Press, 2002.

Bishop, John. Review of *Knowledge of God* by Alvin Plantinga and Michael Tooley. *Mind* 118/471 (2009): 1163–8. [1163–5]

Bosse, Richard. "Wunder's Probability Objection." *International Journal for Philosophy of Religion* 84/1 (2018): 131–42. [141]

Boudry, Maarten. Review of *Where the Conflict Really Lies: Science, Religion and Naturalism* by Alvin Plantinga." *Science and Education* 22/5 (2013): 1219–27. [1224–6]

Boudry, Maarten and Michael Vlerick. "Natural Selection Does Care about Truth." *International Studies in the Philosophy of Science* 28/1 (2014): 65–77.

Brigham, Andrew. "Neural Reuse and the Evolution of Higher Cognition." Ph.D. diss., University of Ottawa, 2019. [95–103]

Cantens, Bernardo. "Cognitive Faculties and Evolutionary Naturalism." *Proceedings of the American Catholic Philosophical Association* 80 (2007): 201–8.

Childers, Geoff. "What's Wrong with the Evolutionary Argument against Naturalism?" *International Journal for Philosophy of Religion* 69/3 (2011): 193–204.

Churchland, Paul M. "Is Evolutionary Naturalism Epistemologically Self-Defeating?" *Philo* 12/2 (2009): 135–41.

Collin, James Henry. "Semantic Inferentialism and the Evolutionary Argument against Naturalism." *Philosophy Compass* 8/9 (2013): 846–56.

Corvi, Roberta. "Methodological and/or Ontological Naturalism: Comment on Plantinga's Paper." In *Analytic Philosophy without Naturalism*, edited by Antonella Corradini, Sergio Galvan, and E. Jonathan Lowe, 45–50. New York: Routledge, 2006.

Crisp, Thomas. "An Evolutionary Objection to the Argument from Evil." In *Evidence and Religious Belief*, edited by Kelly James Clark and Raymond J. VanArragon, 114–34. New York: Oxford University Press, 2011.

Crow, Daniel. "A Plantingian Pickle for a Darwinian Dilemma: Evolutionary Arguments against Atheism and Normative Realism." *Ratio* 29/2 (2016): 130–48.

De Cruz, Helen. "Through a Mind Darkly: An Empirically-Informed Philosophical Perspective on Systematic Knowledge Acquisition and Cognitive Limitations." Ph.D. diss., University of Groningen, 2011. [230–2]

De Cruz, Helen and Johan De Smedt. "Reformed and Evolutionary Epistemology and the Noetic Effects of Sin." *International Journal for Philosophy of Religion* 74/1 (2013): 49–66.

De Cruz, Helen, Maarten Boudry, Johan De Smedt, and Stefaan Blancke, "Evolutionary Approaches to Epistemic Justification." *Dialectica* 64/4 (2011): 517–35. [521–2]

Deem, Michael J. "A Flaw in the Stich–Plantinga Challenge to Evolutionary Reliabilism." *Analysis* 78/2 (2018): 216–25.

Deen, Daniel Richard. "Science, Religion, and Virtue: Toward Excellence in Dialogue." Ph.D. diss., Florida State University, 2015. [20–7]

Deltete, Robert J. Review of *Where the Conflict Really Lies: Science, Religion, and Naturalism* by Alvin Plantinga. *Philosophy in Review* 32/5 (2012): 413–17. [415]

Dennett, Daniel C. "Darwin's 'Strange Inversion of Reasoning.'" *PNAS* (*Proceedings of the National Academy of Science*) 106/supplement 1 (2009): 10061–5.

Dennett, Daniel C. "Truths That Miss Their Mark: Naturalism Unscathed." In *Science and Religion: Are They Compatible?* by Daniel C. Dennett and Alvin Plantinga, 25–37. New York: Oxford University Press, 2011. [35–6]

Dennett, Daniel C. "Habits of Imagination and Their Effect on Incredulity: Reply to Plantinga (Essay 2)." In *Science and Religion: Are They Compatible?* by Daniel C. Dennett and Alvin Plantinga, 45–55. New York: Oxford University Press, 2011. [51–2]

Dennett, Daniel C. "No Miracles Needed." In *Science and Religion: Are They Compatible?* by Daniel C. Dennett and Alvin Plantinga, 73–7. New York: Oxford University Press, 2011.
Dennett, Daniel C. and Alvin Plantinga. *Science and Religion: Are They Compatible?* New York: Oxford University Press, 2011. [*passim*]
DePoe, John M. "The Self-Defeat of Naturalism: A Critical Comparison of Alvin Plantinga and C.S. Lewis." *Christian Scholars Review* 44/1 (2014): 9–26.
Devine, Philip E. "What Is Naturalism?" *Philosophia Christi* 8/1 (2006): 125–39. [132–8]
Diéguez Lucena, Antonio. "El Argumento de Alvin Plantinga contra el Naturalismo Evolucionista: Un Análisis Crítico (Alvin Plantinga's Argument against Evolutionary Naturalism: A Critical Review)." *Éndoxa: Series Filosóficas* 24 (2010): 333–49.
Diéguez Lucena, Antonio. *La evolución del conocimiento. De la mente animal a la mente humana*. Madrid: Biblioteca Nueva, 2011. [170–84]
Diéguez Lucena, Antonio. "La opción naturalista. Una respuesta a Francisco Soler (The Naturalistic Option. A Response to Francisco Soler)." *Naturaleza y Libertad: Revista de estudios interdisciplinares* 1 (2012): 237–64. [248–63]
Diéguez Lucena, Antonio. "Filosofía sin milagros. Comentarios finales a la contrarréplica de Francisco Soler (Philosophy without Miracles. Final Comments on Francisco Soler's Counterreply)." *Naturaleza y Libertad: Revista de estudios interdisciplinares* 1 (2012): 273–9. [278–9]
Di Stasio, Margherita. "Plantinga e l'argomento teleologico: dalla critica a Hume al ruolo del concetto di Proper Function." *Annali del Dipartimento di Filosofia* 11 (2005): 275–301. [295–301]
Di Stasio, Margherita. "Plantinga's Reliabilism between Teleology and Epistemic Naturalization." *European Journal of Analytic Philosophy* 4/1 (2008): 13–23. [14–15]
Di Stasio, Margherita. *Alvin Plantinga: conoscenza religiosa e naturalizzazione epistemologica* (Florence: Firenze University Press, 2011). [33–62, 86–91]
Draper, Paul. "In Defense of Sensible Naturalism." 2007. Available online: https://infidels.org/library/modern/paul_draper/naturalism.html (accessed January 28, 2021).
Draper, Paul and Alvin Plantinga. "God or Blind Nature? Section 2: Evil and Evolution." 2007. Available online: http://infidels.org/library/modern/paul_draper/intro2.html (accessed January 28, 2021).
Fales, Evan. "Plantinga's Case against Naturalistic Epistemology." *Philosophy of Science* 63/3 (1996): 432–51.
Fales, Evan. "Darwin's Doubt, Calvin's Calvary." In *Naturalism Defeated? Essays on Plantinga's Evolutionary Argument against Naturalism*, edited by James Beilby, 43–58. Ithaca, NY: Cornell University Press, 2002.
Fales, Evan. "The Putnamian Argument (the Argument from the Rejection of Global Skepticism) [also (O) The Argument from Reference, and (K) The Argument from the Confluence of Proper Function and Reliability]: Putnam's Semantic Skepticism and the Epistemic Melt-Down of Naturalism: How Defeat of Putnam's Puzzle Provides a Defeater for Plantinga's Self-Defeat Argument against Naturalism." In *Two Dozen (or so) Arguments for God: The Plantinga Project*, edited by Jerry Walls and Trent Dougherty, 198–213. New York: Oxford University Press, 2018. [209–12]
Faria, Domingos. "Será Procedente o Argumento de Plantinga contra o Naturalismo Metafísico?" *Princípios: Revista de filosofia* 22/39 (2015): 121–39.
Feser, Edward. "Conflict Resolution." *First Things: A Monthly Journal of Religion and Public Life* 228 (December 2012): 61–3.

Filatova, M.S. "Vzayemodiya evolyucionizmu ta naturalizmu, yak problema veryfikaciyi viruvan" u teyistychnij antropolohiyi Alvin Plantinga (Interaction of Evolutionism and Naturalism as a Problem of Belief Verification in Alvin Plantinga's Theistic Anthropology)." *Hileya: Naukovyj visnyk (Gilea: The Scientific Bulletin)* 146/7 (2019): 123–7.

Fischer, R.W. Review of *Knowledge of God* by Alvin Plantinga and Michael Tooley. *Heythrop Journal* 50/3 (2009): 513–15.

Fitelson, Branden and Elliot Sober. "Plantinga's Probability Arguments against Evolutionary Naturalism." *Pacific Philosophical Quarterly* 79/2 (1998): 115–29.

Fodor, Jerry. "Is Science Biologically Possible?" In *Naturalism Defeated? Essays on Plantinga's Evolutionary Argument against Naturalism*, edited by James Beilby, 30–42. Ithaca, NY: Cornell University Press, 2002. Originally published as "Is Science Biologically Possible? Comments on some Arguments of Patricia Churchland and of Alvin Plantinga." In *In Critical Condition: Polemical Essays on Cognitive Science and the Philosophy of Mind*, 189–202. Cambridge, MA; London: The MIT Press, 1998.

Ginet, Carl. "Comments on Plantinga's Two-Volume Work on Warrant." *Philosophy and Phenomenological Research* 55/2 (1995): 403–8. [405–8]

Głąb, Anna. "Alvina Plantingi ewolucyjny argument przeciwko naturalizmowi." *Roczniki Filozoficzne* 54/1 (2006): 19–38.

Goetz, Stewart. "The Argument from Reason." *Philosophia Christi* 15/1 (2013): 47–62. [54–8]

Golijanin, Vedran "Hrišćanski filosof Alvin Plantinga i njegov evolucioni argument protiv naturalizma (Christian Philosopher Alvin Plantinga and His Evolutionary Argument against Naturalism)." *Simpleksis: Arhiv za srpsku kulturu i humanistiku (Simplexis: Archive for Serbian Culture and Humanities)* 1 (2018): 156–69.

Graber, Abraham and Luke Goleman. "Plantinga Redux: Is the Scientific Realist Committed to the Rejection of Naturalism?" *Sophia* 59/3 (2020) 395–412.

Griffiths, Paul E. and John S. Wilkins. "Crossing the Milvian Bridge: When Do Evolutionary Explanations of Belief Debunk Belief?" In *Darwin in the Twenty-First Century: Nature, Humanity, and God*, edited by Phillip R. Sloan, Gerald McKenny, and Kathleen Eggleson, 201–31. Notre Dame, IN: University of Notre Dame Press, 2015. [208–13]

Gurmin, John Haydn. "Neo-Darwinism, Evolution, and Meaning." *Yearbook of the Irish Philosophical Society* (2016–17): 98–126. [102–9]

Hardcastle, Valerie Gray. "'The Horrid Doubt': Naturalism and Evolutionary Biology." In *The Blackwell Companion to Naturalism*, edited by Kelly James Clark, 109–23. Malden, MA: Wiley-Blackwell, 2016. [115–17]

Hendricks, Perry. "Response to Wunder: Objective Probability, Non-Contingent Theism, and the EAAN." *Religious Studies* 56/2 (2020): 292–6.

Hendricks, Perry and Tina Anderson. "Does the Evolutionary Argument against Naturalism Defeat God's Beliefs?" *Sophia* 59/3 (2020): 489–99.

Hookway, Christopher. "Naturalized Epistemology and Epistemic Evaluation." *Inquiry* 37/4 (1994): 465–86. [467–8, 479–82]

Hughes, Charles. "Plantinga Defended: A Response to Tedesco's Critique of the Evolutionary Argument Against Naturalism." *Philosophia Christi* 7/1 (2005): 177–88.

Johnson, Adam Lloyd. "Proposing a Trinitarian Metaethical Theory as a Better Explanation for Objective Morality than Erik Wielenberg's Godless Normative Realism." Ph.D. diss., Southeastern Baptist Theological Seminary, 2020. [197–209]

Jong, Jonathan and Aku Visala. "Evolutionary Debunking Arguments against Theism, Reconsidered." *International Journal for Philosophy of Religion* 76/3 (2014): 243–58. [251–5]

Koons, Robert C. "Epistemological Objections to Materialism." In *The Waning of Materialism: New Essays*, edited by Robert C. Koons and George Bealer, 281–306. New York: Oxford University Press, 2009. [289, 294–6]

Koperski, Jeffrey. "Theism, Naturalism, and Scientific Realism." *Epistemology and Philosophy of Science* 53/3 (2017): 152–66.

Koslowski, Adilson. "As origens históricas do argumento evolutivo contra o naturalismo (The Historical Origins of Evolutionary Argument against Naturalism)." *Revista da Unifebe* 1/8 (2010): 35–48.

Lavazza, Andrea. "Conseguenze del fisicalismo sulla mente." *Rivista di estetica* 49 (2012): 355–75. [371–3]

Lavazza, Andrea. "Problems of Physicalism Regarding the Mind." In *Contemporary Dualism: A Defense*, edited by Andrea Lavazza and Howard Robinson, 35–55. New York: Routledge, 2014. [50–2]

Law, Stephen. "Plantinga's Belief-cum-Desire Argument Refuted." *Religious Studies* 47/2 (2011): 245–56.

Law, Stephen. "Naturalism, Evolution and True Belief." *Analysis* 72/1 (2012): 41–8.

Leahy, Brian. "Can Teleosemantics Deflect the EAAN?" *Philosophia* 41/1 (2013): 221–38.

Lee, Wang-Yen. "Does Plantinga's Evolutionary Argument against Naturalism Work?" *Religious Studies* 45/1 (2009): 73–83.

Lehrer, Keith. "Proper Function versus Systematic Coherence." In *Warrant in Contemporary Epistemology: Essays in Honor of Plantinga's Theory of Knowledge*, edited by Jonathan L. Kvanvig, 25–45. Lanham, MD: Rowman & Littlefield, 1996. [28–30]

Lemos, John. "Theism, Evolutionary Epistemology, and Two Theories of Truth." *Zygon* 37/4 (2002): 789–801.

Lemos, John. "A Defense of Naturalistic Naturalized Epistemology (Una defensa de la epistemología naturalizada naturalista)." *Crítica: Revista Hispanoamericana de Filosofía* 35/105 (2003): 49–63.

Levin, Michael. "Plantinga on Functions and the Theory of Evolution." *Australasian Journal of Philosophy* 75/1 (1997): 83–98.

Markie, Peter. "Plantinga, Metaphysical Naturalism and Proper Function." *Southwest Philosophy Review* 15/1 (1999): 65–72.

Mashburn, Emmett Frank. "On Alvin Plantinga's Evolutionary Argument against Naturalism." Ph.D. diss., University of Tennessee, Knoxville, 2010.

McNabb, Tyler Dalton. "Defeating Naturalism: Defending and Reformulating Plantinga's EAAN." *Eleutheria: A Graduate Student Journal* 4/1 (2015): 35–51.

McNabb, Tyler Dalton. "Closing Pandora's Box: A Defence of Alvin Plantinga's Epistemology of Religious Belief." Ph.D. diss., University of Glasgow, 2016. [56–79]

Menuge, Angus J.L. "Beyond Skinnerian Creatures: A Defense of the Lewis and Plantinga Critiques of Evolutionary Naturalism." *Philosophia Christi* 5/1 (2003): 143–65. Republished in *Agents Under Fire: Materialism and the Rationality of Science*, 149–72, Lanham, MD: Rowman & Littlefield, 2004.

Merricks, Trenton. "Conditional Probability and Defeat." In *Naturalism Defeated? Essays on Plantinga's Evolutionary Argument against Naturalism*, edited by James Beilby, 165–75. Ithaca, NY: Cornell University Press, 2002.

Miguel, Felipe M.S. "Theistic Arguments from the Reliability of Our Cognitive Faculties (Argumentos teístas a partir da confiabilidade das nossas faculdades cognitivas)." *Revista Brasileira de Filosofia da Religião* 2/1 (2015): 127–41.

Miller, Calum. "Response to Stephen Law on the Evolutionary Argument against Naturalism." *Philosophia* 43/1 (2015): 147–52.

Mirza, Omar. "Naturalism and Darwin's Doubt: A Study of Plantinga's Evolutionary Argument against Naturalism." Ph.D. diss., University of California, Berkeley, 2003.

Mirza, Omar. "A User's Guide to the Evolutionary Argument Against Naturalism." *Philosophical Studies* 141/2 (2008): 125–46.

Mirza, Omar. "The Evolutionary Argument Against Naturalism." *Philosophy Compass* 6/1 (2011): 78–89.

Moon, Andrew. "Debunking Morality: Lessons from the EAAN Literature." *Pacific Philosophical Quarterly* 98/1 (2017): 208–26.

Moros, Enrique. "¿Es coherente una cosmovisión naturalista? La argumentación de Plantinga contra el naturalismo desde la perspectiva de Artigas (Is a Naturalistic World View Coherent? Plantinga's Argumentation against Naturalism from Artigas' Perspective)." *Scientia et Fides* 4/2 (2016): 343–55.

Morriston, Wes. "Must an 'Origins Skeptic' Be Skeptical about Everything?" *Philo* 11/2 (2008): 165–76.

Motahareh Shohouei Pour Ali Nam and Mohammad Keivanfar. "Berresa asetdelal tekeamela Plantinga 'elah teba'etbawera w neqd Sosa w peasekh Plantinga (Plantinga's Evolutionary Argument against Naturalism, Sosa's Critique, and Plantinga's Response)." *Feslenamh anedashh dana (Journal of Religious Thought)* 19/71 (2019): 71–92.

Naquin, Paul Jude. "Theism's Pyrrhic Victory." *The Southern Journal of Philosophy* 40/4 (2002): 557–71.

Narges Nazarnejad. "Neqd teba'etegurewa az menzer Alvin Plantinga (A Critique of Naturalism from Alvin Plantinga's Point of View)." *Felsefh w kelam aselama (Philosophy and Kalam)* 51/2 (2019): 297–319.

Nathan, N.M.L. "Naturalism and Self-Defeat: Plantinga's Version." *Religious Studies* 33/2 (1997): 135–42.

Nieminen, Petteri, Maarten Boudry, Esko Ryökäs, and Anne-Mari Mustonen. "Biblical and Theistic Arguments against the Evolutionary Argument against Naturalism." *Zygon* 52/1 (2017): 9–23.

Novotný, Daniel D. "How to Save Naturalism from Plantinga?" *Organon F: Medzinárodný Casopis Pre Analytickú Filozofiu* 14/1 (2007): 32–48.

Nunley, Troy M. "A Defense of Alvin Plantinga's Evolutionary Argument against Naturalism." Ph.D. diss., University of Missouri-Columbia, 2005.

Nunley, Troy M. "'Darwin's Doubt' Revisited: Plantinga and His Critics on the Epistemic Implications of Naturalism." *Analysis and Metaphysics* 8 (2009): 44–77.

O'Connor, Timothy. "An Evolutionary Argument against Naturalism?" *Canadian Journal of Philosophy* 24/4 (1994): 527–40.

O'Connor, Timothy. "A House Divided Against Itself Cannot Stand." In *Naturalism Defeated? Essays on Plantinga's Evolutionary Argument against Naturalism*, edited by James Beilby, 129–34. Ithaca, NY: Cornell University Press, 2002.

Oppy, Graham. *Naturalism and Religion: A Contemporary Philosophical Investigation.* New York: Routledge, 2018. [56–85]

Otte, Richard. "Conditional Probabilities in Plantinga's Argument." In *Naturalism Defeated? Essays on Plantinga's Evolutionary Argument against Naturalism*, edited by James Beilby, 135–49. Ithaca, NY: Cornell University Press, 2002.

Palmer, Donald. *Does the Center Hold? An Introduction to Western Philosophy*, 6th ed. New York: McGraw-Hill, 2014. [191–3]

Paolini Paoletti, Michele. "Naturalism (Almost) Self-Defeated." *Proceedings of the XXIII World Congress of Philosophy* 62 (2018): 135–9.

Peressini, Anthony. "Naturalism, Evolution and Self-Defeat." *International Journal for Philosophy of Religion* 44/1 (1998): 41–51.

Peters, Richard. "Naturalism, Knowledge, and Nature: Alvin Plantinga's Evolutionary Argument against Naturalism in Relationalist Cosmological Perspective." Ph.D. diss., Boston University, 2010.

Peters, Richard. Abstract for "Naturalism, Knowledge, and Nature: Alvin Plantinga's Evolutionary Argument against Naturalism in Relationalist Cosmological Perspective." *Process Studies* 40/1 (2011): 206–7.

Peterson, Michael L. *C.S. Lewis and the Christian Worldview*. New York: Oxford University Press, 2020. [53–5]

Plantinga, Alvin. "An Evolutionary Argument against Naturalism." *Logos: Philosophic Issues in Christian Perspective* 12 (1991): 27–49. Republished in *Faith in Theory and Practice: Essays on Justifying Religious Belief*, edited by Elizabeth S. Radcliffe and Carol J. White, 35–65. Chicago: Open Court, 1993.

Plantinga, Alvin. *Warrant and Proper Function*. New York: Oxford University Press, 1993. [216–37]

Plantinga, Alvin. "Naturalism Defeated." 1994. Online at: https://web.archive.org/web/20090930150703/http://www.calvin.edu/academic/philosophy/virtual_library/articles/plantinga_alvin/naturalism_defeated.pdf (accessed January 28, 2021).

Plantinga, Alvin. "Precis of *Warrant: The Current Debate* and *Warrant and Proper Function*." *Philosophy and Phenomenological Research* 55/2 (1995): 393–6. [396]

Plantinga, Alvin. "Reliabilism, Analyses and Defeaters." *Philosophy and Phenomenological Research* 55/2 (1995): 427–64. [438–43]

Plantinga, Alvin. "Respondeo." In *Warrant in Contemporary Epistemology: Essays in Honor of Plantinga's Theory of Knowledge*, edited by Jonathan L. Kvanvig, 307–78. Lanham, MD: Rowman & Littlefield, 1996. [333–7]

Plantinga, Alvin. "Reid, Hume, and God." In *Recovering Nature: Essays in Natural Philosophy, Ethics, and Metaphysics in Honor of Ralph McInerny*, edited by Thomas Hibbs and John O'Callaghan, 201–27. Notre Dame, IN: University of Notre Dame Press, 1999. [215–22]

Plantinga, Alvin. "The Evolutionary Anti-Naturalism Argument: Is Naturalism Irrational?" In *Philosophy of Religion: The Big Questions*, edited by Eleonore Stump and Michael J. Murray, 125–38. Malden, MA: Wiley-Blackwell, 1999.

Plantinga, Alvin. *Warranted Christian Belief*. New York: Oxford University Press, 2000. [227–40, 281–5]

Plantinga, Alvin. "Internalism, Externalism, Defeaters and Arguments for Christian Belief." *Philosophia Christi* 3/2 (2001): 379–400. [391–4]

Plantinga, Alvin. "The Evolutionary Argument against Naturalism: An Initial Statement of the Argument." In *Naturalism Defeated? Essays on Plantinga's Evolutionary Argument against Naturalism*, edited by James Beilby, 1–12. Ithaca, NY: Cornell University Press, 2002.

Plantinga, Alvin. "Reply to Beilby's Cohorts." In *Naturalism Defeated? Essays on Plantinga's Evolutionary Argument against Naturalism*, edited by James Beilby, 204–75. Ithaca, NY: Cornell University Press, 2002.

Plantinga, Alvin. "Probability and Defeaters." *Pacific Philosophical Quarterly* 84/3 (2003): 291–8.

Plantinga, Alvin. "Evolution, Epiphenomenalism, Reductionism." *Philosophy and Phenomenological Research* 58/3 (2004): 602–19.

Plantinga, Alvin. "How Naturalism Implies Skepticism." In *Analytic Philosophy without Naturalism*, edited by Antonella Corradini, Sergio Galvan, and E. Jonathan Lowe, 29–44. New York: Routledge, 2006.

Plantinga, Alvin. "Naturalism vs. Evolution: A Religion/Science Conflict?" 2007. Online at: https://infidels.org/library/modern/alvin_plantinga/conflict.html (accessed January 28, 2021).

Plantinga, Alvin. "Two Dozen (or so) Theistic Arguments." In *Alvin Plantinga*, edited by Deane-Peter Baker, 203–27. Cambridge: Cambridge University Press, 2007. [218–19]

Plantinga, Alvin. "Against 'Sensible' Naturalism." 2007. Online at: https://infidels.org/library/modern/alvin_plantinga/against-naturalism.html (accessed January 28, 2021).

Plantinga, Alvin. "Against Naturalism." In *Knowledge of God*, by Alvin Plantinga and Michael Tooley, 1–69. Malden, MA: Blackwell, 2008. [30–66]

Plantinga, Alvin. "Can Robots Think? Reply to Tooley's Second Statement." In *Knowledge of God*, by Alvin Plantinga and Michael Tooley, 218–32. Malden, MA: Blackwell, 2008. [227–32]

Plantinga, Alvin. "The Evolutionary Argument against Naturalism." In *Science and Religion in Dialogue, volume 1*, edited by Melville Y. Stewart, 324–32. Malden, MA: Wiley-Blackwell, 2010.

Plantinga, Alvin. "Science and Religion: Where the Conflict Really Lies." In *Science and Religion: Are They Compatible?* by Daniel C. Dennett and Alvin Plantinga, 1–23. New York: Oxford University Press, 2011. [16–21]

Plantinga, Alvin. "Superman vs. God?" In *Science and Religion: Are They Compatible?* by Daniel C. Dennett and Alvin Plantinga, 39–43. New York: Oxford University Press, 2011. [42–3]

Plantinga, Alvin. "Naturalism against Science." In *Science and Religion: Are They Compatible?* by Daniel C. Dennett and Alvin Plantinga, 57–72. New York: Oxford University Press, 2011. [66–71]

Plantinga, Alvin. "Evolution versus Naturalism." In *The Nature of Nature: Examining the Role of Naturalism in Science*, edited by Bruce Gordon and William Dembski, 137–51. Wilmington, DE: ISI Books, 2011.

Plantinga, Alvin. "Content and Natural Selection." *Philosophy and Phenomenological Research* 83/2 (2011): 435–58.

Plantinga, Alvin. *Where the Conflict Really Lies: Science, Religion, and Naturalism*. New York: Oxford University Press, 2011. [307–50]

Plantinga, Alvin. "The Evolutionary Argument against Naturalism." In *The Blackwell Companion to Science and Christianity*, edited by J.B. Stump and Alan G. Padgett, 103–15. Malden, MA: Wiley-Blackwell, 2012.

Plantinga, Alvin and Michael Tooley. *Knowledge of God*. Malden, MA: Blackwell, 2008. [*passim*]

Plantinga, Alvin and William Talbott. "Evolutionary Naturalism: Epistemically Unseated or Illusorily Defeated?" In *The Nature of Nature: Examining the Role of Naturalism in Science*, edited by Bruce Gordon and William Dembski, 166–78. Wilmington, DE: ISI Books, 2011.

Post, John F. Review of *Naturalism Defeated?* by James Beilby. *Notre Dame Philosophical Reviews*. 2002. Available online: https://ndpr.nd.edu/news/naturalism-defeated-essays-on-plantinga-s-evolutionary-argument-against-naturalism (accessed January 28, 2021).

Prasetya, Yunus. "An Analysis of Stephen Law's Objection to Alvin Plantinga's Evolutionary Argument against Naturalism." *Polymath: An Interdisciplinary Journal of Arts and Sciences* 4/3 (2014): 22–6.

Ramsey, William. "Naturalism Defended." In *Naturalism Defeated? Essays on Plantinga's Evolutionary Argument against Naturalism*, edited by James Beilby, 15–29. Ithaca, NY: Cornell University Press, 2002.

Rea, Michael. *World without Design: The Ontological Consequences of Naturalism*. Oxford: Clarendon, 2002. [177–95]

Reed, Thomas McHugh. "Evolutionary Skepticism." *International Journal for Philosophy of Religion* 42/2 (1997): 79–96.

Reed, Thomas McHugh. "Christianity and Agnosticism." *International Journal for Philosophy of Religion* 52/2 (2002): 81–95. [85–91]

Reichenbach, Bruce R. and Adam W. Nugent. "Does Plantinga Have His Own Defeater?" *Philosophia Christi* 8/1 (2006): 141–50.

Reiter, David. "Plantinga on the Epistemic Implications of Naturalism." *Journal of Philosophical Research* 25 (2000): 141–7.

Rivera-Novoa, Ángel. "Pragmatismo y evolución: ¿es racional ser teísta y naturalista? (Pragmatism and Evolution: Is It Rational to Be Theist and Naturalist?)." *Topicos: Revisit de Filosofía* 57 (2019): 176–206. [181–91]

Robbins, J. Wesley. "Is Naturalism Irrational?" *Faith and Philosophy* 11/2 (1994): 255–9.

Robinson, William. "Evolution and Epiphenomenalism." *Journal of Consciousness Studies* 14/11 (2007): 27–42. [35–9]

Roeber, D. Blake. "Does the Theist Have an Epistemic Advantage Over the Atheist? Plantinga and Descartes on Theism, Atheism, and Skepticism." *Journal of Philosophical Research* 34 (2009): 305–28.

Rowe, William L. Review of *Knowledge of God* by Alvin Plantinga and Michael Tooley. *Notre Dame Philosophical Reviews*. 2008. Available online: https://ndpr.nd.edu/news/knowledge-of-god/ (accessed January 28, 2021).

Ruse, Michael. *Taking Darwin Seriously: A Naturalistic Approach to Philosophy*, 2nd ed. Amherst, NY: Prometheus, 1998. [295–97]

Ruse, Michael. "Naturalism and the Scientific Method." In *The Oxford Handbook of Atheism*, edited by Stephen Bullivant and Michael Ruse, 383–97. New York: Oxford University Press, 2013. [394–7]

Schmitt, Yann. "L'ontologie réaliste du théisme." Ph.D. diss., École des hautes études en sciences sociales (EHESS), Paris, 2010. [257–75]

Segal, Aaron and Alvin Plantinga. "Response to Churchland." *Philo* 13/2 (2010): 201–7.

Sierra Merchán, Jorge. *¿Crearon los hombres a los dioses? El impacto de la ciencia cognitiva de la religión en la racionalidad del teismo*. Bogotá: Fundación Universidad Autónoma de Colombia, 2016. [126–30]

Sierra Merchán, Jorge. "¿Son válidos los argumentos evolutivos desacreditadores subproductistas de Dennett contra la racionalidad del teísmo?" *Eidos: Revista de Filosofía de la Universidad Del Norte* 26 (2017): 178–209. [203–5]

Silver, David. "Evolutionary Naturalism and the Reliability of Our Cognitive Faculties." *Faith and Philosophy* 20/1 (2003): 50–63.

Slagle, Jim. "Plantinga and the Epistemological Skyhook." Ph.D. diss., Institute of Philosophy, Katholieke Universiteit Leuven, 2012. [210–96]

Slagle, Jim. "Plantinga's Skepticism." *Philosophia* 43/4 (2015): 1133–45.

Slagle, Jim. *The Epistemological Skyhook: Determinism, Naturalism, and Self-Defeat*. New York: Routledge, 2016. [149–63]

Slagle, Jim. "Indicators and Depictors." *The Philosophical Forum* 48/1 (2017): 91–107.

Soares, Emerson Martins. "Naturalismo, função própria e o argumento evolucionário de Plantinga contra o naturalismo (Naturalism, Proper Function and Plantinga's Evolutionary Argument against Naturalism)." *Revista Contemplação* 12 (2015): 96–120.

Soler Gil, Francisco José. "¿Se puede naturalizar la epistemología? Reflexiones al hilode la lectura del libro *La Evolución del Conocimiento* de Antonio Diéguez Lucena (Can Epistemology be Naturalized? Reflections on the Thread of Reading the Book *The Evolution of Knowledge* by Antonio Diéguez Lucena)." *Naturaleza y Libertad: Revista de estudios interdisciplinares* 1 (2012): 215–36. [226–36]

Soler Gil, Francisco José. "¿Qué menos que un milagro podría salvar la epistemología naturalista? Respuesta a Antonio Diéguez Lucena (What Less Than a Miracle Could Save Naturalistic Epistemology? A Response to Antonio Diéguez Lucena)." *Naturaleza y Libertad: Revista de estudios interdisciplinares* 1 (2012): 265–72. [271–2]

Sosa, Ernest. "Plantinga's Evolutionary Meditations." In *Naturalism Defeated? Essays on Plantinga's Evolutionary Argument against Naturalism*, edited by James Beilby, 91–102. Ithaca, NY: Cornell University Press, 2002.

Sosa, Ernest. "Natural Theology and Naturalist Atheology: Plantinga's Evolutionary Argument Against Naturalism." In *Alvin Plantinga*, edited by Deane-Peter Baker, 93–106. Cambridge: Cambridge University Press, 2007.

Sweis, Khaldoun A. "Naturalism Reconsidered." In *God, Freedom and Nature: Proceedings of the 2008 Biennial Conference in Philosophy, Religion and Culture*, edited by Ronald S. Laura, Rachel A. Buchanan and Amy K. Chapman, 150–7. Sydney: Body and Soul Dynamics, 2012. [154–5]

Swinburne, Richard. *The Existence of God*, 2nd ed. Oxford: Oxford University Press, 2004. [350–4]

Szalai, Miklós. "Naturalizmus, szkepticizmus és racionalitás Plantinga evolúciós szkeptikus érve." *Magyar Filozófiai Szemle* 54/1 (2010): 59–78.

Talbott, William J. "The Illusion of Defeat." In *Naturalism Defeated? Essays on Plantinga's Evolutionary Argument against Naturalism*, edited by James Beilby, 153–64. Ithaca, NY: Cornell University Press, 2002.

Talbott, William J. "More on the Illusion of Defeat." In *The Nature of Nature: Examining the Role of Naturalism in Science*, edited by Bruce Gordon and William Dembski, 152–65. Wilmington, DE: ISI Books, 2011.

Talbott, William J. "A New Reliability Defeater for Evolutionary Naturalism." *Philosophy and Phenomenological Research* 113/3 (2016): 538–64. [558–9]

Talbott, William J. "Is Epistemic Circularity a Fallacy?" *Philosophical Studies* 177/8 (2020): 2277–98. [2278–9]

Tedesco, Matthew. "Theism, Naturalistic Evolution and the Probability of Reliable Cognitive Faculties: A Response to Plantinga." *Philo* 5/2 (2002): 235–41.

Thune, Michael. "Plantinga Untouched: A Response to Beilby on the Evolutionary Argument Against Naturalism." *Philosophia Christi* 7/1 (2005): 157–68.

Thune, Michael. "Naturalism, Hope, and Alethic Rationality." *Philo* 9/1 (2006): 5–11.

Tooley, Michael. "Reply to Plantinga's Opening Statement." In *Knowledge of God*, by Alvin Plantinga and Michael Tooley, 184–217. Malden, MA: Blackwell, 2008. [205–17]

Van Cleve, James. "Can Atheists Know Anything?" In *Naturalism Defeated? Essays on Plantinga's Evolutionary Argument against Naturalism*, edited by James Beilby, 103–25. Ithaca, NY: Cornell University Press, 2002.

Vlerick, Michael. "Darwin's Doubt: Implications of the Theory of Evolution for Human Thought." Ph.D. diss., Stellenbosch University, 2012. [50–3]

Voelker, Paul. "Religion, Science, and the Conscious Self: Bio-Psychological Explanation and the Debate Between Dualism and Naturalism." Ph.D. diss., Loyola University, 2011. [180–4]

Vogelstein, Eric. "The Consistency of Plantinga's Argument against Naturalism: A Reply to Tedesco." *Philo* 7/1 (2004): 122–5.

Wielenberg, Erik J. "How to Be an Alethically Rational Naturalist." *Synthese* 131/1 (2002): 81–98.

Wielenberg, Erik J. "Ethics and Evolutionary Theory." *Analysis* 76/4 (2016): 502–15.

Wiertz, Oliver. Review of *Naturalism Defeated?* by James Beilby. Translated by Anna Schneider. *European Journal for Philosophy of Religion* 2/1 (2010): 222–6.

Wilkins, John S. and Paul E. Griffiths. "Evolutionary Debunking Arguments in Three Domains." In *A New Science of Religion*, edited by Gregory W. Dawes and James Maclaurin, 133–46. London: Routledge, 2012. [133, 135–6]

Wunder, Tyler A. "Alvin Plantinga on Paul Draper's Evolutionary Atheology: Implications of Theism's Noncontingency." *International Journal for Philosophy of Religion* 74/1 (2013): 67–75. [72–4]

Wunder, Tyler A. "The Modality of Theism and Probabilistic Natural Theology: A Tension in Alvin Plantinga's Philosophy." *Religious Studies* 51/3 (2015): 391–9.

Xu, Yingjin. "The Troublesome Explanandum in Plantinga's Argument against Naturalism." *International Journal for Philosophy of Religion* 69/1 (2011): 1–15.

Yandell, Keith E. "Is Contemporary Naturalism Self-Referentially Irrational?" *Philosophia Christi* 3/2 (2001): 353–68.

Ye, Feng. "Naturalized Truth and Plantinga's Evolutionary Argument against Naturalism." *International Journal for Philosophy of Religion* 70/1 (2011): 27–46.

Index

a priori and *a posteriori* knowledge 12, 17–19, 24, 40–1, 102–3, 108, 133
abduction *see* inference to the best explanation
A/C model 40–2, 166, 168, 170, 229 n.30
adaptive behavior 64–5, 69, 70–1, 93, 156–7, 182–4, 197–8
ad hocness 5, 51–2, 55, 69–70, 107–8, 114, 117, 146, 152, 170–1, 199–200, 203, 223 n.20, 224 n.43
ad hominem, circumstantial 81, 181
add a bit objection 114–15, 121, 131–4, 146, 147, 188
agnosticism 55–6, 131, 217 n.16, 228 n.8
Agrippa's trilemma 10–12, 20
Alston, William 127–8, 156, 158, 188, 195, 234 n.10
analogy, arguing from 112–13, 130–1, 138, 143–5, 147–8, 226 n.5
analytic
  a posteriori 103, 108
  and synthetic 17–20, 98–9, 102–4, 108, 222 n.48
anti-realism 165, 203, 234 n.13
Aquinas, Thomas 30, 40, 166, 170, 234 n.10
argument from reason 191, 233 n.63
Aristotle 30
Arnauld, Antoine 9
assertion 59, 79–80, 81–2, 84
atheism 53, 67, 105–9, 174, 176, 194, 209 n.7, 217 n.16, 230 n.61
Augustine 30, 234 n.10

Baker, Lynne Rudder 27, 85
barn façades analogy 113
behaviorism 219 n.25
Beilby, James 61
belief-*cum*-desire argument 65, 68–9
beliefs *see* depictors
believed defeaters 57–9
Bergmann, Michael 123–8

Bible 8, 52, 169–71, 176, 229 n.41
BonJour, Laurence 209 n.20
Bosse, Richard 232 n.35
Bradley, F.H. viii
brains in vats 14, 72, 82–3, 113, 124, 127, 129, 130, 136, 145, 160–1, 163, 182, 224 n.7, 226 n.14
Broad, C.D. 222 n.61
by-products/side effects ix, 38, 64–5, 185, 231 n.24

calculator analogy 197–8
Calvin, John 40, 166
Cartesian
  circle 8–9, 149
  doubt 3–9, 12, 14
  epistemology 3–15, 17, 19–20, 23, 25–6, 29–32, 42
category mistakes 76–7
causal theory of reference 83, 227 n.41
causality
  law/principle of 7, 18, 26, 51, 103
  partial 51, 214 n.20
  relationships between causes 51–2, 214 n.20
ceteris paribus clauses 102–3
Chisholm, Roderick 143
Christianity x, 8, 40, 42, 50, 165–7, 169–70, 176, 194, 200–3, 234 n.10
Churchland, Patricia 62, 65, 81
Churchland, Paul 81, 82, 131–4, 225 n.15
circularity
  epistemic 21, 24–5, 129–30, 162, 195
  premise *see* vicious circularity
clear and distinct ideas 7–10, 208 n.10
cogito ergo sum 5–7, 10, 18, 78
cognitive
  disaster 72–3, 191
  dysfunction 34–5, 147–9
  faculties ix-x, 8, 22, 24, 29–44, 47–9, 56–7, 61–3, 65–6, 68–9, 109,

112–27, 129–36, 138–9, 145–9, 151, 155, 157, 160–75, 179–81, 183–91, 193–5, 199–200, 203–4, 216 n.5, 226 n.14
  unreliable 115, 129, 131, 134, 163, 169–71, 184, 204
cognitively inflexible climber analogy 172
coherentism/coherence 10–12, 20–1, 24, 29–30, 149–52, 162, 172, 182, 211 n.3
collective scientific community 131–4, 225 n.15
computational theory 64
computers 77, 152–3, 226 n.15
conditionalization 101, 112–14, 120–1, 132, 138, 144, 186
Conee, Earl 213 n.53
confirmation theory 177
conflict thesis 80–1
contingency *see* necessity and contingency
Copernicus, Nicolaus 81, 190
Crick, Francis 213 n.46

Darwin, Charles 24, 62–3, 81, 217 n.16
Darwin, Francis 62–3
Darwinism xii, 24, 49–51, 54, 152–6
Darwin's doubt 62–3, 66–7, 217 n.12
Davidson, Donald 70, 150–2
Dawkins, Richard 213 n.46
debunking arguments ix-x, xii, 199
defeat/defeaters 55–9
  general principle of 143–5
  mental state 216 n.45
  partial and total 56, 122, 185–6
  rebutting 55–6, 58, 145, 185
  three principles of 226 n.9
  undercutting 55–6, 59, 113, 125, 130, 135, 145, 156, 158, 167, 175, 185–6, 199
defeater thesis 111–28, 164
defeater-defeaters 58–9, 130, 136–7, 224 n.40, 226 n.9
defeater-deflectors 114–20, 224 n.40
definite description 71, 73, 227 n.40
deism 187
de jure and *de facto* arguments 166–7, 171, 229 n.34
Dennett, Daniel viii, 34, 51, 53, 62, 64, 70, 74, 95, 150–1, 197–8, 214 n.17

Denyer, Nicholas 219 n.21
deontology 13, 19, 29
depictors 74, 78, 91–104, 107, 115, 117–18, 132, 134, 138, 148–51, 153, 156, 163–4, 163, 172, 174, 180, 189–90, 192–3, 198, 204, 221 n.31, 222 n.34, 227 n.47
  see also propositional content
Descartes, Rene viii, xiv-xv, 3–15, 17–18, 21, 23, 29–30, 32, 43, 57, 70, 144, 150, 175, 182–3, 190, 192, 200, 202, 208 n.4, 216 n.39, 228 n.11, 232 n.48
description and prescription xi, 13, 17, 19, 23, 26–7, 42, 76, 80, 103, 155, 162
  see also normativity
descriptive psychology 19, 26, 42
design 34, 212 n.22
  arguments *see* teleological arguments
  plan 34–40, 43, 57–8, 123–5, 157–8, 181, 189, 191, 231 n.24
  process/agent 34, 43, 51, 131, 174, 177, 191–2, 231 n.46
  see also God
  see also teleology
determinism and free will viii, 53, 170, 202, 219 n.21
Dewey, John 24
dimensions analogy 72–4, 218 n.55
discrete objects 71–2
divine attributes
  perfectly loving 8, 80, 168, 170–1, 173–4, 176–7, 187, 189, 194
  intellect and will 169, 200–3
  logically necessary 186–7
  omnis 8, 169, 176, 189, 227 n.36
  perfection *see* perfect being
  see also God
Draper, Paul 61, 186
dream argument 4, 6
Duhem-Quine theory 20, 122
Duke of Argyll 62–3

EAAN versions
  Alston's 127–8
  modus ponens and *modus tollens* 128, 195
  Otte's 120–1
  version 0 66–7, 217 n.36, 229 n.34

version 1 67–70, 100, 108, 152–3
version 2 70–4, 153–4
efficient causality 51, 107, 199, 202, 214 n.16
eliminative materialism 27, 75–88, 92, 97–8, 101, 105, 132, 163–4, 180, 182, 219 n.21, 220 n.47, 220 n.48, 223 n.26
emergentism 180
empirical beliefs *see* perceptual beliefs
environment x, xiv, 22, 33–4, 36–42, 50, 64, 69, 78, 96, 101, 106, 113, 151, 155, 157, 162, 164, 166, 182, 197, 221 n.11
   global and local xiv, 22, 39, 106–7, 108, 162, 164, 229 n.20
   see also proper epistemic environment
Epicurus viii
epiphenomenalism 64–5, 107–8, 122, 180
epistemic
   holism 20
   voluntarism 159
ethical beliefs xi–xii, xiv, 118, 127
Euthyphro dilemma 200–2, 234 n.10
evidence relations 106–7, 119, 134
evidentialism 13–14, 21, 31, 41, 161, 166–7
evil (problem of, arguments from) 67, 167, 170–4, 176–7, 186, 189, 194
   demon argument xiv–xv, 5–9, 14, 70, 72, 113, 123–4, 127, 129–31, 136, 144, 146–8, 160–1, 163, 174, 182–4, 192, 200, 224 n.43, 224 n.7, 226 n.14, 228 n.11
     malicious demon 146–7
     revised 147–8
evolution (E) x–xi, xiv–xv, 18–19, 22–4, 27, 34, 36, 47, 49–55, 58, 61–3, 65–70, 75, 79, 81, 91, 93–6, 99, 104, 106–9, 111, 113–14, 117, 119–23, 127–8, 129–39, 144, 148, 152–8, 162, 164, 168–9, 179, 184, 186–91, 193, 197, 204–5, 213 n.46, 217 n.12, 217, n.18, 218 n.2, 227 n.47
evolutionary
   epistemology (EEM) 24, 154–5
   philosophy of science (EET) 154–5, 221 n.14

psychology of religion ix–x, 175, 207 n.5, 230 n.62
experience (EXP) 121, 138
externalism 12, 15, 21, 30–1, 153–4, 161, 163

Fales, Evan 152–3, 232 n.54
fall of humankind 169–70, 172–3
fallibilism and infallibilism 12, 14–15, 20–1, 24, 30–1, 147, 182
fictionalism 192–3
final causality 105–8, 199–200, 202, 214 n.16
   see also teleology
Fitelson, Branden 66, 156–7, 187
Flew, Antony 230 n.59
Fodor, Jerry 72
Foley, Richard 151–2
folk psychology 75, 79, 80–8, 108, 172
foundationalism 9–12, 14–15, 19–21, 29–30, 147, 150, 182, 209 n.18, 211 n.2, 211 n.3
foundherentism 150
free will *see* determinism and free will
Frege, Gottlob 88, 194, 227 n.42
Freudian theist analogy 68, 112–13, 121, 126, 131, 181
Freudianism 83–4
Fumerton, Richard 151–2

Galilei, Galileo 190
Geach, Peter 27
genetic
   drift 217 n.18
   fallacy x, 175, 181
geocentrism and heliocentrism 80–1, 86, 190
Gettier cases 13–15, 30, 32–4, 38–40, 209 n.28
Gifford lectures 216 n.1, 216 n.4
Ginet, Carl 165
God
   as designing agent 43
   as ground of morality and rationality 168–9, 171, 173–4, 176, 200–1
   as infinite substance 7–8
   as worthy of worship 175–7, 201
   unable/unwilling to deceive 8, 169–70, 176–7, 229 n.41
   see also divine attributes

Gödel, Kurt viii, 191
Graber, Abraham and Luke Goleman 119–20, 223 n.26
Graham, William 62
gratuitousness 50–3
　see also Ockham's Razor
Great Pumpkin objection 42

Haack, Susan 150
Hadith 169, 176–7
Hasker, William viii, 121, 220 n.48
Hendricks, Perry 186–7
Hinduism 42
hominid analogy 69, 73, 152–5
Hookway, Christopher 22, 162–3
Hume, David xi, 10, 56, 59, 76, 124–6, 128, 135, 194–5
Humean
　defeaters see under rationality defeaters
　loop 59, 135–7, 184
Husserl, Edmund 4
Huxley, T.H. 24
hypothetical population analogy 63–9, 71–3, 75, 91, 93, 100–1, 109, 112, 117, 121, 138, 144–9, 153–4, 156, 216 n.5

idealism 203
imago Dei (image of God) 169–71, 173, 176, 194, 200–3, 234 n.12
imperatives
　categorical 27, 43, 213 n.52
　hypothetical 26–7, 43
　see also normativity
implicit premise thesis 112, 160
indicators 74, 78, 91–9, 101–4, 107, 115, 117, 132, 138, 148–9, 151, 156, 164, 168, 172, 174, 180, 190, 193, 198, 222 n.34, 227 n.47
induction 10, 23–5, 27, 40, 143, 170, 189
infallibilism see fallibilism and infallibilism
inference to the best explanation (IBE) 10, 106–7, 154–5, 223 n.26, 229 n.20
infinitism 10–12, 20
inscrutability 56, 65–8, 112, 145, 147, 156–8, 175–7, 184–5, 188, 203
　see also probability

internalism 12–15, 21, 30, 40, 161, 163
intuitions, simplicity and conservativeness 22, 162
Islam 42, 50, 169, 176, 203

James, William 24
Japanese car analogy 111–12, 223 n.8
　see also implicit premise thesis
Judaism 50, 167, 169–70, 194, 200
Judeo-Christian tradition see Christianity
justification ix–x, xii, 10–15, 21–2, 25–6, 29–32, 41–1, 55, 119, 128, 161–2, 166–7, 181, 209 n.18

Kant, Immanuel viii
Kim, Jaegwon 13, 51
Klein, Peter 39, 209 n.21
knocked-out pipe analogy 99, 120
Kripke, Saul 103, 222 n.48
Kvanvig, Jonathan 144, 226 n.6

Leahy, Brian 96–8
Leibniz's mill 76, 91–5
Lewis, C.S. viii, 191, 223 n.63
logical
　beliefs xiii–xv, 7, 20, 133–4, 154
　laws xiv, 5, 18, 88, 154, 202
Lorenz, Konrad 24, 72–3
lottery paradox 186, 224 n.44
Lovejoy, Arthur viii
Lucas, J.R. viii, 143–4, 191, 233 n.63
Lucas-Penrose argument 191, 233 n.63

Mach's fallacy 155
magical thinking 95, 120, 180, 198
Malcolm, Norman viii, 102–3
Mascall, E.L. 116
materialism 22, 48–9, 77 92, 95–101, 105–8, 214 n.7, 222 n.58
　see also eliminative, nonreductive, and reductive materialism
max plan 37–8
Mayr, Ernst 33
meaning see propositional content
memory beliefs ix, xiii, 14, 25, 31, 41–2, 48, 69, 111–12, 114–17, 124, 135, 212 n.14

mental
  causality 65–6, 156
    see also syntactic and semantic engines
  handicaps 171–3
Merricks, Trenton 147–9
metaphysical beliefs ix-xiv, 69–70, 74, 91, 109, 118–19, 127, 134, 146, 160, 183, 204
  reliability of (MR) x-xi, xiii, 69–70, 91, 106, 118–19, 203–4
  and science x-xi, 50, 53–4, 106–7, 134, 190
Millikan, Ruth 96–7
mind-body
  dualism 77, 107–8
    and atheism 107–8, 230 n.61
  five possible relations 63–6, 67, 107–8, 122, 180
  problem 94, 97, 138, 153, 174, 190
Mirza, Omar 231 n.22
modal properties 186–7
Modern epistemology see Cartesian epistemology
Moore, G.E. 4, 49, 172, 208 n.4, 222 n.61
moral
  beliefs see ethical beliefs
  laws 200–1, 203
  realism xi-xii
    see also value realism
Mormonism 42

Nagel, Thomas viii
Nathan, n.M.L. 114–15, 160
natural selection 24, 27, 34, 49–52, 63, 76, 93–4, 97–100, 104, 108, 119, 132, 156–7, 183, 190, 217 n.18
  see also Darwinism
natural/physical laws, causality x, 37, 50, 52–4, 102–5, 189, 214 n.20
naturalism (N) viii, x, xiii-xv, 17–21, 24, 27, 43–4, 47–55, 58–9, 61–3, 66–8, 70–2, 75–7, 79, 88, 91, 94–5, 97–101, 103–4, 106, 108–9, 111–24, 127–8, 129–39, 143–9, 151–2, 156–8, 159–65, 167–9, 172–5, 179–95, 197–9, 204–5, 214 n.5, 214 n.7, 218 n.2, 223 n.26, 225 n.15, 228 n.8, 228 n.10, 228 n.11, 229 n.34, 229 n.44, 232 n.37
  methodological 161, 192–3, 228 n.11
  N+ 167–9
  as a stance or research program 192
  plus evolution (N&E) x, xiv, 19, 47, 49–50, 54–5, 61–3, 66–8, 75–9, 91, 108–9, 111, 113–14, 117, 119–23, 127–8, 129–30, 132–9, 144, 148, 151, 156–8, 162, 168–9, 184, 187–91, 193, 204–5, 218 n.2
naturalized epistemology viii, xii, xiv-xv, 14–15, 17–27, 29–44, 106, 155, 161–5, 181–2, 212 n.30, 213 n.53, 229 n.20
  and skepticism xv, 21–2, 162–5
necessity and contingency viii, 7–8, 18, 26, 38, 50, 66–7, 102–8, 119, 121, 123–4, 127, 134, 148, 153, 165, 186–7, 199–200, 202, 214 n.20, 222 n.48
  broadly logical 102–4
  metaphysical 106–8, 119, 134, 165, 199–200
  nomological 50, 104
Neo-Confucianism 42
neurological properties, structures, analyses xiv-xv, 22, 64, 75–8, 80, 85, 92–8, 100–4, 106–8, 155, 182, 189–90, 193–4, 234 n.7
Nietzsche, Friedrich 62
nonclassical logic 88
nonpropositional evidence 123
nonreductive materialism 100–5, 222 n.42
  strong (logical) 101–4
  weak (nomological) 104–5
normative epistemology see Cartesian epistemology
normativity xi-xiii, 13, 17, 19, 21–3, 26–7, 42–3, 96, 164, 182–3, 203–4, 210 n.10, 213 n.52
  technical see imperatives: hypothetical
Nunley, Troy M. 136

Ockham's Razor 51–2, 180
O'Connor, Timothy 113, 123–8, 145
O'Hear, Anthony 92
omniscient interpreter 151–2
optimistic overriders 56–7, 125–6

Orange Catholic Bible 72
original and secondary/derived content 78, 95
other minds xiii, 4–5, 13, 40–1
Otte, Richard 120–1, 138, 144, 217 n.36
overdetermination 51–2

Paley, William 227 n.26
Palmer, Daniel 216 n.43, 225 n.20
pantheism 187
Peirce, C.S. 24
perceptual beliefs ix, xii-xv, 25, 41–2, 69, 117
Peressini, Anthony 122, 136–7
perfect being 7–8, 167, 171, 174, 176–7, 186, 189, 194, 201, 203
  see also divine attributes; God
physical mechanism 50, 214 n.16
physicalism 214 n.7
Plantingian regress 59, 74, 135–7, 184
Plato/Platonism 3, 18, 88, 107, 186
Pollock, John 136
Popper, Karl viii, 186, 221 n.14, 232 n.35
possible worlds 24, 58–9, 66, 96–8, 101–4, 106–7, 121, 123, 186, 187, 190–1, 192, 233 n.60
preface paradox 231 n.31
prevenient grace 173
principles of rationality/humanity 151
probability (P) 36, 47, 49–50, 55–6, 58, 61–2, 64–8, 75, 79, 91, 95, 100, 105, 107–9, 111–12, 114, 117, 119–23, 127–8, 129–30, 132–4, 137–8, 143–7, 151–2, 156–8, 160, 163, 165, 175, 181, 184–8, 191, 193, 197, 214 n.3, 214 n.4, 215 n.32, 216 n.5, 218 n.38, 218 n.2
  Bayesian 47, 58, 66–7, 187, 214 n.4
  global and parochial 156–8
  Kyburgian (statistical) 47, 214 n.4
  logical 47
  objective and epistemic 47, 187–8
  thesis 91–109, 122, 145, 181
  see also inscrutability
proper
  epistemic environment 33–4, 36–7, 39–42
    mini- and maxi- 39–40

function 32–6, 42–3, 56–7, 123–6, 128, 181, 228 n.10
function defeaters see under rationality defeaters
properly basic beliefs x, 29–31, 40–1, 124, 130, 147–8, 161–1, 166, 168–9, 174, 179, 182, 184, 194, 212 n.14
propositional
  attitudes see assertion
  content 48, 64, 68, 75–6, 78–9, 91–8, 102–3, 115, 117, 132, 138, 151, 155, 163–4, 172, 182, 189–90, 193, 197–8, 227 n.47, 234 n.7
psycho-physical laws 104, 107
purloined letter analogy 31, 123–4
Putnam, Hilary 27, 70, 82–3, 150, 227 n.41

quasi-formal causality, laws 106–7, 119, 165, 199–200, 222 n.60
question begging arguments 83–5, 179–80
Quine, Willard Van Orman viii, xv, 17–27, 42–3, 54, 70, 122, 150, 155, 162–4, 168, 182
Qur'an 169, 176–7, 230 n.41

Ramsey, William 85–7, 153–4
random mutations 49–51, 153, 157, 214 n.16
randomness 49–51, 78, 97, 121, 157, 217 n.18
rationality x, xii, 11, 27, 33, 43, 54, 56–8, 84, 87, 117, 122–6, 128, 132–3, 136–7, 139, 144, 148–51, 166–73, 176, 180–1, 189, 192, 194–5, 200–3, 230 n.48, 233 n.75
  defeaters 56–7, 124–6, 128, 181, 185
    Humean 56, 125–6, 128, 145, 216 n.36
    proper function 56–7, 124–5
    internal and external 57–8, 128, 137, 149, 181
    laws of 201–3
Rea, Michael 71, 144, 188, 193
reductive materialism 51, 92–5, 97, 100–1, 105, 221 n.8, 222 n.42
Reid, Thomas 21, 30, 123, 211 n.2, 216 n.5
Reiter, David 122, 149
relativism 164–5
reliabilism xiii, 36, 191

reliability of cognitive faculties (R) 22, 25, 47–50, 54–5, 58, 61–70, 75, 79, 91, 100–1, 108–9, 111–28, 129–39, 143–51, 156, 158, 159–63, 165, 167–77, 179–81, 183–6, 188–95, 198–200, 203–4, 218 n.2, 225 n.15, 226 n.14, 229 n.44
  accidental reliability 35, 184–5, 191
  and irrelevant truths *see* true and relevant beliefs
  R+ 133–4
  as undefeatable 123–7
religion ix–xi, 3, 40–2, 53, 80–1, 169–77, 180, 187, 230 n.62
  evolutionary accounts of 175, 230 n.62
religious
  beliefs ix–xii, 118, 127, 160, 175
    see also theism
  epistemology x, 40–2, 166–7
Reppert, Victor 84
representations *see* depictors; indicators
rhetorical plausibility 71, 183, 203–5
rigid designators 103
  see also analytic *a posteriori*
Robbins, J. Wesley 151
Rosenberg, Alex 220 n.47
rough-and-ready formula 130–1, 143–5
Ruse, Michael 154–5
Russell, Bertrand 71, 73

saving the appearances 84
  see also fictionalism
science x–xiv, 18–22, 26, 33–4, 42–3, 48, 50–5, 62, 65, 80–1, 85–6, 94, 97, 102–3, 106–7, 118–20, 127, 131–4, 148, 155, 162–4, 180, 183, 190, 192, 199–200, 205, 208 n.19, 219 n.25, 221 n.14, 225 n.15, 229 n.20
  and religion 51–2, 80–1
scientific
  beliefs xiii–xv, 118, 127, 131–4, 155, 183, 190
    reliability of (SR) 119–20, 203–4
  realism 80–1, 87, 119–20
Segal, Aaron 133

self-defeat viii, xii, 5, 11, 44, 47, 58–9, 66–8, 79–81, 83–8, 91, 97, 122, 135–7, 139, 163–5, 180, 182–3, 185, 190–3, 198–9, 204–5, 216 n.43, 220 n.47–8, 223 n.26, 225 n.15, 229 n.44
  inherent and accidental 59
self-referential incoherence 14, 25, 27, 85, 88
self-refutation 18, 58–9, 88
semantic externalism 83
sensory beliefs *see* perceptual beliefs
sensus divinitatis 41–2, 166–8, 170, 173, 175
Shoemaker, Sydney 70, 150
Simpsons 227 n.22
singer analogy 64, 94–5, 120, 148, 180, 193, 198
skeptical theism 194
skepticism xii–xv, 3–5, 7, 11–12, 14–15, 20–2, 25, 30, 56, 59, 72, 82–3, 88, 113, 117, 120, 124, 126–8, 130–1, 135–7, 144, 160–5, 174, 182, 194–5, 199, 224 n.7, 228 n.10
  global xii, 14–15, 22, 30, 113, 120, 127, 130–1, 135, 144, 160–5, 174, 182, 224 n.7
  local xii, 120, 131
skyhooks and cranes viii, 99, 104, 219 n.15, 219 n.25
Sober, Elliot 50, 66, 156–7, 187
social epistemology 133
Socrates 201–2
space explorer analogy 113, 149–50
spandrels ix, 119
Stich, Stephen 62–3, 157, 210 n.30
Strawson, Galen 230 n.50
Street, Sharon xi–xiii, 183
Stroud, Barry 62
subjectivism 164–5
successor concepts 80–2
supervenience 19, 51, 100–4, 107, 155, 190, 214 n.20, 234 n.7
synonymy 17–18
syntactic and semantic engines 64–5, 95, 97, 197

Talbott, William xiv, 106–8, 115–20, 134, 146–7, 165, 183, 192, 194–5, 199, 203, 222 n.58, n.60, 223 n.20,

223 n.26, 226 n.6, 229 n.20, 233 n.75
Taylor, A.E. viii
Taylor, Richard 78, 219 n.13
teleological
    arguments 174, 177, 189, 192, 227 n.26
    laws *see* final causality
teleology 105–7, 108, 165, 174, 177, 189, 199–200, 202, 214 n.16
    without intent 105–6, 165, 199
teleosemantic content 95–8
testimonial beliefs 32, 212 n.14
theism 50–5, 67–8, 71, 105–6, 108, 127, 165–77, 179, 186, 188–9, 191, 194, 199–200, 203, 214 n.20, 226 n.9, 228 n.8, 234 n.10
    bare (T) 167–8, 174–7, 194, 203
    broad (T+) 167–77, 194
    as properly basic x, 41, 166, 168
    T– 176–7
    see also Christianity; divine attributes; God; Islam; Judaism; religion
Tooley, Michael 61, 77
Toulmin, Stephen 156
trade-offs and compromises 36, 41–2, 189, 231 n.24
transcendental arguments 199
Trojan horse 116, 223 n.20
true and relevant beliefs 94–5, 101, 104, 138, 148, 150, 189–90, 198
truth value x–xii, xv, 49, 75, 95–6, 101, 181–3
tu quoque arguments 165–77, 226 n.9

ultimately unresolved and undefeated defeaters 59, 129–30, 135–7

value realism xii–xiii
Van Cleve, James 112, 149, 160
van Fraassen, Bas 10, 214 n.5
verificationism 88
vicious circularity *see* circularity: premise
vitalism analogy 83–5, 179

warrant 12, 15, 29–38, 40–3, 56–7, 59, 111–12, 119, 122–3, 125–8, 130, 132–4, 147–9, 158, 161–2, 166–8, 172–3, 181–2, 185, 191, 200, 209 n.29, 215 n.34, 224 n.47, 226 n.9, 231 n.24
    defeaters 56–7, 59, 125–6, 128, 181, 185, 215 n.34, 224 n.47
Watson, J.B. 219 n.25
white rocks on a hillside analogy 78, 99
Whitehead, Alfred North 3
widgets analogy 55, 58, 67–8, 112–13, 129, 144–5, 215 n.31
Wielenberg, Erik 145–6, 157
Williams, George C. 33
wishful thinking/wish-fulfillment 34, 57, 68, 112–13, 115, 126, 131, 145, 181
witch analogy 71–4, 120, 144, 153–4, 156
withhold a bit objection 115–17, 121
Wittgenstein's ladder 87, 138, 220 n.32
Wunder, Tyler 186–8

XX analogy 113, 115–17, 124–5, 129–31, 135–6, 138, 145–6, 149, 195
    Talbott's H 115–16
    Talbott's ZZ 146–47

Ye, Feng 96–8, 155

www.ingramcontent.com/pod-product-compliance
Lightning Source LLC
Chambersburg PA
CBHW062127300426
44115CB00012BA/1836